Toward an Islamic Enlightenment

Toward an Islamic Enlightenment

The Gülen Movement

M. HAKAN YAVUZ

OXFORD
UNIVERSITY PRESS

Oxford University Press is a department of the University of Oxford.
It furthers the University's objective of
excellence in research, scholarship, and education by publishing worldwide.

Oxford   New York
Auckland   Cape Town   Dar es Salaam   Hong Kong   Karachi
Kuala Lumpur   Madrid   Melbourne   Mexico City   Nairobi
New Delhi   Shanghai   Taipei   Toronto

With offices in
Argentina   Austria   Brazil   Chile   Czech Republic   France   Greece
Guatemala   Hungary   Italy   Japan   Poland   Portugal   Singapore
South Korea   Switzerland   Thailand   Turkey   Ukraine   Vietnam

Oxford is a registered trade mark of Oxford University Press in the UK and certain other countries.

Published in the United States of America by
Oxford University Press
198 Madison Avenue, New York, NY 10016

© Oxford University Press 2013

All rights reserved. No part of this publication may be reproduced,
stored in a retrieval system, or transmitted, in any form or by any means,
without the prior permission in writing of Oxford University Press,
or as expressly permitted by law, by license, or under terms agreed with
the appropriate reproduction rights organization.
Inquiries concerning reproduction outside the scope of the above should be sent to
the Rights Department, Oxford University Press, at the address above.

You must not circulate this work in any other form
and you must impose this same condition on any acquirer.

Library of Congress Cataloging-in-Publication Data
Yavuz, M. Hakan.
Toward an Islamic enlightenment : The Gülen movement / M. Hakan Yavuz.
    p. cm.
Includes bibliographical references and index.
ISBN 978–0–19–992799–9 (hardcover : alk. paper)
1. Gülen, Fethullah.   2. Faith and reason—Islam.   3. Social movements—Religious aspects—Islam.   I. Title.
BP80.G8Y39 2013
297.092—dc23   2012006293

5 7 9 8 6

Printed in the United States of America
on acid-free paper

For
Becir (1928–2009) and Nedime Tanovic
and
Edibe Sözen

Contents

Introduction: Islamic Enlightenment 3

PART ONE Man 23

1. Lives in Context 25
2. The Contextual Theology of Gülen: Islamic Enlightenment 47

PART TWO Movement 69

3. The Structure of the Movement: Authority, Networks, and Opportunity Spaces 71
4. Education and the Creation of a "Golden Generation" 92
5. Islamic Ethics and the Spirit of Capitalism: Pietistic Activism in the Market 117

PART THREE Meaning 131

6. Muslim Subjectivities: Islam in the Public Sphere 133
7. Secularism and Science: Gülen's View 152
8. The Theology of Interfaith Dialogue 173
9. The Clash of Political Visions: The Military and the JDP 198
10. The Critics of the Movement 221

Conclusion 243
Notes 249
Bibliography 277
Index 289

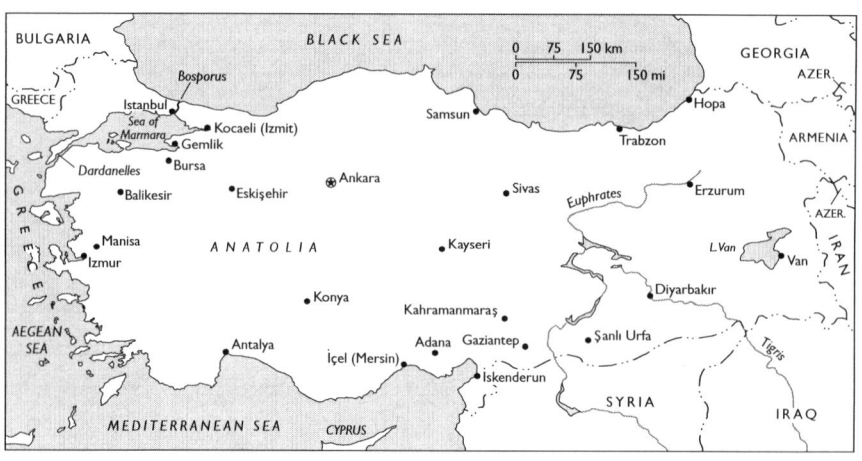

Toward an Islamic Enlightenment

Introduction

Islamic Enlightenment

Abdolkarim Soroush summarizes his notion of Islam as follows:

> First of all we have the phenomenon of Islam. Muslim intellectuals still talk about Islam as if it were a simple, unified entity; a singular object. But in reality the history of Islam, like the history of other religions such as Christianity, is fundamentally a history of different interpretations. Throughout the development of Islam there have been different schools of thought and ideas, different approaches and interpretations of what Islam is and what it means. There is no such thing as a 'pure' Islam that is outside the process of historical development. The actual lived experience of Islam has always been culturally and historically specific and bound by the immediate circumstances of its location in time and space.[1]

Since the Iranian Revolution 1979–80, there has been much intellectual discussion about the compatibility/incompatibility between Islam and various "isms": secularism, liberalism, pluralism, capitalism, and ultimately democratization. The reality is that there is not, and never was, one fixed and authoritative understanding of "Islam" as there is none for secularism, liberalism, and democracy. As in the case of other theologies and belief systems, authoritative attempts at enshrining dogma and praxis have always been contested, and inevitably spawned further permutations and interpretations of what "true" Islam meant. Such contestation in the modern period intensified in the nineteenth and early twentieth century in Muslim lands facing the challenge of Western imperialism, and many of its themes were articulated in the writings and speeches of various and differing luminaries including Ahmad Sirhindi, Sir Sayyid Ahmad Khan, Sayyid Jammaludin Al-Afghani, Muhammad Abduh, Namık Kemal, Muhammad Iqbal, Rashid Rida, Ziya Gökalp, Hassan Al-Bannah, and Maulana Mawdudi, to name only a few.

One prominent cleavage, which in crucial ways itself is a response to the pressures of modernity and global integration, is between literalist/fundamentalists and modernist/reformists. The first group, known as the literalists, has its origins in early Muslim movements of puritanism associated with the thought of Muhammad Ibn Hanbal, Ibn Taymiyyah, and later Muhammad Abdul Wahab. *Neo Salafi* or Wahabi movements posit political and social ills in the Muslim world as resulting from the community of believers straying from the "pure" teaching and practice of an unadulterated Islam exemplified by the Prophet Muhammad and his immediate followers. Such literalists abjure the existence of differing interpretations and insist that a "pure" and literal Islam can be distilled from the Qur'an and the sayings and practices of the Prophet as expounded in the collection of authoritative *hadiths* or sayings of the Prophet. They deny, often willfully, that the Qur'an consists of very general and poetic exhortations toward faith and virtue and that specific political and social legitimacy and practice was always fiercely contested in the immediate wake of the Prophet's death and his successors or *Hilafet*. Literalist and puritanical movements have been able to generate great popular support, particularly in times of intense social and political upheaval, and as a response to the onslaught of external foes from the Mongols to Western Imperialists. In contemporary times, this approach has also greatly benefited from the enormous largesse of the Wahabi Saudi Royal family, which has quite overtly promoted Muslim puritanism and Salafism, as well as sectarian enmity, as a way to neutralize suspicion and hostility over the royal family's own unimaginably decadent lifestyle and reliance on Western military interventions for its own survival. The great pity is that the radical Wahabi-Salafi *Gleichschaltung* of Islam alongside secular-authoritarian ideologies associated with Kemalism, Pahlavism, and Ba'athism elided the more pluralist forms of Islamic revival and reform in the late nineteenth and early twentieth centuries. In the 1920s, Mustafa Kemal implemented a series of radical reforms in an effort to forge a modern (secular) nation-state. The totality of these reforms and practices, which sought to create a European Turkish state and society by removing Islam from the public life, is codified as Kemalism, the founding philosophy of the Turkish Republic.

The second contemporary group, known as the modernists or interpretivists, draws upon the tradition of earlier modernist reformers such as Namık Kemal, Sir Sayyid Ahmad Khan, Sayyid Jammaludin Al-Afghani, Muhammad Abduh, Muhammad Iqbal, and Ali Shariati, to name a few. This contemporary generation of modernists, such as the late Fazlur Rahman, Alija Izetbegovic, Abdur Rahman Wahid, Abdolkarim Soroush, Rachid Al-Ghannoushi, and Fethullah Gülen, sought to free Islamic thought and practice from its rigid and puritanical interpretation and promote revival and reform to meet the modern spiritual and temporal needs of the Muslim world. The second approach had a more limited following in the Arab world until the recent Arab Spring. Reflecting both a higher level of socioeconomic development and the lasting role of Sufi thought and movements, Turkey, Indonesia, Malaysia, and Bosnia-Herzegovina have been more receptive to Islamic Enlightenment and modernist movements. In the following section, I will define Islamic Enlightenment and identify the socioeconomic conditions under which the ideas of Enlightenment are likely to flourish.

ISLAMIC ENLIGHTENMENT

One of the most often cited definitions of Enlightenment was provided by Immanuel Kant. In an article written in 1784, Kant argued that "Enlightenment is man's emergence from his self-imposed immaturity"[2] and he continued by saying that "immaturity is the inability to use one's understanding without guidance from another." In other words, Enlightenment, for Kant, was "the courage to think for oneself." According to Karl Popper, Enlightenment is "the effort of men to free themselves, to break out of the cage of the closed society, and to form an open society."[3]

Thus, there are two aspects of the Enlightenment: use of critical reason, and the evolution of an open progressing society. It is a process of using individual reason to re-interpret the religious and cultural traditions for the advancement of society. For the sake of this book, it might be better to think of Enlightenment as *a bundle of contradictory ideas and debates that are grounded in the faith in reason to bring about social, cultural, and political reforms that would promote democratic society and human rights.* Enlightenment does not mean the rejection of religion or the disenchantment of the world, but rather a new way of understanding the interactions between self and society, society and politics, and science and society. The Enlightenment project has had, since its inception, a major impact on religious debates and shaped a new way of thinking about religious tradition in light of the notions of reason, progress, science, and public deliberation.

Although Ernst Cassirer, Peter Gay, and Jonathan Israel all stress the incompatibility between religion and the Enlightenment, some scholars argue that not only are they compatible, but, moreover, the very foundations of the European Enlightenment are rooted in religion.[4] For instance, Peter Gay's two volume study defines Enlightenment in terms of its hostility to religion and search for freedom and progress through the use of reason. Yet, new research on the Enlightenment stresses the role of religion in the evolution of progressive ideas. J. G. A. Pocock argues that the Enlightenment "was a product of religious debate and not merely a rebellion against it."[5] Pocock does not see a unified narrative of the Enlightenment, but rather a "plurality" and a "family" of the Enlightenment.

On the basis of David Sorkin's influential book,[6] it may be argued that the works of Said Nursi and Fethullah Gülen represent "Islamic Enlightenment" in terms of integrating the roles of reason, tolerance, science and public discussion, and especially in how it facilitates the penetration of these ideas to diverse sectors of society. Although the ideas of the Enlightenment had a major impact among the Muslim intellectuals such as Jammaludin Al Afghani, Muhammad Abduh, Namık Kemal, and Muhammad Iqbal, these ideas, however, were confined to only a small group of intellectuals.[7] While it hardly penetrated the masses, it certainly never became part of the daily Islamic discourse. In the late Ottoman state, some of the key ideas of the Enlightenment were put into practice with the Tanzimat (the period of reorganization) in order to stop the decline of the Ottoman state against rapidly transforming European powers.[8] However, this top-down and relatively imitative process stumbled because the socioeconomic conditions were not enough to provide the necessary social support for these ideas to become a grassroots movement. The significance of the Gülen movement is that it has not only vernacularized the ideas of Enlightenment, but that it has also turned them into a religio-social movement.

The ideas of the Enlightenment are evolving and disseminating within, rather than against, Islamic intellectual spaces. Thus, the new Islamic thinking is very much informed by the key ideas of the Enlightenment in a newly evolving socioeconomic context. In some Muslim countries, such as Turkey, Bosnia, Malaysia, and Tatarstan, one sees the processes of Islamic Enlightenment, which are preconditioned on the use of critical reason to scrutinize the existing Islamic practices and ideas in order to bring about social and cultural reforms that would cultivate a more humane and open society. In other words, Islamic Enlightenment does not mean an imitation of the ideas of European Enlightenment but rather a transmutation and vernacularization of these ideas within an Islamic-Turkish tradition. By focusing on Islamic actors and discourses, one can fully understand how progressive ideas were produced, discussed, and disseminated in the larger society.

Nursi and Gülen, the two intellectual architects of the new Islam, constructed a "reasonable" faith that engages with philosophy and science in the open public arena and, by doing so, they advanced the role of critical reading and diverse texts in the public sphere in lieu of pure emotional devotion or ritual piety. The European Enlightenment was entirely compatible with religious faith, just like the writings of Gülen have argued that since revelation and reason are two God-given "lights," they cannot contradict each other. Adrien Lamourette argues that "Reason and revelation get along infinitely better than their interpreters... These two torches are taken from... the same light; they never spoil each other and conflict except in the hands of man."[9] In fact, Gülen also argues that "religion does not oppose or limit science and scientific work," and insists that science and religion are two definitively separate entities that emanate from the same truth: the Creator. In his writings, Gülen stresses the role that education can play, since "a new style of education [which fuses] religious and scientific knowledge with morality and spirituality will produce genuinely enlightened people with hearts illumined by religious sciences and spirituality, minds illuminated with positive sciences, characterized by all kinds of human merits and moral values, and cognizant of the socioeconomic and political conditions of their time."[10] The enlightened person, for Gülen, is someone who is armed with secular and religious ideas and able to harmonize them in the public debate to advance the communal good; someone who is always polite in his public and private daily life. For Gülen, there is no Enlightenment without God.

It is important to focus more on how and why some pious Muslims adopt the ideas and practices of the Enlightenment, while others totally reject them. In the case of Turkey, the ideas of reason, toleration, progress, science, liberty, and informed public debate have become part of Islamic discourse and this, in turn, helps Islamic actors engage secular and religious public spheres. Thus, the public sphere is more pluralistic with mixed secular and religious ideas and practices. In fact, the ideas closely related to the intellectual ferment of the Enlightenment are becoming the building blocks of new Muslim thinking. Today, more Muslims embrace the ideas of Enlightenment as the defining features of their faith and use these ideas to intervene in the otherwise historically insular, secularist public sphere. Islamic values and convictions do not create insular communities and spaces, but rather build bridges between insular intellectual arguments. In line with his spiritual teacher Said Nursi, Gülen not only stresses the role of reason and public discourse over basic received dogma, but also demands and provides theological arguments for religious toleration and the freedom of religious minorities, even though neither Nursi nor Gülen ever called for state neutrality in religious affairs.

Furthermore, Gülen promotes the process of Islamic thought adopting modern "print technology and communication," drawing attention to the significance of textuality and interpretation in communal solidarity formation. Finally, the Gülen movement has expanded the public sphere in Turkey as Nursi and Gülen, and their followers, engage in secular concerns and use religious terminology to discuss and debate secular issues. Gülen uses this new thinking to accommodate faith with reason and communicate new ideas through religious idioms to the larger masses. Although the Gülen movement is born of religious and social concerns, it redefines and blurs the boundaries between the public and the private, the secular and the religious.

These Muslim actors use reason to support their faith regardless of secularists, who present themselves as the champions of reason and view religion as the cause of Turkey's underdevelopment. By utilizing reason, new Muslim actors present Islam as a sensible and reasonable religion. On the basis of the writings of Gülen, one could argue that the ideas of the Enlightenment helped inform and shape the ideas and practices of the new Islamic thinking in Turkey. Gülen has been more successful than some secularist intellectuals who have sought to promote the ideas of Enlightenment. By casting these universal ideas in Islamic terms, Gülen has made them more accessible to ordinary Muslims. Gülen, just like Nursi, noted that scientific curiosity is compatible with Islamic concerns; the Gülen movement's schools, radio stations, and publications all seek to disseminate knowledge and create an intellectual space for public discourse. The activities of the Gülen movement indicate that one can be a democrat and in favor of civil society out of religious convictions.

One of the long-term effects of the Enlightenment was the emergence of civil society and participatory politics. Civic engagement, interfaith dialogue, participation in political processes, and a deep engagement with education, constitute the key strategies of the Gülen movement to build an "open society." Rather than ritual practice and piety, Gülen and his followers emphasized the priority of service to humanity and the improvement of social conditions without which true faith is impossible to attain. Piety without mercy and charity is incomplete, and faith can only realize its social potential if it is rooted in active involvement in this world for the sake of the other-world. Moreover, the activities of the Gülen movement are also thickening the weak civic culture in Turkey. With its stress on Hizmet and Himmet, the Gülen movement encourages pious people to pay renewed attention to communal duties and responsibilities at the expense of their particularized interests. Islam, in the hands of the Gülen movement, fosters public virtue that allows people to engage in the realization of collective goods and also helps to shape ideas of citizenship by encouraging people to make sacrifices for the attainment of the common good. Gülen's key and controversial assumption is that individuals must be pious in order to be good citizens. Piety, for Gülen, promotes individual thinking to look beyond their narrow interests in support of larger communal goals by fulfilling one's duties to God. In order to promote these virtues, education becomes an important tool to teach public morality rather than externalize one's faith. Contrary to secularist claims, the Gülen movement encourages civic engagement, cultivates civic virtue and promotes the good of the community. Gülen's ideal Muslim is someone who is not consumed by his personal interest and luxury, but rather someone who is defined by the virtues of frugality, moderation and sacrifice for the public good. Gülen always calls upon Muslims to selflessly participate in communal activities and governance. The education system styled by Gülen seeks to develop a sense of common purpose and public spirit for the advancement of one's community and humanity as a whole. Thus, Gülen's ideas of participation, civic engagement, and submission of self-interest to the public good are all defining features of the republican civic tradition.[11] In the case of Turkey, Islamic ideas and practices of mercy and charity, such as helping the needy and improving communal welfare, constitute the normative basis of civic tradition. The activists of the Gülen movement, as virtuous citizens, forge their particularized interests in order to fulfil their mission of fostering a well functioning humane society. Gülen has been transforming and translating Islamic ideas into practice in order to promote the Enlightenment ideas of toleration, pluralism, science and political participation. In recent years, there is more emphasis on social virtues as the basis of becoming a polite society by cultivating proper moral manners by respecting each other, supporting those who are in need, and allowing diverse voices in the public discussion.

The questions remain, why did the Islamic Enlightenment become a powerful societal movement in Turkey but not in some other Muslim-majority countries? What are the major challenges to this process? The sociopolitical conditions of a given country can help us understand why the ideas of Enlightenment have become more acceptable in some Muslim countries than others. Turkey's historical journey from the Tanzimat era to the secular republic under Mustafa Kemal Atatürk, and the powerful state tradition provided the necessary institutional basis for these ideas. In addition to the powerful tradition of the rule of law and the successful policies of modernization such as increasing literacy rates (over 98 percent), the most critical factor in the making of the Islamic Enlightenment is the new emerging Anatolian bourgeoisie. The new conservative business class has closely allied itself with the religious actors and movements in order to counter state power and expand the political and legal space for the development of commerce. Islamic actors, movements, and associations cater to the social and political needs of the new economic class to acquire financial means to fund their activities. In order to understand the context of this still evolving religious transmutation, we need to understand the rapid growth of commerce in Turkey. One of these religious actors who found the support of the Anatolian bourgeoisie is Fethullah Gülen, known as *Hocaefendi* (respected religious teacher), who has emerged as the most effective and powerful Turkish Muslim leader with enormous influence not only in Turkey but also abroad, particularly in regions of the former Ottoman Empire where his foundations run a number of highly successful schools. While he has chosen to live in self-imposed exile in rural Pennsylvania over the last decade, Gülen and his movement represent a particularly dynamic renewalist (*tecdid*) and modernist approach to Islam and the challenge of secularism, liberalism, capitalism, and democratization.[12]

By focusing on the Gülen movement in Turkey, I identify the conditions under which forms of Islamic modernity are likely to emerge. In fact, expanding sociopolitical opportunity spaces, as a result of the introduction of neoliberal economic reforms under Turgut Özal (1980–1993), provided and catalyzed new interpretations of Islam in Turkey that emphasized personal piety as the basis of communal responsibility and collective action in order to build a better world in the here and now. Thus, the juncture between socioeconomic context, textual interpretation and religious practices in modern Turkey led to the evolution of what might be termed the first quasi-Protestant version of Islam. Such understandings and practices of Islam have been reproduced in an increasingly dynamic social context in order to vernacularize and meet the challenges of modernity.

In this paradoxical sense, both Islamism and secularism are aspects of the same phenomenon (i.e., modernity). Even though they are historically not simultaneous, since secularism preceded and spawned its modern Islamist reaction, they eventually became intertwined through mutual interaction and conditioning each other. Different uses of Islamism(s) and secularism(s) have had a profound effect on the evolution of the boundary between state and society. Thus, in order to understand the dynamics of this boundary formation in Turkey, we need to examine the internal and external components of secularism and Islamism together, and indicate the conditions under which they shape and constitute one another. The Gülen movement provides a necessary avenue to study the increasingly intertwined relations between religion and modernity. Gülen, an ethnic Turkish Muslim, was interested in integrating Islamic values into the professional and intellectual sectors (new public universities) of Turkish society. These sectors were crucial from the standpoint of a Turkish Islamic revival as they had been the torchbearers of the Kemalist secular ideology of the Turkish Republic.

The Gülen movement started as a small communal structure in Izmir and has developed into the most influential religio-civic transnational faith-based education movement in modern Turkey. Gülen's movement has been called by different names such as *Fethullahcılar* (partisans of Fethullah Gülen), Gülenciler (Gülenists), *cemaat* (community of Fethullah Gülen), and *hizmet* (amalgam of altruistic service organizations for the realization of the common good).[13] Some call it "*Fethullahcı tarikat*" (Sufi style order of Fethullah Gülen), but as Sufi orders were banned at the onset of the Kemalist period in Turkey, such labeling suggests that the movement is somehow an underground organization. However, while the movement is deeply influenced by the worldview of Turkish Sufism, it would be inaccurate to label it a Sufi *tarikat*. Gülen himself prefers to define the movement as a *hizmet* or social service organization. He told a reporter:

> Even though some call it the "Gülen Movement," I prefer to call it sometimes "Service-Hizmet," sometimes "the Movement of Volunteers," sometimes the "Souls Dedicated to Humanity," and sometimes "a movement that sets its own examples [a movement that does not need to turn back to

a golden age for examples]." Even if it may sound somewhat lengthy, to do justice to its encompassing character, it may be also called "a movement of people who are gathered around high human values."[14]

For the sake of my own study, I have chosen to call it the Gülen movement, which started as a religio-civic movement and has evolved into a transnational sociocultural movement with significant political clout based on Gülen's ideas on education, religion, science, tolerance, dialogue, and morality. I will also sometimes refer to the followers of the movement as Gülenists or "*gönüllüler*" referring to the "volunteers" contributing to the realization of the goals set by the Gülen movement.

The Gülen movement has attracted widespread public attention recently due to its activities in education in various countries, particularly in Central Asia and the Balkans, but also in the United States. For its defenders and promoters, the movement is engaged in the vital task of Islamic reformation and the attempt to provide alternative moderate visions of Islam reconciled with the demands of modernity. For its critics, including the Kemalist secularist bloc in Turkey and neoconservatives in America, the Gülen movement is a sinister wolf in sheep's clothing whose promotion of Muslim modernism and interfaith cooperation hides a radical hardline Islamist agenda.

According to Turkish critics of Gülen, the movement uses its influence in the Turkish police force and the judiciary to intimidate nonreligious and/or antireligious opposition voices in the country.[15] At the same time, the movement has been criticized for being too closely engaged with, and accommodationist toward, the post-Communist authoritarian regimes in Central Asia, even if it hopes to bring about pragmatically, constructive long-term change.

In the United States, on the other hand, the movement is known for its well-publicized campaigns of "interfaith dialogue" and "tolerance" and also for arranging the visit of American opinion-makers to Turkey. The Gülen movement is thus covered by an aura of mystery and secrecy, and is seen as embodying opposed Janus-faced features: liberal yet communitarian; cosmopolitan yet puritan; both a source of hope and a source of fear.

Since the publication of my co-edited volume with John Esposito on the Gülen movement, a series of subsequent books, essays, and even websites, have come out to discuss different aspects of the movement.[16] Four genres of literature or approaches appear to be merging in an effort to analyze it. The first approach is largely academic and examines different facets of the movement. This includes three books by Bayram Balcı, Bekim Agai, and Berna Turam.[17] They all focus on the educational efforts of the movement. Moreover, there are three excellent dissertations that cover different aspects of the movement.[18] In spite of their valuable contribution, there are some limitations with the first genre of academic studies. They are all case studies and limited in their scope of understanding the movement. None of the studies examine the intellectual origins of the movement in the writings of the early twentieth-century Kurdish-Turkish Sufi leader and reformer Bediuzzaman Said Nursi. The studies also tend to downplay the role of Gülen as leader and the force of his ideas and personality, and do not provide a parsimonious understanding of the religio-political changes in Turkey and the Muslim world in which Gülen and similar movements have grown.

The second type of writings on the movement is journalistic in nature and based on either secondary sources or journalistic interviews. This coverage of the movement includes efforts by journalists who are invited to activities of the Gülen movement or provided with paid visits to different countries to see the activities of the movement first hand.[19] The third genre of writings is promotional and apologetic.[20] They are either carried out by the members of the movement or by scholars who are invited to attend the movement's promotional conferences in different settings, and whose expenses are covered.[21]

Finally, there are also alarmist and militantly anti-Gülen writings. They tend to be associated with hardline Kemalist circles tied to the ancient régime.[22] These writings reproduce a vulgar version of Orientalism, claiming that Islamic thought and practice is a reactionary and fixed set of texts, doctrine, and practices, by which the Muslim sense of self is determined.[23] Moreover, in the manner of American neoconservatives with intimate ties to the Islamophobic bloc, such as Charles Krauthammer, Michael Rubin, Daniel Pipes, and even Glenn Beck, they seek to present all Islamic sociopolitical movements as the dark eternal "other" and counterpart to an equally homogeneous and reified Western civilization.[24] Since Gülen is a devout Muslim, they conclude that he must be "reactionary" and "authoritarian" and in spite of claims to the contrary, determined to create a worldwide fundamentalist "Caliphate." The common theme in all of these writings is that the Gülen movement seeks to establish "an Islamist state governed by Shariah law" while "reorienting Turkey towards Iran."[25]

In terms of my own approach in this new study, I seek neither to praise nor to condemn but to understand a religious and sociopolitical movement with the potential for enormous influence not only in Turkey but also in much of the wider Islamic world. I draw upon a series of interviews, the published works of Gülen himself, and other scholarly works in related topics and fields, in order to provide a narrative of the movement, which is neither apologetic nor hostile. In addition to maintaining scholarly objectivity, a fuller and more accurate understanding of the Gülen movement needs to be grounded in the broader social scientific literature on the reciprocal interaction and transformation between religious traditions and the forces of modernity, and above all secularism, liberalism, and capitalist development.

In the interval that followed my first edited academic book on Gülen and his movement, I felt it was necessary to write a new volume to explain the enormous transformations occurring within the movement and broader Turkish state and society.[26] I have met with Fethullah Gülen several times and organized a conference on the movement at Georgetown University in 2001. The edited volume with John Esposito was the outcome of that workshop. I remained a close observer of the movement and its evolution since 2003. The present book aims to critically examine the controversy surrounding the movement and also to account for the broader transformations that both the movement and the Turkish state and society have undergone. Toward this end, I have carried out further interviews in Azerbaijan, Bosnia, Germany, Macedonia, and Turkey, and formed three Gülen focus groups in Aydın, Ankara, and Istanbul. The present book is based on my own observations and interviews, as well as Gülen's speeches and writings and more general newspaper articles, journal articles, and books on the movement.

The movement for its supporters has been a source of hope in terms of aligning modernity (i.e., rationalism, democracy, secularism and the market economy) with Islam in Turkey. However, the very success of the movement and that of the separate Justice and Development Party (JDP) of Recep Tayyip Erdoğan by 2011 also turned the movement into a source of fear for many secular and leftist intellectuals in Turkey. Although the Gülen movement used to be politically neutral and kept an equal distance from various political parties in the past, since 2002, it has increasingly and closely identified itself with the fate of the governing JDP.[27] This politicization further deepened the suspicion about the movement in some Turkish secular and Kemalist circles.

This book aims to bring new material and further examine the intellectual background of Gülen, and to critically analyze his complex and, in some cases, contradictory ideas. It is very important also to examine the changing ideas and positions of Gülen in the sociopolitical context of modern Turkey, rather than view them as fixed and unchanging. By tracing the historical and social influences that have shaped Gülen's ideas, I hope to flesh out such an interactive structure in which Gülen's ideas and their sociopolitical context are in mutually constitutive formation.

The book examines the way in which Gülen's ideas are put into practice at the level of the movement and its followers. I describe how the movement evolved from a small piety-based movement to a large socioeconomic and religious transnational and transformational project. Gülen calls on Muslims to become informed about the problems of their community and the wider world by stressing the importance of being a "concerned pious" personality (*dertli dindar*) who is *in* the world but without becoming fully captured by the world. By calling upon Muslims to be active in the arts, sciences, politics and economy, he seeks to redefine piety as being this-worldly and engaged in easing suffering and antagonism, as well as inextricably linked to salvation in the hereafter. Such pious activism at the level of individuals and also groups committed to social service in education, healthcare, poverty relief, and interfaith understanding are among some of Gülen's most important achievements in recasting traditional understandings of Turkish Islam. His ideas and ethic of social service are put into practice within dense networks of reading circles, schools, associations and media outlets.

Gülen begins his teaching of social ethics by explaining how social justice and the common shared good are foundational for the Islamic faith. He explains how prevailing understandings of Islam and ritual piety are inadequate and states the need for contemporary Muslims to return to a broader spiritual understanding of foundational sources (the Qur'an and Hadith) with an open mind in order to build practical models to meet contemporary challenges, rather than trying to patch old and broken models developed by medieval scholars.

As Gülen addresses many facets of daily life such as education, politics and economics, his writings offer Muslims some useful analytical tools that focus on the significance of individual spiritual development and responsibility. However, it should be noted that there is still a tension between such individualism and the role of Gülenist community leaders who also seek to organize broader and more cohesive faith and service communities. This poses certain more general tensions between communalism and individualism; majoritarian democracy and individual liberty and alternative worldviews. Gülen is at his best when he evaluates the human quest for the "good life." Gülen notes that modern reality reflects such a multitude of paths and conceptions of the good life, not only among different individuals but also within a single movement, that to assume that there is a single path to achieve such ideals is incompatible with modern life. However, he would stress that in as much as hunger, disease, war, injustice, and oppression are ever-present realities for perhaps the majority of humans, their alleviation would be a common goal that could bring together both religious and secular individuals and groups.

Gülen views modernity as posing the most serious challenge to religious faith, but at the same time insists that neither can successfully function without the other. Religious faith cannot hope to survive by retreating tortoise-like into an imagined golden age of the past. Simultaneously, religious faith and ethics are essential for modern societies if they are to avoid alienation, conflict, instrumental rationality, and social predation by the strong against the weak.

Gülen argues that social well-being and modern societies cannot function on the basis of self-interest (*menfaat*) alone, but only become meaningful and stable if they are vernacularized or framed within a particular religious moral worldview (i.e., *ihlas*).[28] Islamic thought, for Gülen, plays an active role in articulating its own claims to normative authority and empowering ordinary people to develop their own individual moral character, which then is tied into the broader social fabric. His success thus far has been based not only on his considerable personal charisma but also on his deep understanding of how to activate the ideas, symbols and emotions of people longing for deeper spiritual and communal connections. He effectively moves from these deeper longings to practical methods and steps of community building, education and transformation.

If we summarize the goal of the Gülen movement and the gist of his thinking over the last four decades, there could be no better formulation than the words promoted by him, "character formation" and community building (*şahsiyet ve kişilik oluşturma hareketi*).[29] This key expression has punctuated Gülen's thought and remained a central principle of the movement itself. In his writings, Gülen sees the process of discovering oneself and becoming attuned to inner spiritual longing as the main way of building individual character and subsequently societal well-being. Knowing oneself, for him, is an inward journey and realization of the spiritual dimension of life; becoming aware that you are God's creature and a part of this systematic universe of creation; knowing one's place in the universe through one's ties with the Creator.

Adab becomes an important concept in the writings of Gülen, who defines it as good morals relate to cosmopolitan life, refined tastes and a cultivated knowledge of wisdom, an overall moral code of conduct for the realization of *insan-ı kamil* or a perfected human being. It is a way of developing one's inner life and relation to others personified by the Muslim belief that the Prophet Muhammad best exemplified such a perfected human being.

In this general outline of Gülen's thought, the influence of Said Nursi is obvious. Whereas Nursi initiated a faith movement with his writings, the *Risale-i Nur Kulliyatı* or Collected Epistles of Light, Gülen has forged a cohesive and well-organized social movement stressing individual character formation and community building, with the goal of catalyzing an Islamic renaissance compatible with the needs of the modern world.[30] In other words, his goal has been to raise an engaged and successful believer and faith-community in this world without being taken hostage by material needs and desires. Gülen says, "We are not here as Turkish Muslims to put ourselves in the service of Islam, but to put Islam in the service of life." The goal here for Gülen is not about a political Islamism focused on assuming political power, a development that he believes would lead to disaster and oppression in a number of Muslim countries.

Rather, the solution to the severe socioeconomic and geopolitical crisis that afflicts the Middle East and the broader Muslim world is the formation of individual moral character and community building, which hopefully, for Gülen, can save both Islam and modernity from the current crisis they face in their own respective terms. Here the German term *Bildung* would be the best concept to capture the essence of the Gülen movement.

This study of the Gülen movement is therefore relevant not only for the study of Islam in modern Turkey but also for the broader existential debate over modernity and religion in the Muslim world. By focusing on Turkey as the most politically and socioeconomically developed Muslim state, and moreover one that under the dynamic leadership of Recep Tayyip Erdoğan is increasingly poised to assume its historic role of leadership in the Muslim world, I seek to illustrate the potential possibilities and pathways of becoming a modern Muslim state and society—a situation that is also faced by less developed Muslim states in the Middle East, Africa, and Asia. There is presently a fierce struggle taking place for the soul of Islam, between neo-Salafists and modernists, which I alluded to at the beginning of the introduction. The consolidation of Turkish democracy and the opening up of public spaces for debate and discussion starting with the liberalizing reforms of Turgut Özal in the 1980s has meant that Salafi and/or radical jihadi-style Islamic revival movements have gained very little public traction. Moreover, due to the lack of direct colonial rule in Anatolia, Turkish political thought (secular or Islamic) did not become suffused with anti-Western reactions to the same extent that can be seen in other Muslim countries. It has always remained an open field for diverse ideas and lifestyles. As the JDP consolidates democratic rule and undertakes a sweeping series of domestic political and constitutional reforms, it remains to be seen whether Islamic discourse and practice will sustain liberal and pluralistic discourse and opportunity spaces or become, as some critics allege, increasingly authoritarian and hegemonic in the face of challenges presented by Turkey's diverse ethnic and social groups. My hope is that this detailed study of the Gülen movement might help shed light on such pressing concerns.

The book will consist of three parts: Man, Movement, and Meaning. The first chapter will explicate the sociohistorical background of the movement by examining Gülen's life story as the man behind the movement and also within the context of larger national and regional forces that were shaping politics in Turkey. Chapter 2 will examine Gülen's intellectual map and key concepts including religion (Islam), morality, the good life and community, on the one hand, and modernity, democracy, pluralism and the politics of identity

(Turkish-Islamic nationalism), on the other. I will explore the following set of questions: How does Gülen define democracy? Is it possible to posit an ideal society and good life without controlling the political process and excluding alternative visions? How do Gülen and his movement participate in politics without reducing Islam to yet another authoritarian ideology seeking hegemony?

The second part, consisting of three chapters, focuses on the structure and activities of the movement. It begins with the third chapter, which explores the sociopolitical features of the movement by examining the role of the leader, the identity of individual followers and the reasons for their recruitment, and concentric networks and their interactions. In chapter 3, I argue that the movement is more organized than diffused, functioning as a lobby or interest group. However, since Gülen is not involved in day-to-day decision-making and the movement does not have a master plan to be implemented in a top-down fashion, the movement is also shaped by local demands and concerns. Yet, the movement still manages to maintain a certain sense of discipline and uniformity at the micro level in terms of dress code, political and social attitudes, roles and internalized normative ideals. Furthermore, the media outlets connected to the Gülen movement play a decisive role in the construction and dissemination of their particular worldview and policy prescriptions. Chapter 4 will focus on the process of cultivating a "golden generation" through examining the discursive and organizational spaces for character formation and communal cohesion within the movement. What is Gülen's notion of modern Muslim education and why is it so central for the movement? Chapter 5 will examine the Gülen movement in terms of the ethics of capitalism and what Max Weber termed as "elective affinity" via the mechanisms in which religion shapes, and, in turn, is transformed by its encounter with capitalist socioeconomic development. This chapter will explore how the values and goals of the Gülen movement have facilitated a quite successful and dynamic capitalist ethos. By underscoring the interaction between "material and ideal interests," this chapter will examine the way in which Turkish Islam has been successfully harmonized with the exigencies of capitalist development. Finally, I will examine whether Gülen offers any criticism of neoliberal economic development policies and what his views are on the imperative of reconciling successful socioeconomic development and social justice.

The third part focuses on Meaning and on the interactions between ideas and practices. Chapter 6 draws on Jürgen Habermas' concepts of the public sphere while seeking to answer the following critical questions: How should we analyze the Abant meetings where the movement gathers a diverse body of intellectuals to discuss controversial issues facing Turkish society? Do these meetings genuinely reflect an openness to tolerance, pluralism and the free flow of ideas? Or, do they, as critics allege, attempt to build legitimacy and coopt more secular intellectuals and opinion-makers? "Consensus-building," "coalition-building," and "intermediation" are critical aspects of the movement. Through a series of interviews, this chapter studies the attempts of the Gülen community to build a bridge between the secularist and Islamist sectors of the Turkish population by utilizing Habermas' concept of the public sphere. In his recent writings, Habermas argues that religion can and should play a role in the "thickening" of public deliberation, and he calls upon religious groups to "frame" their religious concerns and positions with regard to a broader secular language and society. Although some Islamic groups reject the idea that they have to provide secular justifications for their religious positions in the public discourse, there is a need to create a more inclusive and reason-based political language in order to communicate with diverse ethnic, religious, and secularist political discourses and groupings. I will ascertain the Gülen community's efforts in this regard.

Habermas, it should be noted, also argues that not only religious actors but also secular ones must frame their demands and positions in an accessible language that religious sectors of the population can understand as well. By focusing on the Abant meetings, I explain why secular Turkish society also needs to move away from the dogmas of Kemalist secular authoritarianism and learn about Islamic ideals and their role in history in order to make sense of the arguments and beliefs of their fellow citizens as much as the religious Turks need to develop a pluralist cognitive ear for understanding the needs and concerns of secular and heterodox voices. Most of the Abant meetings organized by the Gülen community have been on pressing controversial issues in Turkish society and they resulted in conciliatory and pragmatic lists of proposals. The main themes of the meetings have been: secularism, democracy, tolerance, identity (Kurdish, Alevi, and Islamic), and globalization. The common underlying message of these meetings has been that the Kemalist attempt to impose sociopolitical uniformity via authoritarian diktat has been very damaging to the diverse fabric of historic Ottoman Turkish society, and that a new nonauthoritarian and homogenizing way forward to deal with conflict and diversity must be found.

In order to understand the relation of the Gülen movement with the challenge of secularism and science, chapter 7 will explore the connection between religion and science, on the one hand, and science and secularism, on the other. This chapter will concentrate on the following questions: What is the history of secularism in Turkey? Is there an inevitable connection between science and secularization? How does this history shape Gülen's understandings of these two concepts? How does he examine the interaction between Islam and secularism? Finally, is the concept of secularism inevitably in conflict with Islam? I will briefly examine the intellectual background of this debate over the relationship between science and religion within the late Ottoman Empire by focusing on the works of positivist thinkers from that era. Indeed, there were three reactions to the rationalist and scientific awakening in the Ottoman Empire: rejection of religion as the antinomy to science; rejection of science, especially positivist science, as the enemy of faith; and an accommodationist approach to show that science and religion need not be in inevitable conflict. The last part of this chapter will analyze Gülen's *tevhidi* (unitarian) understanding of the "relationship" between science and religion by critically examining Gülen's thought.

After unpacking Gülen's conceptions of secularism and science, chapter 8 will scrutinize his notion of interfaith dialogue and his approach to globalization, by addressing the following questions: How does Gülen define the "other"? Is it a religious, ethnic, or moral category? How does Gülen integrate his notion of the "other" with Muslim identity? Why is dialogue so important for the movement? The conclusion of the book will set a larger argument about the short- and long-term direction of the movement and its likely impact on Turkish and Muslim society. This examination of the Gülen movement will also hopefully allow the reader to become more fully aware of the larger debates over the main theological and social problems confronting the Muslim world. Gülen himself poignantly raises some of these pressing concerns: Why has the broader Muslim world remained economically and scientifically underdeveloped for the last three centuries? What are the sources of its current geopolitical fragmentation and economic and political weakness?

The last two chapters will analyze the Gülen movement's evasive relations with the Turkish military and civilian governments. In chapter 9, after summarizing the Turkish state's vision of politics as a means of "social engineering" and society as the "homogenous whole and servant of the state," I examine how this vision is in direct conflict with the vision of the Gülen community that argues instead that the state is a "servant" of society, and politics is an instrument allowing each group to bring their definition of the good life to the political sphere to create a consensus. Chapter 10 maps out the societal critics of the Gülen movement, categorized as the secular leftists, Kurds, Alevis, and Islamists. I examine the social and political basis of five major criticisms of the movement. The critics argue that the movement is patriarchal and does not recognize the role of women in the public sphere; it does not promote critical thinking and it has not produced any prominent intellectual; it is communitarian and does not provide space for individual self-construction; it lacks transparency in terms of its financial resources and political connections; and it is a political force that seeks to control state institutions. Although some people in Turkey are afraid of the expanding role of the movement, the majority supports its activities.[31]

To demonstrate the social significance of the Gülen movement, I would like to close this introduction with a summation of a brief exchange I had with Kenan Çamurcu, a young and respected Muslim intellectual. I asked Kenan to discuss "the contribution the Gülen movement has made to the Islamic intellectual debate in Turkey."[32] He gave a terse response: "nothing; absolutely nothing! Because it is not an intellectual movement." When I asked him about the movement's role in social and political life in Turkey, he responded:

> They are playing an important role in bridging Turkey with the outside world and helping internationalize the country. Almost all charity organizations and networks have begun to emulate them in order to develop connections with other countries. They have taught other groups how to collect money and organize themselves in a global context. In short, they have provided the model for other groups in Turkey. While the Gülen community (*cemaat*) was becoming global, it also helped others to become global as well.

In that sense the movement has played a critical role in providing a model for globalization, and has given legitimacy to a more eclectic humanism.

Çamurcu also qualified his statement that the movement "has no place within the literature of Islamism" (*Islamcılığın edebiyatında yerleri yok*). "However, they have succeeded in shifting the discourse from the foundational concepts of Islam such as faith, *umma, dava, jihad* and morality to secular concepts of tolerance, democracy, civil society, dialogue and peace." Indeed, the Gülen movement helped to shift the intellectual landscape of Turkey by drawing upon neoliberal discourses and even creating a secular intellectual ground to discuss religious issues. In other words, they have redefined the ground of public debate in Turkey by stressing secular concepts while also bringing faith back into secular sites to discuss the meaning of virtue and the good life. The movement has been vital to the formation of new reference points for public discussion in Turkey. Moreover, the followers of Gülen all seek to compare Gülen with hallowed Western intellectuals such as Kant, Sartre, and Habermas and not with Muslim thinkers like Ghazali, Rabbani, or Ibn Rushd. In this sense, one sees the internal secularization of the movement. Therefore, what is taking place in Turkey is the paradoxical Islamization of secular society and the internal secularization of Islamic thought. A new form of piety is under construction, unshackled from traditional and literalist Islamic terminology and references. Consequently, I would argue that the movement is one of the main forces for the modernization of the Turkish state and society with further profound implications for other Muslim countries.

This book is an outcome of a ten-year long observation and interviews with different groups and leaders, followers and sympathizers, as well as critics and passionate "haters" of the movement in different countries. There are a number of people whom I would like to thank for their comments, contributions, and questions: Abdullah Antepli, Tal Buenos, Ramazan H. Oztan, William Holt, Ali Aslan, Payam Foroughi, Eric Hooglund, Fevzi Bilgin, Ori Z. Soltes, Amir Duranovic, Edin Radusic, Fatih Yaman, and Umut Uzer. I would also like to thank my three undergraduate students, Alexander Grim, Rachel Flichtbeil, and Nicholas Dutkiewicz, who have read the manuscript and helped to make it more accessible to the general reader. Finally, as usual, I owe a special debt of thanks to my friend and collegue Mujeeb Khan who extensively edited and commented upon the manuscript and provided his customary keen theoretical insights.

M. Hakan Yavuz
Istanbul and Sarajevo

Man

1

Lives in Context

The question of just who Fethullah Gülen is has vexed many. According to his own declaration, he is a stranger in his own land, a political and spiritual exile in his birthplace, as well as not fully at home in any particular era. He is a stranger (*garip*) steeped in anxiety, a religious critic, a social innovator. However, he is much more than an observer; he is a builder, shaper of ideas, and leader of his own movement. Gülen is not a radical activist who would seek to destroy what already exists in order to create a new world. On the contrary, he is conservative and his conservatism leads him to value the preservation of existing institutions and norms—while at the same time working to reform them. He is open to organic change, which reflects the historical identity and moral grammar of his given society. Bridges should be built, not burnt; a new language and cultural identity should not to be introduced as in the case of Ataturk's "Sun Language Theory," but the lexicon may be updated. Gülen values orderly change that seeks to expand and reform traditional values while appreciating the highpoints of Ottoman Islamic history and civilization. He is highly critical of the positivist/Jacobin attempt at a top-down deracination and transformation of Turkish and other Muslim societies associated with the likes of Ataturk and Reza Shah Pahlavi. At the same time, he has also been a strident critic of the Wahabi/Taliban style of fundamentalism and obscurantism.

In order to understand the ideas, goals, and character of Gülen, we need to contextualize his process of becoming a Turkish Muslim leader in the context of larger political and intellectual debates with contemporaries. In other words, Gülen's ideas cannot be separated from the prevailing socioeconomic changes and intellectual debates that transformed Turkish state and society over the last 30 years.

GÜLEN'S FORMATIVE PERIOD (1941–1958)

Gülen was born in the small Anatolian village of Korucuk in the eastern Anatolian province of Erzurum in 1941.[1] On the basis of Gülen's life story, his character was shaped by three formative factors: his family, Sufism and Sufi leaders, and the writings of Said Nursi.

Gülen claims that his ancestors moved to Erzurum from Ahlat, a town located in the Bitlis province (map 1). He highlights the religious and national character of Bitlis by claiming that some of the Prophet Muhammad's grandchildren had settled in Ahlat, along with the first wave of Turkish tribes from central Asia. He argues that these Turkish tribes' understanding of religion intermingled with the spirit of Islam and created a powerful Islamic-Turkish ethos for the people of the region.[2] Gülen argues that eastern Anatolia has been fertile ground for the Sufi vision of Islam and Sufi orders, such as the Abdulkadir Geylani (d. 1116), Mevlevi, and Nakşibendi orders, which dominated the spiritual/intellectual landscape as "followers which blossomed like snow."[3] After highlighting the religio-national aspects of Ahlat, Gülen focuses on the region where he was raised, Erzurum.

According to his memoirs, his boyhood in Erzurum kept his heart pure as his mind matured, allowing him to stand ethically erect in his public life. Born in a community of farmers, young Gülen chose not to farm but to become a religious scholar. Islamic moral principles that informed his early preferences also served as ground for ways of behaving at crucial turning points in later life. In his moral training, his family, especially his mother, and his Sufi teacher, played formative roles.

Gülen's personality has been very much influenced by the regional culture of eastern Anatolia. Communally based Islamic identity in Erzurum existed not in a reified sacred doctrinal form, but rather according to the cadence of everyday life in which Gülen was socialized. Muslim norms and identity here functioned like a vernacular language, allowing intimate communication between members of a community. This form of Islamic identity evolved from historical experience and emerged as people became aware of their own place within a community with a distinct set of historically based practices. Gülen was keenly aware of the power of traditional Muslim norms in shaping the everyday life of people in Anatolia, and his main concern was to bring this formerly excluded identity to the fore in the face of Kemalist efforts to discredit and exorcise it.

The people of Erzurum are also known by the subregional identity of *Dadaş*. This is a regional communitarian form of Islam, punctuated by the culture and needs of frontier conditions. The *Dadaş* variant of Islam stresses the community over the individual and security over other concerns.[4] Erzurum, formerly the eastern frontier of the Ottoman state, was a zone of intense conflict among the Russian, Iranian, and Ottoman empires.[5] Erzurum used to be a religiously and ethnically mixed city before the early twentieth century, with a considerable Armenian Christian population. The city was captured by the Russian Empire in 1829 and remained under Russian occupation for several months before being returned to the Ottoman Empire under the Treaty of Andrianople (Edirne). The second major Russian attempt to capture the city took place during the Crimean War of 1854. However, they failed to take it due to the lack of necessary manpower. Eventually, the Russian forces besieged nearby Kars, disrupting trade routes in the region. During the fatal Ottoman-Russian War of 1877–78, Erzurum was occupied by Russian troops who were aided by local Armenians. Eventually the city was returned to the Ottoman state following the Congress of Berlin in 1878, but the devastation and ethnic cleansing of Ottoman Muslims in the Balkans during the previous war destroyed the trust between the Muslim and Christian populations. The city and its vicinity then became the center of a long-lasting ethno-religious conflict, and the focal point of Armenian nationalism as it boasted a series of Armenian nationalist associations.

In the competitive environment of Erzurum where Muslims and Christian merchants were competing over economic and political resources, the Europeans asserted themselves as the protector of the Christians, as they had in the Balkans, and the Ottoman state had increasingly limited control over these groups. By providing legal immunity to local Christian merchants with whom they desired to control regional trade, the European powers further fueled ethno-sectarian tensions. Local Christian elites developed a close informal alliance with Russia, and some with Britain. The Armenian community in Erzurum gradually recognized Russia as the protector of their community while the Patriarchate regarded the British as the arbiters of their political demands for autonomy and eventual independence. In short, the penetration of European capitalism, the centralization and land policies of the state, the introduction of media and education, Russian occupation, and the collaboration of Armenian groups with the occupying Russian troops, helped to plant the seeds of the ethno-religious conflict in the region. The penetration of European capitalism in Erzurum and its vicinity separated economic from political power. The Armenian community benefited from the expansion of the European capitalist penetration at the expense of Muslim merchants and became the link with the global economic flow of goods. The trade route from Trabzon to Tabriz in Iran, via Erzurum, turned the city into a thriving economy for these traders.[6] Thus, the tension between the Muslims and Armenians of the city developed in tandem with the penetration of capitalism. Moreover, with the Tanzimat process of 1839, and the introduction of the new legal rules to create equality among the subjects of the empire by defining them as Ottoman citizens, the Armenian sense of discrimination was enhanced. There were a series of Armenian protests demanding the full implementation of the legal changes, and on several occasions, the state used force by deploying the military, which regarded itself as a "Muslim army." Growing media outlets, Christian missionaries, and modern education further intensified the Armenian sense of resentment and separatism, and magnified in-group solidarity against the Ottoman state. The Armenian community in Erzurum was much better organized within and outside the city to challenge Ottoman authority. The Ottoman state had limited capacity to deal with the Armenian separatism or a series of uprisings. Following the Balkan wars and the ethnic cleansing of Caucasian Muslim highlanders by Czarist Russia, there were a number of pogroms against the Armenian population between 1894 and 1896.[7] Prior to World War I, the Erzurum province and the city itself had a very vibrant Armenian community with hospitals, schools, printing houses, and associations. It was even the provincial residence of the Archbishop of the Armenian Gregorian Church.

One of the main implications of this geopolitical/communal position was that Islam came to be very much associated with the defense of a particular community and identity. Furthermore, as noted, much of the population of this region by the late nineteenth century was made up of Muslim refugees who were forced out of the Caucasus following a series of genocidal ethnic cleansings resulting from a Russian imperial policy to "pacify" the Muslim Caucasus.[8] The memories of this communal conflict, and Russian occupation, still linger in Erzurum as does, it should be noted, the tragic fate of the Armenian population in 1915 which fell victim to a similar policy of ethnic cleansing. The region was central in the organization of the national movement against the occupation of Anatolia during the War of Independence. Regional Islam, which is marked by *Dadaş* identity, therefore came to be punctuated by the culture of frontier conditions, which stressed security over other concerns, and identified Russian Orthodoxy (and then Communism) as the "other" of Turko-Islamic identity.

Erzurum was the location for one of the bloodiest battles in the Caucasus campaign of World War I, which took place between the Ottoman and Russian forces, aided by the local Armenian population, and which resulted in the fall of the city to Russian troops in 1916.[9] Erzurum was returned to the Ottomans with the Treaty of Brest-Litovsk in 1918. Mustafa Kemal organized the first national congress in Erzurum and the city was a center of the national liberation struggle.[10] As a result of their historical experience, the people of Erzurum tended also to feel that religion cannot survive if the state is not in a strong position to defend it. In his memoirs, Mehmet Kırkıncı, another Nurcu leader of Erzurum, constantly stressed Bediüzzaman Said Nursi's personal heroism in the defense against the Russian and Armenian forces to further legitimize the writings of Nursi in this nationalist region of Turkey.[11] In short, these frontier conditions led to the sense that a strong state and military were a sine qua non for the survival of Muslims and Islamic society. Gülen's conception of Islam is thus conditioned by this nationalism and statism.

Due to its geographic frontier position and the presence of immigrants from the Caucasus, the cultural identity of the region has always been highly politicized, with Islam and Turkish nationalism as its codeterminants. This regional culture, as well as Muhammad Lutfi, Gülen's religious teacher, molded his early personality and his understanding of Islam in significant ways tied to a nationalist and statist framework.[12] A close reading of Gülen's memoir indicates that both his grandmother and mother had a major impact on his emotional understanding of Islam. He witnessed, and was moved by, the stirring power of Islam as an inner force through the conduct and rituals of his grandmother, Munise Hanım. His mother, Rafiya Hanım also played an important role in his religious education by encouraging and supporting the young boy in memorizing the Qur'an at the age of 5. Gülen's religious development took place within a religiously shaped rural community, in which he internalized religious narratives, practices, and symbols. The Prophet Muhammad, for Gülen's rural community, was the perfect man after which all humans are to be modeled, and that the morally proper way of being-in-the-world is to respond to God's calling by living according to Islamic morality. Faith, for Gülen in his rural village, was both a cognitive act and also an emotional and personalized charter that shaped his inner self. His extended family functioned as "the interpreters of religious ideology," and Islam was filtered through their everyday life practices.[13]

Gülen claims that the tenderness and sincerity of his grandmother had a lasting impact upon his own psyche. His family experience and socialization allow us to understand the sources of his emotional understanding of Islam. For Gülen, Islam consists to a great extent of affection and compassionate sentiments. This emotional understanding of religion encouraged Gülen to conclude that the seat of faith lies in the heart more than in the head.

While the young Gülen learned this emotional aspect of faith from his grandmother and mother, he learned a disciplinarian and masculine aspect of Islam from his grandfather (Şamil Ağa), and his father (Ramiz Efendi). For Gülen, Şamil Ağa was a model of a sincere, hard-working, and self-disciplined Muslim; and a teacher of the life stories of Muhammad and his companions. His father's Nakşibendi connections gave him a better understanding of Sufism and Sufi orders. Gülen's early "formal" religious education took place in a Sufi lodge as he argues that "*tekke* was the first place that opened my eye and molded my spirituality."[14] He learned Sufism from the Nakşibendi Sheikh Muhammed Lutfi Efendi, also known as Alvarlı Efe, who was the most influential personality in his early education and paid visits to Gülen's home.[15] His unofficial Sufi education strongly affected his spiritual development. Gülen, unlike nearly all his male friends, never smoked and suppressed his pleasure-oriented passions and erotic feelings. Gülen started more formal education under the tutorship of Lutfi Efendi when he was 10 years old and this continued for six years. Gülen also received religious Sufi (*tasavvuf*) education from Rasim Baba, a leader of the Qadiri order, but he did not remain there long because of their heavy emphasis on outward attire as a sign of piety and also because of the rumor that Rasim Baba wanted his daughter to marry Gülen. After leaving the Sufi lodge, he took two year-long lessons from Osman Bektaş on Islamic jurisprudence, or *fiqh*. In Erzurum, Gülen took further lessons from Solakzade Sadık Efendi, who was the mufti of the city, on Sufism, and from Sıddık Efendi on Islamic jurisprudence.

SAID NURSI'S INFLUENCE ON FETHULLAH GÜLEN

In order to fully understand Gülen's thought and movement, one has to be cognizant of the great debt he owes to the early twentieth-century Ottoman-Kurdish Muslim scholar, reformer, and revivalist, Bediuzzam Said Nursi. It was in Erzurum that Gülen became aware of the writings of Said Nursi in the years 1957–58. This development was crucial in shifting his worldview from a particularized and localized frontier Islamic identity and community to a more cosmopolitan and discursive understanding of Islam. Nursi's collected writings known as the *Risale-i Nur* or *Epistles of Light* empowered Gülen to engage with diverse epistemological systems and a more ecumenical understanding of Islam. However, what most attracted Gülen to the *Risale-i Nur* and the broader Nurcu movement was the exemplary behavior of its followers. When Muzaffer Arslan, a venerable follower and interpreter of the writings of Nursi, came to Erzurum to preach the *Risale-i Nur*, Gülen also attended the lecture.[16] According to Gülen, not only the compelling and logical quality of Arslan's lecture but also his exemplary behavior and moral character deeply touched him; Gülen says:

> In fact, Muzaffer Arslan's sincerity, modesty and his life-style similar to the *Sahabah*, [i.e., the companions of Prophet Muhammad], had a profound effect on me. I have always been of deep affection to the *Sahabah*. When I saw him I told myself I found the people I have been searching for. Since then I never wanted to leave their circle. Both knees of his trouser were patched. His jacket was also in accordance with his modest pants. This modesty inspired different feelings in me.... I went to the mosque and after the prayer, I was burning with desire and an urge that I cannot fully describe. I was imploring: My God, please accept my prayers and help me join this circle of friends; help me to become one of them; and help me to unify with this movement [*hizmet*]; I begged God that night until sunrise. It was only in rare instances of my life, perhaps once or twice, that I prayed to God with such an intimate state of mind. I moaned and sobbed till the morning. That day this was my only plea to God.[17]

Gülen himself would thus become one of the major followers and readers of Nursi. He internalized and fully devoted himself to the texts of Nursi as he had to the memorization of the Qur'an. Today, when Gülen talks about Islam, one hears the voice and message of Nursi.

However, while the spiritual and intellectual debts are clear, there are several major differences between Nursi and Gülen. First, Gülen and those who follow him measure their spiritual success, to a certain extent, in terms of the worldly consequences of their actions. Believing that Gülen is trying to revive the Islamic faith and civilization under the leadership of Anatolian Turks, this newly urbanized group of intellectuals and merchants went into action to translate their worldly success into a heavenly mission and vice versa. Religious ends are achieved through worldly actions rather than purely inward piety, and worldly success through honest hard work and dedication can in turn indicate divine/spiritual blessing. Gülen assumes that the inner transformation of individuals can only take place by impacting and shaping contemporary society and mastering the exigencies of modernity. Indeed, Gülen's method of moving from the inner to the outer may be a reaction to the failure of previous Turkish-Islamic movements to move from the inner individual/spiritual to the outer public/temporal levels.

One of Nursi's main purposes was to avoid reducing faith to politics, that is, using religion to serve particular political factions and ambitions. His main goals were promoting sincerity (*ihlas*) and faith (*iman*) and the belief that lofty religious goals and sentiments should not become an instrument for profane political power. Nursi was skeptical of politics and the political life as being an effective vehicle for bringing positive societal reforms and progress. He felt that even if you succeed politically in enshrining your beliefs, if that success is based on questionable means, it will prove defeat in the long term. From Nursi's perspective, ends do not justify means. The end has to be *ihlas*, not political "victory" and economic success, of which many later Gülenists have been accused. Nursi's understanding of *cemaat* or community is also not that of a "front" or faction as has been the case of some Gülen followers. Moreover, this concept of *cemaat* or community, for Nursi, included not only his followers but all those who believed in God and His divine revelation: the Qur'an. The unity of Muslims is based on the recognition of the Qur'an as God's final revelation. This was a community of believers shaped by the text and tradition. There are several reasons why Nursi remained indifferent to politics and did not try to organize his followers as a potent political force. He did not want to create a separate community or a politicized front so as not to become a target for official Kemalist persecution; he stressed spiritual ties and awakening, not political ones, as central for societal reform and renewal. Nursi was deeply skeptical of political and market-based allegiances and endeavors as the ultimate solution to the human condition in general and Ottoman Muslim decline in particular.

Nursi's main focus was salvation in the afterlife, whereas for Gülen the longing for the afterlife and renouncing of worldly concerns was a traditional Sufi Muslim evasion and "instrument" of fear used to instill obedience and passivity in believers by socioeconomic and political elites. Nursi argued that the ultimate goal for humans is salvation through *ihlas* or high moral conduct that pleases God. For Gülen, the goal is much more worldly: to become politically and economically successful and thus able to shape contemporary Muslim states and societies to successfully grapple with the competitive demands of modernity without discarding one's Islamic faith. Nursi's main task was to serve and promote the message of the Qur'an, while Gülen wants to serve and promote the welfare of this world and success of the Turkish nation and Muslim communities. As far as strategic approaches are concerned, there are differences as well. Nursi stressed the concept of faith and Islamic consciousness; Gülen stresses work, discipline, achievement, and adaptation to modern conditions. Nursi is critical of any movement that stresses power, interest, and struggle to control societal processes. The Qur'an ideally replaces power with "right and truth," *fazilet* (virtue) replaces interest, and struggle is replaced by solidarity and charity. From this perspective, it becomes clear that the contemporary Gülen movement is no longer a gradual progression of the Nurcu movement, but a more modernist and dynamic movement focused on modernity and this-world success. It is a secular modernist movement recasting Islam to conquer the sources of worldly power.

Gülen stresses "action" and "achievement" in contrast to Nursi's focus on "belief." By illustrating the different emphases placed by Gülen on "action," and by Nursi on "belief," one can see the applicability of Alastair MacIntyre's view that the relationship between belief and action are internal and conceptual. MacIntyre argues that "it is because actions express beliefs, because actions are a vehicle for our beliefs that they can be described as consistent or inconsistent with beliefs expressed in avowal."[18] Islam, for Gülen, must be represented by actions geared toward positive achievement in this world, as well as the next, and these actions and achievements, in turn, are seen as genuine expressions of faith. However, the difference between Gülen and Nursi is also related to a newly evolving sociopolitical context within which Turkish Islam is embedded. Social factors that impinge upon this Islamic discourse and influences set the direction of the Gülen movement on a trajectory well beyond traditional Nur movement of Said Nursi.

Although both Nursi and Gülen expressed their views on social and political issues in terms of a perceived assault on Muslim sociopolitical consciousness and tradition during the authoritarian Republican period, each offered different remedies. Nursi, by forming a new religious consciousness, devalued the world in favor of certain spiritual ideals, whereas Gülen stresses praxis as the totality of all human activities through which a person seeks to transform nature into a "human world" (*cemiyet*)—of meanings, consciousness, technologies, and economic forces. One may treat Nursi's understanding of Islam from the "inside out" and Gülen's from the "outside in." These different readings of the role of the Islamic religious tradition are responses to different conditions and needs. In the case of Nursi, the main task was the renewal of religious consciousness and the rejuvenation of faith in the midst of a militantly antireligious state campaign, whereas for Gülen, the challenge of modernity transcends Kemalist ideology and necessitates the wholesale reform of economic and social policy in the Muslim world.

Differences in the stress on the individual and community also differentiate Nursi from Gülen. Nursi's movement remained a faith movement from the beginning to the end. Gülen's movement started as a faith movement but evolved into sociopolitical movement with the goal of shaping modern institutions and spaces. Nursi's writings and activities aimed to deepen religious consciousness, and he preferred to work on the inner core of the self (i.e., *vicdan* (conscience)) by stressing awareness of consciousness in which man is alone with God. Nursi stressed the role of conscience as an inner feeling and revelation about what is morally right and wrong. Nursi's main focus was raising one's religious consciousness to immunize people against the prevailing positivism and materialism of the age.

Gülen's main focus is not on inner individual conscience, but rather action in the public sphere. He thinks that the public collective engagement is the way of raising one's religious consciousness. He wants to move from behavior to belief. In Gülen's conception of the self, one is defined by, and matures through, membership in a community where one becomes fully aware of his duty to the group and broader society. For Gülen, the compelling theme has been action (*aksiyon*) and control over material conditions as a way of enhancing spiritual needs and ends.[19] Gülen presents himself as a contemporary man of praxis, as well as of spiritual contemplation. In the case of Nursi, however, the prevailing conditions of Kemalist persecution forced him to turn away from an externalized message of Islamic reform to an inner contemplative one. The incongruity between the inner and outer spiritual realms conditioned Nursi's understanding of modernity. According to Nursi, there is only one "home" where everyone can feel equal and free, and that is the religious domain in which believers are fully conscious of the existence of God. Members of this inner community view each other as equals. He sought to prevent the assimilation of Muslims to the external world and wanted them to return "home." One sees the perpetuation of this theme of "home" and belonging in the writings of other modern Turkish intellectuals. The notion of "home" was linked intricately with notions of memory, roots, and displacement, within the secularizing and nationalizing Turkish Republic, where the new language of politics was introduced. This notion of "home" was an imagined and mostly invented mythical space for which traditional pious Muslims yearned in response to their marginalization within the Republic. In the case of Gülen, however, "home" is a national-religious one where collective action and worldly success sustains and recasts religious faith in the face of modernity's universal challenges.

GÜLEN: IMAM AND NURCU (1959–1971)

After the local state-licensed examination to become a congregational prayer leader (imam) in mosques, Gülen was appointed to Edirne to offer religious services in the local mosque in 1959. Before performing mandatory military service in Ankara in 1962, Gülen served a two and a half year tenure as imam in Edirne, while remaining very active by participating in a series of cultural activities contesting communism and Darwinism. He supported the writings of anticommunist and nationalist authors. Due to the perceived communist threat at the height of the Cold War, the Turkish state somewhat relaxed its persecution of the Nur movement as a potential barrier against the growing radical leftist movement in Turkey. Indeed, many prominent Nurcus (followers of Said Nursi), like Gülen, became involved in the foundation of the Turkish Associations for the Struggle against Communism (*Türkiye Komunizimle Mücadele Dernekleri*), and the Nur movement itself evolved into a significant pro-NATO and pro-American Muslim group in Turkey.[20]

Gülen did not limit himself to Nursi's writings, but included the books of socially conservative and politically nationalist intellectuals such as Necip Fazıl Kısakürek, Nurettin Topçu, and Sezai Karakoç.[21] Gülen, as a man of action more than ideas, was concerned about the application of ideas and moral norms in public and private spheres. He did not want to confine Islam to the private domain, but rather stressed the role of public religion in the formation of morality, identity, and a just community. After returning from military service in 1963, he visited his family in Erzurum and spent a year there before returning to Edirne in 1964.

Given the relatively liberal and Western outlook of Edirne, Gülen felt socially uneasy there and spent most of his time in the mosque. He interpreted the liberal lifestyle of young women there in terms of their being "free and easy" as an outcome of lack of Islamic beliefs.[22] The young Gülen tended to be uncomfortable around women and his conservative religious worldview conflicted with the emerging secular-modern lifestyle of Edirne and Western Turkey in general and this in turn seemed to encourage a more ascetic personal lifestyle. Gülen eventually decided to leave Edirne and was appointed as an imam in Kırklareli in 1965.

After serving half a year in Kırklareli, Gülen was appointed to the Kestanepazarı Qur'anic School in Izmir to teach and administer courses on Islamic sciences in 1966. While serving as a teacher, Gülen regularly traveled to different coffeehouses, mosques, community centers, and other public spaces, to preach about Islamic ethics and the natural sciences by drawing upon Nursi's ideas. For Gülen, serving God meant striving toward becoming a "perfect individual" who combines spirituality with intellectual attainment, reason with revelation, and mind with heart. Combining his personal abilities with the social resources available in Izmir, he continued to reach out to different students to teach them about Islamic theology and history, while staying engaged with the Said Nursi reading circles. From the perspective of Gülen, early education should focus on the development of spiritual and intellectual capabilities with a Spartan lifestyle. The main task was to plant the seeds of motivation in the hearts and minds of these students to yearn for the "truth" and serve society.

Having become convinced of the importance of role models through the character formation of students (i.e., *Bildung*), in 1968, Gülen decided to organize men-only summer camps for high school and university students in order to teach them Islamic sciences and to cultivate their characters (see more on the summer camps in chapter 2). Gülen always admired military discipline and believed that the best character formation requires discipline:

> The generation to be raised should be well disciplined like the military. The camps should also be similar to the military barracks. However, they should not be closed to the dimension of spiritual yearnings. In this sense, the camps must resemble a Sufi lodge (*tekke*). By reading *Tasbihat*, *Jawshan* and *Evrad-ı Kudsiye*, the participants develop an excellent inner self. On the other hand, it is also necessary to use the intellect alongside the heart. Therefore reading books and taking Arabic lessons made the camps resemble religious seminaries (madrasa). By bringing the best aspects of military discipline, the morality of the Sufi lodge and the religious knowledge of the madrasa in an integrated and holistic way, we take the first step toward our imagined world.[23]

Gülen's primary goal in these summer camps was to cultivate a new generation of Turks who have a holistic understanding of the universe, their society, and their self as Muslims. In the 1960s and 1970s, Gülen also initiated the establishment of the lighthouses (*Işıkevler*) in Izmir where his educational system was fully implemented. These lighthouses provided the necessary space for university students to develop their spiritual capabilities, along with a better and "filtered" understanding of secular knowledge, and most importantly they functioned as spaces where learning and living could take place at the same time (see more on the lighthouses in chapter 2).

Izmir was the place where the ideas and strategies of Gülen were tested and implemented. The movement started as an educational one and stressed self-sacrifice for the greater good of community, Islam, and humanity. Gülen, like Nursi, emphatically presented this movement as *hizmet* (rendering service to someone with the purpose of serving God).

GÜLEN: SEARCH FOR AUTONOMY AND CRITICISM OF ANARCHY (1971–1980)

Following the 1971 coup, Gülen was indicted and convicted of violating Article 163 of the Turkish Penal Code, which strictly criminalized all forms of ideas and activities seen as critical of Kemalism and the secular nature of the state, and he spent seven months in prison. Gülen, along with all prominent leaders of the Nur movement, was arrested and accused of "establishing a clandestine religious association and seeking to change the secular nature of the Turkish Republic." This period in prison made Gülen more autonomous from other Nur movements, since they had close ties with political parties and were the target of Turkey's secular and leftist intellectuals and state institutions. He divorced himself from other Islamic groups in the country and decided to focus solely on education. Moreover, his arrest and experience of state authoritarianism and persecution led Gülen and other Nurcus to withdraw from the public eye and pursue their objectives in a more tacit and concealed fashion. Following the arrest, his life was very much spent in fear and anguish. This traumatic event would mark his future demeanor and conduct. At the height of Kemalist authoritarianism, Turkish citizens were obliged to wear a mask, professing obedience to an ideology that sought to denigrate their faith, identity, and Ottoman heritage. Gülen, like many others, decided to withdraw himself to the inner spiritual sphere of contemplation, where he began to express himself in a highly coded language of ambivalence.

Gülen later appealed his conviction and while the appeal process was in motion, he benefited from an amnesty for people convicted on an ideological basis. Following his amnesty, Gülen was appointed as the imam of Edremit in February 1972 and served two years there. In 1975, he was appointed to Manisa and, in each town he served in, he managed to establish lighthouses and created a web of networks to realize his dream of cultivating a new generation of religious revivalists. In 1975–76, Gülen visited different Anatolian cities and delivered lectures on "Qur'an and Science," "Darwinism," "the Golden Generation," and "Social Justice." In 1976, Gülen was appointed as an imam in Bornova and Izmir, and stayed there until the 1980 military coup. During this period, Gülen searched for opportunities to generate support for his activities among West Germany's growing Turkish community and visited Berlin, Hamburg, Hannover, and Munich lecturing to the Turks there about Islam, work ethics, and family. However, at that time, Turkish communities in Germany did not receive him enthusiastically or give him much support.

In the 1970s, during a period of intense conflict between leftist and right-wing youth movements, Gülen provided intellectual and moral support to the center-right parties, while desperately seeking to keep his followers out of the violent conflicts raging at the time. In the second half of the 1970s, almost all Turkish universities were zones of intense conflict, and the country was on the brink of a civil war between two ideological poles. The lives of prominent intellectuals and politicians were threatened and the daily death toll on university campuses was over 15 students. In this violent and chaotic period, the Nur movement, and Gülen himself, stressed the importance of the power of the state and asked the security forces to be more assertive in establishing law and order. During this critical juncture in modern Turkish history, Gülen supported the center-right and nationalist Turkish political parties against the Kemalist Republican People's Party, since it was perceived to be the surrogate for militant leftist movements in addition to having a reflexive antipathy to religion. During this period, Gülen also wanted to insulate his community from active political involvement in the Islamic political movement led by Necmettin Erbakan and treated such political activity as potentially subverting his reformist religious agenda while inviting the wrath of the state. Gülen would further underscore this conservative nationalist position, by buying into the state's promotion of a Turkish-Islamic synthesis as a way of combating the perceived Communist threat.[24]

In spite of its own experience of persecution at the hands of the Kemalist military-bureaucratic establishment, the Gülen community adopted the security-centric nationalistic outlook of the state in response to growing communal conflict. This underscored the fact that Gülen's main concern has always been avoiding anarchy and the fragmentation of state and society. This also reflects the legacy of the long period of Ottoman decline and foreign invasions of Muslim lands. Gülen defends the state as the central institution to protect society, as well as to secure welfare and development.

During the 1970s and 1980s, the Gülen-guided network communities searched for official legitimacy by adopting the state's line on Islam. The state-centric understanding of Islam among Gülen's followers is the outcome of the culture of insecurity in Anatolia that evolved from the legacy of the disintegrated Ottoman Empire. Said Nursi and his first generation of followers witnessed the elimination of Muslim hegemony in the Balkans and the Caucasus and the partition of Anatolia by the Sèvres Peace Treaty of 1920. Subsequently, the Nurcus, particularly those from eastern Anatolia such as Mehmet Kırkıncı, a prominent Nurcu leader and personal friend of Gülen, and Gülen himself, viewed the state during the Cold War as the first condition for the survival of their religion against the expansionist threats of their Soviet neighbor.

In 1979, in order to prevent the further disintegration of Turkish society, Gülen decided to go public with his own ideas and solutions by establishing *Sızıntı* magazine. During this period of street fights and a very assertive Communist movement in Turkey, Gülen identified the lack of faith and communal solidarity as the source of the violence and polarization of society and proposed his own vision based on Islamic morality as a solution. In addition to establishing *Sızıntı*, Gülen also toured different cities to expound his ideas and reach out to the more traditional Anatolian population.

THE TURKISH-ISLAMIC SYNTHESIS

The 1980 coup was carried out by a group of military officers who sought to overcome the country's political and social divisions and also implement an IMF-led structural adjustment program to curb hyperinflation that was contributing significantly to the political turmoil. The military administration led by General Kenan Evren viewed leftist groups as the greatest threat to their authority in this period and sought to diminish their influence by promoting a "Turkish-Islamic synthesis." This policy garnered considerable support and, more importantly, paved the way for the near revolutionary liberalizing reforms of Turgut Özal.[25]

The rhetoric and policies of the 1980 coup treated a domesticated form of Islam as an element in the service of the nation and nationalism rather than as an autonomous force able to compete with either secularism or nationalism. The idea that Islam is the most important cement of the Turkish national identity was not new. [26] Those nationalist-conservative intellectuals who stressed the ethno-religious aspect of Turkish nationalism had a major opportunity to put their ideas into practice. Islam, for them, inspired, as well as brought a sense of, personal and communal identity to Turks. It is in this nationalist context, in which the issue of the "sacred" as the source of a duty-oriented moral responsibility to community, state, and nation, has been addressed collectively. The military sought to cement national unity by using Islam as its shared social bond. Its ideology of a Turkish-Islamic synthesis was constructed by a group of conservative scholars who were members of the Intellectuals' Hearth Association (*Aydınlar Ocağı*), an organization founded in 1970 to protect Turkish identity and tradition from "alien influences."[27] This new ideology sought to create public consent for the consolidation of state power. The Intellectuals' Hearth Association was sympathetic to the Islamic dimension of modern Turkish identity and also enjoyed good relations with the state-civil apparatus. The military leadership viewed this group of intellectuals as ideal for constructing this new ideology because the sterility of Kemalist positivism as an ideology of state legitimization had become obvious by the 1980s. The Intellectuals' Hearth Association attempted to create a new ideology out of Ottoman, Islamic, and Turkish popular culture in order to justify the hegemony of the ruling elite. They reinterpreted the state as being integral to the nation and society, and their repertoire of Ottoman-Islamic myths and symbols were selectively deployed for the first time in the Republican era to make the past seem relevant to the present. Gülen's vision coalesced with this state project to find an ethno-religious glue to keep society together. He supported the coup and was not critical of the 1980 coup leaders:

> I want to also add that the architects of the coup also took some positive administrative decisions. They shook society to renew itself once again. They defeated the Communist movement which recruited some misguided youth who wanted Turkey to be under Soviet influence. They intentionally or unintentionally prevented our country from entering into quagmire and into a long bloody struggle. Moreover, they gave opportunities to some decent children of our homeland to serve our nation.[28]

THE RISE OF *HOCAEFENDI* AND GÜLEN'S MOVEMENT (1980–1999)

Fethullah Gülen's faith in the new military administrators, however, was not fully requited. Following the 1980 military coup, the military leadership issued an arrest warrant against Gülen on grounds similar to his arrest during the previous coup. Gülen lost his erstwhile inside track with the security forces, and it was only in 1986 that his arrest warrant was revoked by a state security court.[29] Article 163 of the Penal Code, which was used to prosecute Gülen and other religious conservatives, was later abolished by the reforming Özal government in 1991, on the grounds that it violated freedom of expression and religion.

During this period of lying low, Gülen utilized audio cassettes to disseminate his ideas in the form of sermons throughout Turkey. Emotional intensity and release in the form of weeping often epitomize Gülen's sermons. Outwardly, his sermons speak in a triumphant religio-public voice. Yet, beneath these sermons there is a softer and more melancholic voice, audible to those who shared the similar deep religious devotion and the same religious orientation. Due to a more stable and religion-friendly political environment in the 1980s under Turgut Özal's leadership, the Gülen movement put forward its vision of creating a "golden generation" into practice by utilizing new political, legal, and economic opportunity spaces.[30] Gülen developed close ties with Özal, then the Prime Minister, and worked closely with him to transform the sociocultural landscape of Turkey. The liberalization of the political system in the 1980s enabled Gülen's associates and followers for the first time to gain a toehold in the state establishment and emerge openly as one of the most influential sociopolitical movements in Turkey.

After 1983 and the removal of the legal warrant against him, Gülen emerged as one of the dominant figures on the Turkish-Islamic scene. His movement developed close ties with state institutions and became involved in economic, cultural, and media activities. The entry into social, educational, media, and economic fields would in turn also decisively transform the movement itself. The movement quickly came to appreciate the power and significance of the mass media and market economy and tried to become more modernized and professionalize itself by establishing new foundations, broadcasting companies, publishing presses, and cultural foundations. Gülen utilized the opportunity spaces created by Özal's liberalizing reforms and managed to turn his traditional and geographically confined faith movement into a nationwide educational and cultural phenomenon. The Gülen movement attempted to bring "religious" perspectives into the public sphere on social and cultural issues. This, in turn, led to the objectification of a "religious worldview" as an autonomous category to frame public policy debates. The process of "going public" and trying to communicate within the normative domain of the public sphere in Turkey required the Gülen movement to moderate its positions and frame its arguments in terms of broadly accepted reasons and justifications that could persuade secular segments of society as well. This tentative, yet profound, attempt to enter the broader public sphere ultimately facilitated the internal secularization of many Muslim political forces by forcing Nurcu groups to compete with diverse worldviews and frame their arguments to appeal to a broad cross-section of society.

The Gülen movement's attempt to appeal to broader society, however, led more militantly secular segments of Kemalist society to perceive them as an even greater threat. Their activities and especially successful projects in the education of an alternative socioeconomic elite in particular stirred fear and hostility among Kemalist circles. Those who were uncomfortable with the challenges of the Gülen movement and its activities during this period worked hard to project a negative image of the movement in public by accusing them of being "şeriatçı" or promoters of Sharia. This campaign included a vitriolic media campaign in leading Kemalist media outlets. At the same time, the movement was also attacked by more radical Islamists as being too "accommodating" and "pro-American."

EXILE AND FORCED LIBERALIZATION (1999–TO THE PRESENT)

A major turning point in the transformation of Gülen's life and thinking took place within the context of the February 28, 1997, "soft coup" by the military. One of the major consequences of this coup was the further liberalization of Turkey's leading Islamic groups. However, this was an unexpected development at the time. The aim of Turkey's military generals, the self-appointed custodians of Kemalism, was to ban virtually all independent sources of Islamic social, political, and cultural expression to prevent a "fundamentalist" takeover of the state. Instead of Communism and the Left, the new bogeyman was once again traditionally pious sections of Anatolian society. The military-bureaucratic establishment banned the democratically elected Refah/Fazilet Party, restricted Imam Hatip schools, severely curtailed the building of new mosques, and implemented a strict dress code outlawing the wearing of headscarves in institutions of higher education, while suspending and imprisoning elected mayors by order of the Ministry of the Interior.

Rather than opposing the latest round of Kemalist oppression, Gülen controversially and publicly rationalized the military crackdown against the Refah Party and did not oppose the broadening campaign against peaceful Sunni Islamic groups in the country.[31] This failed attempt at appeasement led critics to charge that Gülen had not been very consistent on the issues of democracy and human rights and has sought immunity by promoting his group's interest before the rights of civil society as a whole.[32] Gülen and his community tried to present themselves as "soft" and "moderate" vis-à-vis other Islamic groups within Turkey.

Certain branches of the state and some secular politicians supported the activities of Gülen within and outside of Turkey at the time in order to contain the more "radical" Islamic forces. Gülen, like many others in Turkish Republican history, sought legitimacy as a charitable dispensation from an authoritarian state. Prior to the national elections in April 1999, both President Süleyman Demirel and Prime Minister Bülent Ecevit, the senior leaders in Turkey, defended Gülen's activities and worldview as a "bulwark" against political Islam as represented by the Welfare/Fazilet Party.[33] However, this attempt at appeasement of the Kemalist establishment failed. In 1999, private television stations associated with the Kemalist establishment played a cassette of Gülen in which he asks his followers to be "cautious" and "wait for the ripe time to respond" in the face of the *Kulturkampf*.[34] This led secular critics to conclude that the movement seeks "power and wants to end the secular nature of Turkey." The media, under the leadership of the Kemalist newspaper *Hürriyet*, unleashed a sensationalistic character assassination against Gülen and his movement.[35] In the video recording, Gülen appeared to be saying:

> You must move within the arteries of the system without anyone noticing your existence until you reach all the power centers... until the conditions are ripe, they [the followers] must continue like this. If they do something prematurely, the world will crush our heads, and Muslims will suffer everywhere, like in the tragedies in Algeria, like in 1982 [in] Syria... like in the yearly disasters and tragedies in Egypt. The time is not yet right. You must wait for the time when you are ready and conditions are ripe, until we can shoulder the entire world and carry it.... You must wait until such time as you have gotten all the state power, until you have brought to your side all the power of the constitutional institutions in Turkey.... Until that time, any step taken would be too early—like breaking an egg without waiting the full forty days for it to hatch. It would be like killing the chick inside. The work to be done is [in] confronting the world. Now, I have expressed my feelings and thoughts to you all—in confidence... trusting your loyalty and secrecy. I know that when you leave here—[just] as you discard your empty juice boxes, you must discard the thoughts and the feelings that I expressed here.

He continued:

> When everything was closed and all doors were locked, our houses of *ışık* [light] assumed a mission greater than that of older times. In the past, some of the duties of these houses were carried out by *madrasa*s [Islamic schools], some by schools, some by *tekke*s [Islamist lodges].... These *ışık* homes had to be the schools, had to be *madrasa*s, [had to be] *tekke*s all at the same time. The permission did not come from the state, or the state's laws, or the people who govern us. The permission was given by God... who wanted His name learned and talked about, studied, and discussed in those houses, as it used to be in the mosques.[36]

On the basis of these secretly recorded talks, the Ankara State Security Court prosecutor requested an arrest warrant for Gülen on charges of plotting to overthrow the state by establishing a clandestine organization. The State Security Court rejected the request of the arrest warrant on August 28, 2000. The prosecutor also alleged that "the organization of Fethullah Gülen, which was formed to destroy the secular nature of the state since 1989, weaved itself into the country with its legal and illegal networks that includes advisory boards, regional, city, neighborhood, hostel leaders."[37] The prosecutor was seeking a maximum 10-year sentence based on Turkey's Anti-Terror Law. The prosecutor did not mention a single specific event or "crime" but rather referred to the "destructive" ideas spread by Gülen. The indictment should be read within the political framework of the 1997 coup and its aims to criminalize alternative thinking and movements not part of official Kemalist doctrine.

After the cassette incident, the military-orchestrated media launched an organized and fierce attack on Gülen and his activities as being "reactionary" and a "threat" to the secular nature of the Turkish state.[38] An ambitious and militantly antireligious clique within the Kemalist establishment launched this anti-Gülen campaign by attacking schools, foundations, and the pro-Gülen media. This confrontation was one that Gülen had avidly sought to avoid.[39] Uncharacteristically, however, the attack was met by a sharp and hitherto unprecedented counterattack by Gülen's media outlets.[40] For his part, Gülen had learned a painful lesson that obsequiously catering to the center of military power can breed contempt as much as it does forbearance. To be fair, the attack on Gülen was actually also aimed at eroding civilian authority, particularly the popular leftist Prime Minister Bülent Ecevit. Many journalists and members of Gülen's inner circle believed a militant secularist group within the Turkish army was behind this attempt to further curtail civilian authority.

GLOBALIZATION VIA AMERICANIZATION: GÜLEN IN PENNSYLVANIA (1999–PRESENT)

Fethullah Gülen visited the United States in 1992 and 1997. He was always positive about the nature of the American social and political system. Gülen stated, "When I first came to the US in 1992, I felt it was an outstanding and a very democratic country; the environment was very comfortable and peaceful back then."[41] In 1999, Gülen was finally forced to leave Turkey due to the escalating official media campaign that engaged in character assassination and presented his activities as dangerously subversive. Since then, Gülen has been living at the Golden Generation Worship and Retreat Center, also known as "the Camp," in Saylorsburg, Pennsylvania.

Gülen publicly, however, always explained his continued stay in America as being due to "medical treatment" rather than exile to escape persecution. He says, "I discovered that this country, especially the area where I live, is more serene and quiet in comparison with Turkey. I preferred to stay here because I found it to be more tranquil and thought it to be more convenient to see the doctors under whose care I remain."[42] This was an escape from a situation that was beyond Gülen's control to rectify or even explain himself. This period of exile also marked the beginning of a "new Gülen," who would gradually shed his statist, nationalist, and conservative ideas to adopt a newer universal language of liberalism, human rights, democracy, interfaith dialogue, and tolerance. The American residence marked a decisive rupture for Gülen, who now continuously stresses the need for "bridging" and "connecting" with diverse cultures.

From Gülen's perspective, the future of Turkey cannot be left to chance. He asks his followers and sympathizers not to simply wish what Turkey should ideally become, but rather mobilize to attain it. Gülen tells his followers that they can create their future, but they cannot alter the past and thus they must learn from both the greatness and mistakes of their past. Gülen is not just a visionary; he is also able to combine his vision with sophisticated strategies and international networks to implement them. Thus, Gülen believes that the way to predict the future of Turkey and his community is to have social and political power shape it. In short, his time in the United States has helped him to think with a more universal and holistic vision and further stress the Sufi aspects of Islam. Life in America generated a fresh perspective in Gülen's view of Sufism, pluralism, interreligious dialogue, cultural exchanges, and education.[43]

Fear of state persecution drove Gülen to ultimately withdraw himself into a self-imposed exile, where he learned to express himself in a highly coded language of ambivalence. His interview with Nuriye Akman in America indicates this ambivalence.[44] His writings and speeches in America remind us that the meanings of his statements are esoteric and geared toward different readers or listeners.[45] This esoteric style of writing and talking allowed his followers to decode his real intentions and messages without facing prosecution. Gülen's own experience of prosecution helped forge a complex and contradictory personality. He is capable of both courage and prudence, the two aspects of his personality which have never been reconciled. As of 2004, his last public interview indicates a person worn down by years of living in a state of anxiety, an anxiety that did not go away even in his exile in the United States.

Gülen's application for permanent residence in the United States on the basis of being "an alien of extraordinary abilities" was rejected by the Department of Homeland Security.[46] Immigration officials rejected Gülen's application, arguing that he does not qualify for the "extraordinary ability" exemption because he did not "show that he has achieved sustained national or international acclaim at the very top level." The Immigration Department asked the judge to reject the case since:

> Further, the record contains overwhelming evidence that plaintiff is primarily the leader of a large and influential religious and political movement with immense commercial holdings. The record further shows that much of the acclaim that plaintiff claims to have achieved has been sponsored and financed by plaintiff's own movement. It is the government's

position that the evidence of record permits only one conclusion: that plaintiff has failed to meet the requirements of an alien of extraordinary ability in the field of education.

However, a federal court ruled that immigration authorities improperly rejected Gülen's application, and the court ordered the US government to reverse its decision on July 16, 2008. Gülen provided 29 letters of reference to his motion. Most of the letters came from Turkish scholars of Islamic studies, including several letters from Turkey's Jewish community leaders. Two former CIA officials, Graham Fuller and George Fidas, also wrote letters to support Gülen's motion.

Gülen's personality, as well as his ideas, has gone through significant transformations as a result of his past encounters with adversity. This has certainly been true with his encounter with American style democracy, liberalism, and secularism. Gülen is accommodating new realities by re-creating himself as a "global imam," who is also in tune with the needs of power centers in the United States.[47] This new mode of thinking is more Washington-centered than Ankara-centered. A follower of Gülen who lives in Washington, DC, said, "We have ties with almost all necessary networks in the United States. We have close ties with Hillary Clinton and some senators since the movement contributed to their election campaigns. We need to emulate the Jewish experience in America. Turkey is important but as long as the movement has close ties with the US establishment, Ankara will also listen to Hocaefendi." Indeed, the JDP government, overcoming past mistrust and rivalry, has finally been listening to Gülen on a number of issues, especially appointing pro-Gülen bureaucrats to high positions and supporting Gülen's educational and cultural activities in different Asian, European, and African countries. *The Economist* aptly portrays Gülen as "a farm boy on the World stage" with close connections with politicians both in Turkey and America and a growing financial, media, and educational empire.[48] To see how far Gülen has come in his role as one of the most influential modern Muslim spiritual leaders and reformers, one has to consider the worldview of his cousin Necdet Gülen from the village Korucuk where Fethullah Gülen was born. He proudly told the *Economist* that "God be praised, our village is all Muslim, and we don't have the evil internet." Gülen, who also came out of this conservative and exclusivist milieu, has transformed himself into a "global religio-political leader" and a source of hope and fear for many in and outside of Turkey.

CONCLUSION

Fethullah Gülen, a bachelor and retired functionary of the State's Directorate of Religious Affairs, has emerged as the leader of one of the most dynamic, transnational, and wealthy faith-based Islamic movements in Turkey. He is situated in the particular sociohistorical context of Turkey and his discourse is very much a response to the challenges of his generation. Gülen's thought has evolved over the years in response to his encounter with different sociopolitical contexts and challenges, above all those of modernity and globalization. Islam, for Gülen, not only aims to educate people and ensure their salvation but also to externalize their Islamic consciousness for the moral and intellectual uplifting of human society. Gülen developed a theology of religious activism and encouraged his students, who would later be the core group in the movement, to engage in this faith-motivated sociopolitical ideology and movement. In the constitution of this activism, Gülen evoked the life of Muhammad and also the founders of the Ottoman state as revolutionary exemplars. Gülen has a charismatic appeal that is derived from his intellectual abilities and leadership skills, as well as his reputation for impeccable morality and religious devotion.

Gülen has always been active in the praxis of Turkish social and political life. Resisting the dominant authoritarian Kemalist establishment through conferences, organizing summer camps, building dormitories, and establishing schools, all reflected his engagement and deviation with a long-term vision. Gülen remains deeply concerned with problems of social injustice, illiteracy, and division, and especially what he feels has been the decline of religious moral values in modern Turkish society. In the late 1960s, he thought what he was witnessing could be the eclipse of Turkish-Muslim society with its traditions, values, and dreams echoing from the great Ottoman past. However, unlike some other religious scholars and Sufi masters who opted for an "exit" from the public sphere, Gülen chose to infuse his ideas and leadership within a like-minded community to challenge and transform the Kemalist authoritarian and positivist vision for modern Turkish state and society. For Gülen, the questions of faith and morality were ultimately those of preserving a certain vision of community while reforming it to meet the challenges of modernity.

Until 1983, Gülen's appeal to his followers stemmed mainly from his powerful charismatic qualities. Following his move to America, there has been a pronounced shift from emotional appeals to more rational and routinized ones. As the movement becomes more institutionalized and rationalized, it has expanded to different countries and continents. Although Islamic morality and identity are at the core of the movement, Gülen's discourse is becoming more universal and cosmopolitan and also focused on this-world goals as opposed to the afterlife.

2

The Contextual Theology of Gülen

Islamic Enlightenment

Fethullah Gülen's thoughts and speeches have had a pervasive influence on the course of Turkish Islamic movements and, more generally, state-society relations. This has obliged scholars and experts in several fields to critically examine the questions and interpretations he raises and the answers he provides. In order to comprehend the intellectual map of Gülen and his movement, one must become acquainted with his core concepts, and then, contemplate their varying interactions in the context of a theology that seeks to propose a dialectical relationship between ideas and action. His key concepts are: religion (Islam), morality, the good life, and community, on the one hand, and the politics of identity (Turkish-Islamic nationalism), state, modernity, and democracy, on the other hand. Gülen's exegesis of Islamic tradition provides an intellectual ground for the vernacularization of modernity. Thus, if Said Nursi was the architect of religious enlightenment in Turkey, Gülen is both the contractor and engineer of these ideas in terms of their actualization and implementation. This chapter will explicate his religious thought and its impact in Turkey and abroad.

THE THEOLOGY OF ACTION (*AKSIYON*)

I would like to describe Gülen's system of ideas as a "contextual theology." By contextual theology, I mean a deep concern for the dialectical relationship between the eternal message of Islam and the human condition. Similar to the perspective offered by Protestant German-American theologian Paul Tillich, theology, for Gülen, means understanding the message in its context and while seeking to create a more humane and virtuous world.[1] Gülen is neither as systematic nor as deeply intellectual as Tillich was. However, he is much more successful than Tillich in terms of transforming people's lives and building a series of faith communities. Gülen, like Tillich, has also been known as an autobiographical thinker, that is, his thought tends to be a manifestation of his struggle in life and concern for others. Gülen's interest in updating Islamic dogma and theology, and stressing the idea that "thoughts lead action," was the outcome of his own experiences and struggles, which shaped his understanding of the human condition.

The gist of Gülen's theology is to raise religious consciousness through action in the here and now by building a moral community. His theology provides religious ground for believers to become morally perfect persons (*insan-ı kamil*) by renouncing worldly urges, clearing themselves from all types of desires, and offering themselves to God by acting to please Him. In his writings, Gülen argues that Islam requires hand-in-hand cooperation of self-development and glorification of God through communal actions. Thus, the main purpose of an Islamic life is not self-fulfillment or realization of appetites but consciousness of God through sacrifices and service to Him and His creation. In other words, to be sanctified, one must live and act with constant readiness and willingness to transform one's own thoughts and emotions. This becomes a possibility if believers themselves stay clear from all the pollutions of the flesh and surrender themselves to God. Gülen argues that, by definition, Muslims need to engage in building communities, obeying the Sharia, and responding to socioeconomic challenges through religiously sanctioned actions. According to Gülen, a Muslim is someone who acts to change the social structure because of love for God, not because of self-interest or fulfillment of pleasure. Sacrificing for community and the well-being of others in the name of God is the critical value and ideal in the theology of Gülen. His writings repeatedly stress the act of "sacrifice" as a religious virtue. Indeed, the virtue of sacrifice is an important motivating force for the followers of the movement to overcome their egos and narrow self interests.

Even though he has not explored and systematized his intellectual contribution, Gülen's theological thinking seeks to bring human and divine action together in order to transform people's consciousness by highlighting a vertical believer/God interaction. He then seeks to use this deposited "religious energy" at the horizontal level to externalize that religious consciousness through action. In other words, after raising religio-social consciousness and charging believers with religious passion, he calls those filled with religious enthusiasm to praise God and act collectively for the betterment of their own communities. Gülen, like Tillich, establishes a close "relationship of human and divine action" to improve social conditions. From Gülen's perspective, life and faith are intrinsically related, and his goal is to develop an action-based understanding of Islamic morality. Moreover, Islamic rituals and practices are interpreted within the context of socioeconomic conditions to deepen one's consciousness and find meaning (logos) in life. One's emerging comprehension of that meaning requires that the person not only appreciate the human condition but also participate in communal activities to better it. Gülen's thinking consists of two principles: (1) the core principle is the belief in God and the recognition that God reveals His mysteries through the Holy Books and the Book of Nature; (2) in order to realize this divine potential in each and every person, individual desires must be overcome through self-sacrifice (*fedakarlık*).

Gülen clarifies:

> All of these depend on the existence of unpretentious people with no expectations (*hasbi*), and they are certainly a grace from God. Therefore, people must seriously train themselves in the direction of having no expectation of return (*hasbi*) and altruism. They must be unpretentious and just like the people during the Meccan period who could not see the season of triumph, they should also free themselves from every kind of worldly expectations and seek the pleasure of God. They should never forget that God may not allow them to continue this work until the end. These people of courage should be loyal, but should never hold any expectation. This is because service (*hizmet*) is done not for the reward to be given here, but because it is for the sake of God and salvation. If some reward is given here, then it should be regarded as *ulufe* (paid by the Sultan to some soldiers), but it should never be attributed to any individuals.[2]

Gülen's theology did not evolve from university circles, but rather was born out of his personal and communal experiences in Turkey.

Gülen shared and shaped ideas through wide-reaching networks of acquaintance, correspondence, and publishing, controlled by his movement and also other outlets as well. His close engagement with secular concerns is evident by his many writings on history, philosophy, politics, and current affairs, crossing different intellectual paths. According to Gülen, the Prophet Muhammad embodies logos, the link between God and humanity, and represents a rupture in human history by presenting a new historical consciousness to create an ideal just society. The goal of Islam, for Gülen, is to change people and their engagement, in the world and with others. Thus, Gülen presents "action" as the way in which belief is displayed and shared with another. *Aksiyon*, for Gülen, is similar to praxis, that is, practicing ideas and values or acting while guided by principle. By *aksiyon*, Gülen means "transformative action," to morally improve our communities and our relations with others. It means relating faith to lives by being involved in communal activities. By calling believers to do good works in their communities, Gülen wants believers to realize their "transformative agency" to control their destiny and improve their conditions. His interpretation of Islam seeks to empower Muslims to liberate themselves from confining social, political, and economic conditions. Thus, Gülen's "contextual theology" seeks the transformation of people by introducing a new cognitive map of action from within the Islamic tradition. Gülen's theology is not quietist or submissive, but rather transformative and action-oriented.

CARDINAL PROBLEMS OF MUSLIMS: THE CRISIS OF MORALITY AND COMMUNITY

It is important to study Gülen's intellectual map, since he has become one of the most articulate and influential Muslim scholars today, as well as an important social innovator and educator. Furthermore, he has established a position that is severely critical of the politicization of Islam, and his articulation of the practical problems that Muslims face in modern society is characterized by visionary thinking. Through his writings and actions, Gülen has attempted to persuade his community and countrymen that they cannot simply ignore or reject global trends and the challenge of modernity, of which the Western world has been the primary exemplar. Some Muslim intellectuals have argued that democracy, secularism, and European Union membership are inherently alien and destructive vis-à-vis Islamic faith and tradition. Gülen has never hesitated to give his opinion on the necessity of democracy and modernity for the survival and empowerment of Muslim communities.

However, Gülen also realizes that the liberal enlightenment project is neither adequate nor complete in itself, and therefore, Muslims should not necessarily swallow it whole. Gülen has framed the double nature of Muslim identity in the context of the modern world. At the societal level (*umma* and nation-state level), the problem is mainly that of economic misery and the underdevelopment of Muslim communities, along with the oppressive political systems under which they languish. At the individual level, many Muslims find themselves in moral agony when faced with the failure of enlightened ideals in giving proper answers to the questions of Muslims in the modern world. His goal is to move from the individual level of transformation to the societal level in order to create more humane social and political order.

Thus, the cardinal problem that Muslims face is not how to establish an Islamic state, rather it is how to solve the spiritual crisis, as well as socioeconomic backwardness of Muslim communities that reside in diverse countries around the world. He calls upon Muslims not to search for the top-down Islamization of society as a solution to their agony, but rather he asks them to overcome their own spiritual alienation by creating a deeper and broader understanding of community and salvation in this world and the next. Gülen realizes that alienation and suffering is not a burden of the individual alone, but also of the collective, and realizes that there is no Muslim identity centered solely on the individual, rather the identity of Muslims is communal and linked inextricably to the *umma* or the community of believers. The problem for many Muslims is that along with the loss of their sense of community they lost the deeper sense of Muslim personhood. Gülen finds that in our time cultures have become so rooted in consumerism and insatiable wants, that the believer is estranged and encounters major difficulty in avoiding absorption into the dominant spirit of materialism. Consumerism and narrow nationalism are both avenues for agendas that could blur Muslim identity. Since many contemporary Muslim states are ruled by corrupt authoritarian regimes often backed by external actors and have few authentically Muslim virtues, it is imperative for believers to work for moral renewal at the societal level. Thus, the existence of Muslim identity does not require an Islamic state, rather Muslims and Muslim communities are enough as long as they have the guarantee of legal protection for the development of their moral communities.

Gülen wishes to return to the essence (*öze dönüş*) or sacred center, in order to live a life of spiritual and humane development, and to bring its power into play in every sphere of social life, in order to develop moral individuals. In 2010, Gülen defined the mission as "renewal on the basis of our religio-historical roots and the cultivation of new heroes who are inspired by and connected to the roots of meanings."[3] For this purpose, we do not need an Islamic state or Islamic party, but only morally conscious individuals who develop a humane and virtuous society. Although Gülen does not seek an overtly Islamic state, he realizes the power and the role of Islam in Turkish society. Islam matters to Turkey in a way that few outsiders appreciate. It has been a guide in questions of morality, politics, legitimacy, and identity, and a source of visions for the national future.

Gülen, as a scholar of Islam, thinks that Islam is a rational and divine religion. For Gülen, Islam has a central message or idea, but this message is not an abstract moral desideratum. This message—seeking to strive toward the ideal of the *insan-ı kamil*—is rooted in the Qur'an and shaped by historical conditions. Furthermore, for Gülen, Ottoman history was not only a reflection of this core message of Islam but also the test of its power and a historical manifestation of its universal principles. His main goal has been to turn abstract ideas into concrete practices, institutions, and everyday life (i.e., *Islamiyet*). Thus, for Gülen, the study and appreciation of the accomplishments of the Ottoman Empire is also the study of the application of Islamic ideals in a specific time and place. Indeed, *Islamiyet*, Muslim civilization, cannot be explained solely with reference to the Qur'an and Hadith but also requires the understanding of the concrete historical conduct and accomplishments of Muslims over time.[4] *Islamiyet*, like other civilizations, should only be viewed through the totality of its historical praxis and not through any single interpretive moment or imagined utopian age of Medina. Living Islam informs the rhythms of everyday life and is manifested in action, literature, morality, music, art, and books. Situated Islam reflects the plurality of diverse interpretations and practices and it decenters an Arab-centric ethnic/tribal Islam by emphasizing the more universal context in which Islam evolved. Thus, we need not measure Islam in Turkey against some "authentic" Arab version of Islam.[5]

The Gülen-inspired network community thus differentiated itself from other Islamic groups by stressing the free market, civil society, media, and modern education.[6] Gülen is the engine behind the construction of a "new" Islam in Turkey that is marked by the logic of a market economy and the Ottoman historical and cultural legacy.[7] In order to carry out his mission of reshaping and renewing the future of Turkey, Gülen constantly sharpens his ideas and uses diverse means to disseminate his message of Islamic reform and renewal. Gülen is responding to the contemporary crises of modernity felt by many Anatolian Turks: loss of meaning, identity, and legitimacy and the loss of economic and political power. In fact, many in traditional Turkish society came to believe that they lost a way of being in the world due to the radical Kemalist reforms, in contrast to that of the first Muslim community and the Ottomans, who managed to position themselves as dynamic shapers of the world system. Indeed, there is a crisis of identity and a search for meaning in different Muslim countries. The reason that so many young Muslims feel alienated is that they can neither find meaning in their contemporary societies nor give up the longing to find it somewhere else. Gülen wants to engage with them and provide a set of answers to their search for meaning. Gülen, who is heavily influenced by Sufism, is neither all about action nor a purely abstract thinker, but rather a man who seeks the harmonization of life with ideas, especially Islamic morality. He calls his followers to excel in action yet he also calls them regularly to withdraw into themselves and contemplate the purpose of being here and now. Thus, the study of his ideas is crucial for understanding the broader purpose and appeal of the movement.

THE MEANING OF THE GOOD LIFE

Gülen's works explore the connection between moral life and divine revelation, a theological theme as old as religion. Almost all of his books reflect a deep intellectual commitment to infer some guiding principles from the Qur'an and the Prophetic tradition. In other words, a universal morality, derived from Islamic tradition, prescribing how we ought to live and engage with others is central to his oeuvre.

The good life, for Gülen, is a moral life lived according to shared Islamic morality within the community. In other words, morality and faith in God are knit together to develop the principles of the good life and develop moral responsibility to others, especially to those who are in need. According to many Muslim thinkers, there is a reason why we should live morally, and that is: we are "believers" and we will all be judged by God in the afterlife. In other words, Gülen's justification for living morally is that human existence is a test from God and those who live a moral life will be rewarded for their deeds in the eternal "afterlife."

Although moral categories are derived from Islam with a view toward individual salvation, they are also justified in terms of the long-term interest of coexistence and human flourishing in this world. By stressing the Islamic origins of moral categories and reminding Muslims about their moral duties and responsibilities, Gülen wants "believers" to live an authentic life (i.e., a life prescribed by one's religious tradition) and be respectful of the integrity of other people, since they are all creations of the same God. Indeed, Islam provides a moral code to guide believers to live a worthy life that would please God. He argues that neither self-interest nor utilitarianism can provide a basis for a moral code. In other words, living a good life means pleasing God. Gülen's writings differentiate a good life (i.e., living according to Islamic morality) from living well (i.e., living in comfort and having all the necessary conditions for material well-being). From Gülen's perspective, the meaning of life is not having a materially comfortable one, but the salvation of the soul and winning the struggle against prejudice and appetites. Although Gülen is not opposed to the acquisition of private property, he rejects greed and directs attention to the duty to live by Islamic morality by calling his followers to act in order to please God. Gülen is convinced that life lacks meaning without belief in God. Therefore, faith in God is essential to having a meaningful fulfilling life.

Gülen's conception of morality is rooted in his understanding of religion as doing and acting. Islam is not about abstract professions of faith but rather a way of life and about the concrete and specific. He distrusted what he sees in many Muslim societies, that is, morality in fragmented abstraction and no connection with daily life. Religion, especially Islam, for Gülen, regardless of what others think, is the most powerful force that provides a framework of meaning; a source of social glue in terms of its unifying symbols and especially the sense of belonging that it generates. Gülen, like the majority of Turks, believe that faith is a prerequisite for morality. Many Turks also think that to believe in God is to be a moral person. Gülen and his followers argue that if "God is dead" and Islam is cleansed from the public sphere, society would be awash in a whirlpool of permissiveness. Gülen, along with many Muslim intellectuals, never considers the possibility of maintaining moral seriousness when faith is lost. The difficulty with

Gülen and his teachings is that he offers a comprehensive worldview based on Islam and expects everyone in society to think and act within that framework. It does not occur to him that modern societies have competing worldviews and diverse ethical principles. The main problem of his thinking is that he does not recognize the possibility of a God-free morality or political system. Indeed, modern pluralistic democratic society, which consists of competing visions of the good life, requires a reason-based debate and institutional framework for consensus building.

Although Gülen's conception of religion is not always consonant with secular liberal democracy, his stress on community service is vital to thicken civil society. Gülen is a communitarian who questions the value of individualism, that is, indifference to the concerns of the larger society. Gülen believes that we should all direct our efforts toward some impersonal end—some collective good of building humane conditions for others as well. In other words, we should not reduce the purpose of life to the level of personal desires and appetites. The goal of human life is not about power or pleasure, but rather building decent human relations and just societies with a view toward pleasing God. He thinks this social responsibility and commitment to the "other" can only be realized through a religious morality. In short, he desires engagement with, and the rebuilding of, "modernity" under the aegis of Islamic values and faith, not against or without them. In that sense, one might read Gülen as similar to Karl Barth, a great German neo-orthodox theologian, with the emphasis on resisting both liberalism and Islamic fundamentalism.[8] Gülen's writings on personal relationships, relations with God, and the advancement of a just community stress the negativity of egocentrism and the desire for superiority vis-à-vis other people. He thinks that one achieves perfection when one is capable of suppressing and harnessing egotism through the religious tradition. One has to engage and accept others as equals, respect their worldviews, and seek to learn from their ways of life in order to expand one's own. Egoism and narcissism are two cardinal sins that all Muslims are asked to avoid.

Gülen's writings seek to provide religious motivation to his followers to "achieve and succeed" in their life. Achievement is a desire and commitment to do well, whatever one is doing in life. Since social recognition is important, especially one's prestige in the community, those who follow his ideals are expected to attain an inner feeling of personal accomplishment by best serving their family and community. Achievement is measured in terms of one's exemplary place in the community in earning more and contributing more as well. He always asks for standards of a "perfectionist and disciplined spirit" at work. This religious motive for high achievement has worked quite well within the neoliberal economic policies and privatization of the Turkish economy in the 1980s. Those pious Anatolian merchants and industrialists who are active in the movement are not primarily moved by the "profit" they stand to make, but rather by the prestige and sense of accomplishment they receive within their own faith communities. The profit motive is powerful, but it is only legitimized and qualified by the religious motive of financially serving for the greater good and seeking to please God. On the basis of my interviews with many such merchants, it is confirmed that they are motivated along this line of thinking, as one states:

> Yes, profit is important but there are more important motives than making money. My main purpose is to serve my community, country and my religion. I have enough money to have a comfortable life but I still work and invest even though risks are much higher today. As Hocaefendi says, we need to serve our communities to attain inner satisfaction and make our existence here meaningful to secure a peaceful eternity.[9]

Gülen is a religious communitarian, that is, religious belief helps to create a community, and community shapes the potential of one's own personality and well-being. One might summarize Gülen's mode of thinking in the following way: no religion—no morality, no community—no personality. Religious belief and norms, Gülen thinks, make people treat each other as humans and equals. Ideals from which all believers (citizens) are expected to derive their principles and shared understanding of the good life are in this sense "Islamic."

Gülen's ideas have close similarity with some communitarian theories.[10] Indeed, he does not recognize the individual as an autonomous actor. He argues that democratic institutions and practices should reflect the shared understanding and concerns of the people. Gülen's self is a constituting particle in the community. The individual realizes his or her potentials by fully identifying with the ends of the community. Gülen's individual is not unencumbered, but rather a derivation of his or her community. If we are all shaped by the environment we find ourselves in, we cannot be free to choose our own conception of good or a way of life. In other words, who we are is shaped by our families, schools, and communities, and it is difficult to shed these internalized characteristics.

Gülen rejects the notion of community as an interest group and insists that community is based on a shared collective memory and sense of fate. However, Gülen is cognizant of the continued processes of modernization and individualization. He does not directly deal with the Weberian process of rationalization and "the disenchantment of the world," yet he argues that what is rational is bound by context and time. What Gülen strives for is the rationalization of Islamic values and conduct with the context of this emerging modernity. He differentiates effective and tradition-patterned conduct from value-rational action, à la Weber, that human understanding and conduct should be informed by deliberation and justified values rather than "unquestioned imitative" affective action or patterns of conduct. In other words, religiously informed actions have been shifted from "imitative action and habits" to value-oriented action. Islamic values, for Gülen, should be followed more consciously and deliberately and reexamined on the basis of modern needs and concerns. The nation-state, capitalism, and science are the three major motivating forces behind the rationalization of societies. The values and attitudes, which Gülen defends, provide a powerful breeding ground for a neoliberal economic system. In this vein, he stresses order, honesty, diligence, discipline, punctuality, industriousness, and investment in education. Although these values are all framed in Islamic terms, the form of Islam remains, while its traditional and, some would even say, spiritual aspect is gradually eroded. Some believers seek to overcome the pressures of increasing wealth with generous acts of charity (*himmet*).

THE PAST, MEMORY, AND IDENTITY

The history of the Prophet Muhammad (570–632), the period of four caliphs (632–661), especially the history of the Ottoman Empire, are very important for the inference of a set of authentic moral principles. From Gülen's perspective, history should not restrain our moral imagination, but should enrich it. In short, the past should help us to think anew, since we live in a different "time and space," facing different challenges. However, we should craft a useful past that would help us have a shared memory and language to build communal consensus. Since some of the questions have been vigorously debated by the previous generations, we need to study their responses in order to avoid making similar mistakes. Gülen's position could be considered "eclectic," since his ideas are closely formulated through close consultation of not just the Qur'an and Sunna but also of traditional normative and intellectual sources. He does not ignore the textual treasury of classical Islam, as he finds it a valuable instrument in arriving at answers to questions and problems confronting the Islamic world today. Further, he does not regard these classical Muslim authors to be absolute authorities, since one's understanding also depends on one's particular era and context.

Gülen seeks to restore the Turkish-Muslim nation by "remembering" its past rather than "forgetting" it, and he calls upon people to rediscover the self, which has been embodied within Islam and the Ottoman past. The past from which Gülen wants to derive the contemporary self is not the historical past but rather the past of the present. This cultural revival of Islamic circles in Turkey seeks to criticize the contemporary Kemalist project and its secularizing orientation by positing an alternative pathway to modernity and development. By reimagining the cultural content of the Turkish nation, these Gülen-influenced Islamic groups reconstruct the modern Turkish nation as being Muslim, Ottoman, and Turkish. The politics of nationalism in Turkey have been gradually embedded into the politics of religiosity. There is an attempt to "free" the definition of the nation from that of the "alienated" Kemalist elite. One of the major effects of the politics of culture is the reconceptualization of the nation and its cultural connection with Central Asia, the Caucasus, and the Balkans. Therefore, the Gülen movement, in constructing the present by "remembering" a past of its own choosing, operates simultaneously in modern and non-modern times.

By constructing the cultural past of the Turkish-Muslim community, Gülen attempts to construct his own version of the nation by giving up imitative forms of modernization.[11] Although some Kemalists read this goal as an attempt to form an Islamic state, I would argue that this is a superficial reading of Gülen's project. Gülen and his close circles do not hesitate to offer a critique of the policies of Kemalist westernization as being a poor derivative imitation, which led to the total collapse of the Ottoman state. This movement is constructing its own modernity with its own available means. The Gülen movement aroused justifiable fears of "social conservatism," and unjustifiable fear, though understandable, that this project of "remembering" the past would lead to religious republicanism. There is some evidence to support the latter fear. Yet, a large segment of the Anatolian population has also celebrated and supported Gülen's concept of national identity as drawing on Muslim, Ottoman, and Turkish roots. To feel one's identity, for many followers of Gülen, is to feel a religio-historical emotion, without reifying it. Emotional aspects of identity are not fixed onto a single concept, as an emotional state remains a flowing process.

Gülen in this sense is not only a religious leader but also a Turkish-Ottoman nationalist. His nationalism is an inclusive one that is not based on blood or race, but rather on shared historical experiences and the agreement to live together within one shared polity. The definition of Turk, for Gülen, is not limited to race or ethnicity, but includes those "Muslims who live in Turkey, share the Ottoman legacy as their own, and regard themselves as Turks should be considered as Turks."[12] Islam, for Gülen, remains the basic criterion of national identity and loyalty. Being a Muslim is a sine qua non for being a Turk. For Gülen, there is no difference between being a Turk and of being of Bosnian, Kurdish, or Tatar descent. His first job as a preacher was at the Üçşerefeli Mosque in Edirne, where there are large numbers of Torbesh and Pomak Muslims of Slavic descent. In his memoirs, Gülen hardly differentiates between ethnic and non-ethnic Turks and treats them both as Turks and Muslims. He therefore has a more inclusive notion of identity than many secular nationalist Turks espousing Kemalism; his is a broader one shaped by the Ottoman-Islamic legacy.

Although the Arabs were part of the Ottoman Empire, Gülen is critical of the Arab and Persian understandings of Islam.[13] He accuses the Arabs of having collaborated against the Ottoman Empire and generating a negative image of Islam by reducing Islam to Wahhabism and Gulf Arab norms and practices. Moreover, he differentiates urban Ottoman Islam from tribal Arab Islam, expressing admiration for the Ottoman Sultans and even Mustafa Kemal. Most Gülen schools, therefore, are either in the Balkans or in Central Asia and very few exist in the Arab Middle East.

Gülen is deeply concerned with the debate over the question of national identity in Turkey and the Turkish-Kurdish split. He has tried to redefine Turkishness within the context of the Ottoman Islamic past to include all Muslims residing in the territory of modern-day Turkey. He assumes that this Ottoman legacy can be the basis for overcoming Turkish-Kurdish differences. He talks about the hierarchy of concentric circles of identity, in which the Ottoman past and Turkish nationalism complement Islamic identity and lead to a powerful cohesive Turkey. Gülen prefers to draw not on the ethnic/exclusivist pan-Turkish, or secularist Kemalist sources of national identity, but rather on the cultural and religious roots of Ottoman Turkish civilization. His conceptualization of Turkish identity is always rooted in this shared Ottoman Islamic past.

In Gülen's conception, religious and national communities are fused. In his writings and interviews, he differentiates community (solidarity-based group) from society (interest-based association) and treats Islam as the essential ingredient for the community. Political community, for Gülen, is a union of believers who share the same cosmic interpretive framework of religion and who have joined together freely for the realization of the collective activity of serving God and nation. The ultimate binding force of the community is piety, religiously shaped sentiment, and affections. Self-sacrifice provides the foundation for the survival of the Muslim (Turkish) community. Individuals are expected to sacrifice for the sake of the collective and in the service of religion. Gülen's conception of community absorbs the Turkish nation, since the Turks, for Gülen, are destined to serve Islam and lead their region. Indeed, the state becomes a bridge between religious and national community and an instrument for the realization of these goals. In the writings of Nursi and Gülen, the shared normative charter becomes the necessary foundation for the public sphere and the workings of civil society.

A call for the Turkish future has always been uttered in the context of the discovery of a historical past, or its reinterpretation, to facilitate economic development to empower the community. More than any other contemporary Turkish Muslim scholar, Gülen contributed to the Islamization of nationalism by crafting a religio-social consciousness through education and media more than religious rituals. Moreover, due to his emphasis on modern institutions and concepts, Gülen's notion of *Islamiyet* (not Islam) is not considered an unchanging, dogmatic religious text as maintained by orthodoxy, or a blueprint for the formation of a religious state. To Gülen, living Islam is the articulation of the synthesis between local sociopolitical conditions and the universal principles of Islam. The Muslim *umma* is not an ethnic community rooted in some particular history, but a community of believers possessing both spiritual continuity and an unfolding narrative in relation to different times and places, undergoing transformation by maintaining its sacred core. Islam, in this interpretation, has both a religious and sociopolitical aspect: it is a normative charter (norms and laws) and national identity interwoven into one political community.

Gülen's long and agonizing experience with the leaders of the 1997 "soft coup" had a sobering effect on his thought, transforming his way of thinking in many ways. He became less nationalistic and more cosmopolitan in outlook. In his *Kırık Mızraplar*, Gülen appeals to the moral and national consciousness of the Turks. Consciousness in the writings of Gülen leads to and from God and the state. His notion of "Türkiye Müslümanlığı" or Turkish Muslimness was intended as a reconciliation between ethnic Turkish and Islamist identity, and also as a reconciliation of the ordinary Anatolian people with the Kemalist elite. After moving to the United States, Gülen sought to remain free from the fiercely divided Islamic and Kemalist camps, which preceded the rise of the JDP party in 2002. However, by 2004, Gülen and his followers in Turkey were more willing to respond to challenges from the authoritarian Kemalist core of the Turkish military and "deep state" while reconciling with the post Welfare Party leaders of Recep Tayyip Erdoğan and Abdullah Gül.

GÜLEN AND THE PROBLEM OF MODERNITY

Before examining the ideas of Gülen on modernity, I will utilize Anthony Giddens' definition of the phenomenon. By modernity, Giddens means:

> [A] shorthand term for modern society, or industrial civilization. Portrayed in more detail, it is associated with (1) a certain set of attitudes towards the world, the idea of the world as open to transformation, by human intervention; (2) a complex of economic institutions, especially industrial production and a market economy; (3) a certain range of political institutions, including the nation-state and mass democracy. Largely as a result of these characteristics, modernity is vastly more dynamic than any previous type of social order. It is a society—more technically, a complex of institutions—which, unlike any preceding culture, lives in the future, rather than the past.[14]

Modernity evolved out of a series of tectonic events including the Protestant reformation, the Enlightenment, and the industrial revolution in Europe. It resulted in the radical transformation of society, polity, and individual self-perception. It shifted the basis of political legitimacy from religion to constitutionalism and democracy. This also included the separation of religion and politics in terms of law, education, and social services. This transformation in theory represented the freedom of reason from revelation and it came to be known as secularism. Modernity is based on this different epistemology that stresses reason over revelation. Kant and Hegel were the two leading figures behind of this epistemological shift. However, the Muslim encounter with modernity came through colonialism, subjugation, and military defeat. The question in the nineteenth century was: "What are the causes of this decline and what needs to be done?" Some Muslims totally rejected modernity as a process of dehumanization that created a society free from spirituality and authenticity. Modernity, for some Muslims, remained the root of a global malaise, since it replaced revelation with instrumental reason and turned science and positivism into the lodestars for restructuring society. Some Islamic groups identified secularism and rationalism as the endpoint of modernity, and they tried to overcome it through the spiritualization of society, bringing religion back into society as a guide to daily life while seeking the subordination of modern rationality to revelation.

Gülen is not a wholehearted proponent of modernism, but realizes that many of the changes that it portends are unavoidable. He realizes the power of modern conditions, processes, and discourse, while seeking to reduce their alienating and negative consequences on traditional communities through "bringing God back" into everyday life. Modernity does not negate morality but rather requires rational justifications for it that do not at the same time contradict faith in the divine. Gülen cannot imagine a moral order without belief in God or the afterlife.

A closer examination of Gülen's writings indicates the sanctification of worldly activity especially in the realms of teaching and business. This sanctification of work and full engagement with the world does not preclude the presence of God. Gülen does not support withdrawal from the world and a monastic life. He calls upon his followers to stay involved in the world and sanctify their presence to please God. Through *himmet*, giving charitable dues to the movement, some businessmen feel that they are "buying their salvation." However, for most of the businessmen who provide financial support, they feel that they are not "buying their salvation" but rather freeing themselves from the anxiety of salvation. In short, the Gülen movement seeks to bring privatized Islamic norms and worldview into the public sphere.

Gülen's ideas and activities have initiated a Protestantization of Turkish Islam in terms of its vernacularization, shift in religious authority, and rationalization of Islamic practices. Through the writings of Nursi and Gülen, the movement cultivates the vernacularization of holy scripture into Turkish, and in almost all of their circles the books are read, and commented upon, in Turkish. The writings of Nursi and Gülen are in Turkish and their followers come together to read and comment on what they read. They rarely read the Qur'an alone, but always within the framework of the writings of Nursi or Gülen. In other words, through the vernacularization of Islam, one sees the democratization of religious knowledge—ordinary people can read and interpret their own religious understanding. This indirect vernacularization of Islam also undermines official religious authority and creates a horizontal web of networks for the production of religious interpretation and knowledge. In other words, religious authority has been redefined in terms of the power of arguments and of one's ideas. Thus there is now a major fragmentation of authority in the process of the construction of religious knowledge. As a result of these two processes, one also sees the rationalization of Islamic practices in terms of reason and scientific understanding.

ISLAM AND DEMOCRACY

In the 1980s, Gülen considered the state and nationalism as the main vehicle for achieving an ideal Muslim society. This state consciousness was central to Gülen's earlier thought and activities. However, after the February 1997 soft coup, Gülen was disillusioned with the state and its institutions to such an extent that he became convinced that state power is not the solution but rather a source of the problem that stood in the way of thickening of civil society, consolidating democracy and especially economic development. As a result of his move to America, he increasingly treated civil society as the vehicle for the realization of the divinely shaped good life. Civil society replaced statism and nationalism as a critical reference point. In a series of interviews in America, Gülen has regularly cited the virtues of civil society and democracy and praised American institutions and their commitment to justice.[15] However, Islam, for Gülen, has always remained the all-encompassing belief system, and he examined the world from this Islamic prism coming to the conclusion that Islam requires a well-ordered and dynamic civil society, and not a state. In order to actualize God's will in society and personal life, one needs to have voluntarily organized networks and associations in order to establish a functioning democracy and free society.

Gülen's new civil society-centric thinking is much more in line with democracy than his previous state-centric thinking.[16] In the past, Gülen rather opportunistically claimed, "I am always on the side of the state and military. Without the state, there is anarchy and chaos."[17] By pointing out their differences from other groups as being more "moderate," the Gülen movement tried to gain legitimacy from the Kemalist state. Moreover, Gülen and his followers offered little criticism of the oppressive state policies against nonviolent Kurds and many independent-minded journalists.

In recent years, his thinking on democracy has evolved and he now favors freedom over order. He supports democracy on the basis that it is the best way to secure freedom and the rights of Muslims, an instrument to shape state policies and institutions, and a vehicle for Muslims to live a virtuous life. Gülen does not see Islam as being incompatible with democracy and argues that Islamic principles of *ijtihad* (interpretation), *ijma* (consensus), *biat* (allegiance), and *şura* (consultation) are consonant with a democratic system. Gülen's discourse on politics is not fully developed in a systematic or sophisticated manner. Since he is not a methodical thinker, but rather a leader of a sociopolitical movement, his views on democracy are quite general, yet still exceedingly weighty. In other words, Gülen is neither like Rashid Ghannoushi, a systematic thinker who is the leader of Tunisian's al-Nahda Party, nor the Iranian philosopher Abdolkarim Soroush, but rather a norm entrepreneur,[18] who is recognized as a moral authority by his respective community to initiate and implement new understanding in Islamic theology. He is a theological innovator and articulator of new religious ideas to motivate the people to transform themselves and their social conditions. As such, he has been successful in changing the way in which his followers think and act by reinterpreting Islamic-based moral values. By not only bringing Islamic morality back but also reinterpreting it in light of modern challenges, Gülen wants to link norms and actions.[19]

As an active religious leader, Gülen's views closely define the content of the movement. His followers will find support for both forms of democracy and Islam in his teaching:

> In fact, in a democratic society the source of law is colorblind and free from ethnic prejudice. It promotes the creation of an environment for the development of human rights, political participation, protection of minority rights, and the participation of individuals and society in decision-making institutions which are supposed to be the characteristics of our modern world. Everybody should be allowed to express themselves with the condition that no pressure should be made on others through a variety of means. Also, members of minority communities should be allowed to live according to their beliefs. If these sorts of legislations are made within the norms of international law and international agreements, Islam will have no objection to any of these. No one can ignore the universal values that the

Qur'an and the Sunna have presented with regard to the rights mentioned above. Therefore, it is impossible to prove in any way that Islam opposes democracy. If a state, within the framework mentioned above, gives the opportunity to its citizens to practice their religion and supports them in their thinking, learning, and practice, this system is not considered to be against the teaching of the Qur'an. In the presence of such a state there is no need to seek an alternative state.[20]

Gülen justifies and defends democracy because it serves the interest of Muslim communities and also secures basic liberties for citizens to express themselves. His understanding of democracy is more "instrumental" than principle-based. He differentiates Islam from democracy and offers a nuanced and conditional support for democracy. He argues that Islam as a religion covers the issues of faith, knowledge of God, and doing good things in order to praise God (*ihsan*), while democracy is tasked with the procedural matter of governance.

However, the distinction between religion and democracy should not mean religion cannot play a positive role in democracy. Gülen argues that "an introduction of Islam [into democracy] may play an important role in the Muslim world through enriching local forms of democracy and extending it in such a way that helps humans develop an understanding of the relationship between the spiritual and material worlds. I believe that Islam also would enrich democracy in answering the deep needs of humans, such as spiritual satisfaction, which cannot be fulfilled except through the remembrance of the Eternal One."[21] However, Gülen never expands on how he thinks Islam could enhance democracy and political participation.

The followers of the Gülen movement are generally more disposed to electoral politics, moderation, and a market economy than other Islamic groups in Turkey. There are two contradictory reasons for this. First, Gülen always stressed the communal religious consciousness as the sine qua non for the realization of a just society and, second, he insisted that the democratic state and economically advanced society are absolutely necessary for the survival of the Muslim community. According to the Gülen community, religion is primarily a personal or communal matter as opposed to a political or state matter. Their understanding of Islam is very much conditioned by the influence of the Ottoman state and the Republic of Turkey. Gülen's movement does not seek to negate or challenge the processes of modernization. Rather, it seeks to demonstrate the way in which a properly conceived Muslim project can affirm and further the most crucial ends of modernity, such as the formation of conscious actors who are armed with religious and secular knowledge. Gülen seeks ways to contribute to the vernacularization of modernity by redefining modernity not as Westernization but rather as a set of new economic, technological, and legal opportunities for authentic societal transformation. Modernity, for Gülen, offers new challenges and resources for a renewed Islamic consciousness and Muslim presence in the new public sphere. Gülen's ideas and actions introduce the possibility of being both modern and Muslim at the same time.

Islamic groups rejected the state-led modernization projects of Turkey, Iran, and Tunisia that became the only way to "free" societies from backwardness. These state-led modernization projects were of a totalistic nature implemented by the state regardless of societal resistance. When modernity is closely connected with state policies that seek to transform all of society in order to create a secular and national entity, it reduces modernity to the project of state control of society and denies any agency to societal groups. However, in many Muslim societies, including in Turkey, the state-led modernization projects led to unexpected consequences in opening up new spaces of social and cultural distinctions, leading to bottom-up modernization. In due time, as a result of top-down modernization, which treats society as the "object" of modernization, the new process of bottom-up modernization treats society as the "subject" of modernity. "Modernization-from-below" focuses on the human consciousness, practices, and ability to negotiate the cost of modernity, and utilize modern discourses of human rights and other means to resist the negative impact of the state project of modernization. Thus, what one sees in the works and actions of Gülen is an attempt to negotiate the negative impacts of modernity and use modern means and spaces to transform it. Nursi managed to increase Muslim sensitivities and consciousness about the negative consequences of the modern age of skepticism and positivism. Gülen believes that Muslims have to go beyond this awareness and convince people to organize and act together in the name of Islam to positively shape their sociopolitical environment in accordance with faith. According to Gülen, modern society requires social order and this order can only be sustained through a shared normative consensus that was worked out from shared religion, tradition, and history, to define appropriate conduct in a given social context.

Gülen's notion of politics cannot be considered libertarian, since he gives priority to the community and the state over individual rights. Although Gülen makes political and social claims on the basis of religious distinctions, these are not based on mutual respect and responsibility to other political communities. Further, he has been circumspect around the questions of the oppressive policies of the Turkish state. Agai argues that "his nationalistic, pro-junta state, anti-leftist and anti-Iranian discourse was completely in line with the Turkish-Islamic synthesis promoted by the state after 1980."[22] Gülen's project is a hybrid communitarian movement rooted in the Turko-Islamic state tradition. However, in comparison with the elitist and socially exclusive nature of Turkish intellectual life, Gülen, as a religious leader, is fairly tolerant of the "other." He is open to dialogue with diverse groups in order to promote civility and democracy in Turkey.[23] The Gülen movement has reconciled itself with democratic liberalism and secularism without becoming either fully liberal-democratic or secular. Gülen's vision of Islam is based on both discipline and dialogue. The first principle is imprinted within the community, whereas the latter is an external principle for interaction with other non-Muslim groups. Finally, this pro-democracy and pro-human rights rhetoric of the movement was appealing when the movement was in opposition. As the movement became the partner of the JDP government in the second half of 2000, it became possible to test the commitment of the movement to human rights through their actions. The record of the movement so far has been mixed.

THE CRITICISM OF GÜLEN'S IDEAS

There are two major criticisms of Gülen's ideas. First, Gülen has not been fully successful in empowering individual thinking and reflection. He provides ready-made opinions for the use of his followers, who are thus relieved from the necessity of forming of their own opinions and not much involved in critical thinking. Some sections of his followers are captive to the adulation of Gülen. They reject individualism and stress the role of community and collective action. Gülen argues that individual and collective happiness lie in disciplining three innate faculties of human beings: reason, anger, and lust. The emphasis on disciplining mind, body, and conduct prevents the evolution of critical thinking.

Second, Gülen's ideas are not fully liberal-democratic but are rooted in the Abrahamic tradition of revelation. For Gülen, the eternal precepts of Islam are not only reasonable, but they provide a basis for the universal truths of human rights as well. In other words, revelation is expected to guide and shape what is reasonable and the meaning of the good life. From Gülen's perspective, the universal principles of human rights are rooted in Islamic doctrine. However, he does not consider Islam and Islamic understandings in Turkey to be a more divisive than unifying ground. Islamic tradition and Islamic values constitute a battleground in today's modernizing Turkey. Can controversial religious truth claims be the basis for public reasoning that could appeal to more secular segments of society? Public reasoning, for many Islamists in Turkey, has to be rooted in Islamic values. Gülen seeks to discipline competing lifestyles through Islamic morality and, in the end, his system faces difficulty with aspects of pluralism and individualism. The method of teasing out these norms that would result in consensus is expected to be through participatory politics.

CONCLUSION

Gülen seeks to make religious ideas relevant in contemporary society by reinterpreting them in terms of the global discourse of human rights and modernity. Two texts are central to Gülen: the Qur'an and the writings of Said Nursi. His interpretation of Nursi and the Qur'an reminds us that all "meaning" in religion is socially constructed. Thus, its meaning depends on the location, association, and historical experiences of both interpreter and listeners. This interpretation, for Gülen, takes the historical and cultural context of the Qur'an and Sunna into consideration, as well as the context of modern societies. If Islam can be adequately understood (or reformed), that is, if it can respond positively to the challenge of modernity and rapid social change, then the future for Islam in the twenty-first century can be brighter than any other age in the past. Third, substance or content of belief and practice, for Gülen, is more important than its outer form. Fourth, it is impossible for any person to be certain that he or she understands the will of God better than any other human being. Therefore Muslims must be tolerant toward each other and toward adherents of other faiths.

Moreover, the study of Gülen indicates that religion and secularism are implicated in each other. The contemporary Islamism or Islamic debate evolved out of the Turkish form of secularism and this entangled history of secularism and new form of Islamism has to be imagined in dialectic rather than polar negation. The return of God in the public sphere does not mean the return of "the past or tradition" but rather something very novel. The new action-oriented Islam is incubated in the old concepts and symbols. However, they all have new meanings and functions in the present day. Gülen seeks to legitimize his innovation in the tradition by referring to the old. In short, Gülen's actions and readings are preparing the intellectual ground for the conditions of modernity. The problem of Turkish modernity was that it did not have religious foundations. With the Nur movement, and especially with Gülen, the Turks are developing the religious foundations for modernity. Said Nursi very much sowed the seeds of the Islamic Enlightenment by undermining the authority of the *ulema* (Muslim religious scholars) and empowering ordinary people to read and discuss the meaning of the Qur'an. In the case of Turkey, almost all the "reading public" of the Nur movement started to discuss theological issues from their own perspectives. They constituted the self-conscious rebels against *"taqlidi iman"* and searched for an evidence-based, reasonably justified Islam. Nursi served as a fulcrum for the religious enlightenment and a more modernity-friendly Islam. Gülen is the outcome of this religious enlightenment in Turkey.

In the case of Gülen, one needs to account for the extraordinary powers of persuasion to his ideas and how these ideas provide an emotional link between the experiences of daily life and the future of Turkish society. Thus, one needs to take the social conditions that energize these ideas for the men and women who stood to lose the most in a conflict with modern processes. The followers of the Gülen movement have been reaching out to each other through the channel of print and came to trust one another. They created a religious public sphere and were thus able to construct a more effective and organized religious community.

PART II

Movement

3

The Structure of the Movement

Authority, Networks, and Opportunity Spaces

To understand the inner motivating forces of the Gülen movement, it is important to examine how the movement itself sees its own mission. The followers of Fethullah Gülen compare themselves with the *sahaba* (the companions of Muhammad). During his last sermon, the Prophet Muhammad called upon his believers to spread Islam throughout the world and teach it by example. Later, according to a *hadith*, when the Prophet was asked, "Oh Muhammad! Who are your sincere friends?" He said, "My sincere believers are not here with me. They are the ones who will come when Islam is under attack from within and outside; they will come forward and secure the message of God with moral virtue and exemplary behavior. They are the longed for ones." Many followers of Gülen believe that they are the sincere believers to whom the Prophet was referring. In this religious atmosphere, the movement and its followers believe deeply in their mission and the role of renewing the faith at a time of great challenge and difficulty. Thus, the followers of Gülen believe that they have a mission not necessarily to convert (as do missionary-centered faiths like the Church of Jesus Christ of Latter-day Saints), but at least to convey to others that what they believe is the true enlightened face of Islam.

This chapter will examine the constituent parts of the movement and its strategies for realizing its goals. I will first examine the role of Gülen as a magnetic pole that pulls diverse individuals and social groups together around his mission. After examining Gülen as a spiritual, charismatic, and revered leader of a modern Islamic movement, one who is even referred to as a "saint" by some, I will attempt to critically examine the following questions: Why do people participate in, and donate to, the movement, and what is the attraction of Gülen himself as a charismatic leader? In order to answer these questions, I will unpack the concepts of *hizmet* and *himmet* as the manifestation of inner motivating moral forces of the movement. The last part of the chapter will examine the sociocultural webs of Gülenist networks and also the structure and the workings of the movement.

A RELIGIOUS AUTHORITY: THE "INTELLECTUAL" *HOCAEFENDI*

In order to comprehend contemporary Islamic social movements in Turkey, one has to appreciate how a faith that had been central to society was radically interrupted and disestablished by the reforms of Mustafa Kemal. With the change of the alphabet from Arabic to Latin, a generation of intellectuals lost its ability to communicate in what was once their own idiom, as well as the literature of its Ottoman Islamic heritage. Islamic thought during the Republican era evolved under radically new conditions, which included a deracination from much of its legacy. Many religious leaders and thinkers sought to fill this vacuum by utilizing the translated books of Arab, Iranian and Indian Muslim intellectuals. Yet, the role of these books has been minimal as far as the impact of leading Turkish Islamic scholars and leaders such as Said Nursi, Süleyman Hilmi Tunahan, Abdulhakim Arvasi and Mehmet Zahid Kotku were concerned.[1] As this first generation of Republican era Turkish Muslim intellectuals came to the fore, the text more than the Sufi lodge, or the authority of the book more than the *ulema* (learned scholars of Islam), played an important role in the modernization of Islamic thought in Turkey. Modern Turkish Islam no longer shared an organic link to traditional forms and schools (*mezhep*) of Islam. Not only texts, but modern education and a modern sense of organizational structure, brought about a deeper form of rationalization of faith.

As a leading figure in the second generation of Turkish Muslim intellectuals and leaders, Gülen played an important role in the further revival and rationalization of Islam. An examination of the formation of this new prototype of a *hocaefendi* and his transformation into a modern version of a religious public intellectual reveals more broadly the modernization of traditional religous practices and institutions into modern ones. Gülen, for example, is not a traditional *shaykh*, but rather embodies a series of overlapping roles as a modern intellectual, religious scholar (*alim*) and a social activist. Three main characteristics differentiate Gülen from the traditional Muslim *alim* or religious scholar. First, unlike the traditional *ulema*, whose references are only the Qur'an and Sunna, the reference points for Gülen, and the new class of Muslim intellectuals of his era, include rational reasoning and European Enlightenment thought, along with the Qur'an, Sunna, and important Muslim scholars. Second, Gülen encourages goal-oriented thinking and this-worldly success. While the *ulema* guide the community, and seek to preserve tradition, these new Turkish Muslim intellectuals seek to encourage, rather than discourage, new ways of interpretation of Islamic tradition. Gülen, in fact, has managed to juggle a remarkable mix of these two traditions, which accounts for his enormous popularity with the Turkish middle class and those among the urbanized Muslims of Turkey who hold religious sentiments. By realizing the power of ideas in social change, Gülen stresses education for forming a class of Muslim elite, who are achievement-oriented and rooted in the Turkish-Islamic tradition and able to breach the sharp sociocultural polarization caused by the Kemalist revolution.[2]

Another major characteristic of this modern hybrid of *alim* intellectuality is his ability to interpret Islamic precepts within the context of modern social conditions. He recontextualizes Islamic knowledge across different social boundaries by making use of interpretation in an original and incisive fashion. For example, Gülen is versed in the works of such cosmopolitan writers as Kant, Shakespeare, Hugo, Dostoyevsky, Sartre, and Kafka, and he adopts their general ideas to reinforce his reinterpretations of Islam to meet contemporary needs.[3] However, despite his apparent affinity with Western thought, Gülen's decontextualized verbal borrowing from these critical European scholars can also confuse and blur conventional meanings of concepts such as democracy, human rights and modernity. By referring to major European thinkers, Gülen seeks to familiarize his followers with the ideas of the Enlightenment, and also build a shared language with Turkey's secularist elite.

Gülen's persona and writings have a charismatic appeal that is derived from his intellectual abilities and leadership skills, as is evidenced by his propensity to develop close ties with the state, bourgeoisie and international religious institutions. However, the reasons for the growing influence of his movement go beyond mere charisma. First, Gülen has reproduced a new vision of "contemporary action-oriented Islam" that offers a set of options for people to be both Muslim and modern, Muslim and Turk—the latter being a civic identity composed of national (primarily Turkish-Ottoman) and religious (Sunni Islam) symbols. Second, his movement has adopted a global discourse of interfaith dialogue, civil society, and human rights, developing complex ties with the national bourgeoisie, the state in Turkey and diverse religious groups outside the country. Finally, the movement has activated the inner mobilizing ideas of society by inviting Muslims of Turkey to take part in the construction of a new powerful Turkey.

Two of the most important challenges in modern times that the Islamic tradition as a whole faces are the crisis of religious education and religious leadership throughout the Muslim-majority countries. Religious leadership is a key component in the reproduction and transmission of religious knowledge. Most Muslim states invested little in religious education and reform, and the *ulema* eventually lost authority or became marginalized in many postcolonial Muslim-majority countries. Due to the state's lack of investment in religious education, societal groups (in the way of formal and informal civil society) have often tried to fill the vacuum by establishing their own, albeit informal, seminaries to train religious scholars and leaders.[4] In short, this indifference to religious education resulted in the rise of fundamentalist and reactionary religious seminaries or *medrese*. The fragmentation of religious authority was also the outcome of modern processes of differentiation of social spheres such as education, science, law and medicine. In particular, the development in communication technologies empowered secular intellectuals over religious ones.

Those Muslims who resisted the secularizing projects of modern states turned to a new set of Islamist intellectuals, who popularized themselves and their ideas through newspaper columns or television programs. In Turkey, these new educational and communication networks helped to cultivate a new generation of religious leaders such as Gülen. Gülen represents the evolution of a new Islamic religious authority that blends *alim*, intellectual (*aydın*), and leadership of a socioreligious movement. In the fragmentation of religious authority, new communication technology and print capital have played a transformative role in Islam. Dale F. Eickelman has aptly argued that the religious authority has been questioned and redefined as a result of seismic changes in mass media and communication technology.[5] Both the printing press and new visual communication have transformed the transmission and production of religious knowledge. Gülen has used both print and visual domains in order to disseminate his ideas.

Despite his status as an inspirational religio-secular charismatic leader, Gülen does not involve himself in the minute details of daily decisions and claims:

> I've never called myself a leader. I'm an ordinary man. A leader is someone with capabilities, genius, charisma, and high performance. I don't have any of these.... I insist not on saying "leader" because I expressed my thoughts for 30 years on pulpits, and people sharing the same feelings and thoughts responded. For example, I told them to open university preparatory courses and schools. As an expression of their respect for me, they listened to what I said. This might be a mistake, but they listened and we met at this point. I saw that just as I was saying schools, a lot of people were saying schools. They come to ask about other, mostly religious issues as well. Sometimes they even ask about economic matters. I tell them that such matters require expert knowledge, and send them to experts.[6]

Gülen is cognizant of the socioeconomic differentiation of modern life where each sector of activity has its own specific knowledge and expertise. Indeed, Gülen is right that he is not a "leader" in the ordinary sense of the term, since he does not make decisions and monitor their execution via an established hierarchy. However, he is also more than a leader; he is the Guru/Master/*Hocaefendi*; that is, a charismatic spiritual intellectual saint-like entity for millions of people. In other words, Gülen, like a Zen master or a Guru, stays above and beyond the daily political discussions in seclusion, yet unlike them, Gülen is also deeply involved in major social and political decisions through his messages to the media, or even through his core disciples. For instance, in 2010, Gülen took very critical positions of the JDP government's policies toward Israel and provided full support for the constitutional referendum in Turkey.[7]

As a *Hocaefendi*, Gülen has several characteristics: he is an exemplary model with an ascetic lifestyle; an extraordinary teacher; a source of benevolent power; an intercessor; and a selfless altruist who sacrifices for the welfare of others. Gülen believes that the task of a *Hocaefendi* is to guide and lead the spiritual awakening of his people. It is Gülen's contention that a spiritual awakening has always been the goal of religious leaders. Indeed, one can differentiate Turkish Sufism from other forms of Sufism in Muslim countries where social conditions have led to the development of a lodge (*tekke*), a center where learning and training takes place with the engagement of the surrounding communities.[8] In other words, a Sufi leader and his followers also involve themselves in mundane jobs and attend to the daily issues of the community. In short, religious enlightenment was sought in everyday life, and reflected onto itself through practice.

Gülen's saintly charisma has three sources: many of his followers believe that his knowledge and words are divinely inspired and a gift from God; his successes in education, media, politics and finance have granted him the status of being a sublime leader; and he has acted as a magnetic pole by bringing people together for the commonweal. Gülen as *Hocaefendi*, like Said Nursi, could be considered a charismatic saint who appeals to the collective sociohistorical consciousness of Anatolian Muslims, and through his words and body language, helps to emotionally reestablish ties with the severed Ottoman Islamic past. By utilizing this shared language and memory with the Anatolian heartland, Gülen uses modern communications technology to penetrate not only the minds, but also the hearts of people.

The success of Gülen and the broader movement, however, draws upon much more than personal charisma or Ottoman nostalgia. The movement has been truly transformative in its ability to mobilize followers to reshape the social and economic realms around them. In this regard, the concepts of *hizmet* and *himmet* as the two legs of the Gülen movement must be considered. *Himmet* in Turkish means volunteering, providing welfare assistance, and donating money and service for the welfare of society. *Hizmet* is a related concept and means "rendering service" or working for some higher common good.

Many people also refer to the Gülen movement as a *hizmet* movement to describe its overall activities. People who have been persuaded by Gülen's message help with, and invest in, such activities, especially those related to education. Although these activities are decentralized and the movement itself is loosely knit, because the activities are conducted by like-minded people in different places, it looks like a single organizational structure is directing them from above. This is why critics of the Gülen movement tend to portray it as a single hierarchical "organization" controlled by an *eminence grise* who operates behind the scenes. In short, it would be fair to say that *hizmet* activities are not based on a single hierarchical movement, but on loosely structured and coordinated activities of like-minded individuals and organizations whose actions are directly inspired by Gülen's ideas and encouragement. Finally, *İhlas* is a core religious idea that motivates people to action in order to please God. It is a way of purifying one's soul through good deeds that are intended to please God.

THE THEOLOGY OF ACTION: *HIZMET, HIMMET,* AND *IHLAS*

In terms of his vision of launching an Islamic reformation and rekindling a Muslim renaissance, Gülen wants to influence the full range of social and political processes pertaining to modern life. He therefore emphasizes the vital role of markets, education and the media. A well-ordered society, for Gülen, is based on an effective state and vigorous market that, in turn, presupposes an adequately developed educational system via the general notions of *terbiye* (building character via education) and *talim* (teaching modern sciences) combined with discipline. For Gülen, this moral conviction to promote the advancement of the Turkish public can only be derived from some form or understanding of Islam, which is to serve as the shared cognitive frame for most, if not all, Turkish citizens.[9]

In other words, the morality of conviction and the morality of responsibility create a sort of worldly activism that seeks to transform this world for the sake of the next world. This balance between conviction and responsibility, as propagated by Gülen's philosophy, in the construction of a new *Muslim* Turkey is realized in terms of the decisive quality of self-control and self-discipline under the purposive will to act in the name of religion, thus aiding in the (trans)formation of Turkish civilization. The goal of education, for Gülen, is to inculcate Turkish-Islamic values through *terbiye* and the teaching of the natural and physical sciences. Gülen's following differentiates itself by stressing the importance of ethical norms in politics, education and business. In other words, Gülen moves his focus from personal piety to public ethics, and from traditional religious identity to activist-civic identity, with a well-ordered, disciplined and, yet, faithful society as the logical outcome. Gülen considers education and the media to be key instruments in the formation of both ethics and moral consciousness (*şuur*). To achieve his goal, in addition to *hizmet* and *himmet*, Gülen invokes a third inner mobilizing concept for Turkish-Muslim society: that of *ihlas* (seeking God's appreciation for every action). Gülen not only seeks to mobilize the hearts and minds of millions of Turks but also succeeds in convincing them to commit to the mission of creating a better and more humane society and polity. By stressing social activism and this-worldly accomplishment and success—Gülen is a religious modernist and a social innovator.

Why Do People Join the Movement? The Importance of *Hizmet*

My focus-group discussion with the followers of the Gülen study-circles in Istanbul included seven men from different professional connections and diverse degrees of affiliation within the movement and it produced competing definitions of the concept of *hizmet* or social service. For instance, a businessman who has close ties with the movement said, "*hizmet* requires a type of lifestyle that is based on the values of being honest and that supports the activities to cultivate a generation that would liberate Turkey."[10] However, a teacher who is fully engaged with the movement has a more political definition of *hizmet*. He claims that "*hizmet* is a collective effort to 'liberate' Turkey from the Kemalist/secular establishment and return to the religio-historical roots of the society. This society has been hostage to the Committee of Union and Progress (*İttihat ve Terakki Cemiyeti*) and now wants to free itself through *hizmet*."[11] A graduate from one of the religious *Imam Hatip* schools, who is retired from his job in the municipality, disagreed with the politically oriented definition of *hizmet* and argued that "*hizmet* is not about the 'liberation' of Turkey from the *İttihadcıs* since this country is independent. Rather, it is about investment in the afterlife and securing eternity through good deeds."[12] He provided a more spiritually oriented definition, very much focused on an afterlife and purification of soul through building a religious community, since for him, religion is necessary for both sustained moral action and a moral society. A university student, who studies history, said, "The ideal that *hizmet* is based on is the belief in an afterlife. However, this also means translating religious values to daily life. *Hizmet* requires one to live as a Muslim in the here and now and live in a way to prepare one's eternity through collective efforts with other Muslims."[13] In other words, he said "you are expected to think in terms of an afterlife and invest in the afterlife as well. You prepare yourself for eternity through *hizmet*. *Hizmet* means faith-based action to serve community, nation, and Islam."[14] Although each person offers his own meaning of *hizmet*, the generic definition of *hizmet* is a religiously motivated series of worldly performances in order to secure afterlife through virtuous actions in the here and now. In Gülen's case, *hizmet* is a religiously motivated labor to reform the world and create moral conditions for a just society.

The practice of *hizmet*, or religiously motivated labor, charity and service, is used to restructure society according to religious ideals.[15] *Hizmet* could also be used for civic concerns in education, healthcare, media and new sets of associations to build a public ethics of interaction.[16] The activities of *hizmet* members and groups has been increasingly attractive to ordinary Anatolians who would like to bridge the gap with the urban Westernized elite in the area of education. That is why Gülen's project of raising an intellectually able and morally stable generation was enthusiastically welcomed by many of the lower classes, and marginalized Anatolian Muslim majority in Turkey, also referred to pejoratively as the "Black Turks." Gülen and his associates gave such people the confidence that if they work hard, and pursue modern education, they could catch up socioeconomically with the children of the elite without losing their faith and traditions.

By employing people in its education, media, and other activities, the movement teaches the way in which social capital is built, and how ideally it should be put into practice in Turkey. In short, *hizmet* functions as social capital by bringing people together for a collective goal in terms of rendering their time and resources to create a positive environment for the advancement of society. These *hizmet* activities also help to build interpersonal trust and a code of ethics. *Hizmet* thus becomes the externalization of an internalized belief system. Through *hizmet* the values of community have been transformed, and access to "power" and "domination" is sanctified on moral and religious grounds. One follower of Gülen noted:

> Those "awaited ones" have just emerged to fulfill the glory of the Qur'an by acting according to the teachings of Muhammad by sacrificing themselves to those who need help. Islam flourishes when social, economic and educational achievements of Muslims become daily realities. Thus, any effort in the service of this goal will promote the glory of the Qur'an.[17]

In fact, Gülen defines those "awaited ones" who commit their time and resources to serve humanity as "exalted souls." He says:

> Those who dedicate themselves to illuminating people, struggle to ensure the well-being of people, and extend a hand to them on the verge of life's various pitfalls, are such exalted souls that just like guardian angels of the society, they continuously tackle the problems troubling society, face the hurricanes, step into flames, and remain alert against all threatening disturbances of society.[18]

Gülen further writes:

> [T]he worldly life should be used in order to earn the afterlife and to please the One who has bestowed it. The way to do so is to seek to please Allah and, as an inseparable dimension of it, to serve immediate family members, society, country, and all of humanity accordingly. This service [*hizmet*] is our right, and sharing it with others is our duty.[19]

In Gülen's conception of faith as an internal power to mobilize believers, the lasting piece of work that the believer creates is an *eser*: the materialization of one's good intentions and deeds. In a way, *eser* is the outcome of one's faith and the tangible attributes of one's commitment to God through good works and charity.[20] It could include building a school, hospital, establishing a scholarship, or relieving poverty. *Eser*, for Gülen, reflects one's ability to realize his or her potential, and its creation becomes a religious duty. Revealingly, in this matter of achieving *eser*, Gülen does not call upon people to build more mosques but rather schools, dormitories, hospitals, and media outlets. His concepts of *hizmet* and *eser* lead to an internal secularization of religion in terms of the rationalization of religiously motivated action and the internalization of a particular scientific epistemology. Service, both for personal salvation and for the betterment of humanity, is one of the critical values that constitute the inner motivation for *hizmet*. Gülen calls his followers to overcome their angst by serving others. In his words:

> Suffering in this sense becomes, beyond our own spiritual progress, the dedication of our lives to the happiness of others in both worlds and living for others. In other words, we should seek our spiritual progress in the happiness of others. This is the most advisable and the best approved kind of suffering: that is, we die and are revived a few times a day for the guidance and happiness of others, we feel any fire raging in another heart also in our own heart, and we feel the suffering of all people in our spirits. Rather than only being aware of selfish considerations, such as "One who has not suffered does not know what suffering is," we groan with the afflictions and pains which others in our immediate and distant surroundings endure.[21]

Furthermore, congregational brotherhood and sisterhood circles help to free individuals and the community from the direct influence of the state, and lead them to construct social networks that enhance civil society. My own understanding of the Gülen movement in Germany is the following: Islam provides the normative basis of the lifeworld (*Lebenswelt*) of a believer and he or she will realize human potentials through actions in accordance with Islamic norms. These norms, in turn, require solidarity in coordination with efforts toward the realization of the common good and goals. In this respect, Islamic norms constitute the necessary ethical means in the construction of a certain civil society. In other words, Gülen's vision and networks help to "domesticate" and inculcate civic virtues among members by stressing cooperation, participation, and tolerance. The way of creating an ethical society, for Gülen, is not to offer courses in religion or ethics in schools, but rather to set good examples, known as *temsil*, in one's daily life, whether one is a teacher, policeman, businessman, or journalist. Today, in a modern world where representation and visibility are very important, living an exemplary life and proper conduct are the key to winning people over to Islam.

This formation of "active piety" is at the core of the movement, with the aim of molding this world through Islamic ethics.[22] Redemption through collective action becomes a way for inner salvation. Gülen offers a much needed moral motivation and justification for the increasingly prosperous Anatolian bourgeoisie and educated classes. In the Gülen-led movement, the inner driving forces of Turkish culture such as *hizmet, himmet,* and *ihlas* are utilized to shape the society according to ideals of Islamic ethics. Through *hizmet*, one legitimizes one's social, educational, and economic activities as a way of worshipping God. Gülen's followers do not see themselves as an interest group but rather as a community brought together by their religious commitment to create a more humane society as they understand it. The cultural worldview and religio-economic practices are similar to those in Max Weber's famous thesis on the Protestant ethic: work inspired by religious belief produced the spirit of capitalism, which in turn had dramatic transformative effects in the historical development of the West.[23] With the rise of a well-developed, urban bourgeoisie, the social base of producers and consumers of literacy have expanded. Before the emergence of printing and universal education, reading "circles" were the centers of religious discourse and interpretation. Rather than a worldly public sphere, the reading "public" sphere was centered on the *medreses* and immediate neighborhoods.

Gülen and those who follow him measure their spiritual success, to a certain extent, in terms of the worldly consequences of their actions. Believing that Gülen is trying to revive the Islamic faith and civilization under the leadership of Anatolian Turks, this newly urbanized group of intellectuals and merchants went to action to both translate and validate their worldly success in accordance with their religious ideals and anxiety over achieving this-worldly as well as other-worldly success.

Why Do People Donate to the Movement? The Concept of *Himmet*

The main source of the Gülen movement's financial resources are the fund-raising meetings that are known as *himmet toplantıları*. These meetings are meticulously structured with cultural programs, soft drinks, light food and speeches from different people, especially from successful students of the movement, who recount their path to success. Those who are present are asked to donate for the projects of the movement. In each of these *himmet* meetings, there is a concrete project to which the participants are asked to donate.

Most of the *himmet* meetings are organized by the local leader of the movement, known as the *hadim* or *abi*, and he usually invites the owners of small and medium-sized businesses to participate. Such meetings have become the main source of income for the movement. I have personally participated in four *himmet* meetings in Istanbul as an observer. These meetings are scenes where status and power in society are also displayed vis-à-vis the other (not so powerful) members of the community. Since everybody knows how much each person has declared to donate, these meetings have also become sites for showing off one's wealth, generosity, and, especially, loyalty to the movement. There is indirect pressure on the participants to give and, possibly, give more than they can afford in such fundraising meetings. Those participants who are most generous tend to have their children in the Gülen-run education system, or their businesses linked with the followers of other pro-Gülen business groups.

The meeting usually starts with recitation from the Qur'an, and then a number of short but emotional "testimonial" speeches are delivered to stir up the Turkish-Islamic passions of members, including references to the Ottoman past. After the speeches, the leader of the *himmet* meeting either directly asks the participants to donate, or in some cases, the fundraising follows after the showing of a video about the successful projects of the Gülen community. The participants are asked to become a partner to future projects for the sake of pleasing God, serving Islam, their community, and the wider Turkish nation. In these *himmet* fund raisers, usually one identifies the project and the cost, and then someone starts with matching gifts by declaring and asking, for example, that: "I will donate 20,000 liras for the project. Who wants to take part in its realization?" In a way, this matching gift system has been very successful. It is much easier to collect donations when the projects are in Central Asia, for example, where the Gülen community invokes ethnicity and its members' "historic responsibility" to its "ancestral lands."

The Balkans is a second region where such fundraising appears to be especially fruitful. The leader of the fundraising builds the argument for the safeguarding of the Ottoman presence and role of the Balkans. Moreover, the case of the Bosnian Muslims and their recent genocide at the hands of Serbian forces raises the emotional involvement of the participants, directly and indirectly enticing them to donate because of religion, national honor and the shared Ottoman past. In other words, the *himmet* meetings are also sites of memory (re)construction, and in many cases, indoctrinating the participants about their historic identity, and invoking them to act in accordance with the responsibility of their Islamic, Ottoman and Turkish identity. It should also be noted, that in recent years the Gülen movement has expanded its charitable activities considerably to new locations such as North America and Africa.

Following this, the most respected member of the movement in that region asks people to donate to the *hizmet*, and also declare the amount they have pledged to donate at the meetings. Local sponsors could easily follow the development of the project either in Turkey or outside. There appears to be no paper trail for these fundraisers, or formal accounting of how the proceeds are spent and even the way in which they are wired from one place to the next. From collection to the realization of the project, there is very little public disclosure of spending, making the financial aspects and accounting of the Gülen movement somewhat opaque. Those who are critical of the movement raise questions about the lack of transparency. However, I have personally never heard any complaints about corruption or criticism of how funds are spent from the donors themselves. Almost all financial dealings are based on trust within the community. Indeed, charitable giving by individuals and small to medium-sized businesses has increased dramatically along with the bourgeoning of the Turkish economy after the 1980s.

An obvious question is why middle-class Turkish Muslims are willing to so generously donate to the Gülen movement. Although most of the giving comes from male members of the middle class, there are also female-only fundraising activities as well. People usually donate because they feel an affinity for the cause that the movement is pursuing, and also, "giving" as a religious duty. People often say they donate or volunteer to "make a difference." This phrase means many things to different people. Some of the contributors said, for example, that:

> "I want to donate money for some specific project such as education in Bosnia because I want to make a difference in the lives of these people who were constantly persecuted because they are Muslim. Education will have a lasting and concrete impact on their lives. Rather than providing food, it is more important to offer education to the Bosniaks."[24]

Indeed, many merchants feel that they take an Islamic stand on issues that are important for Muslims and humanity. These merchants are supporting these projects because they care about them and also because some of these groups have business connections with the same countries as well.

One of the major debates within Turkey's secular circles is about the financial sources of the movement. Some Kemalists identify either the Islamic Republic of Iran or the Kingdom of Saudi Arabia as the main sources of the Gülen movement's funds. These unfounded and hyperbolic claims are based on ideological enmity and ignorance about the Ottoman vision of the movement itself. I would argue that nearly all of the Gülen movement's funds come from Turks in Turkey, or expatriate Turks living in Western European countries and the United States. Because of ideological differences, one can be virtually certain that there are neither official Iranian nor Saudi financing of any activities of the movement.

Still, the question remains: Why do many people generously donate money to the movement? On the basis of my interviews, I have arrived at four major reasons: (1) *religious*, to offer religiously required *zekat* (alms tax) or *fitre* (giving to charity), please God, and serve Islam; (2) *patriotic*, to help build a stronger Turkey with friends from outside and fulfill a shared historical responsibility to other Muslim communities in Central Asia and the Balkans; (3) *personal egoistic*, this is the condition of contributing financially to the movement so that one is recognized within the community; (4) *social pressure,* reacting to a communal pressure and expectations. However, in the Gülen movement, internal spiritual motives for giving are more dominant than those stemming from material benefits for the individual. A merchant, originally from Rize on the Black Sea coast, became tired of my questions as to why he regularly gives money to the movement. His response was: "I am not buying something by donating money but rather investing in the afterlife (*ahiret*), serving humanity to please God, and participating in a project to create a better and more livable world."[25] Another staunch supporter of the movement told me: "I give every year because of two reasons: to fulfill my religious duty to remove harm and help those who are in need. When I see that they open schools in different parts of Turkey to educate people, it uplifts me."

THE SOCIAL NETWORKS OF THE GÜLEN MOVEMENT

"Affiliation" or "solidarity" is a much better term to explain the process of "joining" the Gülen movement, more so than membership (or even "follower"), since the latter requires a formal process, membership qualifications, and regular dues. In the Gülen movement, there is no such formal membership, people come and go on the basis of their commitment and abilities to help realize the goals of the movement. Thus, there is a high degree of mobility in both directions, and it is difficult to determine who is in or out of the movement. The term "follower" might be used for some but not all of those active within the movement, since they come and go on the basis of specific projects. People usually become involved in the activities of the movement through the networks of schools, family ties, business connections, or friends. A "part-time" sympathizer of the Gülen movement said: "I only support their educational activities in Turkey since we must have an educated nation to enhance our democracy and also become strong again."[26] When I pointed out other activities to him, he said:

I do not support their TV or newspapers because they are third-rate and also anti-Turkish military. They should stay out of politics. Religious groups should not be involved in politics. I do not read their newspaper Zaman or watch their Samanyolu TV. They should leave it to those who do better coverage of the events, and are not polemical.[27]

On the basis of my interviews, it is possible to argue that a significant minority of participants are not motivated by spiritual goals and the afterlife. For instance, a retired state employee said:

Students who graduate from their schools are successful, and they are very respectful to God and communal values. Moreover, by being involved in their activities I met with many people. Some of these people helped me at the hospital and even in the post office. In Turkey, especially in Istanbul, you need to know people and trust them to get your job done. They help you and you do not feel alone anymore. When they invited me to participate in a demonstration for constitutional change, I did. For the first time in my life, I have participated in a political rally.[28]

Indeed, the movement provides "spaces of socialization" and a web of interactions for different people in cities to build social capital (i.e., trust and coordination in social relations).[29] In fact, trust, cooperation and solidarity are the products of these religio-secular networks of relationships that the Gülen movement provides. In addition, these networks of relations help people to overcome some problems in their daily lives (at the hospital or in the post office) and also to disseminate information about political issues. Furthermore, the widespread local networks provide the flow of information to Gülen about the diverse needs of communities. When there is an acute social problem or need, usually local Gülen communities develop a solution and some of these proposed solutions may run up to Gülen himself for an endorsement. In other words, there is a powerful bottom-up search for solutions; Gülen, rather than developing his own solution, listens to the local leaders, and issues his endorsement or proposes modifications. For instance, when the local Gülen movement in Kurdish inhabited Diyarbakır grew alarmed about the low graduation rates in local high schools, they developed tutoring centers. Before the decision was implemented, they brought it to Gülen, and he endorsed their solution. In this way, even though Gülen lives in self-imposed exile in America, he is well-versed about the local problems in many regions of Turkey and abroad. Such engagements enhance individual civic capacity thereby sustaining regular political participation. In short, religious capital helps to form social capital, and social capital enhances engagement in politics. Social capital generated in religious networks spills over to political activism.

These Gülen movement activities help to train those who come from the periphery and provincial towns, teaching them how to build schools, hospitals and even banks, both within and outside Turkey. The movement provides the necessary social webs of networks to interact and exchange skills, goods, and ideas. These social networks may provide worldly benefits as much as spiritual ones to those who are affiliated. As far as the Turks in different EU countries are concerned, the movement brings them together mainly over the goal of education and the training of children. Although people come together to address the question of education and also problems of the youth, religious solidarity takes civic form through networking and organizing. The movement offers civic education both in and outside Turkey by training people to establish NGOs, collect funds, establish schools, and participate in communal activities. In other words, the religiously informed activities of the movement help to build the values of participation, knowledge, efficacy, tolerance, and trust in institutions. These values enhance democratic culture. The followers of the movement feel that they have the necessary skills and knowledge to participate in public activities, discussions, and processes to change their communities. In short, the movement does not function with a master plan in order to implement it from the top-down, rather it reacts to local bottom-up demands and the needs of a given community. The local community makes a demand and the leaders of the movement move into the community to address those demands and concerns.

Moreover, the movement offers several goods that are competitive in the religious market of Turkey and attractive to a large sector of Anatolians. These "goods" include a disciplined and well-rounded education to pass university exams and a sense of identity and community that shelters its members both materially and spiritually. However, as far as the movement is concerned, one does not become a formal "member" but rather moves in and out of the activities and spaces of the movement. People are free to take part in one activity and refuse, as they wish, to join another one.

The Gülen movement uses new opportunity spaces in the media, market, and education to transform ideas into action. A main question about it, and the Nur movement more generally, is why it has appealed more to urbanites than to the traditional (mostly rural) followers of Sufi orders. The web of social networks it offers is one powerful catalyst. It includes connections with other people, networking for business, social mobility and a sense of community.

Another factor is the movement's utilization of oral-print mediums in the dissemination of their ideas, a medium ideally suited to facilitate the integration of recent migrants into large urban centers. Newcomers to the cities listen to Gülen's cassettes or read his books rather than those of Said Nursi. Much of

Gülen's appeal lies in his integrative and charismatic personality, and his powerful presence as a television orator. He uses the television and radio as skillfully as an American televangelist to vernacularize Islam for the Turkish public. His tremendous oratory and apparent sincerity allows him to mobilize the masses through his sermons. Gülen makes use of lucid Turkish by blending old and new words, Turkish and Islamic phrases, and, where appropriate, the local vernacular to appeal to a broad base of followers regardless of their background, education, or social status. In his discourses on late Ottoman political and religious thought, Gülen examines these issues in terms of their contribution to the formation of national-religious consciousness and the state.[30] Gülen is also an accomplished poet, whose poetry invokes a romantic nostalgia for the Ottoman past and elucidates its relevance for contemporary Turkish society.[31] His poetry further seeks to construct an ethno-religious (Turco-Islamic) consciousness that calls for the mobilization of youth to realize a historical mission, namely the creation of a powerful and prosperous Turkey that once again will play a leadership role in the Islamic heartland.[32]

THE STRUCTURE OF THE MOVEMENT

The Gülen community consists of three circles. At the center of the movement is a core group of believers who leads the activities (*hizmet*) in a spirit of full and unconditional loyalty to the movement and Gülen, the leader. This core includes considerable numbers of university graduates, predominantly specialized in technical subjects (such as engineering), who come from rural areas or small towns in Turkey. The main core of the movement consists of "elder brothers" (*büyük abiler*) and a new generation of leaders with an American or European university education, some of them being Gülen's closest associates and students, who are highly respected and regularly consulted on major policies and day-to-day activities. Most of these elder males are full-time activists who work as professionals with salaries at the movement's institutions. A large number in this core have originated in conservative and patriotic background such as Harun Tokat, Abdullah Aymaz, Şerif Ali Tekalan, and İsmail Büyükçelebi. Although in the past, there were more people at the core group, they were relegated to less important positions. For instance, Hüseyin Gülerce, who presents himself and is also perceived as the spokesperson of the movement, does not have much power over the decision-making processes. People such as Ali Bayram, Alaaddin Kaya, or Latif Erdoğan, who were once prominent personalities, are less visible now. In recent years, there is a growing debate between the older and new generation leaders of the movement. A new generation in leadership is much more aggressive and vocal in their identity, goals, and strategies. This new generation includes Ekrem Dumanlı, Mustafa Yeşil, and Rıza Nur Meral. One of the key aspects of the movement is the constant circulation of the leadership positions and "zero tolerance" in terms of incompetence and mistakes. Thus, there is a major struggle to move up to the decision-making ladder of the movement's institutions.

The second circle of people, *the affiliates*, support Gülen's religio-national goals, and both directly and indirectly participate in the creation of *eser* (good deeds and work) through *himmet* charities. This circle includes small and medium-size merchants (*esnaf*), and businesspeople (*işadamı*), who constitute the board of trustees of the movement's numerous foundations. They support the movement's activities in their area through fundraisings organized by local volunteers. The second circle is organized horizontally in terms of webs of networks in different neighborhoods and led by a leader, known as an imam (in recent years, the movement does not use the term imam but rather *abi* or *hadim*). The second circle is administered through municipal, provincial, or state level leaders, *abis*. These leaders, who are responsible for the implementation of decisions and also facilitate the flow of information from the grassroots to the leadership, are selected by the first circle. One becomes a leader (*abi*) because of his creative thinking, competence, tested sincerity, and sociability. In some cases, sincerity and loyalty are more important as values than capability or competence. Thus, many local leaders are sincere and creative organizers, but they are not intellectuals and some have limited curiosity about other cultures. As the new generation of educated sympathizers join the movement, there is a much richer pool from which to choose local leaders.

Finally, there are those sympathizers who share Gülen's goals but do not participate in their realization. This group is very much involved in the protection of *eser*, whether it involves the schools, newspapers or dormitories. This last and biggest group includes many nominal Muslims, including agnostics and nonbelievers, who nonetheless share some of the key values and goals of the movement. Thus, Gülen's community is less cohesive in its periphery but has a military-like discipline at its core. The connection between the first and the second concentric circle is structured by the norms of loyalty, trust, merit and diligence.[33] Authority is very much distributed outwards from a central first circle to the next circle. In recent years, there has been a decentralization of power and many local Gülen movement leaders have become more autonomous because the movement has grown, and also local needs have started to shape the character of the movement. They have turned into virtual "baron-like" leaders rather than *abis* due to their control of huge funds and properties, including schools. Due to a lack of legal protection in the past and the possibility that the Kemalist state may outlaw the movement and confiscate its assets, almost all funds, properties, and investments of the movement have been under the personal names of leaders rather than of a foundation. However, due to increased political security in Turkey as a result of the JDP government and the legal changes, the movement is undergoing major institutionalization and most of the properties and funds are now placed under legal foundations.

It is important to examine the increasing wealth and influence of the movement since 2002, by which time some important transformations can be observed. The organizational features of the movement are concentric and horizontal. The first circle functions like a "committee of wisemen" of the movement in which there is a constant rivalry over the controlling of the other circles. Since there is no clear second man or deputy to Gülen himself, a few of them in the first circle sometimes imagine themselves as being able to fill this role as the successor after the eventual passing of Gülen himself. Those who overtly indicate their willingness to take on the mantle of succession and leadership are criticized and, if necessary, excluded by the rest of the members of the first circle. Thus, there is a real psychological competition of personalities, and one of the main characteristics of the first circle is that they do not want it opened to additional members.

The second circle is most critical, since it includes regional leaders and organizers of fund raising. As the circle extends outward, its responsibilities get fuzzier, and loyalty requirements get looser. The outer circle is dominated by the movement's sympathizers who express support for the activities of Gülen without becoming active participants in the religious projects of the movement. Each circle is also made up of a bundle of networks of ideas, practices, and instruments of mobility with the purpose of creating the necessary social, economic and political conditions that would allow the realization of their definition of the "good life." Thus, circles are constituted by social networks in which followers form bonds through shared norms and goals. These bonds affect the relations between followers of the movement. The density within circles and networks are not the same, it varies according to their closeness to the leaders, and also sociopolitical cleavages. In the networks the bonds determine the norms and patterns of behavior and lifestyle; while in the case of the circles, norms facilitate the formation of bonds. These networks offer very limited space for individual agency and autonomy. One's position is determined by one's place within the structure of the network. Moreover, these networks are critical in finding a job, promotion, and, especially, gathering information useful to the movement on political, educational and economic activities. These networks constitute the circles, and they, in turn, form the community, what is commonly called *cemaat*, which blends the Weberian notions of *gemeinschaft* (social ties based on shared values and belief) and *gesellschaft* (impersonal and formal instrumental ties) aspects of communalized society.

The unifying glue of these dispersed circles and networks is the shared ideals and goals that are framed by Gülen himself. The depth of feeling within the network, and the moral obligation to the movement to work for the realization of the movement's objectives are two crucial aspects of the Gülen community. The Gülen movement integrates and accommodates a spectrum of ideas and practices as long as they help to realize its goal of creating a Muslim society.

Gülen and his followers are also famous for their open display of emotion and even public weeping. This uncontrolled weeping, and its implication in the broader cultural context of Turkish society, needs to be examined in order to understand the emotional chart of the movement. In Turkish culture, family and neighborhood have been the primary sources of emotion and of the construction of personality. After participating in some gatherings where people weep as they listen to Gülen, I would argue that the depths of religious feeling mustered through such weeping is a non-verbal expression of emotion that recurs when their inner self has been stirred by the speeches and body language of Gülen, constituting devotion to the movement (not necessarily to Gülen but rather to his message).

In recent years, Islam and the Islamic way of life are undergoing significant transformation after the spread and thickening of opportunity spaces in the market, media, education and politics. At the core of this new religiosity is the affectation of public forms of piety. By this, I mean a form of piety that is vivid in terms of ritual, practice and public displays, but not necessarily in terms of deep morality. Although Gülen is seeking to resist this encirclement by stressing morality as the core of Islam, only time will tell if this will succeed.

The movement has also managed to produce a new form of *dava*, which is not carried out by traditional preaching but rather by participation and setting a good example. This new form of Islamic activism is very much formed against a backdrop of the crisis of political Islam. While the movement has evolved into a concentric-hierarchical structure, with Gülen at the top of the movement as a spiritual leader, it does not issue membership cards or offer an official joining ceremony. The movement leaves the door open for those who want to join its activities or, alternatively, leave if they are not satisfied. This free and flexible membership (affiliation) structure helps the movement to project itself as a voluntary civic association. One of Gülen's most remarkable achievements has been shifting Muslim energy away from mosque building and political (and potentially militant) Islam towards building educational networks, media establishments, and financial institutions. In this vein, he identified three areas that are essential for the survival of a powerful Muslim community: *knowledge* via education, *public consensus* via the media and *economic power* through building competitive companies and financial institutions.

The movement has organized itself in several areas. Its followers have established regional, national and international business associations to network among business community, like TUSKON (The Turkish Confederation of Businessmen and Industrialists).

With the support of these entrepreneurs, the movement has opened hundreds of schools and colleges in Turkey and abroad. It has the second largest media conglomeration in Turkey: the two largest daily newspapers (*Zaman*, *Today's Zaman*), six TV channels (Samanyolu, S Haber, Mehtap, Ebru, Yumurcak, Hazar), two radio stations (Burç FM, Dünya Radyo), a worldwide news agency (Cihan News Agency), some publishing houses (Işık Publishing, Nil, Kaynak A.S., Blue Dome) and a number of periodical magazines and journals, such as *Sızıntı* (on culture and science), *The Fountain* (on scientific and spiritual thought), *Yağmur* (on literature), *Ekoloji* (on environmental issues), *Yeni Ümit* (on religious sciences), *Aksiyon* (weekly news magazine) and *Gonca* (a children's magazine). The movement also has private hospitals (e.g., Sema Hospital) and health clinics in different cities, and has set up an insurance company (Işık Sigorta) and a non-interest-bearing bank, Bank Asya. In the following chapters, I shall examine in more detail the educational, media, and business activities of the movement.

Scholars and laymen wonder whether the movement is a religious group, political action pact or civil society organization. In fact, the movement is all of these three. The lack of clear boundaries for religious, political, and social activities is a source of suspicion about the movement. The religiously rooted social and civic associations of Gülen take part in the public debate and expand the boundaries of the public sphere by incorporating diverse ideas and worldviews into the discussion. For instance, the Foundation of Writer and Journalists of Gülen has been an active participant in the public sphere in terms of its yearly and weekly activities and publications. Yet, there are moments when the movement also takes a political position on certain policies and legal arrangements. Since there is no single and centralized institution that governs activities, but rather a cluster of associations and individuals who share the worldview of Gülen, it leads to a speculation about the "hidden structure" of the movement.

CONCLUSION

To understand the network communities of the Gülen movement, it helps to reference Weber's idea of elective affinities in terms of the mutually constituted formations and rationalization of economics, religion and politics. In other words, change in religious understanding and institutions is a function of change in economic structures in Turkey. Gülen argues that salvation cannot be found in the "exit" or "withdrawal" from social life. On the contrary, he advocates salvation in the midst of social and economic activities. The movement is an important case study for examining how religious ideas are put into practice and also how the followers of the movement give subjective meaning to their economic activities. Max Weber, whose ideas deeply influenced my understanding of the Gülen movement, argues that "the human mind...is driven to reflect on ethical and religious questions, driven not by material need but by inner compulsion to understand the world as a meaningful cosmos and to take a position toward it."[34] As the Gülen movement continues to pursue financial and political success, it draws wider groups into its activities. Since 2002, the movement has changed so much that it is no longer only a faith movement. In recent years, its influence has developed into that of a "power network" for accessing certain bureaucratic positions, thus separating it from its theological underpinnings. It is increasingly becoming a useful network for mobility and profit-making. In other words, the movement mirrors our modern cultural neuroses about image, prestige and power. Thus, the movement, which declares itself to be a spirituality based one, could not transform everyone who claims to be Gülenist by turning them into improved moral beings, rather it often provides the necessary means and networks to those who become more of what they already are. In fact, as the movement expands and becomes powerful, many opportunists seek to join it to benefit from its resources. Its transformative role is not the same for every sector of the population; although the movement presupposes the teaching of morality, compassion and mindfulness, it is also preoccupied with the worldly goals of wealth and power.

Thus, the Gülen movement is a multifaceted phenomenon—protean, reflecting the sociocultural crises of Turkish state and society. Politicians can utilize its moderating tendencies while merchants benefit from its networks to distribute their goods and maintain social capital. The poor and marginalized benefit from its production of knowledge industries in terms of providing high level math and science education, while ordinary Turks emphasize its moral vigor in punctuality and excellence. As a result of so many facets to the Gülen movement it could also be viewed as embodying contradictory characteristics: populist and elitist, morally strict and materialistic, communitarian and capitalist.

4

Education and the Creation of a "Golden Generation"

> There is only one road to progress, in education, as in other human affairs, and that is: Science wielded by love. Without science, love is powerless; without love, science is destructive.[1]
>
> BERTRAND RUSSELL (1961)

The most important networks founded by Fethullah Gülen are educational ones, and they are all over the world, and especially concentrated in Central Asia, Africa and the Balkans. Education, in Gülen's eyes, is critical to both his project of contemporary Muslim reform and development, and also to achieving the heights of true spirituality. Knowledge of, and from, God is inherently subject to interpretation by human beings, and thus the Cosmos poses eternal mysteries that knowledge and science may gradually unveil. However, for Gülen, there is no necessary contradiction between science and religion. The accumulation of knowledge about our universe and its creation is in itself an unfolding revelation of God, and contributes to a consciousness of God and his multifarious works. While science may, of course, undermine traditional religious accounts of creation, for Gülen, science by itself cannot encompass the whole mystery of what Heidegger termed being and existence. For Gülen, the bifurcation between traditional religious education and that of modern scientific knowledge lies at the core of modern alienation and its potential lapse into nihilism. At the most exalted level, the vital task of education is to replace ignorance with knowledge without falling into the trap of nihilism or radical relativism and cynicism. At its most practical level, education for Gülen is central for Muslim reform and development.

The Gülen movement itself started in Turkey with educational activities in the early 1980s. Having begun with summer camps, "lighthouses" or discussion groups, and dormitories for university students, it has since expanded to private high schools and several universities today.[2] It is therefore important to understand why the movement has focused so greatly on education and this understanding will, in turn, allow us to better identify and analyze the broader goals of the movement itself. In the first part of this chapter, I will examine the three motivating factors of Gülen's philosophy on education by stressing (a) theological reasons, which maintain that a true spiritual life is only possible via knowledge; (b) socioeconomic reasons, since the source of economic and social backwardness is ignorance, education is the only way to overcome it; and (c) political reasons. Gülen and his followers argue that the main target of educational activities should be the professional and intellectual sectors of Turkish society, since these sectors are the bedrock of Jacobin secularism and those "native aliens" who, imbued with a superficial knowledge of radical positivism, declared war on Turkey's Seljuk and Ottoman Muslim heritage. In the second part of the chapter, I will examine Gülen's remedies for the social and political ailments besetting Turkey in terms of the cultivation of a new generation of elites who are skilled in both religious and natural sciences to help form a new moral and intellectual community. The third part will analyze the arenas and strategies whereby this new generation, termed the "golden generation" by Gülen himself, will be reared. In the last part of the chapter, I will examine both the positive and negative consequences and criticisms concerning the project of developing such a golden generation, and its advance to a position of power.

Gülen endorses the Aristotelian concern for living the good life. However, he differs from Aristotle by arguing that human beings can only realize their fullest and highest nature(s) as "religious beings," and not as simply "political animals." Said Nursi, who influenced Gülen's understanding of human nature and the definition of the good life, had persistently insisted that people can only realize their fullest humanity through piety and serving others. Gülen provides a clear answer in his writings to the question: "What is the meaning of the good life?" He responds that the good life is defined by, and lived according to, Islamic moral precepts, and lived furthermore with the goal of bettering society. At the onset, one criticism may be that for the Gülen movement, the meaning of the good life cannot be determined on an individual subjective basis as is the case of libertarian ideologies, because to some extent, interpretation aside, it has already been defined. The movement does not fully grasp that there are diverse and competing definitions of the good life, which are chosen by individuals with varying sets of values. From the perspective of Gülen, since there is a definition of the purpose of life given by the Qur'an, a believer can realize his or her potential through fulfilling that purpose.

THE CENTRALITY OF EDUCATION

The movement is primarily focused on education, particularly in the Muslim world, as both a religious imperative and vehicle for reform. Indeed, there is a well-known Islamic dictum to pursue knowledge even if one must go to the gates of China. Gülen argues that "the main duty and purpose of human life is to seek understanding. The effort of doing so, is known as education, it is a process of perfection through which we earn, in the spiritual, intellectual, and physical dimensions of our beings, the rank appointed for us as the perfect exemplar of creation."[3] From an Islamic perspective, education is the only path to know the Creator and his creation to the fullest extent possible.

In addition to this theological reason, Gülen identifies the causes of social and economic backwardness in Muslim societies as stemming from ignorance and illiteracy, and regards education as a powerful instrument for overcoming backwardness. By educating a new elite, as well as the masses, he seeks to foster progress and development in the Muslim world. Teachers are asked to educate new elites who are ready to sacrifice themselves for the greater good of the Muslim community. The new educated elites will constitute a new generation of technocrats and intellectuals who are expected to be motivated not by material interests, but rather by concern for the well-being of their community. From Gülen's perspective, the backwardness of many Muslim communities is an outcome of flawed projects of modernization and their alienation from their historic, religious and cultural heritage. This alienation is also the cause of the current crisis of identity, and Muslims may overcome this by seeking a developmental path and reform that allows Muslim societies to modernize without becoming fully alienated or hostile toward their own heritage, as was the case with Kemalism. A proper education is thus a key to the invigoration of society.[4]

Since the Tanzimat period, many Muslims have believed that the Westernizing reforms of the late Ottoman and early Republican period resulted in the evolution of a "native alien" elite that internalized Western notions of superiority and disdain for their own people and heritage. Gülen, like Nursi, believes that the Republican/Kemalist educational system bred relativism and engendered alienation without providing the necessary moral compass for the cohesion and advancement of Turkish state and society. In sum, the Kemalist educational system, from the perspective of Gülen, leads to the impoverishment of the human spirit and fosters alienated and selfish elites who tend to view the rest of society in a colonial fashion. Education is thus central to the creation of a counter-elite, or a "golden generation," to deal with alienation and corruption. In this vein, Gülen has relied heavily upon the resources of the new Anatolian merchant class (*esnaf*) to support his vision of the educational transformation of Turkey and the broader Muslim world by providing dormitories and scholarships to students who come from the lower classes and rural areas.[5]

Finally, education provides an important "space" for Gülen to build his understanding of enlightened Islam within the vital and necessary context of secular schools. A circumscribed Anglo-American form of Enlightenment secularism itself is critical for the Gülenist project of Muslim modernism and reform. These hybrid spaces, where a cross-fertilization of religious and secular ideas takes place, are crucial for the construction of a spiritually and morally oriented society that is at the same time modern and progressive. Schools and education are the essential matrix for fostering such a Muslim renaissance. Thus, by investing in education, the movement seeks both social and political transformation through the transformation of social practices and the political language of a given society. Although the Gülen movement always claims to be apolitical, in the broader sense this cannot be the case.

Many Kemalist/secular groups in Turkey allege that the Gülen movement is Islamizing society through its educational strategies and, also, that it is eventually seeking to control the state. Inevitably, Gülen-inspired vision of modernity and reform rooted in a recast Ottoman-Islamic heritage clashes with that of the Kemalist/Jacobin one seeking to create an a-Islamic, if not actually anti-Islamic Turkish, national identity centered on the speeches and cult of personality surrounding Mustafa Kemal Atatürk as the prophet/founder of a wholly new dispensation. Kemalist critics of the movement view its stress on modern science and education and its distancing from traditional Islamic education as a ploy or tactical maneuver. However, one must appreciate the fact that the Gülenist project of Muslim modernism inevitably entails some forms of internal secularization and a wholesale departure from Salafi-style fundamentalism. This form of secularization, however, has little to do with the Kemalist Jacobin variety.

FORMING THE EDUCATIONAL NETWORKS

There is a close connection between the movement's educational networks that "connect," "disseminate" and, especially, "discipline" conduct and thinking on one hand, and its dominant discourse of ethics and identity, on the other. These solidarity and identity networks seek to channel and shape the actions of the followers through their version of moral responsibility and a strong commitment to the movement. The ideas and codes of these networks constitute the discourse of ethics within the Gülen movement. Gülen uses Islamic ideals to construct and inspire a thicker moral and nationalist shared language for the discussion of modern issues and the interaction with other Muslim and non-Muslim societies. However, almost all Gülenist networks and associations are not directly connected to religious topics and tend to shy away from acknowledging explicit affiliations with Gülen himself or even Islam. Although Gülen has no direct control over the educational networks, during the Kemalist soft coup in Turkey in 1997, he did propose handing them over to the state. Thus, despite the claims of his followers, Gülen is actively involved in these institutions and networks by setting broad goals and possible strategies.

The Gülen network has built or administered hundreds of well-funded and academically high-achieving schools in Anatolia as well as the Balkans, Central Asia, the Middle East, South Asia, Africa, and even the United States. In many of the schools, there is no particular religious teaching or indoctrination. There is also no single organization that administers the far-flung educational networks. However, there are underlying commonalities of discipline, dress, conduct and goals. Personal relations among the followers, shared purpose and understanding about the good life, provide a map of action and orientation for what the followers are supposed to do in different sociopolitical contexts. Through participating in the movement's educational activities, the followers share pride, fellowship and a sense of achievement in terms of fostering an educational system that promotes both academic success and a commitment to morality and social service. They are bound together by the quasi Platonic vision of raising a "golden generation." This goal, which motivates them in everyday life, is put into practice through summer camps, lighthouses, dormitories, tutoring centers, and schools. As Gülen states:

> If the officials running a good and virtuous state are chosen because of their nobility in spirit, ideas and feelings, the state will be good and strong. A government run by officials who lack these high qualities is still a government, but it is neither good nor long-lasting. Sooner or later, its officials' bad behavior will appear as dark spots on its face and blacken it in the people's eyes.[6]

Later, as the movement became increasingly active in providing educational services, especially related to university preparatory education and its students proved to be academic high achievers, the Gülen-sponsored schools were also able to attract children of the established elite. The main attraction of the schools for secular and even non-Muslim parents has been their educational success, especially in scientific and technical subjects. Gülen, like Said Nursi, insists that science and religion are not mutually exclusive or antagonistic, but rather that science can help us to understand God's creation concerning the true nature of the Cosmos. Science, for Gülen, is the most important instrument to comprehend the power and nature of God. Thus, the Gülen network schools put a particular emphasis on science education as opposed to humanities or liberal arts, which may also undermine the foundations of their own moral and religious worldview.⁷

Gülen's educational pedagogy is very much inspired by Said Nursi's writings. He stresses the unity of theological, spiritual, and scientific knowledge, yet at the center of this knowledge is the power and presence of God. The first educational experiment blending these three ways of knowing took place in Gülen-run summer camps in İzmir in the mid-1960s. Rather than escaping modernity and positioning the power of reason against revelation, Gülen has sought to reconcile the two. When university education began spreading to different cities in Turkey in the mid-1970s and early 1980s, Gülen used this as an opportunity to build dormitories for students and use these dormitories as new centers for informal education about Islam. Gülen increasingly started to encourage his followers to invest in the private educational system.⁸ Moreover, when the competition for entrance to universities became stiff, the movement started establishing preparatory schools, along with dormitories, for conservative Muslim students in urban centers. In addition to the summer camps, dormitories, and lighthouses, Gülen unleashed the monthly magazine *Sızıntı* to reach a larger section of the population in 1979. *Sızıntı* contained articles about the connection between science and religion, and attempted to popularize science through an Islamic idiom.

Gülen's ideas and efforts coincided with the critical historical junctures of the new Turkish-Islamic synthesis state policy that the post-1980 military coup leaders sought to deploy and the subsequent rise of the incipient Anatolian Muslim bourgeoisie. With the end of the Cold War in 1991 and Operation Desert Storm, the United States sought to present Turkish Islam as a model to counter the so-called Iranian threat of "radical Islam" in many newly independent states in the former Soviet Union. The Gülen movement was also regarded as a potential bulwark against the more overt Erbakan-led political Islamism by the Turkish state and also by outside countries. In terms of being viewed as a challenge or threat by some power centers, perceptions of the Gülen movement only started to change with the soft coup of 1997, which Gülen ironically supported as a form of appeasement, even though the Kemalist coup plotters had already grown hostile toward him. These changing political contexts have provided opportunities for the repositioning of the Gülen movement, of which they have adroitly taken advantage.⁹

MODERN MUSLIMS AND THE RAISING OF A "GOLDEN GENERATION"

> A nation's future depends on its youth. Any people who want to secure their future should apply as much energy to raising their children as they devote to other issues.... The reasons for the vices observed in today's

generation, as well as the incompetence of some administrators and other nation-wide troubles, lie in the prevailing conditions and ruling elite of 25 years ago. Likewise, those who are charged with educating today's young people will be responsible for the vices and that will appear in another 25 years. Those who wish to predict a nation's virtuous future can do so correctly by taking a full account of the education and upbringing given to its young people. "Real" life is possible only through knowledge. Thus, those who neglect learning and teaching should be counted as "dead" even though they are living, for we were created to learn and communicate to others what we have learned. Right decisions depend on having a sound mind and being capable of sound thought. Science and knowledge illuminate and develop the mind. For this reason, a mind deprived of science and knowledge cannot reach right decisions, is always exposed to deception, and is subject to being misled.[10]

Gülen's golden generation is to be constituted from those who are educated in sciences and religion and who have reconciled the tensions of living in modern secular societies without compromising their faith in religion.[11] Gülen's golden generation is expected to fulfill the daunting task of reconciling religion and science while promoting universal moral values against the specter of postmodern relativism and nihilism. The defining characteristics of the golden generation, for Gülen, are faithfulness, responsibility, tenacity and an abundance of idealism and selflessness.[12] Here, Gülen speaks in almost Nietzschean terms:

> They will think, investigate, believe and overflow with spiritual pleasure. While making the fullest use of modern facilities, they will not neglect their traditional and spiritual values in building their own world.... These new people will unite profound spirituality, diverse knowledge, sound thinking, a scientific temperament and wise activism. Never content with what they know, they will continuously increase in knowledge: knowledge of self, of nature and of God.[13]

In the education and preparation of this new generation, Gülen has assigned a special mission to teachers and defined their teaching activity as akin to a religious mission. He has called upon the best minds to participate in the preparation of the golden generation, and has asked his followers to invest in education rather than mosque building. Gülen framed this teaching activity in Islamic terms by calling their mission an *irşad* (moral guidance) and a struggle to save souls by teaching them how to comprehend the glory of God and creation. From Gülen's perspective, the teachers perform the highest aspect of *hizmet* by teaching and preparing future generations. Gülen identifies schools as new "holy spaces" and teachers as "saintly people":

> Teachers should know how to find a way to the student's heart and leave indelible imprints upon his or her mind. They should test the information to be passed on to students by refining their own minds and the prisms of their hearts. A good lesson is one that does more than provide pupils with useful information or skills; it should elevate them into the presence of the unknown. This enables the students to acquire a penetrating vision into the reality of things, and to see each event as a sign of the unseen world.[14]

MORAL IDENTITY AND PUBLIC MISSION OF THE GOLDEN GENERATION

Gülen believes that a free and just society requires public morality, and this morality cannot come into effect without a form of religious faith and accountability. Gülen sees holistic and moral education drawing upon Islam as the answer to this problem. Indeed, in recent decades, the Turkish political sphere has been "naked" and free from any moral concerns, and it is dominated by narrow selfish interests and pop-nationalism which cover up violations of basic rights. Gülen wants an educational system that is rooted in Islamic morality. Gülen believes that "a bureaucrat or a businessman could do more to change society than could a preacher, because the purely religious part of society was so marginalized that people with solely religious knowledge were not in a position to influence society."[15]

Due to Turkey's new liberal political environment and growing Anatolian Muslim bourgeoisie, Gülen, unlike Said Nursi, has had an opportunity to implement his ideas about education as the most important tool for engineering a new type of society. Moreover, Gülen, unlike Nursi, stresses religious activism, not only knowing or believing, but rather "behaving" and "doing," and translating his ideas into action. His religious activism calls for his followers to not passively wait for things to occur, but to actively seek their realization through *hizmet* (engagement for the realization of the collective good). Believers are constantly reminded that avoiding sin is not enough; rather, engaging to change and create a more humane world is an obligation.[16]

EDUCATIONAL OPPORTUNITY SPACES

There are several locations in which educational activities take place toward the development of the golden generation. These started with the Gülen summer camps in the late 1960s, but continued with the "lighthouses," dormitories, tutoring centers and schools. I will now examine each of these spaces with its own distinctive pedagogical program in detail.

Through the summer camps, young people learned the values of caring, sharing and cooperation. Through summer camps in İzmir, Gülen formulated, tested and adjusted his approaches to teaching religion and science together to build a new type of person who would be in the service of his goal to create an Islamic way of life. The key principle that Gülen championed is teamwork. It teaches young people how to come together as a group to work toward achieving a common objective. These camps, which are all for males, provide the necessary spaces for social network formation, group readings and discussion, religious fellowship and sporting activities.

Lighthouses and *Dershanes*

These "lighthouses," as Gülen argues, are as the "home of Ibn-i Erkam," who was an early convert to Islam, and who provided a place where believers of Islam could go to discuss and learn about their new faith. Gülen describes lighthouses as: "Private shelters for the youth against disbelief and the corrupting influences of the system.... I hope they help each and every young person to create and improve their personality by living together and enhancing their environment with Islamic ideals."[17] Lighthouses, where same-sex roommates from different social and economic backgrounds live in a culture of harmony, brotherhood, and spirituality, provide a clean and safe alternative for university students from socially and politically conservative and/or insecure milieus in Turkey. Many of the students who have received scholarships from the Gülen movement's foundations are cared for in lighthouses for the duration of their education. Later on, they volunteer or work in movement-affiliated institutions as teachers, journalists, clerks, or they establish their own private companies and work in the market while remaining connected to the movement as new sponsors.

These informal social settings are devoted to fostering piety and fellowship among its followers. In these lighthouses, mostly young students come together to read the writings of Said Nursi and Gülen, and later discuss them among themselves. Prayer sessions always accompany these meetings. The central element of these gatherings is the spiritual conviction to change themselves and their sociocultural environment. These lighthouses are centers where Puritan values are cultivated, along with the balance between the external and internal aspects of religiosity. Inner conviction becomes the necessary condition for outward observance. From the perspective of Gülen, good collective works of *hizmet* and *himmet* are evidence of the spiritual renewal of the Turkish nation. One of the leaders of the focus group, who has been very active in Maltepe,

Istanbul, said "faith in Islam and conviction of the Qur'an has to be verified through personal and collective actions. Islam without action is like having a bank account without any deposit."[18] In other words, good works and deeds would be sacred if they follow from faith, and these good deeds are the investment of believers in the afterlife. He further said, "You cannot separate faith and work; they are indivisible; if you believe in God, you need to do something to please God." The emphasis on discipline and pietism is very much in line with the authoritarian value structure of modern Turkey. Gülen always stresses the virtues of work discipline, obedience, and commitment to one's profession. Such a value structure, as in the case of Weber's *Protestant Ethics*, laid the foundation for Turkey's neoliberal economic takeoff.

In the evolution of the post-Kemalist Turkish public sphere, religious debate and Islamic printing played a vital role. The writings of Gülen and the evolution of the textual communities on the basis of Gülen's writings promoted a literate devotional culture. Islamic revival in Turkey is closely linked with print and mass education, both as a cause and effect of this expanding print culture that the nation-building process necessitated. Gülen's books required ordinary people to read and discuss among themselves. Although an expanding print culture did not stop oral traditions and the memorization of the Qur'an, the reading of religious texts, especially Nursi and Gülen's writings, became more common. Thus, pietism and revival of Islam played an important positive role in the expanding of print culture, and a new mode of sociability that evolved through these reading circles. Just like conventicles in Germany in the eighteenth century, the lighthouses provided a space for devotional gatherings in homes.[19] People read, discuss, and pray together in these homes. These devotional gatherings outside the mosque helped to foster piety, promote work discipline, and develop trust-based social ties among the followers that would eventually spill over to other spheres of social life. Thus, these homes became the agents of social change and reconstitution of Islam in light of modern social and economic needs.

Lighthouses are informal, spontaneous conversational centers of debate and exchange of information. However, there is always a degree of "authority" that is maintained by those who lead the debate. Both the *dershanes* of Said Nursi and the lighthouses of Gülen are very important vehicles for the reception and diffusion of religiously shaped ideas and practices. Throughout Turkey, lighthouses are information networks through which books were read and discussed, and information about economy and politics has been exchanged. These lighthouses were also associational incubators from which new intellectuals and leaders could emerge and gain legitimacy

In the lighthouses, students regularly attend the "lessons or conversations" (*ders* or *sohbet*) that are presided over by an "elder brother or sister" (*abi* or *abla*) and they read either from Gülen's books or watch his videos, and contextualize his message both in daily life and in dominant political discourse. The elder brother functions as a leader of the group, and also a tutor who seeks to instill Islamic values in students. There are always discussions that seek to clarify concepts, and summarize the moral message in terms of "what needs to be done." The dominant mode in these discussions is always "narrative-based," and there is always a story about the life of Prophet Muhammad or some prominent Muslim personality. The main goal of these lessons and discussions is to make Islamic moral principles relevant to everyday life, and develop strategies of addressing moral dilemmas in modern society. However, daily newspapers, except the dailies *Zaman* and *Bugün*, or books that are regarded as not Islamic, are discouraged due to two reasons: "newspapers cover politics too much and they are also tabloids with too many stories about the lifestyle of movie stars and ultimately have corrupting consequences, which could lead to divisiveness among the students."[20] Although leaders of the movement seek to explain this "prevention" or censorship of alternative newspapers and books by pointing at the merit of keeping students from being distracted, and keeping them focused on religious values, this pedagogy also points to the limits of independent and critical thinking fostered by the movement.

The lighthouses function as semi-sacred spaces where piety and religious duties are carefully fulfilled. Students are expected to participate in daily religious prayers. In many cases, due to their respect for the elder brother, they develop a sense of solidarity and internalize the moral code and rituals of the lighthouses. Students who are coming from conservative religious milieus, or who are in search of spiritual fulfillment, find great comfort in these houses. They provide a moral compass and necessary shelter against the strange environments of large urban centers. For those students who are coming from the small towns and villages of Anatolia, the lighthouses do not represent a major rupture, but rather a "modernized version of their moral world."

As this author observed, in the lighthouse in Paderborn, Germany, a group of 15 students from diverse backgrounds come together to read an essay by Gülen from *Asrın Getirdiği Tereddütler*, which calls upon Muslims to read and examine the universe as if it were a book to be deciphered. When one seeks to understand the wonder of nature and the universe, one also opens doors to comprehend the will of God and His revelation (i.e., the Qur'an). The students then raise a series of questions about the interaction between Islam and the wonders of the universe. One elder *abi* says, "We need to study the universe through the signs and attributes of God." The conclusion of this lecture was that the Qur'an reveals the signs of *ahiret* (afterlife), the universe, nature, and human beings (*insan*). I asked a student why he comes to these lectures, and he responded:

I come here because I learn new things that I didn't know. I never thought of nature, universe, and human beings, within this holistic view. I have been in hunger of spirituality in the last several years and my father does not know much about these things, and in the schools you cannot ask because German schools are "free of God." In addition, I make some friends here and we talk about Islam and learn how it relates to our life and thinking. I renew my "memory" (*hafızamı yeniliyorum*) here by thinking who I am and why I am here.

He also said, "The people here are in peace of mind (*huzur*) and they are very peaceful and I wonder about the sources of these soft-tone and humane relations as well. Yes I am here because I learn something new and also for peace of mind."[21]

The lighthouses in Germany carry out several functions: they help Turkish students with their homework assignments, and tutor the students to get better grades; they also teach them about Islam and Turkish history; provide an arena of friendship with other Muslim Turkish students; and have discussions and prayers together. These spaces are both public and private where the young Turks come together to discuss Islam and relate it to their everyday life. Some of the students who attend these places are not followers of Gülen, but they are there because these houses are run by Turkish Muslims, and offer useful communal spaces. However, the leaders, called *rehber* and not *abi*, call upon the young Turks to distance themselves from sex, drugs, gangs and un-Islamic ways of life. They expect the students to pray and differentiate themselves from the more liberal and hedonistic German "ways of life." In one sense, the Gülen movement has played an important integrative role for young Turks in Germany by stressing education and public participation in German political and social processes. However, the movement has not been fully successful in Germany due to its authoritarian and conservative attitude and efforts to simultaneously discourage too much assimilation into broader society. German-Turkish youth frequently criticize the *abis/rehbers* who come from Turkey and "do not know much about Germany, and seek to preach and control how we should live here."[22]

In Cologne, I visited a lighthouse with seven students, three from Turkey, who lived together. One student who was born in Germany and not a "full time" follower of the movement said:

Gülen gives *feeling*, not knowledge (*Gülen his veriyor, bilgi değil*). It raises and molds our feelings by providing examples from Islamic and Turkish history. These feelings do not lead to thinking but to action and this is what the movement is all about: action. There is not much thinking if you define thinking in terms of challenging established norms and trying to be different. However, the movement is a bundle of actions and practices. *Hocaefendi* is the one who thinks and tells the rest of the followers what is right and what is wrong. You see in the recent constitutional referendum in Turkey, *Hocaefendi* played an important role by mobilizing his followers to vote, and vote "yes."[23]

Indeed, the movement is steeped in nostalgia and deep feelings about Islam and the glories of the Muslim past, especially the Ottomans. Thought would excel with critical thinking and questioning. However, where the pedagogy falls short is again in the area of critical and independent thinking. Ironically, in this regard, Said Nursi, Gülen's own inspirational guide, sought to open more cognitive spaces for critical thinking and the reexamination of Islamic texts and discourses. It seems that Gülen's fixation on preparing the new elite of "the golden generation" via discipline and devotion has sacrificed the perhaps equally vital values of critical thinking and openness to alternative ways of being, though of course such criticism can also be leveled at nonreligious forms of belief and living as well.

In Turkey, these lighthouses are highly valued and supported by rural parents who are worried about sending their children for education to large cities all alone and without communal support structures. A father from Demirözü, a small town in the Bayburt province in conservative Eastern Anatolia, whose son was staying in one of the lighthouses, affirmed that:

> The lighthouses are what encouraged me to send my son away from home to Istanbul where all kinds of temptations are present and would easily besiege these vulnerable young souls. I know for a fact that my son will be under moral supervision of someone who would protect him and remind him what is *halal* and what is *haram*. These houses are surrounded by Islamic values.[24]

Indeed, the lighthouse I visited had an elder brother who regularly reminded the students to remain conscious (*şuurlu*) Muslims (*Müslüman*).

The students who stay in these centers eventually develop their own circles through activities and draw newcomers into them and develop a collective identity. The students I have interviewed in these houses do not desire an Iranian-style "Islamic Republic" or Saudi type of "Shari'a state" in Turkey, but rather a modern (not necessarily a secular) state where Islamic morality and appreciation of Ottoman history and culture will be restored in the face of the Kemalist Kulturkampf. One student told me, "We are Muslim by name, but we should become conscious Muslims with the purpose of building a humane and

Education and the Golden Generation

democratic society like the Ottomans did. The issue is not Sharia or an Islamic Republic, but rather creating an environment in which each community can live as they want without one community imposing their way of life on the rest."

In the lighthouses, some books are just *read*, some are *studied* such as the writings of Said Nursi, and some are asked to be taken whole such as the Qur'an. Although the young students read Gülen's books, they study Nursi's writings with particular devotion. There are books that are read to learn new information, which includes interpretations about historical events. There are also books like the Qur'an, which are foundational texts that seek to ground a certain worldview for the students.

The main priority is not to get students to believe in God, since they all come from religious family backgrounds, but more importantly instruct them how to live as Muslims within the deracinating milieu of the modern age. One student said, "In Turkey we all believe in God, including many leftists who believe in God, so the problem is how to make Turkey a better place where we can live as better Muslims."[25] Thus, the main focus was not only belief, but also—and I would say more importantly—how to live and comport oneself as an ideal Muslim and citizen. The students of the lighthouses were not living in religious or ideological ghettos, many could be critical about the limitations of the Gülen movement and leadership and were keen to reach out and interact with different groups in society. However, the movement has its own moral code and conception of the good life, and expects all students to live by this, limiting the room for internal dissent and deviation. The lighthouses, in this sense, are typical Anatolian *mahalle*s or neighborhoods with a single vision of the moral world and a clear-cut hierarchical structure. Moreover, the role of women is still subordinated to men, and women are esteemed more as mothers of the next generation than they are as the intellectual and political equals of men.

A closer examination of the Gülen educational networks indicates that in these spaces, neither the teacher nor the students were fully aware of the politics that surround their education. Rather than encouraging critical thinking (i.e., challenging the established traditional norms), the Gülen educational system focuses on conformity with tradition and the power structure. Inasmuch as the educational goals of the movement seek to foster a certain worldview and modes of conduct, it narrows serious consideration or understanding of alternative lifestyles and values. Knowledge is enhanced by, and requires some, authority of transmission. At the beginning stages, students are treated as a clean page to be indoctrinated and shaped by Islamic values. The Gülen educational system is what Paulo Freire, a Brazilian educator, criticized in terms of its treatment of students as an empty account to be filled by the teachers. Freire argues that "it transforms students into receiving objects. It attempts to control thinking and action, leads men and women to adjust to the world, and inhibits their creative power."[26] In such an educational system, there are limits to how knowledge can serve as an instrument of emancipation. After graduation, those who have stayed in these lighthouses are expected to provide financial support for the activities of the movement, especially by opening new schools and more lighthouses. More importantly, those who stay in these houses develop a shared sense of solidarity and identity, and they use these connections for their own individual and communal advancement.

Dormitories (Yurt)

In addition to these lighthouses, the movement is also connected throughout Turkey with its university preparation centers where high school seniors and graduates prepare for university exams. Students who attend these centers usually pay high fees and some students who cannot pay receive financial support. In many Anatolian cities, the movement usually provides volunteer teachers to tutor at these centers. In some cases, a new university graduate would be sent to different centers in Anatolia to tutor students, similar to the function of Peace Corps volunteers, in cities that are lacking a good educational system. These centers play an important role in terms of leveling the educational gap and providing opportunities for lower-middle class provincial students to succeed at the university level. The centers are highly popular and productive in terms of national integration and offering opportunities to Anatolian students who otherwise may not have better educational facilities.

The Gülen Schools

The movement has been very skilled in establishing schools, lighthouses, and university preparation centers. In many cases, the movement sends its skilled representatives to different cities and countries to advise and counsel locals in establishing their own schools. The movement provides training on how to raise funds, manage the schools and carry out its educational programs. The success of the educational institution depends on the degree of the community's support and, therefore, the movement focuses a great deal of attention on this. Contrary to common wisdom, an in-depth analysis of the establishment of these schools shows that most of them are locally funded and administered. In short, this is very much a bottom-up, not top-down, process, as some critics claim. However, the situation is very different outside Turkey. In different countries, especially in Central Asia and the Balkans, where the tradition of civic initiative is weak, or in which people lack economic means, these schools are mostly funded by Turkish contributors, who are investors or businessmen having some connection to those countries. However, the main challenge in these schools has been to make them self-sustaining, and they usually charge differential tuition to the students. The salaries of the teachers are quite low and, to an extent, much like US Peace Corp volunteers, the teachers find purpose in the social-service aspect of their work, rather than the payment. In countries abroad, the main missions of these volunteer teachers are: help those interested communities in improving the educational level of their students, promote a better and more modernist understanding of Islam, and promote Turkish business interests if possible. On the basis of my interviews with teachers in Bosnia, Macedonia and Azerbaijan, I identified three moral characteristics of these teachers: self-sacrifice, compassion and determination. Gülen's Islam is about "doing something for other people." There is a deep sense of altruistic activity that aims to improve the quality of life. It is not self-serving expectations, but rather this altruism that guides these teachers. They sacrifice their time, energy and wealth, for the benefit of those communities, especially Muslim communities, in need of help. However, this altruism has a missionary basis.

On the basis of my research in these three countries, there appears to be a prepackaged plan for how these schools are established. The first step is that those who are connected with Gülenist educational interests visit these countries, and talk with local and national state officials about establishing private schools that will improve the quality of education in their schools. Following this, they invite these state officials to come and inspect such schools either in Turkey, or in some cases, a third country to prove the success of their model. When these state officials are convinced about the quality of these schools, the movement sends teachers and administrators to open the schools. The final stage, which is the most important for the survivability of these schools, is to get local communities to become involved and supportive of these schools. When parents see the quality of these schools, in contrast to the usually dismal condition of the existing educational system, they usually support the schools, and gradually provide funding and other forms of support. The movement especially seeks to appeal to the children of the political elite in these countries in order to open doors, and maintain good relations. My own research indicates that the children of the elite in Bosnia, Macedonia, and Azerbaijan, are indeed highly represented.

One significant limitation of the teachers in the Gülen schools, however, is that they seldom learn the local language. No former teacher has written a book on the basis of his experience in these schools. This indicates an indifference to the local culture where they may have lived for three to ten years, and the lack of an attempt to learn something from those cultures. This also indicates that these teachers are not reflective individuals, but rather servants of the movement, and they are part of this faceless collectivity called "collective personality" (*şahs-ı manevi*).²⁷ The followers are asked to display the same belief, behavior, feelings, and ideas. The movement's sociologist argues that it is "like a piece of ice melting in the ocean and thus becoming the ocean."²⁸ In other words, the movement calls its followers to negate their individual identity for the sake of collective oneness.

Mehmet Ergene, a follower of Gülen and a sociologist who writes promotional books about the movement, which are distributed by networks of the movement free of charge, argues that the biggest problem in the Muslim world is that the Muslim societies are "besieged by Western influence." Ergene, like some more traditional followers of the movement, claims that "besieged by Western civilization, the Muslim world experiences a deep identity and personality crisis, and subsequently experiences political, cultural and social transformation."²⁹ This mode of thinking shared by Salafist and their neoconservative counterparts in the West stands in contrasts with a more Muslim modernist approach espoused by Gülen himself. It creates a sharp dichotomy between Western and Muslim civilization and elides the fact that modernity is a force that is deeply destabilizing for all forms of tradition and religious faith.³⁰ Such an Occidentalist reading of the West, however, is not uncommon among lower level followers of the movement. The Kemalists were not liberal reformers but attempted a Jacobin Kuturkampf, which everyone is well aware of and has now challenged in Turkey. To point this out is not Occidentalism, nor is it a sign of intolerance any more than criticism of Mao or Stalin for what they did to Russian or Chinese history and culture. If phrased in such sweeping terms, the intellectual integrity of the broader project will be undermined, and the movement will be accused of wanting to play all sides at the same time.

Ergene, an official sociologist of the movement, argues that as "the Turkish modernist intellectual builds his identity he inclines towards the West, not towards his own history and past. Therefore, whenever Gülen refers to resurrection and a new Renaissance, he always emphasizes the past, tradition, and cultural legacy."³¹ Indeed, Gülen stresses the role of vernacular culture and nostalgia for the Ottoman past. However, he does not make these claims in opposition to an implacable and homogenized West arrayed against the East in a crude counter-thesis to the simplistic and ideologically tinged writings of Bernard Lewis or Samuel Huntington. Gülen argues that the core of Turkish moral and ethical life, just as in the case of many countries, is a religious tradition and culture that provides a basis for identity, ethical norms and societal solidarity. Education, for Gülen, is not about affirming one tradition and identity in opposition to another, but rather teach in a way to indicate their connections and similarities, and the fact that the crisis of modernity or postmodernity and the search for meaning and solidarity is shared by all human communities. However, the ideological divergence between the writings of a prominent follower like Ergene, and those of Gülen himself, indicates the potential for a growing distance between Gülen in America and his many grassroots followers in Turkey.

EDUCATION AND THE SHAPING OF MORAL VALUES

Fethullah Gülen asks the teachers in his educational outlets not to simply lecture on Islam (*teblig*) but to represent and teach Islam through exemplary conduct. The Gülen movement prefers to teach Islam and moral reasoning through the concept of *temsil* (i.e., setting a good example through one's deeds). Furthermore, in the context of the secular schools run by the Gülen community, they are strictly prohibited from proselytizing. These official restrictions in terms of school pedagogy (as opposed to the private after-school lighthouses or *dershanes*) are further underscored by Gülen's own philosophy of pedagogy. Teachers are expected to promote respect for Islam in a secular educational setting not by indoctrination, but by setting an example of exemplary behavior and altruistic idealism for their students. The intent to "bring Islam in" is different from lecturing about Islam. This intent is based on the assumption that "true" Islam is about exemplary conduct and the explanation of the origin of that conduct should come afterward. Gülen sums up his position in the following way: "There can be no room for language, explanation next to showing by living (*hal*)! Once *temsil* speaks, there can be no need for *tebliğ*!"[32] Students internalize the attitudes and behavioral patterns of their teachers, whom they consciously or subconsciously wish to emulate. In other words, by emphasizing conduct, especially virtuous conduct, Gülen seeks to shift the focus from explanation to conduct. Bringing in Islam *qua* conduct seeks to earn the sympathies of the students, and then allow students to wonder about the principles behind the conduct. For instance, a teacher in Istanbul explained:

> There are many ways of bringing one to Islam: first, you need to get the student's sympathy by setting a good example and making him or her admire your lifestyle, method of work, honesty and discipline. You do not need to use books to teach Islam. Rather, you use your body language; how you dress; how you interact with your students and others as a way of communicating the Islamic way of life without openly discussing Islam as a religion. When the students like your behavior, they would gradually internalize and mimic your pattern of conduct and mode of thinking, and then slowly you discuss the intellectual reasons behind your conduct, and finally, if they are ready, you can introduce Islamic literature.[33]

Thus, teaching Islam through good deeds is much more effective on young minds than teaching Islam through dry texts. *Temsil* (teaching by exemplary conduct) constitutes the most important method of the Gülen educational movement. Kocabaş argues that "this hidden curriculum makes the transfer of Islamic ethical norms and values to the students possible by the behavior or interpretations of teachers."[34] Indeed, an Orthodox Macedonian student in Skopje said:

> I understand and appreciate Muslims more now. Even though my teachers don't discuss religion in our courses, I know they are Muslims and also followers of a Turkish Sufi order, led by Fethullah Gülen, who lives in America. I admire their behavior and commitment to teaching. They have very good moral values and I'm always impressed by their tenderness and care for the students. I wish our Macedonian teachers were as serious and honest as they are. They're very committed to teaching us and are always ready to help.[35]

I have collected a series of interviews from students of Gülen-run schools in the Balkans which I visited and which comprised both Muslim and non-Muslim students. They were all overwhelmingly supportive of the schools and had very positive opinions of their teachers. An Albanian student in Skopje said: "The Turks are back again! However, this time they do not want to occupy our land or send a pasha to rule us; this time they focus on our minds, and send us teachers. I think this time will be different." When I asked him what he means he said:

> I think this might be a more effective way of maintaining Turkish-Muslim presence, since they want to educate the indigenous population and want to help us to become better Albanians, and help us to rebuild our communities. They (Turks) do not hold a sword in their hands but a pen and a book. However, to be honest with you, I wonder why they're here? I know they help our education, but why do they spend their money and time on us? Albanians from Albania and Kosovo would not do for us what they're doing here. I really like them, and I support Galatasaray!"[36]

This statement indicates a simultaneous sense of appreciation and puzzlement. The student wonders about the "purpose of this investment," and thinks that there must be something Turkey will get in return. The comparative success and high level of education has already enhanced the Muslim consciousness of many of these Albanian students—that they are Albanian yet Muslim—and that they also played an important role in the running of the Ottoman state. In this way, the schools definitely enhance the "soft power" of Turkey and the appeal of its secular culture in addition to that of Islam.

In Sarajevo, a Bosnian Catholic student told me:

> I've got problems with Bosnian Muslims. They're nationalist, aggressive, and always care about themselves. My teachers are also Muslim from Turkey but they're kinder and always ready to give something to you. I wonder whether Bosniak Muslims are Muslim, or maybe they simply don't know Islam! I really don't know what to make of these two types of Muslims. I like the school and teachers there. They always help you and never say "no." My math teacher explained to me four times and I finally understood on the fifth try! No teacher here would do what our teachers are doing for us. I will be going to Istanbul this summer with our teachers.[37]

This indicates that the teachers are very successful in terms of instilling admirable models of behavior into students and also encouraging students to rethink Islam and view the Turks more positively.

A Bosniak Muslim had a slightly different view of the educational system in his school:

> The Turkish schools are the best high schools in Bosnia. It is not easy to pass their entrance exam. When you pass the exam, you have to work hard to pass your classes. I work hard and I am very pleased that they are here. They show that Islam is about education and learning. We Muslims were not given the opportunity under Yugoslavia to control our life and live as Muslims. Now we are learning Islam, and we want to be good teachers and scientists, and show that Islam and science are not mutually exclusive. They complement each other.

From the terminology the student uses, one easily detects that he has been introduced to the writings of Gülen. When I asked him if that is true, he said he and his father go to a different Bosnian home every week and they collectively read the books of "Said Nursi, who was the teacher of Fethullah Efendija."[38]

For Bosniak Muslims, the schools are perceived as institutions of rebuilding Bosnian Muslim heritage in the wake of the recent genocide and advancing a "modern Islam that is European and Ottoman at the same time." In Bosnia, the schools have widespread support, and the teachers have the support and admiration of the students.[39] Almost all the students know that these schools are established by Turkish Muslims, and a Muslim from Sandjak said "The Turks are in Bosnia to bring Islam back into the Balkans."

NARRATIVE AND ORAL TRADITION AS MORAL DIDACTICISM

Gülen rarely discusses theology in the form of a defence of key Islamic doctrine. Instead, his writings are a journey of exploration of the key concepts of Islam through stories. Gülen is presently the best religious storyteller in Turkey. Nearly all his lectures and writings entail stories about the first Muslim community.[40] These stories play an important role in the development of the personal identity of Muslims. These stories, if repeated several times, constitute a shared vocabulary and an interpretive scheme for the young Turkish Muslims to understand their own lives. In these reading circles, the movement uses stories to organize ideas and knowledge. Thus, storytelling is fundamental to their method of teaching and helping students to develop their cognition. Stories of Muhammad and major Islamic personalities excite, explain, and teach the students about the meaning of life and mold their character. In the case of Gülen, he uses stories as a framework for building memory, stirring up emotions, and connecting them to the origins of Islam by giving them a sense that they are part of an "unfolding revelation" to be realized through living and acting. When I asked a student, who listens to these religious stories, about their impact on his understanding of Islam, he said:

> These religious stories bring abstract Islam back to our daily life and it becomes relevant to what we do and why we do it. These stories help me understand, through memory, the origins and evolutions of my society. When they are told in the group by a respected authority/*abi*, we all feel we are on the same page, since we relate to it and imagine together that we are brothers. Look, I like stories more than reading verses of the Qur'an. Those stories reach within each of us in the room and they incite similar passion in us.[41]

By invoking the life stories of religious figures, Gülen expects that those who listen will internalize these religiously informed roles and convert them into action. Indeed, Gülen's stories do not pose a moral dilemma, and thus students are not taught how to overcome moral dilemmas, but rather asked to internalize and obey Islamic moral codes of conduct. However, Gülen's stories help his followers to frame their identity and conduct in accordance with an Islamically sanctioned worldview. These stories provide a moral compass for the students on how to deal with daily challenges. According to Gülen, morality requires faith in God, and if the students are faithful, they will be moral. Thus, Islam is inseparably bound with his understanding of morality, and religion provides reason to be moral. Gülen's religiously rooted stories help his followers make sense of their world, organize their experiences, and provide a compass for their future actions.

The stories of the first Muslim community repeated in Gülen's writings and cassettes generate a set of categories to discuss the present situation, and the community come together outside the lighthouses because they share the same stories. Furthermore, Gülen weaves Islamic and Ottoman stories together to sharpen Islamic and nationalist consciousness and offer a bundle of acceptable roles that his followers may play. His stories have deep moral consequences and help his followers to conceive of their lives as a web of stories. Indeed, storytelling is one of the most effective ways of moral development and a vehicle for memory building and connecting to God. Through stories we understand our place in the world and construct shared values. Religious and historical stories help us to construct meaning and organize our everyday life. However, as stated, Gülen's stories are always moralistic and do not allow room for the listener to make his or her own choice, but rather show the model that they must follow.

Belonging to the Gülen community means sharing the stories that Gülen preaches in his sermons and writings, and these stories, in turn, shape the identity and vision of the followers. The stories of the Prophet Mohammad and the first Muslim community form a dynamic vision and a shared language for the articulation of the "good life" among the followers of Gülen. During an interview, Gülen argued that "Islam is not about 'being,' but rather 'becoming' a moral person by internalizing the Muslim model of *insan-ı kamil*, a perfect human being." The model for this moral personality is rooted in the stories of the Prophet Muhammad and the first Muslim community. Thus, becoming Muslim means learning the stories of the first Meccan and Medinan communities well enough to interpret and judge one's own life experiences. This interpretation must be communal, and consensus must be respected. In the movement, personal and collective actions are informed by the shared stories told by Gülen.

CRITICISMS OF THE GÜLEN EDUCATIONAL SYSTEM

An in-depth examination of the Gülen educational system indicates that the schools are very successful at teaching natural sciences, and also in instilling discipline in the students. In the case of Turkey, the lighthouses and dormitories provide indispensable financial support for needy students; they also offer a formative shelter for those students who come from provincial towns and villages of Turkey; and supply a vital social support network. Many former and current students of the lighthouses argue that the Gülen networks "gave them a sense of identity and grounding; and opened their intellectual and political consciousness."[42]

However, the Gülen educational network is also subject to criticism. Ahmet İnsel raises several criticisms of the Gülen educational system, pointing out that they are conservative and potentially authoritarian in that they stress obedience more than critical thinking, while equating morality with Islam and assuming that morality requires faith in religion. They also tend to promote traditional gender roles and segregation.[43] In this regard, however, Özdalga, who is sympathetic to the movement, argues that the movement is trying to make its message and teachings more universal, and this has effectively diluted its Islamic message. She argues that this practice "renders the Islamic doctrine more shallow."[44] The pragmatism of the movement forced it to adopt several competing languages and agendas in a given context without fully investing in anyone.

Opponents and proponents of the Gülen educational system disagree over the long-term implications and success of the educational project. Although Kocabaş praises the methods of teaching the natural sciences, she criticizes the educational program for stressing its disciplinarian aspects.[45] The critics of the Gülen movement's educational activities tend to separate the character-building process, or *Bildung*, from the transmission of accumulated knowledge and skills, although Gülen himself sees both as inextricably linked.[46]

In the case of Nursi, and also Gülen, the purpose of education is to cultivate the inner self of students to allow them to make their own moral choices within the parameters of the acceptable moral-religious framework of society. Thus, individual moral choices are expected to be in line with the Islamic conception of the good life. In other words, the primary purpose of schooling is not to educate students to develop overly critical approaches to their past, tradition, and faith, but rather to seek worldly success and reform without losing one's faith as a whole, and lapsing into relativism. By teaching foreign languages, providing state of the art laboratories and computer technologies, the Gülen schools also arm students with the skills and knowledge to become competitive both in their own society and outside. Their educational mission is thus both secular and religious at the same time.

In line with its goal of Muslim modernism and reform, it is perhaps best seen as a continuation and culmination of the Jadidist movement in the late Russian and Ottoman empires led by Ismail Gasperinski.[47] Gasperinski was a Crimean Tatar and the outstanding intellectual, leader and pedagogue of early Islamic movements of modernism and educational reform. His "*jadid*" movement of educational reform sought to oppose both Western Imperialism and their own obscurantist traditional political and religious elites by launching a Muslim renaissance via modern education. In this vein, Gasperinski traveled through Central Asia, the Ottoman Empire, and even among the Muslims of British India, seeking to establish modern schools. As such, he was the direct intellectual godfather and role model for the Gülenist movement of educational reform in the Muslim world. The Jadidists believed that modern education and science did not inevitably lead to atheism, though it did call into question traditional beliefs and practices, which was not necessarily a negative thing. The Jadidists viewed educational reform as central to launching a Muslim reformation and renaissance, which would allow Muslims to liberate themselves from Western imperialism.[48] Their program failed both due to obscurantist opposition from traditionalist Mullahs, who viewed such reforms as a threat to their power-base, and also eventually due to the Bolshevik and Kemalist revolutions. However, now with the collapse and failure of both Bolshevik and Kemalist ideologies, it seems that Jadidism via the Gülen movement may have a new lease on life with significant implications for Muslim countries outside Turkey as well.

In short, Gülen's education provides the necessary skills, values, and knowledge to the students to meet the needs of a neoliberal competitive system and also to build a powerful Turkish society. Moses Mendelssohn (1729–1786), the founding father of the Jewish Enlightenment, wrote an important article, "What is Enlightenment?", and identified education with Enlightenment itself. In the case of Gülen, education is a way of becoming aware of the presence of God and not the freedom of reason from revelation. Education is not only self-realization, but rather realizing the power of God and serving for the betterment of one's own community. One may argue that the Gülen educational system is preparing the students for more jobs and less for life by telling them "what" to think more than "how" to think. In other words, the educational system does not cultivate an inner character that could guide and choose decisions, thus leading to a self-formed personality. Here the goal is to orient followers toward the interest of the movement or the needs of a neoliberal economic system. The Gülen educational system does not liberate one from tradition, authority or conservative morality.

Due to the movement's alliance with the JDP government, the movement's networks are becoming much more attractive to those who are seeking social mobility and promotion, either in national or local governments. In recent years, the educational networks of the movement are facing overwhelming demand, since many people see great advantages in becoming connected to the new centers of Turkish power. Yet, it begs the question of whether many new individuals within the movement are seeking to further Islam or their own ambitions.

CONCLUSION

The main goal of Gülen's education is to teach students about the purpose of their communal life and to live according to Islamic morality. His educational system seeks to bridge science and religion and treats them as mutually reinforcing modes of thinking to define the meaning of the good life.[49] Gülen's movement seeks to foster a "golden generation" in order to create the necessary sociopolitical environment in which believers can live their life "meaningfully." In the Turkish context, the Gülen educational system has played an important positive role in bringing education to a broader and disadvantaged sector of Turkish society; facilitating the urbanization of provincial and rural youth; and developing connections with the outside world. It has also protected the youth against radical Islamic discourses and rejected violence under all conditions. Although the movement is quite successful in instilling moral and emotional values of self-control, asceticism, discipline and self-sacrifice, the movement has fallen short of encouraging critical thinking and being truly open to alternative lifestyles and modes of being.

5

Islamic Ethics and the Spirit of Capitalism

Pietistic Activism in the Market

One of the most interesting elements about the Gülen movement is its deep involvement in the economic development of Turkey. The movement is well positioned to benefit from the current economic revival. Thus, one wonders: What are the values and ideas that facilitate the current capitalist culture in Turkey? How does the Gülen network shape the evolution of Turkey's bourgeoning economy? Since religious ideas affect human conduct, and shape social relations, one needs to examine religio-psychological conditions that induce its affiliates to search for spiritual and material fulfillment in the market.

By studying the interaction between capitalism and Islam within the context of the Gülen movement, one is thus capable of shedding more light on how "material and ideal interests" à la Max Weber work together in the daily life of the community.[1] Gülen's ideas and actions dispute Max Weber's thesis that Islamic doctrine does not allow for the evolution of capitalism because (1) asceticism was necessary for the development of capitalism, and Islam prevented the evolution of asceticism primarily because the warrior group, which was the promoter of Islam, stressed not inward, but rather outward salvation by urging jihad to capture more lands; and also because Sufi orders stressed mystical, but not ascetic, morality; (2) Islamic law, which was not flexible, and the *qadi* justice (arbitrary rulings and rulings based on personal whim) prevented the evolution of a formal and rational legal system, which was one of the preconditions for the development of capitalism, along with ownership of land, the development of autonomous cities, free movement of labor, and free markets. Islam, for Weber, was the warrior religion of Arabs. In other words, according to Weber the concept of inner salvation in Islam was ignored in favor of outward rituals and behaviors.[2]

Although some parts of the Weberian thesis have been undermined by Maxime Rodinson's seminal work, I believe Weber's methodology and his stress on "elective affinity" are critical for understanding this transformation and the role of Islam. The relations between the Gülen movement and the market economy indicate that Gülen's ideas provide the necessary Islamic ethics for taming and enhancing the spirit of capitalism in Turkey.[3] However, this "modern capitalism-friendly Islamic morality" is not the cause, but rather the outcome of sociopolitical pressures on Muslim actors to reimagine Islamic tradition. Thus, unlike the argument put forward by Weber, Islam is neither hostile to rationalism nor capitalism, but rather a flexible religious tradition open to diverse interpretations within its doctrinal and social context. Gülen, in contrast to Weber, treats Islam as a religion of the city (Mecca and Medina), commerce, and literature.[4]

Islam, according to Gülen, aimed to build a new civilization based on commerce, science and education. Neither has it been overlooked that the ascetic life also played a part in the Prophet Muhammad's own role as exemplar. Thus, Gülen's Islam is both activist and ascetic, while focusing on bringing about change here and now without rejecting otherworldly salvation. Gülen often reminds his followers that the Prophet Muhammad was a successful merchant who engaged in the competitive and free market economy in Mecca and Medina. Having said this, we need to know why contemporary Muslim countries are less developed, less educated and dominated by poverty. Some scholars, such as Toby E. Huff, rightly wonder why there is no Muslim Hong Kong, Singapore or Japan.[5] What explains the current miserable economic and political situation in the Muslim world? What is it in the Muslim world that hinders economic development? These questions make the study of the Gülen movement even more pressing and necessary. The problem, for Gülen, is not inherent in Islam as a doctrine, but rather the facile "imitative modernity" found in places like the UAE and the ongoing legacy of Western colonialism.

Modern capitalism, Wolfgang Schluchter argues, is an outcome of motivational and institutional factors. According to Weber, there is an intrinsic connection between an ascetic lifestyle and a capitalist form of economic activity. In short, Protestant asceticism is regarded as an inner force that transformed economic activity and supported the emergence of modern capitalism, along with the rationalization of law, city, and bureaucracy. In Turkey, the "Protestantization" of Islam is not a point of departure, but rather a consequence of a configuration of economic and political liberalism and economic opportunity spaces. Through reinterpreting Islam, Gülen, and other Muslim scholars, provide the necessary cultural and moral impetus for the vernacularization of modern capitalism as a resource to build their own variant of a "city on a hill." The Gülen movement promotes inner-worldly asceticism, rationalization of daily life, and hard work and austere lifestyle. The movement has been seeking to transform the world by humanizing socioeconomic conditions for the glory of God. Gülen's proposed lifestyle includes a series of practices and norms that echo puritan injunctions, such as hard work, disciplined life and abstinence from pleasures and excessive consumption.

VANGUARD OF ISLAMIC ENLIGHTENMENT

Gülen calls on Anatolian Muslims to bring their wealth to establish powerful firms so that they could compete in the world market. Not only does he seek to mobilize resources but he also calls on Muslims to hire educated technocrats to run these companies. Thus, in the 1990s, the most important development was the evolution of the Islamic bourgeoisie, which fuels the locomotive of Islamic Enlightenment by providing necessary economic resources for the creation of critical spaces in the media, education system, as well as think-thanks to promote market and democracy-friendly religious interpretations and new work ethics. This new class became the vanguard of Turkey's recent democratization. The expansion of the economic opportunity spaces did not only facilitate the evolution of more moderate political forces, but also enhanced civil society and private education. Autonomous economic groups supported a number of cultural projects, along with new TV stations, radio channels and magazines.

The Islamic bourgeoisie evolved out of the state's neoliberal economic policies that created economic conditions conducive to emerging transnational financial networks as a result of deregulation and the opening of the Turkish economy. The Islamic bourgeoisie have also benefited from the local governments (*belediyeler*) of the Welfare Party, especially after 1994. This new actor is both a cause and an outcome of the neoliberal economic policies of Özal, the former reformist, Turkish Prime Minister and President who died in 1993. The symbiotic relationship between the state and the large Istanbul-based capitalists had been based on agreement over secularism and Kemalist ideology. The emergence of an Anatolian-based Islamic bourgeoisie ran counter to the existing economic and cultural alliance between the state and the Istanbul-based capitalists.

Islamic entrepreneurs consist mostly of a first generation of college graduates who are the children of an Anatolian-based petite bourgeoisie who benefited from Özal's neoliberal economic policies, which increased their social mobility and allowed them to establish their own medium and small-size firms. They are the first generation of urbanizing economic elites who continue to maintain strong ties with the provincial towns and villages of Anatolia. Most of them were born and raised in provincial towns and villages, and only settled in the big cities of Turkey after their college education.

They were first introduced to Islamic values in their provincial towns and villages and later spent several years in university dormitories, mostly run by the Gülen movement or Nakşibendi Sufi orders. They objectified Islam as an alternative project, and became conscious Muslims who had a clear and concise notion of what constituted an Islamic identity. They were, and are, critical of state subsidies for the Istanbul-based republican business class and have always been disgruntled with Turkey's history between state and big businesses. The Anatolian-based petite bourgeoisie were mostly excluded and marginalized by the import-substitution policies (ISI) of the state, and the state, from the foundation of the Turkish Republic onward, always favored a secular-oriented, big city-based bourgeoisie as the carrier of its modernization projects and purveyor of its prescribed lifestyles. Most of this new urbanizing economic elite became involved in the growing textile and construction trade. Eventually, services, transportation and tourism became important fields of activity. Most of these small and medium firms are family owned, and they maintain family structures with conservative religious values. They identified the state's interventionist policies and its ties to big business as being responsible for Turkey's uneven economic development and socioeconomic problems that excluded large sectors of the bourgeoisie. Islamic identity, which was marginalized, and identified as the cause of Turkey's backwardness by the Kemalist elite, was mobilized by these new actors to challenge state policies, and form a new organization to articulate their policies. In other words, Islamic identity was not a cause, but rather a lubricant to prime the workings of market forces, and an instrument for carving their share of the market. This new bourgeoisie, steeped in Islamic ethics and networks, supported the pietistic activism of Gülen, and they became the main supporters of the Gülen movement. This entrepreneurial Islam is the outcome of this new elite who critique Istanbul-based secularist elite and traditional Islamic conception of *esnaf*, small merchants.

There is a close "ellective affinity" between the ideas of Gülen and the new Anatolian bourgeoisie acting as implementers of Gülen's ideas. In other words, pro-market, pro-democracy, and human rights oriented Islamic values converged with this emerging economic class. These new constellations of ideal and material interests constitute a new beginning for Turkey. This unfolding experience of the Gülen movement in Turkey indicates that the value structure is socially constructed by Muslim intellectuals (such as Gülen) and the new economic class in response to socioeconomic challenges and the needs of modernity. Özdalga argues that "The perspective taught by Gülen is based on activism which is both stirred up and by pietism. I argue that this 'activist pietism' (or Weber's 'in-worldly asceticism') describes a new feature in Turkish religious life."[6] Indeed, Gülen's "pietistic activism" does not reject the world, but rather provides religious motive for its cultivation and rationalization.

Although Gülen did not write directly about capitalism, it is possible to piece together Gülen's position on capitalism and the market economy from fragments of his writings.[7] Gülen develops two general principles that would help to understand his position on the market economy. These principles are that believers should work hard and live an ascetic life in order to leave "*eser*" (testament) to please God, and that economic development is necessary for the spiritual well-being of society. It is important to examine these principles separately.

ASCETICISM, GÜLEN, AND MUSLIM CALVINISM

Islam, according to Gülen, is more about behaving than believing. Indeed, Islam, as a message, seeks to create a new community and identity, and therefore it stresses "action," what one actually does, more than passive contemplation. Thus, Gülen's understanding of faith is based more on action than on contemplation. In a way, Gülen's understanding of contemporary Islam is very similar to the Calvinist emphasis on work and action. Weber writes that for the Calvinists,

> "Waste of time is thus the first and in principle the deadliest of sins. The span of human life is infinitely short and precious to make sure of one's own election. Loss of time through sociability, idle talk, luxury, even more sleep than is necessary for health... is worthy of absolute moral condemnation.... [Time] is infinitely valuable because every hour lost is lost to labour for the glory of God. Thus inactive contemplation is also valueless, or even directly reprehensible if it is at the expense of one's daily work. For it is less pleasing to God than the active performance of His will in a calling."[8]

Gülen would also argue that engagement in daily life and seeking to transform it in order to glorify God is more important than just contemplation. Gülen therefore calls his followers to work and never waste any of their time over worthless things. Thus, there is a close association between the ascetic lifestyle that Gülen seeks to promote, and the spirit of modern capitalism. Gülen brings Islam into daily life by highlighting active living, and arguing that serving the community and humanity is a sacred duty. Gülen strives to bring the spheres of economy and religion together in order to control some destructive aspects of the market. He inspires businessmen who follow the movement to work and earn money to participate in religiously informed communal activities with selfless diligence. The main purpose of such activities, including those of an economic nature, is the glorification of God more than personal salvation. Gülen wants Muslims to complement their prayers with actions that aim to create better conditions and understanding with different sectors of the society. In a way, Gülen's discourse on faith-informed action wishes to sanctify labor and enterprise. Gülen's attempt to inject religious values of hard work into the economy has had a major influence on the development of the economy. As the Turkish economy grows to become the sixteenth largest global economy in the world, this growth in prosperity is viewed as evidence of God's blessing upon those who devoted their labor and wealth to please God.

The Gülen movement has a dual goal of social and religious transformation. Gülen has opened the floodgates for a radical conscientious transformation that offers the possibility of salvation only through rendering service to others and working to improve the human condition. The followers of the movement believe that only hard work, along with ritual activities, could glorify God. A merchant from Adana, who supports Gülen's activities, summarized the economic philosophy of the movement in terms of two goals:

> "Believers must act always with the purpose of the glorification of God. There is nothing wrong, on the contrary it is a blessing, in being rich as long as you know the ultimate goal: serving others (*hizmet*). Second, believers must work to improve socio-political conditions to live their conception of the good life".

The businessmen I have interviewed, usually see themselves first as "believers" (*inananlar; inananlar olarak*) and "volunteers of the movement" (*hizmet erleri*) with the responsibility to transform the world in accordance with their vision of the good life. In order to succeed, they all stress the role of economic power. They all believe that one cannot live his or her own good life if there are no economic means to sustain it. The local leader of TUSKON in Istanbul summed up their position by saying "we live in the world with economic and social challenges and in a competitive setting. We must work and become the master of our own life by controlling the resources but never become part '*of*' it." By referring to a commonly cited biblical verse, he argues that "we must be involved 'in' the world in order to serve those who need help and improve our living conditions and work for the glory of God." In other words, the business members of the movement share the idea that *hizmet* is a divine assignment; one's duty toward God and this, in turn, require disciplined engagement with the world. However, they also realize that the danger of being involved "in" the world may lead to a "captivity" by worldly appetites.

Gülen asks followers to avoid spending time leisurely, and to abstain from consuming luxurious goods. Followers should shun personal glorification and, instead, seek to identify with the community. Gülen offered the following definition of asceticism:

> Asceticism, which literally means renouncing worldly pleasures and resisting carnal desires, is defined by Sufis as indifference to worldly appetites, living an austere life, choosing to refrain from sin in fear of God, and despising the world's carnal and material aspects.... Like fear and hope,

asceticism is an action of the heart; however, asceticism differs in that it affects one's acts and is displayed through them. Whether consciously or unconsciously, a true ascetic tries to follow the rules of asceticism in all acts, such as eating and drinking, going to bed and getting up, talking and keeping silent, and remaining in retreat or with people. An ascetic shows no inclination toward worldly attractions.[9]

Asceticism, for Gülen, does not mean seclusion or retreat from daily life, responsibility, or struggle to build "just community."[10] The critical building block of the Gülen movement's success in the expanding economic market is the stress on inner-worldly asceticism (*zuhd*) in which religious discipline, hard work and capital accumulation have been encouraged. However, significantly, this accumulated capital is to be channeled in a particular manner, as followers are asked to spend their acquired wealth in the glorification of God through improving the human condition. There is an emergence of elective affinity between the spirit of capitalism and the ascetic morality of the Gülen movement, as Weber argued in the case of Europe. Inner-worldly asceticism of the movement provided the much needed religious justification for the emerging class of Anatolian bourgeoisie. In other words, piety, for Gülen, is not only about fulfilling basic religious rituals, but most importantly, it is about acting collectively to change the misfortunes of the people. It is therefore observed that Gülen is assembling the foundation blocks for the construction of Calvinist Islam (i.e., glorification of God through hard work and discipline). Elizabeth Özdalga aptly argues that there are close parallels between the Protestant ethics and the Gülen movement:

> belief in the individual study of holy scriptures; the urge to live a life of piety and self-sacrifice; the enthusiasm for knowledge in general and knowledge of the natural sciences in particular; the urge to carry this knowledge to others through various educational projects; an enterprising spirit; the urge to do good deeds (activism); and a strong impulse to break open the borders of one's own national milieu to reach out to other countries and places around the globe.[11]

With the introduction of neoliberal economic policies in January 1980, the Islamic concept of business, trade, profit and wealth all gradually underwent radical change. This, in turn, created a new "elective affinity," that is, the ways in which certain socio-institutional processes and religious ideas coalesced to create a functioning system.[12] In other words, the shift from the other-worldly Islam to this-worldly Islam occurred. Rewards and punishment are not confined to the graveyard and beyond but also to the here and now. Many Sufi groups, especially the Nurcus, came to the conclusion that believers are God's agents to bring about change to build a more humane world. No religious Turkish scholar was as open to free enterprise as Gülen. He realized that many people are motivated to engage in the market because of self-interest, greed, the will to survive, glory, the enjoyment of riches and honor. However, he wanted to bring about a different notion of capitalism that would stress the entrepreneurial spirit, the desire to serve others, and the use of wealth to make a permanent contribution (*eser*) for the well-being of the community. A businessman who is a member of TUSKON said:

> You need to tell God that I used all my means to bring about change to improve the conditions of people. Business is not all about "me" making money, but rather its purpose is to provide material means to pursue higher spiritual ends. *Hocaefendi* says business is a noble activity as long as one is morally concerned and socially committed to the well-being of humanity.[13]

A textile merchant, also a member of TUSKON, said:

> Free enterprise will be good for our Islam, since economic well-being bring openness, new opportunities for people to live their religion, will help to create more tolerance towards diverse views, goods, lifestyles, and encourage social mobility and commitment to moral rules. Islam will flourish in the market with proper morality.[14]

In my interview with this textile merchant, I came to the conclusion that he has more faith in "money-theism" than "monotheism," a term coined by a Malay social critic, Chandra Muzaffer. This merchant said:

> Capitalism is good for Islam. It makes us freer and richer to build a Muslim society. I cannot imagine a fully developed Islam outside of the free market environment. I think only with freedom and within the free market context can Islam be better understood.

Another merchant said:

> Islam has values to motivate wealth creation, and also some values which impede capitalism. I think that as long as our motive in the market is to produce and distribute goods and services to meet spiritual and material needs of the people and improve the living conditions, it is a noble activity.[15]

A member of TUSKON who had a business management degree from an American university said:

Islamic Ethics and the Spirit of Capitalism

> You need to know that many scholars such as Frederick Hayek argue that the engine of capitalism is discovery, innovation and invention. This is only possible with a good education system. This is also the reason why *Hocaefendi* doesn't say capitalism is the solution, but he says education is the solution! In a way, he is right that the path to sound capitalism goes through education and the free entrepreneurial spirit.[16]

These statements indicate that the Islam of Turkey is much more this-worldly than other-worldly and that believers want to reap benefits from their work here and now without ignoring the afterlife. In short, there are two competing visions of the role of economy within the movement. Some support the idea of "enterprise Islam," which aims to expand the free market to provide more opportunities for believers to be "free" and make "choices." This group wants to see an effective and limited state carry out its role of the rule of law and defense. In other words, enterprise Islam consists of a set of loose religious values selectively picked on the basis of the market needs. Their vision of enterprise Islam consists of values of responsibility, initiative, industrious efforts and hard work. Economic performance becomes an important sanctified activity to generate wealth. In a way, for the "enterprising Muslim," it becomes the goal to display or buy one's religiosity through material goods or through supporting Gülen-inspired projects.

The second group of entrepreneurs, who are older than the first group, emphasizes the "sharing" and "distribution" of the wealth, and stresses communal and religious responsibility. This group seeks to contain economic rationality within the framework of moral values such as social responsibility. In short, economic activity turns into a religious "calling" to serve for an Islamically defined public good. The central motivating value is service to God, meaning, serving humanity for the glorification of God. Those who actively involve themselves in the terms of *hizmet* or *himmet* are blessed and elected Muslims who fulfill God's commands in building a "new world" in which God is brought back into the public sphere.

Gülen's interpretation of Islamic values has provided incentives for the expansion of capitalism. Indeed, many Gülen-inspired business associations seek to expand their share in the national and international market. Inside Turkey, sharing the same religious networks and being followers of the same movement helps to create networks of trust and familiarity that lubricate economic transactions and the flow of goods. However, it is important to study the Gülen movement, not only in terms of its effect on economic development, but also in terms of the effect of economic development on religious networks and values. Just like Nursi, Gülen also recognizes that capitalism drives people to greed, materialism and egoism. They both believe that religion is the only way to rescue people from the siege of capitalism by calling on businessmen to reinvest their richness in good deeds and to avoid pleasure.

One of the main sources of controversy surrounding the Gülen movement has been its acquisition of financial resources. The movement's finances are collected from merchants and a smaller number of business groups. These groups collect religiously mandated alms (*zekat*), personal alms (*fitre*), and the hides of animals (*kurban derisi*) that are sacrificed during *Kurban Bayramı* or the Muslim festival of sacrifice. In a way, his movement's reliance on domestic sources of funding has forced Gülen to distance his group from political parties.

The typical Gülen "follower" tends to be a professional or merchant and his identity is a mixture of Islamic and Turkish national idioms. New merchants and small-scale industrialists support Gülen's missionary zeal for creating a powerful Muslim Turkey. For example, Gülen's wealthy followers established the Asya Finance Corporation in September 1996 to support social and educational activities inside Turkey and among Muslim populations in the Balkans, the Caucasus, and Central Asia.[17] These pro-Gülen businessmen established the TUSKON, the Confederation of Businessmen and Industrialists of Turkey includes several regional associations such as the Association for Solidarity in Business Life (İŞHAD)[18] and the Businessmen's Association for Freedom (HÜRSİAD)[19] to compete with the more Islamically oriented MÜSİAD and secularist TÜSİAD.

Since 2002, TUSKON has emerged as the most activist business organization in Turkey. It stresses know-how, experience and communication networks with world business communities. TUSKON works as an umbrella organization for 7 regional federations and 151 business associations with more than 15,000 business people in Turkey, and it has been very active in Asia, Africa and the Balkan countries.[20] It has offices in Beijing, Brussels, Moscow and Washington, DC. This economic infrastructure is necessary to support 400 private high schools, universities and colleges, dormitories, summer camps and over 100 foundations. Day-to-day activities are organized by a loosely structured local management based on the tenets of charity, trust, obedience and duty to the community. This structure is composed of businessmen, teachers, journalists and students. Gülen is well aware of the opportunities available in a free market economy. His philosophy is very much in tune with this growing business community. He stresses education and engagement in the market economy as an essential part of becoming a good Muslim. Gülen emphasizes the role of culture as the most important factor in the success of a society. Cultural values, more than politics, are regarded as most effective in the transformation of society. Since cultural values, practices, institutions and attitudes shape economic and political development, Gülen wants to reinvent positive values to promote the development of the society. The main negative attitude that is regarded as the obstacle to development, for Gülen, is "defeatism" and the "lack of self-confidence" in the Turkish society. Although Gülen does not deal with the causes of this defeatist mood in Turkey, he conjures up nostalgic feelings about the classical age of Islam, and also the Ottoman state, to mobilize "thirsty" Anatolian masses in whose reach it is to restore their greatness. However, Gülen always argues that this "greatness" or becoming a regional power requires outward activism, cross-fertilization of ideas and institutions, and investment in education.

Gülen has been very clear about his views of democracy as being essential for civil society, since through democratic institutions excessive power of the state is balanced. After the soft coup of 1997, and the military memorandum during the presidential elections in 2007, the Gülen movement has adopted a more critical position and started a systematic criticism of the Turkish military's role in politics. There is more stress on associational life and encouragement for the followers to establish associations, NGOs, and foundations to create an integrated civil-religious society to balance the state power. The Gülen movement encourages the formation of associations and independence of civil society from the state. Although it is very encouraging to see more criticism of the excessive use of power by the state, the Gülen community is hesitant to defend the group rights of other marginalized societies such as the Alevis, Kurds, and labor groups. As the movement expands its reach to different state institutions under the JDP government, it does not hesitate to use its access to power for its own reasons.

Despite the decrease in state power due to a solidifying civil society, the creation of a more transparent state due to EU-led reforms, and the emergence of a new Anatolian bourgeoisie, the market, as a model of governance and distribution of goods and services, has nonetheless taken over. There is little criticism of the market society or the hegemony of market forces. After 2002, the market logic prevailed in society. Social responsibility and moral values have been reduced to self-interest and cost-benefit calculation. The movement does not realize that the moral ethos of Turkish society has been undermined and subordinated by market values of self-interest, competition and commoditization of relations. Since social justice and poverty are not the main concern of the movement, they do not think that the market logic would undermine political society and if the state is too weak to protect the marginalized sector of society, this would end up in chaos and an unjust society. A follower of Said Nursi, who was a sympathizer of Gülen in the past, criticized the Gülenist faith in the market by saying that "by entering business in terms of banks, construction and media companies in order to market Islam, they turned Islam into a commodity." An American Muslim also told me that "the followers of Gülen are the most successful in turning Prophet into profit." Although these are two extreme comments, the movement has a positive view of capitalism and there is faith that the market model is the best framework to realize human potentials.

Today, the market society fosters a kind of egoism that leads to fragmentation instead of communality. The Gülen movement easily surrendered the Islamic public language of justice to market forces. Islamic discourses of justice, community and the well-being of the weak, have been either ignored or deliberately excluded from the public debate. For instance, there is no call by the movement to redefine state power to nurture social justice and balance the expansion of special interests at the expense of the public good. It is not clear that the Gülen movement will be any more successful than its Protestant, Jewish, or Mormon counterparts in resisting the rise of a new "prosperity gospel" where the original spiritual motivation to achieve material success only to serve God and the commonweal falls by the wayside and the accumulation of wealth becomes an end toward lavish consumption.

While the market is regarded as the solution to social and political problems, and a new "heaven," the state is treated as a source of the problem and the enemy of religious freedoms.

In summation, contemporary Turkey is shaped by the configuration of forces of the state, organized civil society, and the market. In recent years, there has been a major shift in the public discourse of the Gülen movement. This discourse could be recapitulated in the following manner: the overbearing state is the problem and the reason why Turkey failed to reach its historic potential; civil society is a force for good and needs to organize itself and bring Islamic communal values back into the public sphere; and the market is the solution to many socioeconomic problems and only with and within the market-created opportunity spaces can Islam realize its full potential.

CONCLUSION

As a result of Turgut Özal's political and economic liberalization, the Republican fears about the role of Islam have been lessened, and new socioeconomic opportunity spaces for the construction of Muslim self and community were opened, these spaces energized competing aspirations for change. Opportunity spaces, such as the public sphere, which became more accessible as a result of the neoliberal economic and political reforms of Özal in 1980, provided necessary spaces for citizens to deliberate over the public issues and the exchange of goods, while developing a new comprehensive shared political language. Moreover, the competing views and doctrine in the public sphere required a new imagination of Islam that emphasizes a religiously rooted public morality of engagement with the "others," a collective initiative to realize common goals and a new sense of political identity and loyalty. In the formation of the Gülen network communities, newspapers, magazines, books and new means of communication technology played a formative and differentiating role.

The cultural/intellectual transformation of Turkey involved a revolution through the widespread dissemination of journals and magazines among an increasingly literate and worldly public. The expanding influence of grassroots activities coordinated through Gülenist media prepared the necessary soil for the diffusion and construction of a market-friendly and moderate Islamic identity. These "network communities," interconnected by a shared code of ethics and social vision, are now found all over Turkey, having also spread to Central Asia, Europe, America and the Balkans. Further, the network communities have been an important matrix for the formation of a new intellectual class that has differentiated itself by being highly educated while maintaining an Islamic outlook toward daily life and politics.

These economic and cultural spaces have allowed the Muslims of Turkey to articulate their own vision of modernity and authenticity. As Turkey moves to a market economy and feels the effects of globalization, its Muslim groups reimagine their cultural vocabulary within the framework of global discourses. These spaces are not only instrumental in redefining tradition but also in integrating the cultural periphery. Moreover, multiple public spaces have simultaneously led to the pluralization and fragmentation of groups, and the interpenetration of diverse identities and cultures in Turkey.

PART THREE

Meaning

6

Muslim Subjectivities

Islam in the Public Sphere

> What I want to say is that during the secular era (still predominant in Europe), religion did not disappear, but instead took a form that was invisible at a public level. No one talks about religion, and religious groups don't dare to enter the public sphere because they do not feel legitimate. Secularization is nothing more than a phenomenon that has hushed up religion: seizure of land, interventions, censorship in schools. Therefore, religion has left the public sphere and entered the private. But this is not to say that it has disappeared. It has simply become invisible.
>
> KLAUSE EDER[1]

Despite the exclusionary and delegitimizing efforts of the Kemalist state, a gradual yet profound social transformation has been taking place at the grassroots level in Turkey as a result of the emergence of new alternative social, cultural, and economic public spaces. The economic and political liberalization policies of Turgut Özal accelerated the formation and expansion of such spaces. Muslim groups have used these alternative spaces to create their own "parallel society" to attract culturally and economically excluded groups. For instance, the deregulation of broadcasting has empowered Islamic voices to express themselves on diverse radio stations and television channels and in magazines and newspapers. Moreover, the growing Anatolian bourgeoisie, commonly referred to as the Anatolian "tigers," has formed its own associations and has been involved in the rebuilding of a new Turkey by supporting educational, cultural, and political projects. New alternative spaces, such as business associations, newspapers, NGOs, private schools, and television stations, have served to empower Islamic groups in Turkey. With the activation of the free market economy and the liberalization of the legal system to allow marginalized identities and worldviews to become public, the Gülen movement used these opportunities to create new (counter) public spheres or transformed the "official" public sphere. By doing so, the followers of the Gülen movement have used the media to speak back to the state and challenge its hegemonic discourse.

Yet, as a result of economic liberalization, the introduction of private media, and the changing legal system, Islamic movements have also been transformed in terms of their goals and strategies. The evolution of the Gülen movement illustrates this transformation and the expansion of Islamic practices and discourses in diverse spheres of social and economic life. By examining the Gülen movement and its involvement in publication, finance, media, broadcasting, and business associations, I argue that one can see the formation of a new Muslim consciousness, alongside a recasting and powerful sense of the Muslim self. The case of the Gülen movement challenges the argument that Islam and modernity are inherently contradictory and antagonistic. Rather, I show the way in which they interact and transform each other. New opportunity spaces in the media, education, and economy both empower and transform Muslim actors and help the process of cross-fertilization of the universal and the particular: modernity and Islam; secular ideology and religious practice. As a result of the formation of more dynamic spaces of cross-fertilization in the media, economy, education, and politics, the Gülen movement has become an identity- and ethics-oriented faith movement with major instruments of social control and empowerment.

On the basis of the Gülen movement's experience, one could argue that Islamic movements are not necessarily a rupture or revolution, but rather a reinterpretation of tradition in light of modern debates. Thus, the Gülen movement is not necessarily formed in reaction to modernity, but rather represents participation in its vernacular production. Religion has provided both solidarity and ethics to facilitate the incorporation of positive aspects of modernity. The Gülen movement demonstrates this modernizing potential of religion. By focusing on the public sphere and the market, this chapter argues that Islam in Turkey operates as a source of social stability and a motivational force for socioeconomic development rather than as a fundamentalist return to the past or a radical political project. I begin my argument that religious ideas are not fixed in practice but are protean and open to change, by examining the Gülen movement's role in the redefinition of the public sphere and its bridging role in the construction of a new political language in Turkey. The case of Gülen illustrates the ability of religious traditions to absorb and rearticulate the global discourse of democracy, human rights, and the market economy. This protean nature of religious traditions encourages many secular thinkers to reevaluate the role of religion in the public sphere, deepening moral discussions. Followers of Gülen, just like many Muslim scholars, selectively borrow from the ideas, practices, and institutions of Western civilization. However, this borrowing takes place in a decidedly different context, channeling ideas only through a filter that comprises their own cultural tradition. Thus, in the end, they follow their own historical trajectory without becoming uncritical subscribers to European culture.

THE PUBLIC SPHERE AND THE GÜLEN MOVEMENT

One of the most substantial fault lines of Turkey is the role of religion in the public sphere. There is a lively and a significantly polarizing debate developing over the relationship between Islam and the public sphere via dilemmas concerning headscarves, the presence of religious parties in the parliament, religious education in the public schools, and the state funding of religious institutions. The main questions are: When, and to what extent, should Islamic actors be permitted to play a role in the public sphere? What should the role of religious discourse be in the formulation of public policy or the law? The Gülen movement provides an important avenue for examining and answering these questions. Before addressing the argument and practices of the Gülen movement, it bears mentioning that Gülen himself sought to reconcile Islamic values with secular discourses on human rights, democracy, and the rule of law, by excavating the core message of Islamic humanism and building deliberative bridges between tradition and modernity, reason and revelation, and economic development and social justice.

Here it would be theoretically useful to bring into the debate Jürgen Habermas' recent writings on the political role of religion in the public sphere, to better understand how Gülen seeks to bridge secular and religious arguments over common concerns to form a religio-secular language. It is imperative to ask, what we can learn from Habermas' conception of the public sphere and the role of religion in public deliberation. Is it possible to build a bridge between secular and religious discourse and worldviews? Gülen, like Habermas, is deeply committed to the public discussion and he tries to examine how, and to what extent, Islam can contribute to economic development, democracy, and the vibrancy of civil society. Are religious and secular worldviews incommensurable when it comes to fundamental notions of justice, legitimation, representation, and the good life?

Diverse groups in Turkey are in the process of redefining its future identity by reimagining religion and history within the context of new regional and international opportunities. The Gülen movement is the most important actor in the evolution of this new Turkey by redefining a public sphere in which diverse ideas, identities, and lifestyles are in competition. By public sphere, I mean places where groups and autonomous individuals come together as a public to deliberate over common concerns, rules, and values, in order to attempt to craft policies and solutions for challenges that confront society as a whole.[2] However, it should be noted that the dominant official definition of the public sphere in Turkey, in contrast to Habermas and liberal theory, is derived from the robustly centralized and top-down French tradition of the state.[3]

Habermas distinguishes publicity (i.e., media) and prominent celebrities who are visible and become public personalities,[4] from the public sphere whose spotlights is not on a single person or the media, but rather on the articulation and power of public discourse that impacts society as a whole. The public sphere is vital in the creation of legitimacy and the formation of public opinion that leads to political cognitive change in the existing political, cultural, and socio-economic system. Importantly, Habermas also distinguishes between the informal public sphere and the formal public sphere. He argues that religious people are allowed to refer to their sacral and comprehensive religious doctrines when they participate in the informal public debate but may not expect to deploy them as self-evident and incontestable truths in a formal public sphere made up of many alternative worldviews. In the latter, they need to accept the fact that their arguments and prescriptions must be debated and won within the boundaries of public reason. For John Rawls, public reason only covers the debates and discussions in "the public political forum" that is restricted to the discourses of judges, politicians, bureaucrats, candidates running for public positions, their managers, and party platforms.[5]

The Gülen movement has utilized its informal network of reading circles as a stepping stone for the construction of new (counter) public spheres and discourses.[6] *Işıkevler* (lighthouses) are spaces for socialization in community-oriented practices and outlooks through conversational readings, discussions, and prayers. For instance, the *Işıkevler* reading circles in dormitories, and the Abant Platform of the Gülen movement, constitute an informal public sphere where people freely bring their religious arguments and views forward for discussion and feedback. In order to utilize and promote these new public spaces, the Gülen movement stresses both religious and secular arguments for creating an inclusive language of discussion. In these reading circles, the movement incorporates and contends with critical views of religious faith and practice while cross-fertilizing religion with reason and the natural sciences.

In response to the question of religion's relationship with reason in the past, Habermas argued against the use of "religiously informed moral argument" in the public sphere and defended secular reasoning as the legitimate basis for modern societies. However, in recent years, Habermas has gradually changed his views about the role of religion in the informal public sphere.[7] He argues that religious discourse should be a part of the informal public sphere in order to have a more inclusive, pluralistic, and dynamic public debate. Furthermore, Habermas actually calls upon both secular and religious citizens to understand the background and views of each discourse and prepare for well-informed discussion, instructing that:

> This requirement of translation must be conceived as a cooperative task in which the non-religious citizens must likewise participate, if their religious fellow citizens are not to be encumbered with an asymmetrical burden.... Secular citizens must open their minds to the possible truth content of those presentations and enter dialogues from which religious reasons then might well emerge in the transformed guise of generally accessible arguments.[8]

Habermas not only restores the freedom of religious reasoning but also asks secularists to respect and listen while recognizing arguments from both sides of the spectrum and reciprocating tolerance. In other words, the public sphere needs diverse religious reasoning to be inclusive. Habermas believes that basic ideas of human dignity, freedom, equality, and justice have deep roots in religious traditions. In 2004, he argued,

"Christianity, and nothing else is the ultimate foundation of liberty, conscience, human rights, and democracy, the benchmarks of western civilization. To this day, we have no other options [to Christianity]. We continue to nourish ourselves from this source. Everything else is postmodern chatter."[9]

However, Habermas limits these views to the domain of opinion formation, arguing that they should not provide justification for parliamentary decisions (formal public sphere). He insists that the state must remain secular, and that religious people should bring their religious views when forming opinions but not solely rely on them as self-evident truths when it comes to the decision-making formal public forums.

In 2004, Habermas conducted a fascinating debate with Pope Benedict over the relationship between the secular and the religious.[10] Habermas argued there that most of our secular ideas about human rights, human dignity, and justice are rooted in religious traditions. He says, "in the past, many of our most powerful conceptions derived from religious sources."[11] By stressing religious foundations of human dignity, responsibility, compassion, and justice, Gülen, like Habermas, is also seeking to develop a shared political language drawing upon an ontological wellspring among Turkish citizens. As it is becoming a part of Turkey's bourgeoning public sphere, Islam is forced to enter into a dialogue with diverse and competing ideas and lifestyles. Religious citizens needed to justify their arguments in a more broadly secular language to be able to engage in discussion and debate with other segments of society. However, in this vein it has often been the hegemonic secular sectors of the population who needed to be socialized into tolerance for alternative worldviews and practices. With the support of the Kemalist political and media establishment, they have often stridently opposed the legitimacy of Islamically informed norms and concepts in arriving at a consensus on issues of human rights, social justice, and democracy. As a result of entering the public sphere, Islamic worldviews in Turkey have opened themselves to criticism and dialogue with secular ideas, while some militantly secular circles have been trying to continue to either exclude or criminalize all religious voices. As in the case of the broader Muslim world, this has been particularly shortsighted and self-defeating, since such opportunity spaces provided necessary sites for Muslim actors to reinterpret Islamic tradition in order to vernacularize and incorporate themselves modern discourses of human rights, pluralism, and democracy.[12]

The Gülen movement has been active and vocal in the democratization of the Turkish public sphere in terms of its diversification and has also attempted to create a more inclusive political language to deliberate common issues. In fact, the major diversification of the media took place in the early 1980s with the establishment of new newspapers, magazines, and publishing houses. The time period 1983–1993 has been termed "the period of restoration" by some followers of Gülen. It is more appropriate, however, to treat this era, not as a period of restoration, but rather as a time of invention and renaissance. In this period, Muslim intellectuals engaged in a novel reformulation of their Islamic beliefs vis-à-vis the contemporary social, cultural, economic, and political issues confronting modern Turkish society.[13] They employed the print and the communications media widely to shape the exterior social world and manifest a plural, though not necessarily liberal Islamic discourse.

In Turkey, Islamic actors and Islamic debates played a formative role in the evolution of alternative religious public spheres outside the control of the state and its official Kemalist ideology. Islamic movements, especially the Nurcu movement and the Nakşibendi Sufi orders, were crucial in the evolution of the growing Turkish national public sphere. Indeed, the history of this public sphere, and the role played by Muslim intellectuals and movements in its evolution, challenges some of the critical assumptions of Habermas' earlier studies.[14] According to Habermas, the public sphere evolved in the eighteenth century via private individuals who came together to discuss the uses of power. The expansion of the market for newspapers and books played an important role in the evolution of the public sphere. Those who engaged in the public debate over the use of power and the common good were secular liberals who were challenging the hegemony of traditional political and religious orders. In other words, there was a close affinity between the Enlightenment and the new group of intellectuals who wanted to open cognitive spaces for critical thinking.

Habermas disregarded religious public opinion in his earlier writings, since he considered it to have stood against rationalism, tolerance, and enlightenment. Indeed, this new public sphere was instrumental both in the evolution and the expansion of secular ideas and practices against prevailing religious and traditional orders and worldviews.

MODERN HISTORY OF THE PUBLIC SPHERE IN TURKEY

In the late nineteenth century, the newly emerging public sphere in the Ottoman state was dominated by ideas borrowed from Europe, and there was a major debate over the future of the state and the role of nationalism within it.[15] With the establishment of the modern Turkish nation-state, religion as the societal glue was to be replaced by nationalism.

The history of the modern public sphere in Turkey is linked to the shift from a cosmopolitan empire to a homogenous nation-state. The Turkish Republic was to be a centralizing and homogenizing entity, organized and legitimated by mass mobilization in the spirit of a constructed monolithic ethnic and ideological nationalism. Since this Kemalist nationalism tried very hard to suppress particularistic and diverse identities and beliefs in favor of this top-down homogenized Turkish nationalism, it created a Republican public sphere with its own clear inner rules of inclusion and exclusion. In order to be allowed to participate in this Kemalist public sphere, one was expected to shed one's particularistic ethnic, regional, linguistic, and religious identity in favor of the official republican one. The task of this new public sphere was not to bring diverse voices to the fore in dialogue but to force homogenization from the top-down and zealously police and exclude any identities and narratives that deviated from the official one. This highly intrusive modernizing project sought to invade the private domain as well, within traditional Turkish Muslim society, which created, in turn, a strong counterreaction that further fueled zealous Kemalist efforts at suppression. In other words, this official "modernizing" public sphere was not a domain for deliberation and dialogue among diverse individuals and groups, but rather an arena for monitoring and controlling "politically correct" visibilities, discourses, and performances.

The Turkish Republic did claim that this official public sphere was a "universal and rationalistic" arena meant to be inclusive of all of Turkey citizens. However, rationalism in this case was read as an antireligious form of secularism and became the organizing principle of the Turkish Republican public sphere in terms of what was "rationally" acceptable discourse and what was not. Islamic or Kurdish identity claims were not tolerated. This secularizing and modernizing *mission civilicatrice* has been the legitimizing ideology of the ruling Kemalist elite even though the organic Seljuk/Ottoman-Islamic civilization they tried to depose would always enjoy much greater societal depth and historic resonance than their, at times bizarre, synthesis of European, Hittite, and Altaic forms of identity and legitimation. Since traditional Ottoman Turkish society was the problem that had to be overcome in this radical cultural revolution, political parties or civic associations were tolerated only as long as they served to promote the Kemalist vision of laicism and nationalism. Since their military-bureaucratic guardians knew better, Turkish political and civil society had no right to imagine a different polity or redefine the public good. These civilizing reforms did not tolerate the formation of alternative discourses let alone alternative public spheres and much of the cultural and intellectual politics of the new republic centered on policing the boundary between acceptable modern, secular, and rational discourses and those deemed their opposite.

Indeed, the Kemalist modernizing reforms aimed to transform society by strengthening the power of the secularizing state, but the meaning and role of Islam was transformed as well. In other words, the radically secularizing reforms of the Turkish Republic breathed new life into "old" religious discourses of opposition and the content of Islamic dogma was itself redefined in this fateful encounter. The modernizing reforms contributed to the formation of a counter Islamic public sphere. Islamic language and institutions were redefined by these Turkish Muslim counter-elite as an oppositional identity to challenge the radical antireligious nature of the Kemalist reforms. Thus, religion became the most powerful ideology to challenge the new modernizing and authoritarian leviathan on issues of civil rights, justice, and political representation.

The revolutionary change in regard to the public sphere took place when the reforms of Prime Minister Turgut Özal created a link between a liberalizing public sphere and a liberalizing market. The emergence of a new Anatolian bourgeoisie, along with new technologies of communication and patterns of consumption, led to the proliferation of independent TV, radio, newspaper outlets. These new sites encouraged and even required Islamic groups to engage with other groups and diverse issues. As a result of this political and economic liberalization in Turkey, an Islamic public sphere was formed as a counter or an alternative public arena to that of the Kemalist state. In these new public spheres, a belief system and idioms were reconstituted to meet the needs of a freer market economy, democracy, globalization, and the growing universal discourse of human rights. Gradually, with the new reforms of the Özal period, the public sphere was freed from the ideological dominance of the state. The new Islamic intellectuals, communication networks, and bourgeoisie very much played a role in the emancipation of the public sphere from the control of the state. The new public sphere was constituted by dissent and opposition and the processes of conflict and negotiation were at the center of the formation of new Muslim subjectivities. By moving into the new public sphere and taking advantage of new opportunity spaces, diverse Islamic groups competed over monitoring, representing, and disciplining the new public sphere. This competition, in turn, led to the pluralization and cross-fertilization of the Islamic and secular discourses and identities. One of the by-products of this cross-fertilization is the realization of pluralism and diversity among the Turkish Muslim community. New public spaces and growing wealth allowed Anatolian Muslims to carve out their own cultural, symbolic, and economic locations of representation and articulation with their own movies, novels, poetry, music, fashion shows, entertainment, magazines, restaurants and hotels. Thus, new hybrid nationalistic–Islamic, modern–traditional identities and roles were under construction. Although Islamic movements, such as the Gülen community, still seek to heavily influence this public sphere, they themselves are also eventually transformed and shaped by their encounters with diverse alternative ideologies and representations.

With political and economic liberalization, and the introduction of a new legal framework to allow private media to be established, Turkey has been experiencing the evolution of a new political language that is both secular and religious. The Gülen movement's media outlets are at the forefront of this new "mix," cultivating a public language that does not criminalize religious voices. Gülen believes that only through exchange of ideas Muslims are able to enlighten themselves and expand their understanding. He says "it's all up to people being able to get together and talk and enlighten themselves and view each other with tolerance."[16] The development of a new pluralist and modern Islamic idiom through the print and electronic media has played a key role in promoting the influence of Gülen's followers. The movement purchased the newspaper *Zaman* and turned it into one of Turkey's leading dailies.[17] *Zaman* is unique among Turkish newspapers in that it is printed in 13 different countries that have large Muslim Turkic populations. It is a conscious effort to promote an "imperial Ottoman Muslim vision."[18] Also, *Zaman* was the first Turkish newspaper to be available free through the Internet. By 2011, *Zaman* was the largest Turkish daily newspaper circulated online. Likewise, there is *Today's Zaman* published by the same group (http://www.todayszaman.com).

In addition to the newspaper *Zaman*, the Gülen movement has launched a national television channel, known as *Samanyolu*, and popular radio stations such as *Dünya* (World) and *Burç* (Tower). The movement also owns *Sızıntı* (a scientific monthly), *Ekoloji* (an environment-related magazine), *Yeni Ümit* (a theological journal), *Aksiyon* (a weekly magazine), and *The Fountain* (English language religious publication). Gülen's activities are aimed at molding a cohesive and disciplined community through education, mass media, and financial networks. In the United States, the movement has established Blue Dome Press and has been active in the book publishing business.[19]

Once a month, Gülen writes a long column in *Sızıntı*, and once every three months in *Yeni Ümit*; these essays are reprinted in *Zaman*, and in them, he deals with a wide range of issues. The pedagogical form of his essays indicates that his readers are familiar with print culture while still being receptive to the appeal of an oral cultural style of production. His form of argumentation is very allegorical and constantly refers to natural and divine truths as being derived from "the book."[20] Gülen does not offer literal interpretations of the Qur'an, but rather reads it through the lens of the phenomenal world. This literary and allegorical hermeneutic softens the orthodox language of Islam as a religion and makes it more amenable to flexible interpretations and the practical exigencies of modern life. Moreover, in order to appeal to Turkey's secular intellectuals, and build a bridge across the secular and religious divide, Gülen constantly refers to major European thinkers in his writings. Gülen realizes the difference between diverse epistemic and religious traditions. However, he believes that underneath this diversity there is a shared human aspiration for dignity, justice, compassion, and meaning.

Since 2002, Gülen's discourse has increasingly privileged individual rights over collectivist goals and solidarity. This cognitive shift is not only confined to the Gülen movement, but rather reflects an emerging general consensus in Turkish society according to which individual rights must prevail over collective understandings and goods. This shift is increasingly internalized by various religious groups as well. They tend to frame their religious rituals and behavior in terms of the "language of rights" rather than the obedience to God. Indeed, at this juncture, the public debate over the meaning of the good life and recognition of diverse lifestyles becomes significant. The issue to examine is how the "public use of reason" is going to shape and be shaped by religious discourse. In the thickening and burgeoning public sphere of Turkey, we see a radical change in the form and content of Islamic consciousness in response to its encounter with alternative ideologies and modernities and also expanding opportunity spaces. However, one problem in recent years with the electoral triumph of the JDP has been that despite the growing emphasis on individual rights and pluralism, there have also been attempts to silence secular voices by some affiliated with the political Islamic movement of Necmettin Erbakan on the basis that it is just to reciprocate past Kemalist intolerance and oppression with a counter-Islamic one. In this ongoing struggle highlighted by the Ergenekon controversy and trials, the Gülen movement has been more restrained and circumspect than those more politically inclined Muslim movements tied to Erbakan's old *Refah* or Welfare Party. In other words, in terms of the Gülenists, their discourse concerning these controversies has been more inclusive and "reasonable," allowing diverse sectors of the population, including secularist intellectuals highly critical of aspects of JDP governance to engage in that part of the public sphere represented by the Gülen movement's media outlets.

The new political discourse of Turkey is evolving within the framework of a dialogue between the secular and the religious arguments that is going to be more inclusive of and accessible to the public. A closer examination of the Abant Conference and accords of the Gülen movement shows that it has been quite successful in both relating to the collective and accessible languages of competing views, and maintaining its own distinct Islamic perspective. Having a particular Islamically informed perspective on diverse social and political issues does not exclude them from Habermas' ideal of the public sphere, but rather has encouraged them to develop a more comprehensive and pluralist understanding of the needs for diverse societies. As a result of interactions with diverse religious and secular doctrines, the Gülen community has been developing a more integrative, reflexive, and tolerant epistemic position.

THE ABANT PLATFORM FOR DIALOGUE AND THE SEARCH FOR COMMON COMMUNICATIVE ACTION

In spite of the ferocious state-directed anti-Gülen campaigns of the 1990s, Gülen guided the Writers and Journalists Foundation, which became more active in terms of organizing conferences, meetings, and dialogue symposiums to build a new social contract, stressing the need for tolerance and pluralism in Turkish society and an understanding of secularism more in line with the Anglo-American tradition. Gülen brought many diverse groups together to discuss contemporary Turkish challenges and present possible solutions. In this regard, the Journalists and Writers Foundation identified major "divisive" political issues confronting Turkey: the relationship between Islam and secularism (1998);[21] religion and the state (1999); democracy and human rights (2000); and pluralism and reconciliation (2001). The Gülen movement brought many leading scholars, intellectuals, and policy makers together, as the Nurcus do in their *dershanes*, to discuss these divisive issues and author consensus-building charters, known as *Abant Bildirisi*. The main points of the 1998 Declaration were: "revelation and reason do not conflict; individuals should use their reason to organize their social life; the state should be neutral regarding citizens and their beliefs, faith and the overall philosophical orientation of society; governance of the state should not be based on explicitly religious or secularist ideologies but should expand individual freedoms and rights and should not deprive any person from public participation."[22] The 4th Abant Conference Platform of 2001 examined the subject of pluralism and its political consequences and the question of social reconciliation.[23] It concluded that "pluralism can only be realized in a democratic and secular regime that takes the supremacy of the law as its basis and which is based on human rights. Civil and political freedoms, headed by the freedoms of belief, thought and expression, education and organization, are the prerequisites of pluralism."[24]

The Gülen movement has continued to organize this series of regular and well-publicized meetings by bringing some of Turkey's most prominent journalists, public intellectuals, bureaucrats, and politicians, together to discuss challenges and issues facing Turkey and the larger Muslim world. These meetings have included people from diverse ethnic, sectarian, and ideological backgrounds. Although the Abant Conferences were originally started to overcome the suspicion and legitimacy problem faced by the Gülen community from the Kemalist and secularist establishment, they have become pathbreaking public forums for debate and discussion among diverse and contending segments of society that had rarely entered into dialogue before. They have played a vital role in easing tensions by bridging diverse epistemic communities and creating a shared language over common concerns. I attended two of the meetings in Abant and Washington, DC, and also carried out 23 individual interviews with the participants. Later, a professor of constitutional law who was an organizing member of several meetings said to me:

> I am a liberal and also an agnostic. I took part in these meetings because they were the first organized meetings that brought people from diverse backgrounds to show that the political language of the country can also be shaped by bottom-up, civil society initiatives. In Turkey, our political language of what is politically "right" and "wrong" is usually determined by the state. For the first time, civil society has come together to challenge this state-dominated discourse and also provide societal solutions to the common problems of the role of religion in politics, the Kurdish issue, the Alevi question, war and peace in the Middle East, and democracy.[25]

Another participant, who is a follower of Said Nursi, and a professor at the divinity faculty in Ankara, said:

> These meetings have played an important role in terms of creating a liberal-Islamic discourse which is used nowadays by the governing JDP. These meetings have provided an intellectual map, forming new boundaries between the state and society, and have stressed that state is a servant for the needs of society.[26]

A diplomat who is both a member of a nationalist Turkish party and a columnist, said:

> I have always been in pain due to the polarized intellectual life experienced in Turkey. These meetings did not only bring diverse groups together to create a consensus on the basis of our social needs and shared history but also provided new arguments for politicians. I always attend their [Gülen's] meetings. I feel that I am a different person at the end of

these meetings. They expand my horizons and enhance my courage and expectations of the future of Turkey.[27]

Indeed, Gülen's public meetings appear to have helped to bring Gülen's ideas to the larger public sphere and also have provided a context for diverse "voices" to harmonize their arguments and solutions over common issues. All such meetings were organized by the Journalists and Writers Foundation, which was established by some followers of Gülen. They started their public debates through organizing *iftars* (fast-breaking) during Ramadan as early as 1994. The JWF institutionalized three platforms with specific goals: the annual Abant Platform meetings, which also organized meetings in the United States, Europe, and some Arab countries; the Intercultural Dialogue Platform, which focuses on interactions and mutual understandings of diverse religious faiths and cultures; and the Dialogue Eurasia Platform, which works in former Soviet republics to create a better understanding between Turkey and these republics, especially the Turkic ones in Central Asia and the Caucasus.[28]

THE ABANT MEETINGS

These meetings stress intellectual engagement among diverse voices based on identities and ideological positions. Mete Tuncay, President of the Abant Platform, who has authored several books critical of Kemalism, says:

> The Abant Platform meetings have been held six times since 1998. I participated in the last three of them. In order for our country to be able to lead a democratic and free life [today], also in the future, in harmony with the contemporary world, I view it as a must that the dialogue spirit that dominates these meetings becomes widespread. Our discussions at these meetings have revealed that, while there are differences among us as regards the solutions to the problems, we all share the fundamental values of humanity. This definitely arose from having been brought up within the same cultural traditions.[29]

Examples of *Gülen*-Abant Conferences for Dialogue have included:

1. 2010 (Abant) Democracy and Tutelage
2. 2010 (Cairo) Egypt, Turkey, and Stability in the Middle East
3. 2010 (Ankara) Democratization for a New Social Contract
4. 2009 (Abant) Democratization: Political Parties
5. 2009 (Erbil, Iraq) Searching for Peace and a Common Future
6. 2008 (Abant) Kurdish Problem: Seeking Peace and a Future Together

7. 2007 (İstanbul) Turkey as a Civilizational Bridge in the EU
8. 2007 (Istanbul) New Constitution
9. 2007 (Istanbul) Turkey–France Conversations 2: Perceptions and Realities
10. 2007 (Istanbul) Historic, Cultural, Folkloric, and Contemporary Dimensions of Alevism
11. 2007 (Cairo) Islam, the West, and Modernization
12. 2006 (Abant) Global Policies and the Future of the Middle East
13. 2006 (Paris) Turkey–France Discussions: Republic, Cultural Pluralism, and Europe
14. 2005 (Erzurum) On the Verge of a New Age: New Searches in Education
15. 2004 (Brussels) Turkey's EU Membership Process: Culture–Identity and Religion
16. 2004 (Washington) Islam–Democracy and Secularism: The Turkish Experience
17. 2003 (Abant) War and Democracy
18. 2002 (Abant) Globalization: Political–Economic and Cultural Dimensions
19. 2001 (Abant) Pluralism and Societal Reconciliation
20. 2000 (Abant) Democratic State of Law
21. 1999 (Abant) Religion, State, and Society
22. 1998 (Abant) Islam and Secularism

Since almost all proceedings of such meetings are published, closer readings indicate the intellectual strengths and weaknesses of the participants. The journalists, more than academics and professors, play an important role in terms of setting the parameters of the debate. Indeed, the intellectual "vigor" of the meetings appears to have gradually declined, and has turned into what can be termed talk-shows or less intellectually critical conversations to highlight the concerns of the Gülen movement. However, these meetings all start with a set of critical assumptions: (1) religious traditions are both a positive and negative source, they could become an instrument of social cohesion and peace-building or a source of division and conflict; (2) the modernization of Turkey (new opportunity spaces) leads to more Islamic activism and the return of religion into the public sphere; and (3) religion is both a source of legitimacy and a dissent against oppressive government.

On the basis of these shared assumptions, I would like to identify three major conclusions of these meetings: one major conclusion is that in order to bridge the division between the secular and religious fault line in Turkey, both sides must agree that the rationality of reason is the only avenue toward societal (democratic) problem-solving. Only through reasonable arguments can the citizens of Turkey develop a cohesive and shared language for addressing public controversies and challenges. In order to maintain deliberative discussions over the public issue, all sides must tolerate each other and share moral responsibility to make their arguments accessible to the other side. The second major conclusion is that all sides must accept the legitimacy of the constitutional state that is based on human rights and protection of the rule of law. Lastly, it is concluded that all sides must tolerate and accept the plurality of worldviews (either informed by religion or secular ideologies) as legitimate voices.

However, there have been major disagreements about the sources of values and norms. Secular participants insist that these values are collectively determined as a result of public discourse; more religious participants want to present them as rooted in religion and more fixed. The intellectual level of these meetings has gradually weakened because the Gülen movement became more politically partisan by allying itself with the governing JDP. This openly partisan profile has in turn engendered opposition and criticism from more secularist factions.

In fact, since 2004, many critical intellectuals, except those who are either the followers of the movement or connected to its media outlets, have stayed away from these meetings. A professor who has participated in several meetings said:

> I do not participate anymore. When they had a legitimacy problem, they invited me and I always found the meetings very useful. However, as of 2010, I feel that these people are not sincere at all. They seek to co-opt intellectual thinking. They talk about secularism, democracy, tolerance, equality, but they all preach and never implement. Now they are a part of the government and control most of the university administrations, they are the least tolerant bunch. They [for example] actively prevent any left-leaning academic from working in the universities![30]

Another journalist who is a columnist for a major secularist newspaper said:

> I have participated in two meetings before the movement became aggressive and assertive against critical voices in the country. I am a columnist in a Doğan Media Corporation owned newspaper. I had thought the movement created an environment of debate and discussion. However, the most aggressive and intimidating broadcasting is taking place at the TV stations of the Gülen movement. Look at Samanyolu TV, their news reporting is very sensational with no respect for human dignity. If they target you, there is no way to defend yourself. Is this what they mean by mercy, justice,

and morality? I am seeing a different movement today than the one which organized those meetings [in earlier times]. I wonder what their goal is. What do they seek to achieve? As you know, the movement is now organizing a series of promotional meetings in American universities to promote their image. I follow these papers and wonder why these professors are taking part in these meetings.[31]

A female sociologist, who used to be sympathetic with the Gülen movement and maintained friendly relations with it, said:

> I participated in their *iftar* and even made several comments. I've come to the conclusion that they constitute a threat to my liberal lifestyle and seek to control what I say. Moreover, the intellectual level of those who are running the JWF is very dismal. You learn nothing from them. They are all respectful but they really do not fully understand what you say. No concept or curiosity about ideas. What made me the most upset was that they care "who you are" in terms of your visibility and position, not what you say or the power of your argument.[32]

A journalist who writes for a pro-government newspaper said:

> The concepts of democracy, secularism, reason, tolerance, and liberalism are understood as much as the United Arab Emirates understands the logic behind high technology. They merely use and consume them. For the movement, these concepts are to be "consumed" for their own community goals of controlling society, and then the state. There's not much internalization of those concepts.[33]

These criticisms raise the question of "sincerity" and also growing dissent toward the "intellectual" agenda of the Gülen movement. However, these individuals appear to have also recognized that the meetings helped different groups come together to discuss public issues. Critics raised questions about the politicization of the movement since 2004. One of them said:

> It is too bad that the movement could not remain neutral to all political parties but decided to ally with the JDP. It might have been more effective in the long-run and also constructive if it had stayed less political. I used to write for their Zaman newspaper. Now I do not like writing any op-eds for them because [they represent only] "one-side" of the current political struggle in Turkey. Having said this, I also think the earlier Abant meetings were positive in terms of seeking to bridge diverse groups.[34]

The main debate has been to what extent the Abant Conferences have been aimed at creating a "deliberative context" in order to develop a new shared political language to bridge the religious-secular divide or a tactical move to fend off Kemalist persecution following the February 28, 1997 "soft coup" and also increase the legitimacy of the movement. I would argue that even though there is an element of truth in this criticism of the Gülen movement, even if motivated by tactical reasons, it still played an important and constructive role in terms of expanding the public debate over the role of religion and secularism in the public sphere and also helped to develop an ethics of pluralism and tolerance in the public sphere. Some debate and dialogue is better than no debate and dialogue at all. Such debates become all the more important in Muslim societies as the majority is precisely lacking any significant forums to discuss religion, secularism, democracy, and other critical subjects. Despite its problematic areas, it must be conceded that the Gülen movement has helped take both secular and religious Turkish public spheres to a level of pluralistic discourse and critical thinking that is well beyond most Muslim-majority peer countries. These meetings have resulted in the realization that reason and revelation are not inherently conflicting. By providing the necessary deliberative forums for Islamic discourses to compete and interact with secular ones, the Gülen movement led to a significant internal modernization of Islam. In other words, bringing Islam (or the syncretic Islam of a given country or region) into the public sphere helps to transform it through empowering different Islamic intellectual interpretations to evolve in relation to secular ones. As these various visions enter into debate and dialogue, the main source of evaluation of these multiple worldviews becomes the power of reason and persuasion.

Habermas also hopes to open the way for the diversification of religious voices and transformation of religious discourse along liberal constitutional lines by inviting religious voices to play a role in the "informal public sphere."[35] However, Habermas' invitation to religious voices to play a role in a secular society is confined to those societies where democratic and constitutional rules are fully internalized and they are all multi-religious societies. The question remains: What should be done in a mono-ideological religious society where secularism has not been fully internalized and a large sector of the population still wants to see Islamic law play a role? This form of society continues to exist in mostly rural traditional areas of many Muslim countries in the Middle East, Central Asia, and North Africa. Habermas is vehemently against allowing religion to play a role in the political public sphere where laws are enacted. Is it possible, however, to draw a boundary between the informal and formal political public sphere? Since secular, liberal, and constitutional systems in many Western societies are deeply entrenched, they can allow religious voices to play a role in the formation of political opinion without putting the liberal constitutional system at risk.

Since many Islamist groups reject liberalism and insist on the implementation of shari'a as interpreted by Salafi-inspired *ulema*, would Habermas endorse the exclusion of religious voices from the informal public sphere and the establishment of a religious party from the formal public sphere?

I would fully support the presence of religious voices in the formation of public opinion even though Turkey has a dominant Sunni-Hanafi Islam with a weak tradition of liberal secular practices, though that is clearly changing. There are two reasons why religious groups, especially the Gülen movement, should be encouraged to continue taking part in public deliberations. First, various interpretations of Islam have been the most important source of cultural and political concepts, norms, and legitimation to deliberate the meaning of the good life and moral truths. The secular concepts of human rights, constitutionalism, democracy, and human dignity would only be fully vernacularized through, and within, debates with a long religious tradition, which has marked Muslim majority states. Such Islamic narratives and framed moral truths in Muslim majority societies long pre-dated secular notions of justice, human dignity, and opposition to cruelty and oppression. We need to realize that secularism is one perspective among other religio-spiritual perspectives. Second, the exclusion and criminalization of Islamic dissenting voices limits public discussion and leads to the polarization of society while forestalling public deliberation. In the long run, it leads to the delegitimization of political authority and helps to create aggressive, even extremist, or possibly terroristic, opposition groups. It is much healthier to incorporate religious voices into the public sphere. That is indeed the comparative advantage of today's Turkey over its Muslim-majority peer states, and why it has emerged as a vital model for and inspiration behind Arab Spring. Encouraging the incorporation of both religious and secular voices, including a vigorous open societal debate among them, can only lead to a healthier Turkish society that is more at peace with itself, and a soft-power model that appeals to both the Muslim East and the Christian West. It also leads through discourse to reciprocity and the modulation of stark oppositional frames on the part of both secularist and religious groups and individuals.

CONCLUSION

In conclusion, a constructive deliberation between religious and secularist citizens of Turkey requires the democratic obligation of both sides to make their argument accessible on the basis of mutual dialogue and reasoned persuasion if they desire to convince the other side of the virtues of their contending worldviews. If their point of view and arguments are not accessible via appeals to reason, or if it is perceived as not being appealing due to fear and ignorance, they will not be able to engage in an intellectual debate, resulting in the collapse of broader public deliberation and the public sphere. It is very important, therefore, to have shared ethics of deliberation and responsibility to engage with rival ideological groups. Seeking to frame one's argument in religious or secular form to make it accessible to others imposes a necessary cognitive burden on all participants. If one is living in a Muslim-majority country, where the secular language and debate is very thin or mostly borrowed from outside, and where the prevailing political language is steeped in Islamic symbolism and morality, religious citizens have the moral responsibility to make their language accessible to the secular minority so that they can achieve tolerance in the public sphere. The Gülen movement, by publishing several national daily newspapers, magazines, and websites, and having its own TV stations open to diverse viewpoints, seeks to systematically construct and participate in an open public sphere. By "going public" or deciding to participate in a public dialogue, Gülen has constructed an accessible modernist interpretation of Islam and also framed Islamic issues and concerns in a universal language of rights that can appeal to a broad spectrum of the citizenry via reasoned persuasion. Gülen tries to show that we can arrive at the common goal of restoring human dignity, justice, and democracy, through a religious epistemic path, as well as a secular liberal one.

7

Secularism and Science

Gülen's View

> Science without religion is lame, religion without science is blind.
> — ALBERT EINSTEIN

> Men never do evil so completely and cheerfully as when they do it with religious conviction.
> — BLAISE PASCAL

There are two reasons why the relationship between science and religion is central to the Gülen movement. First, the main fault line in Turkey is between Islamic and secular sectors of the population, and this fault line is drawn, and regularly contested, over the debate on science and religion. Second, Turkish secularism has built its legitimacy on the claims of scientific positivism and the creation of a modern and progressive society through scientific thinking by excluding religion and the religious masses from centers of power and authority. Thus, it is vital to understand the relationship between the two in order to comprehend the intellectual origins of the current polarization of society. In fact, the relationship between science and religion, and secularism and democracy, informs many competing political positions in regard to the Muslim world.

In the wake of 9/11, and the lack of democratization in many Muslim countries, the connection between secularism and democracy, on the one hand, and Islam and modernization, on the other, has been at the center of scholarly and public debate. Some politicians in the West have called for the Western-style democratization of Muslim countries to contain and undermine Islamist political movements. The key assumption behind this debate is that Islam is impeding, if not totally preventing, the processes of development and democratization by hindering the secularization of Islamic countries. In short, the debate in the West regards secularism as a necessary, but not sufficient, condition of democracy. Both politicians and some orientalist influenced scholars, regard the contemporary understanding of Islam as a negative force that hinders progress and destroys critical thinking. Samuel Huntington's "The Clash of Civilization" article argues that Islam and Islamism provide antagonistic ground for the democratization of Muslim countries. Huntington regards secularism as the most important condition of democratization. These Huntingtonian assumptions, which dominate Western public discourse over Islam, and orient many scholarly works as well, are quite dubious. While, some Islamic leaders and intellectuals consider the very term "secularism" as alien and democracy as a Western invention inimical to Islam, many Muslim intellectuals argue that Islam and democracy are fully compatible, and they seek to redefine the meaning and role of secularism itself as a concept not inimical to the influence of religious faith in society.

Fethullah Gülen is an important voice in this debate over science, secularism, and Islam. Before I lay out the key assumptions of Gülen's metaphysical scheme, it is imperative to sum up his position which is: Islam as a tradition is not in conflict with science and is compatible with democracy; Jacobin style secularism is neither compatible with democracy nor with any religion; and Islam as a religion provides necessary ideational ground for a scientific mode of thinking. In practice, the followers of Gülen prove that one could remain Muslim and live a "modern" life. In other words, he advocates modernization within Islam, not without it.

While Said Nursi and Fethullah Gülen do not recognize the complete autonomy and separation of religious and scientific modes of understanding, by seeking to ally Islamic beliefs and science, which is based on questioning and skepticism, they unintentionally injected critical inquiry into religious dogma. The irony of their approach has been the ongoing rationalization and secularization of their Islamic worldview. Thus, both men, more than Kemalist adversaries in Turkey, promoted an Islamic Enlightenment by encouraging the internal and inadvertent development of secular thinking. Nursi and Gülen's thought and practices celebrate progress via science, utilize deistic arguments by using the laws of nature as the sign of God's existence and power, and also stress tolerance to allow different views to compete. The goals of the Enlightenment (i.e., progress, tolerance, and science) are expressed and promoted in Islamic terminology within the particular Turkish sociohistorical context.

This chapter will first explore the connection between religion and science, on the one hand, and science and secularism, on the other. In the second part,

I will briefly examine the intellectual background of the debate over the relationship between science and religion within the late Ottoman Empire by focusing on the work of Ottoman intellectuals. Indeed, there were three reactions to the revolution in rationalist and scientific thinking in the Ottoman Empire: rejection of religion where it is viewed as the "other" from the perspective of science; rejection of science, especially positivist science, as the enemy of the Qur'anic/revelation mode of thinking; and the accommodationist approach to show that science and religion are not inherently in conflict. The last part of the chapter will analyze Gülen's *tevhidi* (Unitarian) understanding of the relationship between science and religion by critically examining Gülen's thought.

INTELLECTUAL CONFLICT IN THE EARLY TURKISH REPUBLIC: THE NURCU MOVEMENT

One of the perennial debates in the Turkish public sphere has been the virtues and tribulations of secularism.[1] This debate is closely linked to how the Turks reacted to the collapse of the Ottoman state and challenges posed by Western economic, scientific, and political power. The origins of this debate are rooted in the Tanzimat period, and it was sharpened with the reforms of Mustafa Kemal to create a *secular* nation-state with the authority and help of scientific 'truth.' Thus, in the Turkish context, secularism meant the removal of the domination of religious authority from diverse spheres of society and public spaces, and building new authority through scientific positivism.[2]

Through secularism, the Republic sought to reposition itself in a Western-dominated international system in a more favorable and powerful way by distancing itself from the Ottoman *Islamic* legacy, since it carried a very negative image in the Western public sphere. Because the main goal of the new Republic was to consolidate its authority and create a new society and identity, it sought to weaken religious institutions and identity as obstacles to its reform agenda. The leaders of the Republic asserted their sovereignty by dismantling religious institutions. The words *laik/laikçilik/laikçi* defy transliteration, not because it is borrowed from French but rather because its meaning underwent a significant mutation during the last 90 years of the Turkish Republic. These terms have much broader connotation than the Anglo-American meaning of secularism. Laic/laicism means a form of lifestyle and identity, a type of polity, a project of becoming "civilized" and modern, a process of displacing religion with scientific positivism, and also a strategy of criminalizing religious opposition. In Turkey, those who see themselves as guardians of *laiklik* believe that they have the right to shape, lead, and guide society, since they represent a progressive worldview with the mission of "civilizing" society.

Kemalists who adhere to the ideology and cult of personality surrounding Mustafa Kemal Atatürk, as a new blueprint to engineer a "modern" society, argue that Islam as a totalistic, in some cases totalitarian, religious tradition must be, if not abolished outright, kept under strict state control, and estranged from the public sphere. From a Kemalist perspective, the only successful path to modernity would be the aggressive transformation of society along contemporary European practices and principles that are based on science and secularism. Bekim Agai sums up the Kemalist perspective well: "They claimed that as long as religion and its institutions had a strong influence on society, superstition would predominate over reason and the advancement of society would be impossible."[3] The major issue that was also framed over the debate of secularism was the competing perspective on science. The radical secularists, or Kemalists, argued that science and scientific thinking cannot be separated from the European experience of secularism. In short, secularism means freedom of reason from the hegemony of revelation, and the scientific mode of thinking could not be separated from secular European culture and practices. If Turkey wanted to become a modern society, it had to adopt secular European culture and practices. The Kemalist discourse of secularism evolved out of two interrelated reactions to the demise of the Ottoman state and also a reaction to the traditionalist Islamist prescriptions to the Western challenge.

The Islamists' discourse has also evolved in opposition to the Kemalist one. This group of Islamic intellectuals explained the weakening, and eventual dissolution, of the Ottoman Empire in terms of "moving away from Islam," especially the Sharia. They identified the Tanzimat reforms of the nineteenth century as the "direct cause" of the failure of Ottoman Muslim society. The traditionalists, or Islamists, presented Westernization as an alienating and morally repugnant process of denying the existence of God and His eternal laws. They used every opportunity to derail the reforms and developed a reactionary discourse against everything Western. In response to these two extreme debates between the Kemalists, who wanted to cleanse Islam from the public sphere, and the traditional Islamists, who rejected any modernizing reforms or modernization, the third group evolved. This group includes some, though not all, Nakşibendi orders and the Nurcu movement of Said Nursi. The third group, which includes the Gülen movement, seeks to bridge the chasm between revelation and reason, religion and science, and Islam and modernity. I will analyze Nursi and Gülen in terms of their arguments about religion, science, and modernity.

THE LATE OTTOMAN DEBATE ON SCIENCE AND RELIGION

From the perspective of Said Nursi, a scientific interpretation of the world is not necessarily in contradiction with a religious understanding of the world. However,

Nursi was very critical of scientism as a discourse with its own assumptions, values, and conclusions about the universe. Indeed, in the late Ottoman period, the intellectuals were in search of a solution to the political and social problems of the decaying Ottoman state and society. He argued that the Ottoman intellectuals were reading their own society through the lenses of European intellectuals who sought to explain the decay in Muslim societies as the outcome of Islam, and especially non-reformed Islam. Thus, the solution, for these intellectuals was to either leave Islam aside or to create a form of "enlightened Islam."

Although most of the religious scholars, *ulema*, tried to explain this decline in terms of the weakening of Islamic values and proposed a return to traditional Islam as a solution, some members of the *ulema* vehemently disagreed and called for the modernization of state and society. Thus, there was not a unified Islamic front about the causes of social and political problems, and diverse solutions were offered. However, a small yet very influential group of Ottoman intellectuals insisted on the total rejection of religious values and practices, and defended a society and polity that was free from Islam.

Following the 1908 Young Turk revolution, which institutionalized the suspended 1876 Constitution and reopened the parliament, the intellectual debate focused more on how to become a modern society by carrying out a "civilizing mission" on the basis of the European Enlightenment and industrialization.[4] The previous generation of intellectuals, known as Young Ottomans, had a very practical question: How to save the state, along with Islam? The post-1908 intellectuals posed more theoretical questions: How to renew society through adopting a scientific worldview that would exclude religion as a basis of public order. The Young Turk leaders under the influence of German materialism and French positivism attacked Islam as the source of social and economic "backwardness" and called for a society based upon logical positivism. Logical positivism argued that the scientific method (observation, deduction, and rationalism) is the only way to build objective knowledge about the processes and institutions of social life.[5] It claims that "scientific knowledge" is testable and must be verified by evidence rather than "arguments" or "rhetoric." The purpose of scientific knowledge is to develop general laws (i.e., determining necessary and sufficient conditions for social events such as suicide, revolution, secularism, and democracy) about social events and test them in different cases. Positivism turned science into an ideology (scientism) and rejected metaphysical speculations and emphasized validity and reliability. It argued that the methods we use to study nature should be used in understanding social events as well. If modernity is an outcome of certain conditions, the state should create those conditions to have the same outcome of a secular nation-state.

Şükrü Hanioğlu, who studies the role of this new scientific understanding of Ottoman society, argues that "the salient characteristic of late Ottoman materialism is the belief in science as the exclusive foundation of a new Ottoman society."⁶ The Ottoman intellectuals who sought to replace religion with logical positivism were Beşir Fuat (1852–1887), Abdullah Cevdet (1869–1931), Ahmet Rıza (1859–1930), Baha Tevfik (1881–1914), and Rıza Tevfik (1869–1949).⁷ They, and their followers, made the following argument: the Ottoman state and society were in decay because of the negative power and role of Islam; in order to become a progressive society and a powerful state, religion needs to be cleansed and science must take the place of religion as the new guide and compass of human life.

They imagined science as a new religion to address all problems of the individual and society, and even constructed a new scientific Islam that would serve secularism. However, the new generation of intellectuals under the influence of French Jacobinism was even more radical and demanded a society that was cleansed from religion. The radical Kemalist reforms were very much informed by this debate, and Mustafa Kemal's project aimed to create this new society. The most famous aphorism of Mustafa Kemal is: "the only guide in life is science" (*Hayatta en hakiki mürşit ilimdir*). In short, the founding fathers of the Republic of Turkey planned to create a new Turkish and secular society that would have full faith in science, and this faith in science, in return, was projected to create a secular society that was free from religion.

Are science and religion in conflict as claimed by positivist Turkish scholars? I will argue that they are not in conflict, but rather two separate modes of understanding and experiencing. However, I will further argue in the following section that they cannot be seamlessly integrated as Gülen and his followers want them to be. Religion and science are two rival epistemic systems. Some religious scholars argue that the Qur'an is not only telling us religious truths but also reveals the laws of natural science. However, increasingly some "scientific fundamentalists" like Richard Dawkins also reject religion totally and claiming that faith and spirituality have nothing to offer. They even claim that many of the worst mass killings and atrocities stem from religion while omitting the fact that many of the twentieth century's greatest mass killers like Stalin, Hitler, and Pol Pot were actually militantly antireligious. Even though religious and scientific enquiries are not the same in terms of their epistemological and ontological foundations and methodologies, they both enhance our understanding about the world we live in. Being rival modes of understanding does not mean they are in conflict or that one exists at the expense of the other. Science is concerned with nature, facts, and events, while religion focuses on the values and meaning of the good life and the potential for this-worldly and other-worldly salvation. Scientific thinking deepens and rationalizes our religious understanding, and science plays an important role in the evolution of theology. By expanding our knowledge in nonreligious spheres, our understanding of religion expands as well.

THE ISLAMIC REACTION TO POSITIVISM: SAID NURSI AND FETHULLAH GÜLEN

There was a major reaction to scientism in the late Ottoman period. Those who defended the claims of science argued it was science that turned Europe into the world's leading power center. They also argued that science meant power, and Europe copied this science from earlier contributions from Islamic civilization. Therefore, it was the duty of Muslims to reclaim science back in order to become a powerful civilization once again. They hardly questioned the philosophical ideas behind the scientific revolution in Europe. They failed to see that Western-originated modern science has its own worldview and requires a different perspective on the nature of reality. Their guiding question was: why did the Muslim world, in general, and the Ottoman state, in particular, remain underdeveloped? Said Halim Paşa (1863–1921) was the first Ottoman intellectual to confront this question from an Islamic perspective by focusing on a Muslim understanding of Islam. He wanted to know why Muslims misunderstood their faith and were subordinated by colonial powers. Although he was against "imitative Westernization," he supported selective borrowings from Europe. The second response to positivism came from Said Nursi. Since Gülen's ideas of the relationship between science and religion are directly derived from Nursi, I will first summarize Gülen's position on science, and then shuttle between Nursi and Gülen to display their role in the current Turkish Muslim understanding of the relationship between science and religion.

Gülen's understanding of science, and its relationship with religion, is not original, but rather derived from Nursi. This perspective is based on a set of presumptions: God is the Creator of the universe, and He is constantly present in the motion of natural and social events; God endowed humans with reason to search for the truth (*hakikat*); since God created the universe, all knowledge and laws emanate from God's will. God "willed the world into being"[8] and our task, as scientists, is to study and understand the workings of this universe in order to decipher God's power. Although Nursi provided the ideas, it was Gülen who put them into practice and turned ideas into action.

Nursi and Gülen sought to overcome scientific skepticism by enhancing Muslim faith in God through science and scientific discoveries. Nursi's writing on the relationship between science and religion took place during the period in which positivism was ascendant and becoming the hegemonic discourse against religion. Instead of rejecting science, as the positivist of the late Ottoman era rejected religion, he tried to display the spiritual origins of scientific discoveries. Nursi's main struggle was to develop an argument convincing skeptical Muslims that Islam and science are not in conflict. Nursi never questioned the universal objectivity of science, and realized the power of science to improve, not to guide, human conditions. Thus, Nursi invited his readers to read the verses of the Qur'an through the lenses of scientific discoveries in order to disarm positivist arguments and enhance Muslim faith in religion. Rather than rejecting the Newtonian mechanistic understanding of the world, Nursi found a close parallel between the Qur'an and the Newtonian worldview: there is an eternal order that is designed according to certain rational laws by a Creator. In his famous book, *Sözler*, Nursi presents God as the Absolute Artisan (*sani-i mutlak*) of the universe. On the basis of Nursi's writings, the Turkish academic Şerif Mardin argues that Nursi does not shy away from even incorporating the deistic interpretation of the universe in terms of a machine or clock.[9] Thus, nineteenth century scientific vocabulary becomes very dominant among the followers of Nursi to understand the physical world. Nursi's approach created a renewed interest in natural science among his followers, and they used new scientific discoveries to decode the sacred verses of the Qur'an. When a group of students visited Nursi and asked him to speak about God since their teachers did not talk about the Creator, he said: "All the sciences you study continuously speak of God and make known the Creator, each with its own particular tongue. Do not listen to your teachers; listen to them."[10] Thus, it is not surprising that most of his followers went on to study chemistry, physics, biology, and engineering. Gülen's first major monthly magazine *Sızıntı* popularized the "scientific reading of the verses" by stressing the parallels between the verses and new scientific discoveries. Each scientific discovery was framed in terms of one or more verification, cosmological verses of the Qur'an as proof of the Creator. Even though this Islamic apologetic position tried to validate the verses through scientific discoveries, it helped to generate a new wave of curiosity among the young Muslims to focus on natural sciences and technology.

Nursi's God, unlike the deist God, is not only the ontological Creator but also continuously present in the universe; present, yet separate. From the perspective of Nursi, Muslims should read the universe in terms of its fragments and universality by differentiation between the meaning of material existence as such (*mana-yi ismi*) and its indicative meaning (*mana-yi harfi*), that is, as the manifestation of the attributes of God. This theoretical distinction allows Nursi to swing between the two analytically separate yet unified meanings. Science should focus on the material existence of things and study their nature and evolution, while religion would offer more abstract and holistic understandings of their purpose in the universe. Nursi is against a heartless science and mindless religion. He wants a dialectical relation between religion and science. Pope John Paul II, like Nursi, argues that "science can purify religion from error and superstition; religion can purify science from idolatry and false absolutes. Each can draw the other into a wider world, a world in which both can flourish.... We need each other to be what we must be, what we are called to be."

For Gülen, God had two revelations: Nature and the Holy Book, particularly the Qur'an. God expresses himself in, and through, these two books. The metaphor of the two books played an important role in the Religious Enlightenment in Europe. Indeed, in the seventeenth century, some scientists and theologians alike urged "exploration of the vast library of creation as a necessary complement to the knowledge of the Scriptures."[11] According to Bacon, Locke, and Newton, natural science and revelation were not competing epistemological domains, but they were "harmonious endeavors where the rationality of science occurred with the 'oracle of God'."[12] Gülen believes that these two books are the creation of God and, therefore, whatever knowledge exists in the one has to be compatible with the other.

Gülen's metaphysical scheme informs his understanding of science and he seeks to create a unified (*tevhidi*) account to subordinate science to the Qur'an. He argues that God is always part of creation and His will is part of the events. Gülen's ideas of creation are deeply influenced by Asharite theologians, who developed Islamic occasionalism in the eleventh century, by arguing that every motion in the world is the direct outcome of God's will. God's actions create the laws of nature and provide equilibrium and stability to His creation. God, as the Creator, constantly sustains His creation.[13] Scientific knowledge is accumulated through using logic in concert with evidence of the senses. However, religious knowledge is not about logic used with evidence, but rather it is about faith and belief in the Qur'an. On the basis of a religious mode of understanding, which is based on a set of assumptions, one can believe that Christ walked over water or that Moses parted the sea to lead his people. However, these are difficult to sustain in light of historical evidence and scientific rationality. Although the followers of Gülen tend to justify the existence of God through analogical reasoning such as arguing that since things are made or come from another thing—for example, a home being designed by an architect or a computer by an engineer, so there must be a creator of the universe—it cannot be random or accidental. However, this regressive thinking also begs the question: Who created the Creator if there is always a creator? This rhetorical reasoning is less likely to lead us to a convincing conclusion. It is more intellectually stimulating to think of religion and science as independent spheres that are nonetheless in dialogue to shed light on our quest for the origins and evolution of being and the universe.

A closer examination of the writings of Gülen leads us to conclude that his understanding of science and religion is both dialogical and confrontational. However, he is very clear that science must be subordinated to religion and its mission is to enhance our faith in the Creator. In order to unpack Gülen's understanding of this relationship, one needs to take a three-step examination: What does Gülen mean by religious and scientific "truth" (*hakikat*)? Are they the same quality of "truth"? What are the building blocks of his understanding of nature? Is the task of science to develop necessary knowledge to control and exploit nature, or is it to preserve nature in harmony with human existence? How does he construct an Islamic understanding of science on the basis of his reading of the Qur'an?

Truths: Scientific and Religious

HAKIKAT

Gülen's analysis is rooted in the mainstream Muslim understanding of the relationship between science and religion. Gülen, like Nursi, argues that since God's names are manifested in the universe, it is the Divine Book of Creation. By arguing that creation is the manifestation of God's names and product of God's will, scholars need to study nature in order to serve God. From this assumption, Gülen seeks to distinguish absolute and eternal truth from relative truth. By truth, Gülen means "truth is not something the human mind produces. Truth exists independently of man and man's task is to seek it."[14] In other words, absolute truth is unchanging and above or outside of our visible world, since it is about the essence of existence and involves eternal verities.[15] Thus, there is a set of absolute truths outside our human reasoning. We are asked to accept them as "given" and "perennial." Gülen argues that modern science "is very far from finding out the full truth behind existence and explaining it."[16] In other words, Gülen very much creates this mysterious world beyond our visible world and outside the grasp of scientific methodology. For instance, Gülen argues that truths in the Qur'an are absolute and not open to debate. One wonders what Gülen means by those truths in the Qur'an. As far as his conceptualization of relative truth is concerned, he argues that this is the realm of change and evolution where truths are discovered through the scientific method. Gülen argues that scientific truths are in constant modification, and change in light of empirical evidence and rational reasoning. Gülen states:

> [T]he universe, the subject-matter of the sciences, is the realm where God's names are manifested and therefore has some sort of sanctity. Everything in the universe is a letter from God Almighty inviting us to study it to have knowledge of Him. Thus, the universe is the collection of those letters or, as Muslim sages call it, the Divine Book of Creation issuing primarily from the Divine Attributes of Will and Power. The Qur'an, issuing from the Divine Will of Speech is the counterpart of the universe in verbal form. Just as there can be no conflict between a palace and the paper written to describe it, there can also be no conflict between the universe and the Qur'an, which are two expressions of the same truth.[17]

Gülen believes that scientific inquiry should be "used to expound Islamic facts."[18] He calls for a missionary science in the service of religion. For instance, he says, "our primary aim when introducing science and scientific facts must be to win the pleasure of God." However, in Europe, the rational study of nature became more important, and science as the most significant avenue for understanding the will of God was dropped. The conservative nature of the Church and the lack of proper education of the clergy played a significant role in the devaluation of the Scriptures. Here Gülen makes his view about the subordination of free inquiry to religion very clear:

> Our position must be clear, and it is this: the Qur'an and *hadith* are true and absolute. Science and scientific facts are true as long as they are in agreement with the Qur'an and *hadith*, and are false inasmuch as they differ or lead away from the truth of the Qur'an and *hadith*. Even definitely established scientific facts cannot be pillars to uphold the truths of *iman* (faith).[19]

Gülen refers to those scientists who do not subordinate science to religion as materialistic who seek to "exploit science as a means of defying religion and use its prestige to spread their thinking." In other words, Gülen is very uneasy about those scientists who are free from religious concerns. In order to stop this "exploitation," Gülen calls his followers to use science to support the existence of God and deepen faith in the Creator. His main goal has been "employing science" to serve Islam. This "utilization" of science to enhance religious argument also has the possibility of analyzing religious doctrine from a scientific mode of understanding.

Nature

Said Nursi's understanding of science informs Gülen's conception of science and scientific thinking. According to Nursi, "science should be pursued to understand the laws of nature and thus the art of its creator: God."[20] Thus, Nursi tried to demonstrate through his writings that, by studying science, Muslims would develop a better understanding of God and the Qur'an. It was Nursi who stressed a more inclusive education that would teach Islamic sciences along with the natural sciences. Nursi believed that an education that focused solely on religion would breed narrow-mindedness, if not bigotry, while an education that only focused on natural sciences would breed atheism. As a solution to this rift between Islamic and natural sciences, he called for an integrative education by urging students to research belief and knowledge at the same time. Nursi's novel approach to science and religion as mutually constitutive fields of inquiry helped many conservative pious Turkish Muslims to redefine their position on science and technology, and pursue scientific education. However, what has worked in practice in terms of reconciling science and religion did not offer a convincing theoretical argument. The tension between science and religion is not easy to resolve as long as religious groups seek to impose their own "understanding of nature and creation" from their own religious perspective.

Since Gülen believes that the Qur'an contains everything by referring to the Qur'anic verse, "With Him are the keys of the unseen. None but He knows them. And He knows what is in the land and the sea. Not a leaf falls but with His knowledge, not a grain amid the darkness of the earth, nothing of wet or dry but (it is noted) in a manifest Book."[21] However, Gülen also argues that even though the Qur'an contains all knowledge, it contains them "in the form of seeds or nuclei or summaries or as principles or signs, and they are found either explicitly or implicitly, or allusively, or vaguely, or suggestively. One or other of these forms is preferred according to the occasion of revelation, in a way fitting for the purposes of the Qur'an and in connection with the requirements of the context."[22]

Gülen's followers believe that as our knowledge in other fields grows so does our understanding of these verses. Therefore, it is science which is expected to shape and deepen our understanding, and not the other way around. Gülen argues that "while the Qur'an contains allusions to many scientific truths, it is not to be read as a book of science or scientific explanations."[23]

Gülen creates an imagined "Western" science and criticizes it because it does not serve religion:

> Positivistic and materialistic theories have permanently suppressed the domain of science and thought for the last few centuries. Metaphysical ideas have been ignored while interpreting existence, the universe, worldly and heavenly phenomena. Instead, the positivist approach has been employed all the time. This materialistic interpretation of the universe has pointed to just one way of thinking and it has narrowed the ways leading to reality. The West examined the universe and nature in detail, exercising an empirical method which placed great emphasis on reason, but it could not manage to develop a unity of physics and metaphysics. Thus, in the end, human beings have been taken to a position where they contradict their own selves, intellect, and soul. And this position has estranged their soul from their subjective senses.[24]

Moreover, he takes "skepticism" as the source of the problem that led to the decline of religion. Gülen states:

> Neither science nor the intellect of human beings offered a serious explanation of the beginning and end of the universe, creation or the secrets of

life. Such issues, which humankind has been occupied with since the beginning, remain the eeriest puzzle for their intellect.

Indeed, this challenge of explaining "the beginning and end of the universe" remains not only one for the scientific community but also for religious scholars. Various religions provide a sensible argument about the beginning of the universe, but they do so within a set of "metaphorical" statements. Gülen continues by saying:

> Today's science and man's intellect do not seem to explain extra-sensory perceptions, revelation, inspiration, intuition, dreams, extra-sensory sources of knowledge, the penetration of metaphysics into physics, miraculous occurrences, or prayers. Humanity today still seeks help and references from the explanations offered by religion.[25]

This important statement rejects treating science and religion as two separate epistemological systems with different modes of understanding. Science cannot claim to explain "revelation" and accordingly it never does. The problem here is very much Gülen's understanding of science and religion, which is based on a *tevhidi* conception of Islam. Like Nursi, he does not separate and treat them as two different modes of human experiences. In short, Gülen has a very totalistic conception of religion as the force to organize human life, comprehend existence and the universe, as well as an afterlife. He wants all human activities to be guided by this set of absolute truths, derived from the Qur'an. There is limited room for debate or experiment, but rather scholars are expected to read the universe in terms of the verities of religious texts.

Gülen searches for absolute truths and he wants societies to be governed by these absolute truths of religion. He is very uneasy about building knowledge through falsifiability and thinks that scientific truths are always open to change, and since religious truths are absolute, science should not be used to justify the meaning of certain verses. He says:

> It is hard to say that science has reached the remarkable conclusion with regard to man, the universe, and divinity, about what prophets let their people know ages ago. Science today is still like a creeping child and it changes its conclusions everyday. It regards many of its old conclusions as wrong, and it makes other mistakes as it reaches still other conclusions. Moreover, it cannot go beyond its boundaries, where it deals with limited issues. It is not wrong to state that science has produced no theory that has not been replaced by itself again. Thus, it has never been able to find reality. This statement does not aim to consider science as unimportant or to

ignore scientific research. We rather consider both science and its outcomes to be important and they deserve respect. Thus we are supposed to appreciate them. What, then, we endeavour to maintain is that revelation is also a source of knowledge with regard to man, existence, and creation. And this source is available in the Books revealed to the Prophets by God, though some were distorted.[26]

Gülen's philosophy of education, religious knowledge, and imagination of God is different from most of his contemporaries. His approach is more hermeneutical, à la Gadamer, saying that there is no *"facta bruta,"* that is, no existence-in-itself but rather socially constructed and imagined realities within the context of one's worldview. In other words, understanding is always about interpretation and seeing from one's own internalized cognitive map. Thus, Gülen, like Gadamer, thinks that understanding is a projection of our core beliefs onto what is to be understood. In a way, an understanding of the universe and the Qur'an at some level is self-understanding. Gülen's interpretive "horizon," or cognitive map of understanding, consists of Islamic ideas and history. He wants all understandings to start within this "horizon" that would start the process of understanding but will not end there. Gülen, like Nursi, believes that the interaction between the Qur'anic view of creation and its encounter with new ideas will enrich our understanding and raise religious consciousness. As a result of the process of understanding the new phenomenon through one's internalized "horizon," a person who is seeking to understand is not where he was in the beginning.

Due to this close connection between understanding and religious consciousness, Gülen calls his followers to invest in education, especially the natural sciences. By projecting one's core religious beliefs unto the events, one does not necessarily close off the new meaning, but anticipates new meaning to deepen one's worldview. In other words, understanding involves reflecting our current questions and interpretations back onto tradition and constantly modifying the tradition. In a way, each interpretive engagement starts with tradition but is expected to lead to modification of that same tradition. This is the reason why Gadamer argues that "in the final analysis, all understanding is self-understanding." Each interpretive process has an impact on our worldview. However, Gülen anticipates that each encounter with new ideas could undermine faith, however, for him even a scientific worldview, without God, would be inherently flawed.

Nursi and Gülen's vision of the universe and revelations as the divine manifestation of God is similar to that of Joseph Butler (1692–1752). Butler, a Bishop of Durham, had major impact upon John Newman, the most prominent Catholic theologian of the last century. It would be useful to compare the ideas of

Butler and Newman with those of Gülen. According to Thomas K. Carr, who studied the intellectual background of Newman, Butler played a formative role in forming Newman's ideas.[27] A similar connection exists between Said Nursi and Gülen himself. Moreover, these four theologians all started with the ontological basis of the existence of God but developed different pathways from there. Butler argued that:

> [B]y studying nature one should expect to find confirmation for the revealed doctrine of Christianity. Moreover, he determines that so great is this analogical connection between nature and revelation that simply by studying nature alone, one should be able to arrive at an adequate acknowledgement of God, which would then prepare the way for a fuller indoctrination into Christian teaching.[28]

Nursi, like Butler, also argues that both the universe and nature are a reflection of God, reaffirming the existence of God, while saying that our understanding of material things cannot be limited to our observations per se. Nursi, like Newman, insists that religious understanding is an internal aspect of a person's character. One's personal character is deeply attached to one's argument about the existence of God. In other words, knowledge about God cannot be only book-based and transmitted from teacher to pupil, but rather it has to be lived, internalized, imagined, and turned into a character formation. This pedagogical influence of religious tradition on the formation of a believer's character is an important aspect of Gülen's education program. Religious knowledge, for Gülen, comprehends all diverse forms of knowledge and is a type of knowledge that a believer is assimilated into and becomes intimate with character formation. In a way, religious principles that constitute one's worldview are not outside oneself, but rather are part and parcel of one's very existence. They constitute the "horizon of understanding" and a believer uses them to make sense of his or her environment, as well as life experiences. Gülen, like Nursi, believes that faith in God structures the way in which we process acquiring knowledge by the use of reasoning, intuition, or perception. This belief, in turn, orients our conduct and social relations.

The main weakness of Nursi and Gülen's epistemology is that they both ignore the fact that the unveiling of God requires different modes of imagination than that of understanding the laws of nature. The universe and events of nature could be construed through imagination as the manifestation of God. However, this religious "imagination" is very different from scientific understanding. Indeed, a believer could use religious symbols and arguments to integrate "the world as lived and the world as imagined."[29] Nonetheless, this religious imagination cannot supplement critical and scientific understanding.

From the perspective of Nursi, our knowledge of God depends on our engagement with religious rituals, practices, and symbols. In other words, acting and behaving in terms of an Islamic worldview is the way to expand our understanding of Islam and raise our religious consciousness. Religious experience is oriented inward and inspires human imagination through a set of symbols: love, beauty, light, and justice.

Nursi and Gülen argue that human reason can only comprehend fragments of the whole of the universe and nature.[30] In order to have a holistic understanding, one needs to examine them from the perspective of revelation. In other words, reason in itself is not sufficient, but necessary, to understand nature. We could use reason and scientific inquiry to better understand the messages of the Qur'an. By employing reason and science to understand the Qur'an, Nursi and Gülen are attempting to reconcile reason with revelation, and eventually inadvertently open a cognitive space for the internal secularization of Islam.[31]

According to Nursi, the Qur'an provides an Islamic understanding about the purposes of the existence of the universe. Şükran Vahide, in his authoritative study on the thought of Said Nursi, argues:

> The Qur'an instructs man on how to read the words of being "inscribed by the pen of power" on its pages. The reading and comprehension of its words in turn expound or lead to deeper understanding of the Qur'an's verses, demonstrating the complementary relationship between them.[32]

Neither Nursi nor Gülen want to replace religion with science; they both understand that these are distinct yet related epistemologies, but they do not see them as two fully autonomous modes of understanding. Nursi claims that science promotes better understanding of the Qur'an and through the study of the Qur'an one understands the purpose of existence and the universe. The Qur'an is not a scientific book, yet it helps us decipher the purpose of our existence and role in the world. This is the reason why Nursi insists that the understanding of the Qur'an would vary on the basis of the accumulation of scientific knowledge.

The Qur'an is always open to "interpretations" and its meanings vary in terms of space and time. This intertextual relationship between the universe of the manifestation of God's power and the Qur'an as the words of God help us to develop a holistic understanding of our existence and the role of human beings in this world. Nursi seeks to subordinate reason to revelation. He provides a set of hermeneutical tools to move back and forth between the two texts: the Qur'an and the universe. Kelton Cobb argues that Nursi "has made use of a hermeneutic that shuttles between the Qur'anic text and the observable world in both directions."[33] Nursi claims:

Even, although all the centuries are different with regard to ideas and capacity.... Man's works and laws grow old like a man, they change and are changed. But the rulings and laws of the Qur'an are so firm and well-founded that they increase in strength as the centuries pass. Indeed, this present age and the People of the Book in this age, who have more than any other relied on themselves and stopped up their ears heedless to the words of the Qur'an, are so in need of its guiding address of, *O People of the Book! O People of the Book!* that it is as if it addresses this age directly, and the *phrase O People of the Book!* (*ehli kitab*) comprises also the meaning of *O People of the Modern Science Books!* (*ehli mektep/schools*)."[34]

Nursi's understanding of the Qur'an is dynamic and poetic with its own rules of deciphering. There are some minor differences between Gülen and Nursi. In the writings of Nursi, one sees almost no reference to Western thinkers, but in the case of Gülen there is a constant attempt to embellish and link his thought with that of major Western thinkers. For instance, almost all Gülen promotional conferences have some articles comparing Gülen with some major Western thinkers. In other words, there is a well-organized attempt to familiarize Gülen and his framework for understanding and promoting Islam through some references to Western thought as a way of appealing to both well-educated Muslims and Westerners more generally. The followers of Gülen who organize annual conferences in different universities, even though none of these universities provide funding for such endeavors, seek to deploy a Western academic pedigree to provide credibility and legitimacy to their movement. This is an added dimension in comparison to Nursi and his followers. Although Nursi's main concern were ideas and the inner transformation of the self, Gülen's primary focus is on action and service (*hizmet*) in order to build a moral community with its own vernacular moral charter that would be derived from Islam and Turkish history. With the cultivation of the "golden generation," Gülen wants to have access to critical global political, economic, and educational institutions.

Fethullah Gülen, like Nursi, emphasizes the centrality of nature, and calls upon his followers to examine nature in the light of Islamic reasoning (i.e., understanding of nature as the script of God and His will). By studying the Qur'an and the expression of God's laws, one can comprehend profound aspects of the universe (creation). Gülen contends that God "has subjected creation to constant flux and renewal through the cycle of death and life, to an incessant motion towards its final perfection."[35]

Gülen even believes that the study of the Qur'an can aid scientists in gaining a deeper understanding of existence and the universe. For instance, Gülen argues that "Islam is the religion of the whole universe. That is, the entire universe obeys the laws laid down by God, so everything in the universe is 'Muslim' and obeys God by submitting to his laws."[36]

From the perspective of Gülen, knowledge (i.e., information about the Creator and His creation) is essential to living a fully virtuous and meaningful life. Gülen sums up his argument:

> The purpose of learning is to make knowledge a guide for your life, to illuminate the road to human perfection. Any knowledge that does not fulfill these functions is a burden for the learner, and any science that does not direct one toward sublime goals is only deception.[37]

Gülen defines his mission in terms of educating the Muslim world, especially the Turkish Muslims, so that they are intellectually and materially equipped to live in the modern world. From this perspective, there is no incommensurable contradiction between science and religion; science studies creation (e.g., the universe and the laws of nature), while religion seeks to comprehend the Creator. Therefore, creation and its mysteries are avenues to understanding the Creator and vice versa. By studying science and religion together, the believers, Gülen argues, would have a greater level of understanding about themselves and their cosmic mission on earth. Like Nursi, Gülen argues that the study of science and religion is necessary to overcome atheism and materialism, which is identified as the source of many social ills, and fanaticism that alienates people from religion.

Gülen claims, "Science and knowledge should seek to uncover the nature of men and women and the mysteries of creation. Any knowledge, however scientific, is not true knowledge if it does not shed light on the mysteries of human nature and the dark areas of existence."[38] A close reading of Gülen's thinking about the connection between religion and science indicates his instrumental and subordinating reading of science as a tool for understanding aspects of nature and the universe while not being able to contravene the religious fact of some providential power or creator. Thus, Gülen rejects the positivist argument that religion is superstition and science is the truth. Gülen is also critical of the simple explanation of the universe in terms of the rules of causation and reaction. Moreover, Gülen argues that science and technology are useful "as long as they serve human values, bring peace and happiness, contribute to international harmony, and help address humanity's material and spiritual problems."[39]

Gülen is fully aware of the negative potential of science and technology. He calls for the moralization of science and technology so that they cannot be misused as in the case of Nazi Germany, the Soviet Union, and the American nuclear bombings of Japan. He argues:

> Despite the disasters caused by science and technology, their mistaken approach to the truth, and their failure to bring human happiness, we cannot condemn them outright and become pure idealists. Science and technology do not bear the full responsibility for humanity being devalued, human feelings being diminished, and certain human virtues, along with health and the ability to think, being seriously weakened. Rather, the fault lies with scientists who avoid their responsibilities, who cause science to develop in a materialistic and almost purely scientistific atmosphere, and then let it be exploited by an irresponsible minority. Many worrying conditions probably would not exist if scientists had remained aware of their social responsibility, and if the Church had not forced it to develop in opposition to religion."[40]

For Gülen, the scientific method always presents the danger of rule according to instrumental rationality divorced from any divinely sanctioned morality. Gülen is of course not the first to point to the danger that this focus on instrumental and materialistic goals may lead to the rational and scientific construction of death camps and nuclear weapons whose deployment within a certain modern relativistic or value neutral realpolitik worldview may make perfect sense.

CONCLUSION

From the perspective of Gülen, the Qur'an becomes a guide for the uncovering of the mysteries of existence and the universe, itself the creation of the divine Creator. This intertextuality between the Qur'an and the immanent universe is expected to reconcile the tension between reason and revelation; science and religion. While these are deeply profound ontological insights and questions that can be traced back all the way to pre-Socratic philosophy, there is of course the danger that Gülen's attempt at reconciling religion and science may more likely lead to farcical constructs of "pseudo-science" where instead of the scientific method and empirical experimentation and observation leading to truths about nature and existence, a patina of scientific legitimacy and claims are deployed to ostensibly "prove" traditional, scientifically unsupported, religious beliefs concerning, for example, the origin of human life in Adam and Eve.

This mode of thinking poses the danger of an a priori subordination of science to religion and reason to revelation. Thus, it constrains true free inquiry and critical thinking by creating mental boundaries with regard to what types of questions and conclusions may be considered legitimate based as much as humanly possible on certain objective criteria. When scientists are educated to think that all the things in our universe are the manifestation of God's existence, they would naturally put off limits on certain types of questions and organize the facts in accordance with pre-given religious verities. For instance, such a schema would not allow scientists to imagine a world or a universe without some form of providential design or creator. In the West, such controversies have raged in particular concerning the teaching of Darwinian evolution and religiously based alternatives such as "creationism" or "intelligent design." In the Muslim world such pseudo-scientific efforts at legitimation involved the controversial Turkish writer Harun Yahya, known as Adnan Hoca, and his polemics against Darwinian evolutionary theory, as well as the Saudi funded project promoted by the American based International Institute of Islamic Thought (IIIT) for the "Islamization of Knowledge," which sought to reconcile scientific knowledge and the laws of nature with "revealed" Islamic "truths," rather than the other way around.

Gülen's main problem is that he does not separate "understanding" from "explanation" and his doctrine of Oneness (*tevhid*) or a holistic truth in accordance with divine creation limits independent inquiry. His reading of the universe from the Qur'anic perspective destroys the objectivity of a scientific attempt at comprehending "truth" and requires the researcher to subordinate his or her own hermeneutic situatedness (i.e., within the framework of an a priori revealed Islamic truth claim). In the end, Gülen is not able to reconcile this inherent tension and his epistemology undermines the scientific basis of critical inquiry and the notion that a researcher has to observe the universe free from all pre-given and unproven authority and truth claims. This tension, it should be noted, well pre-dated the modern Newtonian and Darwinian scientific revolutions and can be traced all the way back to the quarrel between Jerusalem and Athens or reason and revelation most profoundly elaborated by the great Muslim philosopher Al-Farabi and his followers.[41] The core problem in the case of both Said Nursi and Fethullah Gülen is that they both regard scientific understanding as *reading into the universe* their religious worldview rather than *reading off of the universe* from the standpoint of skeptical reasoning, which admittedly has its own limitations.

Nonetheless, it should be noted that both men have contributed a great deal to the modernization and development of Turkish education by vernacularizing scientific approaches and discourses, framing them in Islamic idioms. Furthermore, their contention with the age-old tension between religious and scientific/philosophic truth claims and the inherent limitations of both approaches is in many ways far more sophisticated than the vulgar logical positivism still espoused by many Kemalist circles. Their holistic process of understanding allows us to move back and forth between divine revelation and the multiple manifestations of a wondrous Cosmos and natural existence.

Both Nursi and Gülen's writings have provided a profound impetus to the popularization of science, and the engagement with the processes of modernity within Turkish society. This reinterpretation of Islamic values in order to tease out a more activist pietism is a significant factor in the thickening of civil society and the mutual transformation of religion and modernity. Gülen's epistemology and interpretation of Islam differs from that of other Sufi orders because of its affinity for highly emotional, heartfelt religiosity, and communal actions, to improve prevailing socioeconomic conditions. Moreover, Gülen has developed and disseminated a harmonious understanding between religious and secular knowledge. Gülen's propensity for promoting the centrality of scientific achievements in human material and intellectual progress has helped to develop a more rational system of values favorable to the pursuit of well-being here and now.

Concisely put, the movement's unintended and unforeseen consequence of stressing science as an avenue for understanding the immanent majesty of God sparked the process of the internal modernization and secularization of religious faith and values. Thus, Gülen and his ideas are neither the implacable enemy of modernity nor even that of secularism in Turkey. As has been seen, given his life story and the evolution of his ideas, Gülen never adopted a reactionary stance toward the pillars of modernity such as science, the market economy, religious pluralism, or democracy. Gülen considers religion and science ultimately reconcilable, since both refer to quite distinct yet intertwined facets of reality: science seeks to understand the objective world, while religion focuses on giving meaning to existence and also seeks to establish normative truth claims. Under the deep influence of Nursi, Gülen concludes that science is not inimical to religious traditions, not the least because science and human rationality themselves are inherently limited in giving a comprehensive and final account of Being and the Cosmos. Furthermore, both Nursi and Gülen aptly underscore the dangers of modern instrumental rationality and the ever present need for its restraint by moral claims and traditions, especially those derived from religion.

8

The Theology of Interfaith Dialogue

Dr. Hans Küng, a Swiss Catholic theologian and professor at Tübingen University, argues that there is "no human life without a world ethic for the nations. No peace among the nations without peace among the religions. No peace among the religions without dialogue among the nations."[1] Gülen concurs with Küng's vision that social cohesion and peace require close cooperation between religious institutions and scholars. Moreover, due to the insidious debate over the "clash of civilizations" and increasing Islamophobia after the events of 9/11, interfaith dialogue gained urgency. In response to this and the exclusion of Turkey from EU membership on the basis of religious "otherness," corresponding with Europe's historical suspicion of Judaism and Islam, Gülen became restless and initiated several projects to increase interfaith dialogue and understanding.[2] Given the Western media's general negative portrayal of Islam and Islamic movements, many non-Muslims may be inclined to view the Gülen movement as inherently intolerant, and thus as an unlikely vehicle to promote dialogue, tolerance, and, consequently, bridge-building between different cultures and religions. However, the case of Gülen provides an important counterpoint to such views. Indeed, it showcases an Islam that, like other religious traditions, has necessary symbolic and religious ideas upon which a more ecumenical moral understanding may be built, which is fertile soil for a democratic and pluralist political system.

Although Gülen's interest in interfaith dialogue evolved and intensified in the mid-1990s and early 2000s, his theology of dialogue aims to build social relationships to promote tolerance and peace rather than probing and reconciling theological differences. Gülen's interfaith dialogue is also part of his larger conception of education, and he puts an emphasis on exemplary conduct (*temsil*), rather than preaching or focusing on conversion (*tebliğ*). Gülen believes that preaching alienates others and prevents bridge-building between faiths. His interfaith dialogue focuses on representation through good conduct and especially well-formed moral character, not presentation through preaching. Thus, everyday life is a constant examination for believers to display their good moral character in the public sphere, be it as a teacher at school, a businessman at a meeting, or a doctor at the hospital. There is no specific space that exempts this exemplary conduct. According to Gülen, interfaith dialogue is not limited to the mosque, church, or university, but rather it is possible to turn every place where people meet into a site of interfaith dialogue. The Gülen movement has three goals in interfaith dialogue: building relationships and networks, promoting social cohesion and peace, and transforming others' perceptions of Islam.

This chapter will first offer an examination of the meanings and functions of interfaith dialogue and will then proceed to map out diverse Muslim positions in order to give an understanding of where Gülen's own position fits. In the second part, after defining Gülen's approach to interfaith dialogue, I will lay out the intellectual origins of Gülen's position and then demonstrate how his ideas are manifested in different contexts. Then, I will offer four criticisms of the interfaith dialogue approach of the Gülen movement.

INTERFAITH DIALOGUE

By interfaith dialogue, I mean an attempt by religious groups to harmonize their competing and conflicting voices to create a shared grammar of interfaith communication for the discussion of common issues in the transnational public sphere. It is an attempt to cross-fertilize diverse religious claims in a common ground. The purpose of the dialogue is to understand the perspective of each tradition, demonstrate respect in spite of differences, and create a basis for continuing communication. A constructive dialogue requires tolerance and recognition of difference in order to develop an ecumenical public language to address common concerns. There are several immediate benefits of interfaith dialogue. It allows participant believers to express what it is that they believe and prevent misunderstandings. Moreover, interfaith dialogue provides opportunities to express and explain one's faith by using the concepts and metaphors of other religious traditions. However, there is no single meaning or model of dialogue. Some define dialogue as a mode of inquiry, a process of will formation, or the formation of a shared understanding of commitment or consensus. Interfaith dialogue does not expect to uncover new divine truths or ask for a compromise of religious beliefs. It does, however, extend the horizons of people by encouraging participants to realize the inconsistencies of their positions and develop more coherent and ideally more pluralist positions.[3] In other words, dialogue may lead to self-reflection and even self-transformation. By understanding each other and achieving common normative grounds, having a dialogue increases social integration and enhances cohesion within multireligious communities.

Participants, with their collective faiths and histories, have identities that are determined to a great extent by religious traditions, and they engage with each other because of the shared challenges of modernity and also because of a concern for the suffering and welfare of others.[4] Since interfaith engagement is a public activity, it is open to public (both religious and secular) scrutiny. By deciding to discuss their differences in the public sphere, these religious traditions become subject to rational-critical discourse. As Charles Taylor argues, the discussions in the public sphere seek to create a "common mindset" that would then shape policies and future discussions.[5] One of the expected outcomes from having debates in the public sphere is the development of social integration and a shared language among the participants. There are many motives that explain why people participate in interfaith engagements. Some are interested in it because they believe that it is a religious duty to understand others. For others, it is a strategy for conversion or at least for winning sympathy to their faith. Also there are those who engage in interfaith dialogues for social, economic, and civic reasons rather than purely theological ones. As a form of public conversation and exchange, interfaith engagement is variegated and narrative-oriented (i.e., life and social problems are integral to it).

These engagements with varying depths have a direct impact on the evolution of civil society and the thickening of democracy, and its effects are not limited to religions. By virtue of engaging other faith communities, one becomes involved in a collective action of creating practices, networks, and discourses of sociability. In other words, as a result of interfaith engagement, people build norms, trust, and resource networks that could be utilized for secular purposes: peace building, justice, and the environment. James Coleman's idea of building social capital and its consequences serves as a useful tool to understand the major effects of interfaith engagements.[6] Looking at social capital, Coleman offers a dual typology: bonding and bridging. Whereas bonding takes place within primordial ties of family, tribe, and religious community, bridging results from interactions with other groups or communities due to their common interest and shared space, be it the same city or the same world. Although bonding is important for in-group discipline and cohesiveness, it is the bridging, for Mark Granovetter, that is the most powerful and effective in terms of providing mobility, civility, and social integration across diverse communities.[7] Indeed, interfaith engagement constructs bridges, opening access to social capital among diverse faith communities, and this, in turn, has a major positive effect on the thickening of civil society in multireligious states and overcoming misunderstandings of different faith systems. Interfaith engagement does not result in assimilation or indifference, but rather becomes a vehicle to deepen one's religious identity in relation to, not in opposition to, other religious traditions. It becomes a vehicle for marginalized and new groups to gain recognition and respect. Gülen realizes that in order to engage and shape public opinion, interfaith dialogue is necessary. Reciprocity, recognition, and civility are critical values of interfaith dialogue. Diverse religious groups interact in the public sphere and establish interfaith networks of people and religious institutions in order to create a better framework of coexistence in multicultural societies.

MODELS OF INTERFAITH DIALOGUE

The first known organized interfaith initiative was the World Parliament of Religions, which was held in Chicago in 1893. The second crucial event, which redefined interfaith dialogue, was the Vatican II of the Catholic Church, which recognized elements of truth in other religions. Yet another major event was a centennial celebration of the World Parliament of Religions in 1993. The keynote speech was drafted by Hans Küng, who stressed the purpose of interfaith dialogue, in the promotion of justice and peace in the world.[8]

There are several generic typologies of interfaith dialogue that map out positions of religious groups.[9] In order to map out different Muslim perspectives on interfaith dialogue, I utilize the typology of Alan Race, a formative scholar in the development of interfaith dialogue. He sees three types, which he classifies as exclusivist, inclusivist, and pluralist. As in other religious traditions, exclusivist Muslim leaders insist that truth can only be found in Islam and others are wrong and misleading; interfaith dialogue is a way of presenting Islam with an opportunity to convert the others to the one true religion (Islam). The main motive here behind the interfaith engagement is proselytizing. Some other Islamic groups totally reject interfaith dialogue by arguing that given the power structure in the international system, interfaith dialogue is a sinister plan by the West to convert Muslims, create an ecumenical faith by blending them together, and diluting and undermining the authenticity of Islam in the process. They insist that there is one truth, which is their interpretation of true Islam. They insist that since there is a major power gap between the Muslim countries and the West, any form of dialogue will be skewed at the expense of Muslims and it is likely to become a dialogue of power. Haydar Baş, a leader of a small nationalist Islamic group with a media outlet, is against interfaith dialogue and claims that the Gülen movement is helping Christian missionaries through interfaith dialogue to blend Islam with rival religions. Moreover, Turkey's leading political Islamist newspaper, *Milli Gazete*, and its columnists, such as Mehmet Şevket Eygi, even argues that Gülen in his fervent ecumenism has made an alliance with the Vatican to sell out Turkey and Islam.[10] One of their major criticisms is that the framework of the dialogue is defined and imposed by a Western/European understanding of religion, secularism, and liberal values; it does not recognize each tradition as distinct but rather seeks to reduce them to a single framework within a dominant religion (Western Christianity).

Inclusivists are those who argue that "our religion is ultimately true and other religions may have some fraction of the truth." They favor dialogue within certain limited space. They argue that we can evaluate other faith systems on the basis of the "last and most complete" faith: Islam. They seek to understand other faith systems within Islam and through Islamic lenses. Those who stress dialogue, similar to Vatican II (1962–65), argue that other faith systems may be a legitimate path to God but they are not all equal. Some inclusivist Muslims argue that the members of other faiths have religio-moral values and all persons of faith can achieve salvation if their intentions are to serve God. These scholars recognize the spiritual value of other faiths. However, they insist that complete salvation is reached through faith in Islam and the Qur'an alone.

In the case of Turkey, the writings of Said Nursi provide a framework of interfaith dialogue within the context of believing in God, and in building an alliance with other faith systems against materialism and a Godless human existence.[11] Nursi argues that faith in God is universal and the main purpose of Islam has been to build moral personalities in order to have a well-ordered community. These moral values have a universal appeal and other religious systems also share essential values. This means that Christians or Jews could share these values which are defined as Islamic. A Muslim could have ungodly virtues as much as a Christian could have moral virtues informed by faith. One does not need to be within Islam to achieve ultimate salvation, since God's Grace (*Allah'ın rahmeti*) permeates human existence and creation. All religious traditions experience God's grace and act with the idea of pleasing God. As the concepts contained in German Roman Catholic theologian Karl Rahner's *Anonymous Christian* have played an important role in ecumenical understanding within the Catholic Church,[12] Nursi's ecumenism has also greatly shaped the interfaith activities of the Gülen movement. For instance, the Declaration of Vatican II states, "Those also can attain to everlasting salvation who through no fault of their own do not know the gospel of Christ or his church, yet sincerely seek God and, moved by grace, strive by their deeds to do his will as it is known to them through the dictates of conscience."[13]

Said Nursi accepts that salvation is possible through other paths to God, but insists that Islam is the complete faith and the most direct route to salvation. Nursi claims that:

> When urging the People of the Book to believe in Islam, the Qur'an makes it appear familiar to them, and easy. That is, it implies: *O People of the Book!*

> You should experience no difficulty in accepting Islam: it should not appear hard for you. For the Qu'ran does not order you to abandon your religion completely, it proposes only that you should complete your faith and build upon the fundamentals of religion you already possess. For the Qu'ran combines in itself the virtues of all previous books and the essentials of all previous religions; it modifies and perfects existent principles.[14]

Nursi further states:

> A mighty religious revolution occurred in the time of the Prophet, and because all the peoples' minds revolved around religion, love and hatred were concentrated on that point and they loved or hated accordingly. For this reason, love for non-Muslims inferred dissembling. But now...what preoccupies people's minds are progress and this world.... In any event most of them are not so bound to their religions. In which case, our being friendly to them springs from our admiration for their civilization and progress, and our borrowing these. Such friendship is certainly not included in the Qur'anic prohibition.[15]

Nursi always defended alliances with different religious groups against ignorance, poverty, and enmity.[16] His main goal was to protect "faith and transcendence" in our daily life and live according to religious morality. Nursi did not criticize other Abrahamic religions, and his main targets of criticism were: materialism, positivism, atheism, and consumerism.

In short, inclusivists emphasize the specificity of each religious tradition and recognize particular theological differences. However, they are in favor of interfaith dialogue with the purpose of coming to know differences yet acknowledging them and seeking to create a stable working environment for coexistence. In other words, the second perspective stresses difference more than commonality; and seeks to maintain "differences" as a result of interaction; they seek social stability and foster respect and tolerance toward diverse religious groups. This group includes Tariq Ramadan (b. 1962), Sayyid Fadlullah (1935–2010), Hamza Yusuf (b.1958), a founder of Zaytuna Islamic Center in California, Sherman Jackson, a professor of Islamic law and ethics, and Ingrid Mattson (b.1963), the past president of the Islamic Society of North America.

The third type is the pluralists. The core assumption of the pluralist approach is that all religions represent different paths to the ultimate truth.[17] By "truth," some of them insist that each religion leads to salvation and they emphasize theocentrism (God is central to our thoughts and feelings) as opposed to anthropocentrism (human beings as the measure of all things) or existentialism (personal experience as the focal point of existence). Moreover, the pluralist perspective argues that the diversity of religions indicates that there are multiple pathways that lead to God. It stresses God's Grace as a shared basis of humanity. In other words, pluralism does not mean assimilation but rather recognition that all religions offer a potential parallel journey to meet the ultimate reality: God. John Hick, a philosopher of religion, has become one of the most important proponents of the pluralist position.[18] In his writings, Hick argues that all religions seek to enhance the human soul and lead to the same ultimate reality. Hick believes that shared groups of interfaith dialogue should not be restricted to religions, but should focus on theocentric perspectives, meaning that all religious groups need to take a step back from their Islamocentric or Christocentric views toward theocentric positions in order to create a shared ground to address common sufferings and needs of humanity. Thus, all religious traditions must realize that at the center is God. Pluralists support dialogue by arguing that the process of interaction with other religious faiths opens an opportunity to deepen faith by getting to know the other and realizing that these diverse paths lead to the same destination. The interaction and engagement with other religious groups are treated as necessary conditions to create a shared religious language in order to discuss differences. The lack of a shared language is likely to lead to conflict and the dehumanization of different religious groups. Thus, dialogue aims to transform the conflict and encourage participants to humanize the other. Ultimately, this, is the essence of establishing relationships: humanizing the other. In *I and Thou*, Martin Buber argues that individual existence and consciousness is based on engagement and interaction with other people. Buber treats the "I and Thou" relationship as dialogical and mutually transformative.[19] When the "I" encounters the "Thou" in informal settings such as coffee shops, stores, halls, or factories, without expectation, they share stories, experiences, and ideas. Gülen, like Buber, believes that dialogue is not between faiths but believers; and dialogue would become more transformative if it is informal and open-ended.

These intellectuals who stress theism and the commonality of all religious traditions seek to transcend particularities and focus on the universal aspect of religions. The diversity of religious traditions is surmounted by a similar conception of God. Thus, through interaction with, and a study of, other religious traditions, believers will expand the knowledge of their own tradition. The basis of interfaith dialogue, for the pluralist, is the realization that "we are all creature of God and we are all part of humanity." There are several prominent Muslim personalities and scholars, past and present, who support the theistic basis of interreligious dialogue and a pluralistic understanding. They include: Jalal-udin Rumi (1207–1273), Yunus Emre (1240?–1320?), Muhaiyaddeen, and Syed Hussein Nasr.[20] The famous Sufi Poet Rumi states:

What is to be done, O Moslems? for I do not recognize myself.
I am neither Christian, nor Jew, nor Gabr [Magian], nor Moslem.

I am not of the East, nor of the West, nor of the land, nor of the sea;
My place is the Placeless, my trace is the Traceless;
'Tis neither body nor soul, for I belong to the soul of the Beloved.
I have put duality away, I have seen that the two worlds are one;
One I seek, One I know, One I see, One I call.[21]

Yunus Emre, a prominent folk poet, grounds his faith around the ecumenical God more than any specific religious traditions. He writes:

With the mountains and rocks
I call you out, my God;
With the birds as daybreaks
I call you out, my God.
With Jesus in the sky.
Moses on Mount Sinai,
Raising my sceptre high,
I call you out, my God.[22]

Although Gülen's philosophy of interfaith dialogue is deeply informed by Rumi and Yunus Emre, he is more exclusive than both of them. Especially, before Gülen moved to the United States, belief in God (*La ilaha illallah*: there is no God, but God) used to be necessary to build a foundation for interfaith cooperation. He also insisted on the distinctive authenticity of Islam by stressing: *Muhammedan Rasullullah*—Muhammad as the last prophet with the complete revelation. However, there has been a gradual shift from an exclusivist perspective to a more inclusive one starting in the late 1990s. His interaction with different religious leaders and his life in America played an important role in this transformation. Having one foot in the exclusivist camp and another in the inclusivist, Gülen constantly moves back and forth between the two positions as the situation requires. Gülen's position is based on following two Qur'anic verses: "If God had so willed, He would have made all of you one community, but He has not done so that He may test you in what He has given you; so compete in goodness" (Qur'an, 16:93). The second verse states that "O mankind! We created you from a single (pair) of a male and a female, and made you into nations and tribes, that ye may know each other (not that ye may despise (each other)" (Qur'an 49:13). Due to these two verses, Gülen believes that unity in diversity, not unity via homogenization, is the design of God's creation. Thus, dialogue, for Gülen, is the recognition of this diversity and establishment of relationship between diverse faiths in order to serve humanity.

Since Gülen's understanding of interfaith dialogue is informed by the powerful intellectual tradition of Turkish Sufi Islam and the relatively tolerant history of the Ottoman state, this motion between the two camps of interfaith dialogue is also rooted in the traditional Islam of his followers. He is always a step ahead of his community, but if necessary he would step back and wait in order to prepare the community to take a more progressive stand.[23] Although Gülen is theologically not a pluralist, sociologically he is one (i.e., he regards human diversity as the blessing of God and fully supports joint action to address common issues). This sociological pluralism is an important avenue for studying the long-term evolution of the Gülen movement toward inclusivism, and it even involves some interaction with the pluralist camp.[24]

GÜLEN'S DIALOGUE

Gülen's interfaith dialogue is based on his understanding of human beings and human identity. What it means to be human (*insan*) and live a human life is determined in large part by our religious identities. These identities are formed and expanded as a result of encounters with other traditions and in relation to God. The latter relationship unifies us with other traditions. The former relationship involves encounters with other traditions, and this encounter helps us to mold our self-identity. There is always a spiritual "home" (i.e., an internalized tradition) that helps us to go out and interact with others and return having been enriched. We are not the same when we come back "home." In other words, through reading a text and conversing with others, we transform our understanding and enrich our own tradition. In fact, Gülen insists on the authenticity of each tradition and calls upon his followers to respect each tradition as it is and invite people to study theirs in order to appreciate the difference and to realize their human potential. Dialogue, for Gülen, becomes essential for identity formation and self-enrichment. Dialogue should focus on our particular understandings and situated stories of God. Gülen has a dynamic sense of transcendence: it is simultaneously particular and universal.

For Gülen, humans derive their identities from their tradition and historical particularities. Since we live in a globalized world in which time and space seem to be collapsing, we have to engage and deal with diverse cultural, religious, and civilizational "others." The question is what should be the ethical basis of our engagements with these different forms of "others." Gülen proposes to view "others" as friends by recognizing their identities and opening up one's own identity to relate, not necessarily absorb, and work with others.

Gülen argues that the main purpose of religions is to bridge, to unify, humanity on the path to virtue, not to divide it. However, he realizes that each faith system has its own traditions, and interfaith dialogue should not aim to reduce this diversity into a single belief system. Interfaith dialogue, for Gülen, is neither a "melting pot" nor a mosaic of religions, but rather it is a toolbox for building bridges between humanity's continents and isles. Gülen argues that "interfaith dialogue is a must today, and the first step in establishing it is forgetting the past, ignoring polemical arguments, and giving precedence to common points, which far outnumber polemical ones."[25] It is a "must" because of theological and pressing sociopolitical reasons. However, the call to "forget the past" is wishful thinking, since all believers are situated in their own history and have collective and often antagonistic memories about other religious groups. It might be more constructive to call for a "reconciliation of the memories" rather than for a willful forgetting in order to develop fulfilling dialogue.[26] Dialogue brings forth Gülen's emphasis on persuasion as a way of building consensus and disseminating one's ideas. Persuasion, not force, is the way. Due to the constant flow of ideas and people all over the globe, Gülen suggests that his followers engage with other faith communities to build bridges through persuasion and the exchange of ideas. In this process of persuasion and developing intellectual and emotional bridges, Gülen always stresses narratives and symbols, in essence proving himself to be a powerful storyteller.

Gülen differentiates between interfaith dialogue and the generic practice of dialogue. Dialogue, for Gülen, "means two or more people coming together to talk and meet on certain subjects and, by means of this, to draw closer together to one another."[27] Gülen identifies tolerance as the most critical condition of dialogue. Tolerance, for Gülen, "does not mean being influenced by others and joining them; it means accepting others as they are and knowing how to get along with them."[28] As far as interfaith dialogue is concerned, Gülen shies away from discussing theological differences and stresses the humanitarian aspect of dialogue to facilitate coexistence among diverse cultures and nations.

Gülen understands Islam to be a lived faith with its inner (faith, values, and passions) and outer dimensions of human life. The goal of the Gülen movement is to connect these two dimensions of faith in everyday life. In fact, the Qur'an, calls upon Muslims to live out their faith in everyday practices. Faith, for Gülen, is not about religious doctrines, but rather a way of "living" and "being" in this world. By endeavoring to recognize every believer in her/his own unique conditions and seeking mutual self-transformation through conversation and establishing friendship, Gülen both respects the individual and obliges the believer to do likewise with others, including those holding other beliefs.

Gülen is very sensitive to the sociopolitical context of each society, and his form of interfaith dialogue is shaped by praxis and the prevailing socioeconomic context of each society. A closer examination of the writings and activities of Gülen indicates that his main goal is to reinterpret Islam, within its own tradition, with the purpose of making its message relevant to modern society. His contextual theology shapes his understanding of dialogue. In other words, in the case of the Gülen movement, theology becomes a transformative and critical conversation not only at the individual level but also at the societal level.

Rather than nationalism or some secular ideology, Islam, upon its shared origins with the other two Abrahamic religions, provides a much stronger bridge to other cultures and civilizations. Moreover, given the forces of globalization and flows of people to diverse states, religious pluralism becomes a fact of life. Then, the main questions become: What should be the ethics of the relationship with existing diverse cultures and religions? Is there an Islamic responsibility toward the believers of other religions? How could Muslims, especially the followers of Gülen, realize dialogue as an "Islamic" practice? How does the practice of dialogue shape Islamic identity? To what degree do actions taken by the Gülen movement involve a consideration of how the movement is perceived by non-Muslims? Islamic principles of mercy, love, grace, justice, and being creatures of one God provide a formative role in interfaith dialogue.

Due to his stress on the context and sufferings of humanity as a result of poverty, illiteracy, and chaos, Gülen understands dialogue as being a "transformative" practice. It seeks to address the socioeconomic conditions of humanity to restore human dignity. In other words, the process of self-transformation in terms of the "fusion of horizon" or expansion of one's worldviews is possible if believers open themselves to different views and engage with them through reason. Even though we all participate in a dialogue with our prejudices, by the end of the dialogue our understanding has expanded and our self-transformation becomes apparent. Gülen, like Gadamer, argues that dialogue transforms people by transforming their self-understanding and stretching their earlier cognitive maps of understanding.[29]

His idea of dialogue is not only to have an abstract theological debate but also a social practice to restore justice on the basis of shared theistic ideas of mercy and grace. In the contextual theology of Gülen, faith is always translated into action in light of the pressing needs of a given society. Islam, thus, becomes a language to speak about human needs and concerns as much as the content of these beliefs are shaped and understood by the prevailing context. Interfaith dialogue offers a powerful and dynamic framework of identity transformation on the part of participants. Since identity formation is a relational and contextual process, dialogue is an important process in the evolution of Islamic identity among the followers of the Gülen movement. Practice of dialogue becomes an integral part of contemporary Islamic identity formation. A practice of interfaith dialogue consists of a set of ideas that informs shared patterns of activities that are related to social goals.

THEOLOGICAL FOUNDATIONS OF GÜLEN'S INTERFAITH DIALOGUE

The interfaith dialogue of the movement is based on Gülen's four core ideas: love, tolerance, recognition, and sharing or constructing a new language of understanding as an outcome. Gülen's position on interfaith dialogue is based on his understandings of religion and human nature, on the one hand, and modernity and common concerns of humanity, on the other. Interfaith dialogue, for Gülen, is an integral part of becoming human and a key principle of his Islamic worldview.[30] Since Islam stresses peace and harmony and living together with diverse faith communities, dialogue is the necessary condition for realizing this Islamic goal.

Love

Gülen identifies the lack of faith in God, thus, the lack of love of God as the source of international conflicts. Gülen argues:

> [Love] is an elixir; a human lives with love, is made happy by love and makes those around him or her happy with love. In the vocabulary of humanity, love is life; we feel and sense each other with love. God Almighty has not created a stronger relation than love, this chain that binds humans one to another. In fact, the Earth is nothing but a ruin without love to keep it fresh and alive.

Love, thus, "is the rose in our belief, a realm of the heart that never withers." He says:

> As a matter of fact, we have forsaken God, and thus, He has disbanded us. Because we could not believe in Him and love Him to the degree required, He withdrew the feeling of love from our hearts. What we are now doing, deep in the abyss of our bosoms where we are condemned to suffer yearning for Him, is to utter the egotistic nonsense of "I," "you," and to label each other as "reactionary," "infidel fanatic," and to constantly produce scenarios to dethrone one another. It is as though we have been cursed, as if we have indeed been deprived of loving and being loved, and we are craving mercy, compassion, and bliss. We did not love Him, so He took love away. No matter how long we wait, He will make us love one another if only we turn to Him and love Him. However, we are distant from the source of love. The roads we are on do not lead to Him, not at all. On the contrary, they are leading us away from Him. Our spirits, which used to receive streams of love, receive nothing now. Our hearts are like dry deserts; there are caves in our inner worlds, resembling the dens of wild animals. The love of God is the only remedy for all these negative things.[31]

Gülen believes that it is possible for humanity to come together around shared universal values and address the common concerns of humanity if we are to requite God's love for us. His solution is to create a theistic view around the Love of God. He claims:

The Theology of Interfaith Dialogue

> The love of God is the essence of everything and is the purest and cleanest source of all love. Compassion and love flow to our hearts from Him. Any kind of human relation will develop in accordance with our relation to Him. Love of God is our faith, our belief, and our spirits in the physical body. He made us live when we did. If we are to live today it is only through him. The essence of all existence is His love, and the end is an expansion of that divine love in the form of Paradise. Everything He created depends on love and He has bound His relationship with humankind to the holy pleasure of being loved.[32]

The critical building blocks of dialogue are his integrative understanding of religion and human beings. Gülen argues that all religions are sent by God to help humans create a just and humane society. Since we are all created by God with different physical features and levels of understandings, we have to respect and love every human person because of our love for the Creator. By referring to Yunus Emre, an Anatolian Sufi, we have to "love everyone because of our Love for God." He explains:

> Indeed, without taking God into consideration, any love for this or that object is futile, unpromising, indecisive, and fruitless. Above all else, a believer must love Him, and have a liking for all others only because they are colourful manifestations and reflections of His divine names and attributes.[33]

This is the most basic foundation of Gülen's idea of dialogue. Love, for him, is the essence of our humanity and existence. The feeling of love that manifests itself in different forms is a God-given virtue that we all share. Love remains the most powerful instinct and motive that cannot be defeated by sociopolitical forces. Those who lack this virtue "live in their egotistic labyrinths of personality and they are travelers of darkness." Gülen argues:

> [W]e need love and mercy as we need water or air. We seem to have forgotten love; what is more, compassion is a word rarely used. We have no mercy for each other, nor love for people. Our feeling of pity has diminished, our hearts are adamant and our horizon is pitch black from hostility; it is for this reason that we see everything and everybody as being bleak.[34]

Gülen believes that Islam is not a religion of exclusion or seclusion, but rather both a bridge and a vehicle, reaching out to different cultures and societies.[35] He argues:

If we start our efforts for dialogue with the belief that "peace is better'" (Qur'an 4:128), then we must demonstrate that we are on the side of peace at home and abroad. Indeed, peace is of the utmost importance to Islam; fighting and war are only secondary occurrences which are bound to specific reasons and conditions. In that respect, we can say that if an environment of peace where all can live in peace and security cannot be achieved in this land, then it would be impossible for us to do any good service for society or for humanity.[36]

Indeed, the Gülen movement has been the most successful contemporary Islamic movement to build bridges with diverse religious and cultural groups.

Tolerance

Gülen argues that a dialogue's sine qua non condition is tolerance (i.e., respecting the other), since we all share the same human dignity and diverse manifestations of creation. On the basis of his theistic view of humanity, Gülen argues that there are more bonds and common issues to bring diverse religious groups together than those that separate them. He offers a broad definition of tolerance and seeks its application in the sense that:

> We should have such tolerance that we are able to close our eyes to the faults of others, to have respect for different ideas, and to forgive everything that is forgivable...have so much tolerance that we can benefit from opposing ideas in that they force us to keep our heart, spirit, and conscience active and aware, even if these ideas do not directly teach us anything.[37]

He backs his argument by citing the Qur'an, by associating tolerance with other values such as respect and forgiveness: "If you behave tolerantly, overlook, and forgive (their faults)" (Qur'an, 64:14).

From his perspective, tolerance is an exalted human value that springs from the nature of God:

> Tolerance is not something that was invented by us. Tolerance was first introduced on this Earth by the prophets whose teacher was God. Even if it would not be correct to attribute tolerance to God, He has attributes that are rooted in tolerance, like forgiveness, the forgiveness of sins, compassion and mercy for all creatures, and the veiling of the shame and faults of others. The All-Forgiving, the All Merciful, and the All-Veiling of faults are among the most frequently mentioned names of God in the Qur'an.[38]

Yet, Gülen also defines tolerance by what it is and what it is not. Gülen's main sources of dialogue are the Qur'an, the hadith, and the writings of the Muslim scholars. He utilizes several hadith references to provide religious legitimacy for interfaith dialogue. Gülen says that according to the prophet, his most important acts are to be "feeding others" and "giving salaam" (peace) "to those you know or do not know."

Gülen also gives a number of examples from Islamic history to prove the need for tolerance to make positive contribution to interfaith dialogue. He argues that after defeating the Byzantine emperor, the Seljuk ruler Alparslan proved magnanimous, and his commanders escorted them to their own territory. Similarly, Saladin, who was even celebrated for his chivalry by his Crusader foes, offered aid to wounded soldiers and allowed the Christian population of Jerusalem to leave the area in peace, in contrast to the bloody massacres perpetrated by the Crusaders against Muslims earlier. He also provides a series of examples from Ottoman history to show that tolerance was a critical virtue in Islamic states. Gülen argues:

> We are the children of a culture that produced such people. We are the heirs of the culture that has the world's broadest, most comprehensive and most universal tolerance. This understanding and view is spreading today like waves in the sea, and reaching the four corners of the Earth. I fully believe that the coming years will be years of tolerance and love. In this framework, we're giving to the world a lot and receive a lot. Let alone fighting with our own people, we will not even be fighting with other cultures, civilizations, or people of other beliefs and worldviews. Issues leading to argument and opposition will be resolved completely, and once again understanding the power of love, will open our hearts to everyone with love and compassion. With God's help, we will realize the important matters of dialogue and tolerance, which today's world needs so much.[39]

By referring to the verse in the Qur'an, which says "They who swallow their anger and forgive people. God loves those who do good" (3:134), Gülen stresses forgiveness as an important aspect of tolerance.

In recent years, Gülen uses the concept of tolerance reluctantly and less frequently. Indeed, tolerance in itself is a negative virtue. To tolerate someone or another faith is to put up with their ways of thinking. Due to these issues, Gülen also stresses recognition of the other as the third founding principle of dialogue. Although Gülen and his movement used to stress the concept of tolerance more often in the past, Gülen has been using the concept more selectively in recent years. When I asked a close associate of Gülen why this has been so, he said:

Yes, there is less emphasis on the concept of tolerance because it does not capture what Gülen wants to say. For instance, tolerance is a reaction to a person, conduct or a tradition that you judge negatively but you are willing to bear it. Gülen believes that dialogue is not only "tolerating" each other but rather appreciating each other and working to develop a shared language to enhance social cohesion.

When I asked him if it is still in use in some of Gülen's speeches, he said:

Yes, I told you the limited meaning of the concept in terms of endurance or bearing something you don't like. However, it is also a key concept of peace-building and social cohesion. It means commitment to the principles of respecting one's dignity and exercising self-control. Because of this latter meaning, the concept is still necessary but not sufficient to make our position clear.

The primary goal of Gülen's dialogue project is not to find common ground for existing religions, but rather to develop a framework for coexistence despite clear differences. Interfaith dialogue, for Gülen, becomes citizenship training with responsibilities and rights to build a shared future through collective actions. In recent years, the Gülen movement has been stressing recognition and social cohesion as key aspects of dialogue to build a peaceful society.

Recognition

Gulen's third idea grows out of the first, and that is recognizing the other as equal, including an acceptance of the other's definition of the good life as legitimate. In recent years, Gülen has stressed recognition more than tolerance and his simple definition of recognition is "to accept everyone as they are and get them to appreciate you" (*herkesi olduğu konumda kabul etmek ve sizin temsilinizle sizleri yakın görmesini sağlamak*). A closer study of Gülen's writings, mostly collected from his preaching and Q & As, shows that, by recognition, he means admitting or acknowledging a person or a community as they are. By acknowledging each believer as the creation of the same God and of a tradition sharing the same sacred origin, Gülen wants to build the framework of communication within the principles of respect and esteem. From Gülen's perspective, respect and esteem follows from his idea of love of God and seeking to please God. In short, love is essential for the recognition of one's identity and tradition. Through the process of recognition, one could also see one's own tradition through the mirror of others. Failure to recognize one's tradition or identity results in distortion and disrespect, which, in turn, facilitates conflict.

Gülen believes that the cities, countries, and regions of the world are in major demographic transformation as a result of the forces of globalization. We live in plural societies with different languages, races, cultures, and religious traditions. The main challenge is to find a way to live together peacefully by enhancing social cohesion. Since every group demands universal rights, as well as seeks recognition of their identity and specific tradition, Gülen stresses dialogue as an instrument of social cohesion. Gülen, like Charles Taylor, believes that our identities (religious or ethnic) are not constructed within and in isolation. Rather, we construct our identities through dialogue with other traditions and always negotiate it as a result of our interactions with others. Indeed, other religious traditions played a constitutive role in the formation and reformation of our religious identities. Accordingly, the history of Islam, which consists of Muslims' encounters with diverse religious traditions and cultures, is the story of refining Islamic civilization and identity. Islamic identity evolved as a result of historical interactions with different religious civilizations.

By highlighting the role of interaction with diverse cultures, Gülen also brings his concept of *temsil* to the contemporary debate by arguing that "how others see and evaluate us is an important part of how we understand who we are." In other words, the most effective way to get others to recognize our identity in a positive way is to set an exemplary lifestyle in every sphere. Thus, the struggle over recognition should be carried out through good conduct rather than preaching to other cultures. In fact, we come to learn the meaning and role of our religious identity from the perspective of a religious partner during the interaction.

Gülen is a man who is constantly restless over the negative understanding of Islam as a religion of conflict or violence. This negative view of Islam by other traditions undermines Muslim self-esteem, and Gülen wants to transform this perception through dialogue and through good conduct in daily practices, not by words per se. He also argues that we all have particular traditions and practices and they must be recognized as well. No religious tradition or cultural group should be ostracized by other dominant groups, especially those who exert economic and political power. If a group is humiliated, and as a result this humiliation is also internalized by an oppressed group, he considers this situation as the worst form of denial of one's dignity.

Shared Language of Common Concerns

The purpose of dialogue according to Gülen is also to form a shared language to address pressing problems of humanity. In other words, there is an expectation of cross-fertilization of ideas and the evolution of ecumenical understanding that would allow diverse faiths to cooperate for the improvement of human conditions. In an interview, Gülen said:

Our age is a time of addressing intellects and hearts, an undertaking that requires a peaceful atmosphere with mutual trust and respect.... In the peaceful atmosphere engendered by this treaty [Hudaybiyya], the doors of hearts were opened to Islamic truths. We have no intention of conquering lands or peoples, but we are resolved to contribute to world peace and a peaceful order and harmony by which our old world will find a last happiness before its final destruction.[40]

Gülen identifies materialism, ignorance, and poverty as the causes of conflict and imperialism in the world. He believes that religion and religious alliances can address the destructive nature of secular ideologies of materialism. He further explains this in the following way:

The goal of dialogue among world religions is not simply to destroy scientific materialism and the destructive materialistic worldview; rather, the very nature of religion demands this dialogue. Judaism, Christianity, and Islam, and even Hinduism and other world religions accept the same source for themselves, and including Buddhism, pursue the same goal. As a Muslim, I accept all Prophets and Books sent to different peoples throughout history, and regard belief in them as an essential principle of being Muslim.... Regardless of how adherents (of different religions) implement their faith in their daily lives, such generally accepted values as love, respect, tolerance, forgiveness, mercy, human rights, peace, brotherhood, and freedom are exalted by religion. Most of them accorded the highest precedence in the messages brought by Moses, Jesus, and Muhammad, as well as in the messages of Buddha and even Zarathustra, Lao-Tzu, Confucius, and the Hindu scholars.[41]

Gülen states that "in truth, except for certain special cases, the Qur'an and Sunnah always advocate tolerance. The shielding canopy of this tolerance extends not only to the People of the Book, but in a sense to all people."[42] From the perspective of Gülen, not all religious paths end up at the same hill. A closer reading of his writings and a set of Gülen-inspired activities encourage us to make the following conclusion: God is not present in every religious tradition but rather every tradition is present in God. In other words, having a *tavhidi* perspective (i.e., seeing everything as the manifestation of a single God's power), one could perceive the existing diversity as a different attempt to relate to God. All particularities and diverse traditions are contained within God. There is a recognition that human reality is diverse and multiple, but divine reality is One existing in unity. The universal and the particular are human realities. On the basis of this perspective, we should treat each tradition with respect and care without denying their authenticity. The actions of the Gülen movement, in terms of promoting interfaith dialogue, indicate that they seek to understand the meaning of Islam and Islamic tradition in light of their engagement with other religious traditions without forgoing their own.

PRACTICES OF DIALOGUE

On the basis of my studies of Gülen's discourse of interfaith dialogue and the practices of the Gülen movement, I would conclude that the movement stresses practical and dialogical over intellectual engagement. Practical dialogue seeks to build relationships between ordinary people, allowing them to work together to solve problems and improve human conditions and understanding. It is well intentioned and based on sharing personal stories and helping one another for the realization of a common good. This practical dialogue is different from formal scholarly interfaith dialogue. Intellectual dialogue, unlike the practical one, is limited to the churches, mosques, or synagogues and to scholars of religion. It concentrates on comparing, studying, and sorting out different religious traditions to learn more about the nature of religion and its evolution. The scholarly dialogue takes place either in the houses of worship or universities and indeed may include many individuals who are agnostic or even atheist intellectuals and scholars. The Gülen movement activities involve mostly ordinary people from different walks of life, and people come together to share worldly concerns, not necessarily religious concerns per se, to find common ground for cooperation. They consider human suffering and the search for existential meaning as more important than doctrinal differences. People, who participate in these lay-person exchanges, share stories, feelings, and their experience with the sacred in order to create shared emotional bonds. A volunteer of the Gülen movement interfaith dialogue in Germany said, "People shy away from direct theological discussion over religious issues. It is better to build confidence. One earns trust of people through cooperative action over issues. After building trust with one another, one can start to talk about theological issues."[43]

A closer examination of the interfaith dialogue of the movement indicates that the movement focuses on the mobilization of shared concerns about the conditions of daily life more than a concept of a shared God. Another activist in Chicago said:

> The most important issue is not to remind other groups that we share the same God, but rather that we share the same concerns, such as education, well-functioning of the public services, and peace. People may not believe in God or are not ready to discuss theological issues. Moreover, our main interlocutors are not religious scholars but rather ordinary people who confront daily issues.[44]

Through these worldly concerns the Gülen community seeks to find shared spiritual ground. Most interfaith activists of the movement are teachers, community leaders, and engineers, while actual scholars of Islam are underrepresented. One of the most characteristic elements of the interfaith dialogue is the representation of Islam through exemplary conduct and excellence in one's vocation. They stress Islamic virtues in fulfilling one's job and a frugal and disciplined lifestyle. An activist of interfaith dialogue in Salt Lake City said:

> The issue is to break the ice between different religious groups. The only way we can do this is to present Islam not in terms of words or in the form of preaching or getting into deep theological discussions. Rather, displaying genuine concerns over our common humanity and having virtuous work habit and lifestyle in our daily life. The secret is to be good in conduct and disposition not only with words.[45]

In fact, almost all of the Gülen movement's interfaith activities are focused on the grassroots and the purpose is to "relate to people" and develop an environment of trust.

Gülen has had some success in this regard. He has met with Patriarch Bartholomeos, the head of the Orthodox Fener Patriarchate in Istanbul, and other leaders of the Orthodox churches. He has also met with other Christian and Jewish religious leaders, including David Aseo, the former Chief Rabbi of Turkey, and even Pope John Paul II, in an effort to advance interfaith dialogue.[46] Moreover, the Gülen-inspired Foundation of Journalists and Writers of Turkey has organized a number of conferences on interfaith dialogue meetings.[47]

One of the most successful structures of the movement is the Intercultural Dialogue Platform (IDP). Its founding declaration says:

> We praise and thank God Almighty who has brought us together on this soil, the cradle of religions and civilizations, and enabled us to get to know each other and exchange ideas. We all are members of the family of humanity, created, protected and guided by God. As one of the results of planting seeds of hostility, as well as growing them for centuries, among persons and societies of different religious convictions by exploiting cultural differences throughout the history of humanity, which are related to religion and faith in particular, for this or that purpose, is that humanity has been subjected to tremendous negativities.[48]

IDP has several local branches with the purpose of promoting dialogue among diverse ethnic and cultural groups in Turkey. Gülen calls upon his followers all over the world to engage in interfaith dialogue. For instance, IDP organized the

International Symposium in Urfa on April 13–16, 2000, to promote dialogue, tolerance, and peace around the shared legacy of Abraham. The meeting concurred that "Abraham is the symbol of rationalism in the search of truth, a deep sincere faith of monotheism, being devoted to God with love, serving humanity with love, combining faith and affection, patience, courage, the effort to attain result in determination, and peace and dialogue." The second symposium took place in 2006 with a large number of scholars and they all stressed the commonalities of the three faiths.[49] The Dialogue Eurasia Platform, with its popular DA Magazine, focuses on the intercultural and interreligious dialogues in Russia, Central Asia, and the Caucasus. It regularly organizes the conferences, panels, and a series of art shows in these places to promote the movement as a "bridge builder." Gülen says:

> Be so tolerant that your heart becomes wide like the ocean.... Approach unbelievers so gently that their envy and hatred melt away. Like a Messiah, revive people with your breath. Return good for evil, and disregard discourteous treatment.... Choose tolerance, and be magnanimous toward the ill-mannered.[50]

In another situation, he declared:

> We must be as if handless to those who hit us and tongueless to those who curse us. If they try and fracture us into pieces even fifty times, still we are going to remain unbroken and embrace everyone with love and compassion. And, with love toward one another, we will walk toward tomorrow.[51]

The Gülen movement is also active in America and Canada. It runs over 50 local interfaith dialogue groups in virtually every state in America. These groups are motivated by the writings of Gülen and organized under his auspices. The largest one is the Institute of Interfaith Dialogue for World Peace, Inc. (IID) based in Austin, Texas, and has 17 chapters in other American cities. IID organizes interfaith Ramadan dinners in every major city in the United States and awards local religious leaders who are active in interfaith dialogue. Almost all of these activities are financed and supported by the Gülen movement. The organizational structures of these activities are heavily Turkish and teachers from Turkish charter schools play important roles in the organization of these activities. In Washington, DC, the movement established the Rumi Forum in 1999, with the goal of promoting interfaith and intercultural dialogue. The Rumi Forum organizes lectures, distributes the writings of Gülen, and also participates in interfaith dialogue with different religious institutions. It has several branches in different cities.

CRITICISM OF THE INTERFAITH APPROACH

There are four criticisms directed at the interfaith dialogue of the movement: (1) it engages in very little *intra*religious dialogue within and between Islamic sects and focuses more on interreligious dialogue; (2) its interfaith dialogue groups include few women and is a mostly male-dominated activity; (3) it does not engage deep theological issues and regards the interfaith dialogue as an instrument for the promotion of Islam or the movement itself; and (4) there is very little curiosity among the members of the Gülen movement to deeply study and learn other religious traditions and cultures.

If one compares interfaith versus intrafaith dialogue, there are striking disparities. There has not been a single Gülenist meeting with the Shia or other Islamic sects. The movement shies away from intra-Islamic debates and takes a skeptical attitude toward Shiism and especially regarding Iran. The Ottoman legacy and rivalry with the Safavids are still very powerful forces which partially explain the Gülen movement's distance from Shia communities and also from Arab societies with a strong Salafi presence. The historical rivalry between the Ottomans (Sunni) and Safavids (Shia) play a critical role behind the suspicion toward the Shia. The movement seems to distance itself from the other Middle Eastern communities in the United States and also in Europe. The movement also so far did not make major inroads into non-Turkish/Balkan Muslim communities. In fact, interfaith dinners that the movement organizes in major American cities seldom include Iranians or Arabs, and they shy away from those Muslims whose attire is non-Western.

Moreover, most of the interfaith dialogue activities are carried out by men and male-dominated interpretations of Islam perpetuated by the Gülen movement. Although all interfaith dialogue is overall dominated by men from different religious groups, the Gülen community in recent years has encouraged women to establish women-only interfaith activities in terms of connecting with other women groups. There is not a single woman, or *abla*, among the first circle of Gülen, or in any high position of the movement. Again, the conservative norms of this Anatolian Turkish-Muslim context hinder the leadership role of women.

The movement is more interested in cooperation and establishing relationships than abstract debate over doctrinal differences. There are very few people who can engage in comparative religious debate. Most of those active in the Gülen movement consist of ordinary teachers, engineers, doctors, and businessmen. These people relate with other religious believers through their personal stories and feelings. Moreover, the decision not to get involved in doctrinal discussions is a deliberate one. A prominent member of the movement said "*Hocaefendi* does not want formal or elaborate onstage interfaith meetings, but prefers something else."[52] When I asked him "what do you mean by something else" he offered the following explanation:

Gülen's main concern is joint action with other members of religions to improve socioeconomic conditions of people. He believes that formal on-stage interfaith dialogue could turn into a performative act by the participants to send their message to the audience rather than seek to understand each other. In fact, I have also witnessed a number of times on the stage, those who participate in the debate are under pressure to impress the audience especially their own co-religionist. Thus, interfaith meeting becomes a performative acts and impressions.

Although the Gülen communities' interfaith activities have not produced a major text or a shattering initiative, in fact it has allayed many non-Muslim people's attitude toward Islam and increased people's curiosity about the possibility of an enlightened Islam. Thus, it is the case that the Gülen movement tries actively not to get involved in controversial theological debates, since it does not foresee productive outcomes. Moreover, the Gülen community's stress on the representation more than the presentation of Islam limits interfaith dialogue and deep intellectual engagement. Moreover, especially after the 9/11 attacks on the United States, there has been a deliberate promotion of anti-Muslim bigotry in many European countries and the United States on the part of neoconservatives, their erstwhile allies in Christian Zionist Armageddon churches represented by the likes of Pat Robertson and John Hagee, and the European neofascist right.[53] As a result, Gülen has come to the conclusion that instead of formal theological discussions and debates, interfaith dialogue could also be carried out by setting exemplary conduct in different social arenas and welfare work. One does not need to organize interfaith meetings in order to build bridges, but rather one can communicate ideas through good conduct. A follower of Gülen in Washington said:

Remember! Silence in some circumstances is the most powerful communication. Actions, such as joining people organized to realize better education and helping the poor and the needy, can be much louder than words. Silence speaks and an action embodies words of dialogue.[54]

When I tried to press him on the issue of silence, to get at what he means by it, he said:

There are different meanings of silence in different societies. In some societies, silence means disagreement; in some cases, you prefer silence because of memories that are hard to cope with and ideas that are unsettling; in our case, silence means it is time for action, not only words; it also means contemplation and spiritual enlightenment.[55]

In fact, in the post-9/11 context of America, exemplary conduct or joining other faith groups to achieve a concrete social goal becomes more effective than organizing a formal interfaith dialogue meeting. In recent years, there is a shift from interfaith to intercultural dialogue along with more emphasis on joint action rather than on debate over theological issues.

In order to fully understand the Gülen movement's endeavors in this regard, one has to differentiate between Gülen, the inspirational leader, and the activities of the movement. Gülen is a sincere believer in interfaith dialogue, and he has been very effective in transforming his conservative grassroots followers by encouraging them to reach out to different religions and cultures. However, not every follower of Gülen internalizes this message, and especially given the current sociopolitical conflicts in Turkey, the spirit of interfaith dialogue is drowned out by the pursuit of self-interest or power, which guides some in the Gülen movement's actions. Although the interfaith activities have not produced a major text or a shattering initiative, it, in fact, softened many people's attitudes toward Islam and increased people's curiosity about the possibility of an enlightened Islam.

CONCLUSION

Under the current sense of siege that many Muslim communities harbor, the main challenge is: how to turn Islam into a "bridge" to reach other traditions. Gülen's solution to this challenge is to engage with other traditions and their specific histories and theologies. His concepts of *care* for others' needs and *respect* for others' identities provide the necessary foundations for bridge building. The main objective is mutual self-transformation and better understanding of one's own tradition as well. We realize our human potential and enrich ourselves through engaging with others. Interfaith dialogue begins with the process of engagement more than with abstract intellectual conversation among small groups of religious scholars. Gülen proposes learning *qua* engagement with other religious communities over concrete projects of social welfare.

Through dialogue, the Gülen movement brings misunderstood beliefs, doctrines, and convictions to the public's attention and thus comes under public's scrutiny. Dialogue becomes a process of turning the stranger into a friend. In fact, people always meet as strangers before they become friends through dialogue. Be it relief organizations, educational institutions, or a network of interfaith meetings, the Gülen movement is not only treating dialogue as a practice but rather a praxis to alleviate human suffering by providing better education, healthcare, and promoting the establishment of a just and peaceful world. And the purpose of the Gülen movement's activities in different parts of the world is indeed to ascertain that upon meeting the "stranger," one's inclination would be to navigate the encounter down the road of friendship and understanding rather than alienation and enmity. Likewise, Gülen's interpretation of Islam is not confined to the mosque; it is a praxis that seeks to ameliorate human suffering and build bonds among different cultures. Gülen-inspired schools, NGOs, and networks provide a fertile ground for such interfaith dialogue. They seek to build bridges between diverse cultures. If love is the cement, compassion and exemplary works are the iron of the bridge that Gülen seeks to build between religions.

9

The Clash of Political Visions

The Military and the JDP

In Turkey, the Republican/Kemalist elite, especially the military, has historically posed as the guardian of official ideology, as well as the state. They therefore regarded policy making as the exclusive domain of the state elite and bureaucracy until the "backward" Turkish civil society could be molded into their image. These Kemalist elites developed a mystical faith in the power and righteousness of state institutions to civilize the population. The guiding principle, or legitimizing basis, of the bureaucracy has always been to reach the standard of Western European civilization by establishing a secular European nation-state. The state elite therefore set out on a mission to even get the populace to "look and act European," down to the smallest detail in dress and decorum.[1] Moreover, they viewed any challenge to this top-down modernization as obstructionism, reactionism and religious fanaticism. In particular, Islamically mobilized groups were considered as the main impediment to the state-led modernization project. All of the military coups in 1960, 1971, 1980 and 1997 were aimed at protecting the power of the Kemalist bureaucratic/military elite by insulating key decision-making bodies from the influence of Turkish civil society. As civil society started to develop and demand more rights, the Republican establishment became more radicalized and evoked a series of strategies to repress and eliminate autonomous religious movements.

Said Nursi himself fell victim early on to this Kemalist Kulturkampf, being forced to spend the remainder of his life (d.1960) either in jail or harsh internal exile. Since the Gülen movement was seen as a direct descendent of Nursi's efforts at promoting a modernized but still religious Turkish civil society, it also faced suspicion and persecution at the hands of the Kemalist military-bureaucratic establishment until the JDP's historic electoral victory in 2002.[2]

This chapter will focus on four major questions: What do politics mean for the Gülen movement? What are the main political goals and strategies that make it a target of the Kemalist establishment? To what degree is the movement overtly *political*, considering that its supporters often claim that they have no overt political agenda, and while its detractors view it as a sinister movement with a hidden political agenda? What is the relationship between the state institutions and the movement, with particular attention to the perceived animosity between the military and the movement?

THE GOALS AND STRATEGIES OF POLITICS

Fethullah Gülen is often portrayed as the quintessential idealist, relying on spirituality, ideas and engagement rather than political power. Gülen, in fact, is a far more complicated man than such a simplistic portrayal would lead us to believe. He has an astute sense of hard and soft power, and understands power in terms of its various components and limits. He is cautiously pragmatic about the balance between ideals and power, and can be critical of those who are motivated by religious ideals without taking into consideration the limits placed on them in the existing power structure. The movement has at various times broken with, and sought accommodation from, both the Kemalist establishment, as well as overtly Muslim political movements such as the one led by the late Necmettin Erbakan.

The political engagements of the movement with Turkish state and society are complex and multifaceted. Even though the movement officially rejects any engagement in politics, and works diligently to present itself as an *apolitical faith movement*, the fact is that such an apolitical stance has proved impossible even if sincerely sought.[3] Yet, at the same time, it would be problematic to present the Gülen community as a purely political movement committed to turning Turkey into some form of an Islamic state. The truth lies, as often is the case, somewhere in between. The members of the Gülen movement, like the other citizens of Turkey, participate in political process; however, the guiding principle of the movement in politics is not partisanship, or unquestioned alliance with any party, but rather pragmatism. The Gülen movement has offered support to political parties ranging from the center-right to the center-left, and even the Nationalist Movement Party as long as they would not be prevented from pursuing their religious, educational and welfare projects. For example, when Bülent Ecevit, Turkey's most charismatic leftist and social-democrat leader, publicly supported the educational activities of the Gülen community and met with Gülen himself, significant numbers of Gülen supporters voted for Ecevit's party.

Given the wide-ranging activities of the Gülen movement, it would be a mistake to solely categorize it merely as a social, religious or political movement. It is, in fact, all of these at the same time. Since it is an amalgamation of diverse socio-religio-political ideas and interests which defy traditional categorizations, we are not always capable of fully grasping the multiple trends within the movement itself. It is essentially a religious movement with its own agenda for shaping the public sphere by introducing ideas and promoting programs informed by Islamic values in order to transform society and the state. In other words, a sharply delineated boundary between what is religious or what is profane may not be very helpful in categorizing the movement, since it transgresses these arbitrary boundaries of secular and religious, social and political, national and transnational, and private and public. Some of the criticism against the movement is based on a strict Kemalist secular paradigm, which argues that since it is a faith-based movement, it should not get involved in public debates or seek to influence public policy and legislation.

Politics, for Gülen, is not confined to "political parties, propaganda, elections and the struggle for power" alone, but more importantly "politics is the art of management, based on a broad perspective of today, tomorrow and the day after, which seeks to satisfy the people and win God's approval."[4] Politics, thus, is not only about the "management" of conflicting interests, but most importantly building a consensus and serving the commonwealth. Political society as such for Gülen is not made of laws, which seek to reconcile conflicting interests, but it is made of sentiments, beliefs, historical memories and ideas. This definition of politics, indeed, requires a different mode of political engagement. The effort to locate the Gülen movement's politics and political engagement begins with an identification of the various forms of political engagement that exist in Turkey. There are four such forms: (1) the politics of election, (2) the politics of the street (protest movements), (3) the politics of violence (insurgency, terrorism, targeting the civilian population or state officials), and (4) social movements and informal/network politics. The Gülen movement rejects types (2) and (3) and gives more preference to informal politics as a networked social movement. However, in recent years it has gradually become more overtly and formally active in electoral politics.

By informal politics, I mean behind-the-scenes politics and maneuvering, that is, the procurement of interests via backdoor channels, which stresses communal interests, and seek to influence public debates by putting forward new ideas. Through this form of politics, the Gülen movement has managed to bring new issues to the public's attention and have them debated in the public sphere without the cost entailed in being seen as an overtly partisan political party. Although Gülen does not want to use politics and legislation to create his conception of the good society directly, he wants to employ political tactics in order to remove those obstacles that would otherwise hinder the process of a bottom-up moralization of society. He wants a state that does not exclude people from government jobs, or prevents entrepreneurs from engaging fully in the marketplace because of their religious beliefs and socioeconomic backgrounds. He prefers his vision of reform, social development and welfare to be achieved from a bottom-up societal impetus, and complains that the draconian top-down Kemalist model of secular authoritarianism violates the sanctity of freedom of thought and association. Thus, the movement has been very active in Turkish political life to lift the exclusionary restrictions, which exist in the name of protecting the secular nature of state and society, but which in reality have served to entrench a Kemalist political and socioeconomic elite composed of key families and institutions of similar background. The actions, statements and literature of the Gülen community do not indicate any desire to establish traditional Islamic law or Shari'a or an Islamic state per se. Rather, they are geared toward creating a sociopolitical environment for diverse identity groups to pursue their conception of the good life free of authoritarian imposition. This awareness is reflected in, and stems from, Turkey's economy where, as entrepreneurship has become increasingly valued, and people have begun to harvest the fruits of a freer market, the market itself has become a blueprint for a new imagined society open to increasingly diverse voices and people who have, in short, become increasingly skeptical about the power and the role of the state in their country.[5]

Since Gülen is seeking to bring about the moral transformation and integration of society through raising religious consciousness and empowerment of voices that had been previously marginalized, his project is not purely political in terms of uniquely stressing institutional and legislative change. Gülen, like many secular and religious scholars, thinks that the social disintegration of societies generates a series of crises of identity and justice, meaning and morality. Alasdair MacIntyre's *After Virtue* aptly describes such a crisis of belief.[6] MacIntyre locates this existential crisis in the decay of religious faith and morality. Although Gülen agrees with MacIntyre about the origins of the current crisis, unlike MacIntyre, he proposes a return to religion, and does not consider a return to Aristotle to be a solution. While MacIntyre and many scholars hold that the Owl of Minerva had fled without the possibility of a return, Gülen believes that is not the case. However, John Neuhaus, a Lutheran, and later a Catholic minister who was engaged in sociopolitical life, argues that the American public square is naked because of the decline of religious faith and morality.[7] Neuhaus, like Gülen, sees religion as an integral and essential part of the fabric of American society, and he therefore seeks to overcome the cultural crisis in America by reintroducing theistic morality to the public square. Neuhaus, like Gülen, is convinced that modern society requires a morality that is derived from religion in order to overcome the pernicious consequences of social disintegration.

Gülen believes that if a given society consisted of individuals with moral virtues, it would become a society of love and tolerance, and its institutions would eventually reflect that societal contract. From Gülen's perspective, the problems of modern societies are moral and not political. Modern societies are held in thrall by the forces of materialism, egoism and hedonism. Therefore, he proposes that the solution to the problem is a return to spirituality, a recentering of daily life around the love of God, and the development of a citizenry that is knowledgeable about the power of science, technology and economic forces. His main opponents are materialists and antireligious positivists, who deny any social role for religion and stress science as the new religion for establishing normative truth claims and for guiding humanity. He identifies his community in terms of love and selflessness, educated both in knowledge and wisdom, and regards the Golden Generation as the builders of his imagined society. Thus, the strategy of Gülen has been to educate the golden generation to restore an ideal of Islamic civilization that is based on love, tolerance, human dignity and scientific and economic achievements. This is a religio-social project par excellence but with different means and political goals.

On the basis of Gülen movement activism, it is possible to identify four general sociopolitical goals of the movement: (1) engagement, (2) social justice and welfare, (3) sociopolitical integration, and (4) empowerment. The most important goal is *engagement* with political processes, institutions and groups to improve governance, and set an inclusive political agenda. Politics for Gülen is a mode of *conversation* to convince people about shared human values of dignity, love and better social conditions.[8] His conversation involves both an intellectual engagement and a setting of exemplary conduct. Indeed, the movement helps to expand the "public sphere" and "participation" by encouraging people to discuss their common issues and challenges, and to develop a shared vision of the past and future of the society. Religiously-informed values provide a shared language in which diverse groups articulate their own vision of the good life and diverse lifestyles. Indeed, variants of Islam, as the *lingua franca* of Turkish society, facilitates public conversation and debate and empowers different groups to form their own political arguments concerning the public good. Dialogue, and thus political negotiation, depends on the continued use of familiar terms and narratives. Gülen does not deny the fact that people are motivated by a desire for wealth and power. However, he believes that the greatest long-term and most peaceful relations are likely to be formed if the spiritual side of human identity is also taken into account. By recognizing that our diversity, shared human dignity and love, are all manifestations of divine virtue, we could, according to Gülen, achieve much greater harmony.

The second goal concerns *social justice*, which as discussed previously, forms, along with education, the core of the central commitment to social service or *hizmet* with which most of the movement's social engagements are concerned. The third goal of the Gülen movement is the *social integration* of society by removing exclusionary legal obstacles from the realization of one's own definition of the good life. The movement is active in politics in order to eliminate obstacles, barriers or constraints that seek to impose one specific definition of the good life (secular) against diverse and more traditional lifestyles. Finally, its strategy has been the *empowerment* of people with knowledge, skills and the necessary resources to build sound communities.

When we examine the political engagement of the movement, we need to realize that the movement is constantly evolving and transforming itself. This is especially true as the movement has become internationalized, and has started working within, and among, diverse cultures and political systems. In so doing, its understanding of politics, identity and especially religion has also been transformed. That is to say, the movement of 2012 is not the same as the movement of the 1970s, 1980s or 1990s. The movement differentiates itself from other religious movements in terms of its successful learning curve and its ability to adapt and evolve under new conditions. The Gülen movement used to be accused of being apolitical, ineffective and not sufficiently aggressive to challenge authoritarianism and human rights violations in Turkey. Today, many people claim that the movement is too political, confrontational and assertive vis-à-vis state institutions. How can we then explain this transformation, and does this pattern of transformation suggest a future trend for the movement?

The reason that rival actors from both civil society and the state complain about the Gülen movement's increasing power has to do with several issues. First, the movement offers a new sociopolitical language to expand and deepen public discussion, and mobilize traditional social sectors that had hitherto been strictly marginalized. Its rival vision of society did threaten the official authoritarian Kemalist dogma. The Gülen movement posed an alternative mode of modernity; one that does not exclude religious norms and lifestyle. It sought to ameliorate ideological, sectarian, class and ethnic cleavages by condemning the Kemalist military-bureaucratic establishment's efforts at maintaining hegemony by pitting Turkish societal groupings against one another; it stressed politics as a means to remove obstacles to socioeconomic and political development and not to engineer a radically new society at war with its own history and traditions; and it related to the Ottoman Islamic past not as cause of economic and social backwardness, but rather as a brilliant world civilization and an instrument for contemporary social integration and a catalyst for capitalist development. Second, the Gülen movement became the target of certain Kemalist state institutions and their societal allies because it offered very effective rival networks of social mobility that insisted on the redistribution of resources and the democratization of political power. Those who benefited the most from the status quo with its ongoing cycles of corruption and nepotism between the media, corporations, politicians, businessmen, as well as the state-and military-owned public companies, which received generous subsidies, all turned against the Gülen movement. Media groups with long-standing ties to the Kemalist establishment and the Turkish "deep state" such as the Doğan media group sought to criminalize Gülen and his movement, and portray it as a sinister force that sought to infiltrate state institutions and the economy with the purpose of restoring the Caliphate or an Islamic state. Third, the affinity between the ideas of Gülen and the new emerging Turkish Sunni entrepreneurs of Anatolia made the old Kemalist business establishment and economic elite uneasy. The "Anatolian tigers," who emerged in the wake of Turgut Özal's liberalizing reforms became the vanguard of the Gülen movement and its main source of funding for its growing social and educational activities. This Anatolian bourgeoisie became the main force demanding economic and political liberalization and an end to the corrupt and exclusionary nepotism between the established political and business elites. It should also be noted that it was this Turkish Sunni Muslim Anatolian middle class, and not the Turkish left or would-be-revolutionaries, which achieved the greatest success in promoting democratization, human rights, pluralism and civilian rule in the authoritarian Republican period.

The Gülen movement sought to avoid being overtly political so it could focus on its educational and social activities. A central part of this strategy was to try to appease the military and bureaucratic establishment by distancing the movement from overtly political Muslim parties like those led by Necmettin Erbakan. However, this strategy failed, and the movement's attempt to portray itself as apolitical, moderate and patriotic only infuriated the Kemalist establishment even more.

Individual supporters of the Gülen movement inevitably gravitated toward Muslim democratic political movements, and sought to expand the limited liberalizing reforms that Turgut Özal managed to introduce following the 1980 military coup. Because of their business interest and growing role in the liberalizing and globalizing Turkish economy, this "Anatolian tigers" vanguard of the movement both funded the Gülen movement's educational and social activities, and separately mobilized followers to support both Erbakan's Welfare Party and its successor, the Justice and Development Party (JDP). The increasing influence of the entrepreneurial class and its close connections with the JDP government, in turn, mobilized many rival groups in Turkey against Gülen and his community. The gradual rise in the 1980s of an alternative Anatolian Turkish Muslim economic and political elite became a source of great anxiety for the Republican old-guard political and economic establishment. To further illustrate these points, the following section will examine the ideological confrontation between the military and the Gülen movement by examining the cognitive map of the military and its fear of society. Ironically, it is the military's aggressive and criminalizing strategies that forced the Gülen community, after much hesitation, to closely ally itself with the JDP.

THE MILITARY VS. THE MOVEMENT

It is important to differentiate between Islam as a political ideology (political Islam) and Islam as a source of morality, identity and tradition. In order to understand the military's hostility toward the movement, we need to understand the historical background of the formation of the military's view on Islam and Islamic politics.[9] The Turkish military could not completely reject Islam as a source of morality nor even as an element of national identity, as exemplified by the Turkish-Islamic Synthesis following the 1980 coup, because they knew that if the military totally denied the Islamic sentiment shared by the majority of the population, it would face a severe backlash from society and suffer a loss of legitimacy. One of the defining features of the modern Turkish military has been its enmity toward any variant of political Islam and its public manifestations.[10] As far as the "political" aspect is concerned, the military regards political Islam at odds with the goal of its bureaucratic elite to retain the reins of power and engineer a homogenized and Westernized nation.

There are two dimensions to the military's skepticism toward Islam and religious movements in Turkey. The military, as the guardians of Kemalist ideology, are the most nationalistic and secularist (Jacobin) institution in Turkey and regard religion as the source of economic and political backwardness within the Ottoman state and society. Moreover, the military regards its corporate identity, that is, professionalism, positivism (faith in technology and science), to be in direct conflict with Islamic political identity, such that an Islamic identity could lead to fragmentation and polarization within the military institutions themselves by providing a legitimating ideology that would supersede Kemalism and achieve vast inbuilt support. After the defeat in the Balkan Wars (1912-1913), the military moral code was developed around the core concepts of duty, homeland and the protection of the state, along with stress on science as the only guides to life.[11] In other words, the military started to see competing ideologies (religious and ethnic) as a threat to its cohesion, and started to define military unity by keeping religious ideologies and loyalties outside. Thus, Islam in general, and Islamism in particular, became regarded as a polarizing and fissiparous force for the unity of the military.[12]

The military schools adopted a positivist education and stressed nationalism as a solution to the decomposition of the Ottoman Empire. Because traditional institutions, which were rooted in Islamic worldview, had opposed the modernizing reforms in the early nineteenth century, many

Young Turks, and later Kemalist radicals, saw religion as a whole as a force for backwardness. Military professional ethics were also in conflict with religious identity in terms of loyalty and duty to the state rather than Islam. While it was seeking to create a set of ethics based on professionalism, the military did not shy away from subordinating Islam to the larger nation-building project. Through professionalism, the military wanted to claim its autonomy vis-à-vis the religious establishment and the dynasty. In the Balkans, the military examined the manner in which the Balkan churches became the repository of nation-building and institutions in the service of the state. Later on, the Turkish generals imitated the Balkan experience by attempting to create a nationalized Islam to enhance state power, and discipline the citizenry to serve the nation. In other words, the military wanted to utilize Islam in order to cultivate a sense of duty, loyalty and discipline of the body and mind for service to the nation. From 1923 to 1950, Turkey remained a single-party system, and the military became one of the main instruments in the hands of the ruling establishment. The Turkish military's understanding of religion and its perceptions and fears were shaped by the Kemalist Republican People's Party (CHP) leadership. The military was both the guardian and an extension of single-party politics, and it became the main institution for the creation of the new nation. It therefore sought to remove all obstacles standing in the way of its secular nation-building project. There were a number of rebellions in the name of Islam that were led by religious leaders against modernization. The 1925 Shaykh Said and 1930 Menemen rebellions were turning points in the relationship between the state and Islam.[13] The military became more radical after the rebellions, sought to remove Islam from the public domain. Thus, it became more rigidly in favor of secularism and the secularization of society. In due time, the military developed its own understanding of Islam. Even though the matrix of understanding was shaped by Jacobin secularism, a commitment to scientism, and desire to become ultimately a European nation-state, where religion would be forced out of the public sphere in favor of science and reason, the military also recognized the role of religion as a cohesive element for social integration and as a potential resource that could enhance civic-mindedness and as an ideology that could be used to mobilize ordinary soldiers during times of conflict by stressing the great martial history of the Seljuks and Ottomans, and the spirit of the *ghazi*'s and *sehid*'s as defenders of the faith and nation.[14] However, the same military-backed Kemalist ideology rejected any public role for Islamic institutions or networks in the new Republican Turkey.

With the coming of the multiparty system, Islam as an oppositional identity to Kemalist authoritarianism inevitably returned to the political fore. The Republic's efforts to coerce a complete secularization of social and political life naturally generated intense hostility and resistance that could not be erased through sheer force. The Kemalist elite did not properly take into account the fact that Turkish Islam was embedded in various layers of social life and was more conducive to mass mobilization than either a constructed ethnic nationalism or socialism. The Democrat Party (DP), the first viable opposition party, which came to power in the 1950 elections, used religion as a tool to counter the power of the Republican People's Party (RPP; CHP) and the military in order to open more space for itself. This new economic and political class redefined Islam as an electoral factor to mobilize more support for their political agenda. With the multiparty system, religious groups also reemerged, and were reactivated. Moreover, as the DP tried to expand the freedom of religion by criticizing the radical reforms of Mustafa Kemal, this led the military to conclude that the DP was in fact opposed to the very ideology and cult of personality surrounding Mustafa Kemal himself, as well as their own central role as guardians of the state. The DP at times withheld raises to military officials and used a number of means to marginalize the military's role within the civilian political domain. The revival of a Turkish Muslim identity, and the perceived marginalization of Kemalist ideology, led to the radicalization of the higher echelons of the officer corps.

The 1960 military coup that resulted in the removal of the DP from the political stage, and the hanging of the popular and democratically elected Prime Minister Adnan Menderes along with two prominent ministers, underscored the brutality with which the Kemalist establishment was willing to maintain power, and hardened attitudes between the establishment and the majority Anatolian Turkish Sunni society over which they sought to rule. The military became suspicious of electoral power, and unsure whether Turkish society could be "trusted with democracy." It created parallel governance through autonomous state institutions, the constitutional court, and the National Security Council to limit the power of elected civilian governments. Moreover, the military started to valorize Kemalism as the main source of national identity and allegiance, and as a model of governance and progress in opposition to Islamic and leftist ideologies. For the first time in the 1970s, an autonomous Islamic movement, under the leadership of Necmettin Erbakan, entered the parliament from outside the purview of the official center-right in the political spectrum, and it even became the key coalition partner in a series of such governments. This in turn further radicalized the military against the renewed vigor of Muslim democratic political movements which the 1960 coup failed to suppress.

In the 1970s, Turkish society faced an economic crisis, and intense and bloody street battles between leftist and rightist forces. During the height of the Cold War, the Turkish military came to view Communism, and not Islam, as the leading threat. The uneasy dialectic between Islamism and Kemalist secularism constituted a parallel, yet interconnected, development. When another military coup took place in 1980, led by General Kenan Evren, the military promoted Kemalism along with, for the first time, a new Turkish-Islamic Synthesis as a supplementary ideology, to end the social fragmentation of the nation along class, sectarian and ethnic lines. This novel shift underscored the extent to which Kemalist ideology had failed to hold Turkish society together or gain deep-rooted legitimacy.

With the Soviet invasion of Afghanistan in 1979, the NATO alliance even started to tolerate and use political Islam as a tool against Communism. Given the sharp left–right cleavages in Turkish society in the 1970s, the 1980 coup actually served to bring the conservative masses closer to the military. The coup leaders this time mainly targeted leftist and Kurdish groups, and tried to use a tamed Turkish-Islamic synthesis as an antidote against the alleged Communist threat in Turkey. Moreover, the military realized a possible role for Islam as a new type of glue that could overcome the growing ethnic divisions within Turkish society presented by Kurdish separatism. Thus, Islam was reintroduced through public education to inculcate a new generation to be loyal to the state, and proud to be Muslim Turks. The Turkish-Islamic thesis became the main ideology of the military to redefine the nation, and gain the legitimacy that hard-line Kemalism had failed to accomplish. It is thus no coincidence that in the early 1980s the Gülen community held a very positive attitude toward the military, and Gülen himself took the military as a model for the organization of his community even asking his followers to have a similar discipline and commitment to duty.[15] Gülen, like most of the Sunni *ulema*, had a deferential view toward the military due to its central role in the Ottoman state, and his fear of anarchy and external threats to the Turkish nation. This deferential view would only be overcome in the last decade in the face of renewed Kemalist military persecution, leading Gülen and his followers to become more publicly critical of the military's self-bestowed mission of becoming a guardian of an ideology rather than the defender of the country.

After the 1980 coup, the first civilian government was formed and led by Prime Minister Turgut Özal, who was from the Nakşibendi Sufi order, and had close ties with Anatolian Muslim networks. Özal's liberalizing and globalizing economic policies greatly helped to create a new Anatolian Sunni bourgeoisie and industrial class, which would eventually eclipse the Kemalist "white Turk" rival economic and political establishment in Istanbul and Ankara. The Anatolian Sunni Muslim networks were much better positioned to utilize these new political and economic opportunity spaces than were other groups. Islamic identity, which was marginalized and identified as the cause of Turkey's backwardness by the Kemalist elite, was mobilized by these new actors to challenge state authoritarianism and a closed economy. It also formed new rival political, economic and cultural power centers to give voice to the demands for representation by the Anatolian Sunni majority. In other words, Islamic identity by itself was not the catalyst for change, instead it was used as a lubricant vis-à-vis the workings of market forces, and an instrument whereby this new elite was able to carve out its dominance in the globalizing market and eventually the Presidential Palace in the Ankara neighborhood of Cankaya. When Turgut Özal eventually became president, as a modern Nakşibendi with close ties to Anatolian Sunni groupings, including the Gülen community, he protected them from persecution by hard-liners in the bureaucracy and the military. This new bourgeoisie seized the opportunity and became a highly educated, upwardly mobile and culturally very confident force in challenging Kemalist authoritarianism, and its anachronistic and embarrassing cult of personality surrounding "the great leader" while positing its alternative path to modernity and progress.

When the Kemalist establishment failed to proactively coopt these new forces that it had unwittingly helped to unleash with the liberalizing reforms of the 1980s, it sought to criminalize them through what became known as the February 28 "soft coup" process. The events of February 28, 1997, are categorized as a soft coup because the major establishment business associations and media cartels were mobilized by the military, bureaucracy and judiciary, to force Prime Minister Necmettin Erbakan, Turkey's first explicit leader of a Muslim political coalition, to resign. Behind this public campaign was the unmistaken message that Erbakan's government would "voluntarily" resign or be forced out by the generals. On that day, at the National Security Council meeting, the Chief of Staff made Prime Minister Erbakan sign and approve a list of precautionary actions against so-called "Islamic reactionaries" or "*irtica*," before being eventually forced to resign himself in June 1997. This soft coup is also known as the "February 28 process" because the coup was not only limited to the removal of the Welfare Party led coalition-government, but was also a process that allowed for the state establishment, mainly the military and bureaucracy, to monitor, control and criminalize all Islamic activism deemed by them as a security threat. The Kemalist establishment even desperately tried to institutionalize a permanent legal framework that would ostracize devout and/or active Turkish Muslims from the commercial, educational and political spheres. According to Andrew Mango, a leading expert on Turkish politics and society, the process of February 28 was "a campaign, concerted by the military, to eradicate political Islam from education, business and other activities."[16]

Furthermore, the "securitization" of Kurdish and Islamic identity claims increasingly politicized the society. Securitization is hereby referred to as a concept articulated by Barry Buzan and Ole Waever whereby the state brands certain religious, ethnic, class or ideological groups and movements as a national security or even existential threats, thus justifying coercive and often extrajudicial measures against them.[17] Assertive Kurdish and Islamic identity claims reinforced the securitization of domestic politics in Turkey and the institutionalization of a national security state, in which the military expanded its overseer role to include such civilian areas as the judiciary, economy, education and foreign policy.

In addition to the Welfare Party of Erbakan, the Gülen movement was the most powerful Muslim actor within Turkish society, and thus Kemalist hardliners declared war against the Gülen community's efforts to influence Turkish state and society. According to the internal reports of the military, the movement used every opportunity to infiltrate the military high schools in Istanbul, Bursa and Izmir. In the late 1980s, the military high schools and colleges started to purge some cadets from the schools because of their alleged ties with the Gülen movement. In fact, rather than it being an organized conspiracy to infiltrate the military schools, some students with sympathetic views of Gülen or Islam entered these schools just like any citizen of the country. However, in order to exclude pious or conservative Turks from the military schools, Kemalists always portrayed this basic right of citizens as a form of infiltration. The generals sought to keep the military immune from rival societal identities and divisions. Ersel Aydınlı, a scholar of the military, aptly summarizes the mindset of the military:

> The Turkish army holds absolute control over the internal indoctrination of its personnel, drawing its members from the heart of the society, but then doing its best to keep them independent from popular national and international ideas and trends. The Turkish army is not the army of the elite, but is rather an elite-*making* institution. It recruits cadets largely from rural Anatolian towns, but with its carefully crafted and closed institutions, turns these Anatolian kids into a unique new societal elite—a group neither completely inside nor outside of society. In many cases, while the immediate relatives of this new elite carry socially common ethnic and religious identities, the officers themselves become stripped of these identities through the military's own "eliticization" process and absorb the institutional identity.[18]

By purging traditionally pious Anatolian Turks from the military, the generals, in fact, isolated themselves from the majority within their own society, and gradually suffered from diminished legitimacy as a result.

In the 1990s, in order to prevent any recruitment of Gülen sympathizers, the military developed a sophisticated surveillance system. One of the ways to determine whether someone was affiliated with the movement was to check whether he read any of Gülen's books, listened to his sermons, subscribed to publications like *Sızıntı*, read the leading daily newspaper *Zaman*, watched the movement's

TV programs, or sent his children to Gülen-inspired schools. There was a systematic witch-hunt in the military, as well as in other crucial state institutions to purge and keep the Gülen sympathizers out. If there was any suspicion that a military officer sympathized with the activities of Turkish Muslim reform movements, the military would launch an internal investigation that included psychological, and in some cases physical torture. Any sign of religiosity could be used against the accused officer and he would be expelled without any right to take his case to the court. From the perspective of the military establishment, those officers who simply prayed regularly, and did not consume alcohol or socialize with the higher echelons of the military, would be suspected of having ties with the Gülen movement or other religious organizations, and often would be purged no matter their professionalism or patriotism. A retired military officer told the author:

> When I was a sergeant in 1997 in Polatlı, I had to ask my mother and sisters not to visit me since they were all covered. I stopped attending Cuma [Friday afternoon] prayers not to be targeted as a member of religious groups. It is difficult to make sense of those years. How did the Turkish military get to the point that it declared any form of piety or religious observance as a threat to national unity and the discipline of the army? Who would organize such a thing? The February 28 coup was a turning point in terms of the end of the military's legitimacy amongst more conservative Turks.

In fact, since the mid-1980s, almost all higher promotions in the military were determined based on the candidate's ideological purity and devotion to Kemalist ideology rather than on merit. The intellectual quality of the Turkish general staff had been in serious decline as a result, and eventually the military lost the support of Turkey's conservative religious grassroots, which comprised the vast majority of society. In short, when the military defined basic Turkish Sunni religiosity as a security threat, it fatally undermined its legitimacy among the majority of Turks as the "hearth of Prophet Muhammad."[19]

The February 28 decisions were inherently antidemocratic, and a violation of civil and human rights, not only in their conception, but in their implementation as well. Although the military refuses to acknowledge it publicly, it established a special task force to carry out purges in the military ranks. Termed the "Western Working Group," its task was to determine and direct policies in the war against any manifestation of Islam in the public sphere.[20] In order to keep track of whether those decisions were being implemented or not, the military establishment pushed hard for the creation of a special bureau called the "Monitoring Board for Implementation" under the Office of the Prime Minister. Most decisions were taken secretly in such government monitoring institutions. The Monitoring

Board started sending special groups of inspectors, in which sometimes military officers were also represented, to institutions with suspected ties to religious groups, even though most of them were nonviolent, nonpolitical and moderate. Schools and dormitories affiliated with the Gülen movement were especially targeted. A number of people were arrested, bureaucrats were fired, and private companies owned by pious Anatolian Turks faced organized boycotts and harassment. After the February 28, 1997, coup directives, the Higher Education Board took administrative actions against Fatih University, an institution of higher education affiliated with the Gülen movement, and those academics who were critical of Kemalist authoritarianism or had perceived sympathies to the movement were punished, some of them being summarily removed from their positions. In addition, a state prosecutor, backed by the military establishment, launched an investigation which later in 1999 turned into an indictment against Gülen himself. According to the Anti-Terror Law, Gülen was accused of forming an "illegal organization" to change the secular nature of the Turkish state, and according to the prosecutor, very prominent national and Turkish Sunni institutions like the daily *Zaman*, Samanyolu TV channel, Asia Finance, Işık Insurance Company were treated as part of an "illegal network."

In response, Gülen adopted a strategy of appeasement, which greatly disappointed liberal as well as Muslim groups who were seeking to defeat authoritarianism in Turkey.[21] Although Gülen adopted a deferential and compromising position by publicly suggesting that Prime Minister Erbakan's pro-Islamic government should step down in order to ease tensions, the military coup leaders were not appeased. However, the rest of Turkish society, which did not subscribe to Kemalist authoritarianism, refused to be cowed any longer. Kemalist hard-liners severely miscalculated in thinking that Turkish society at the turn of the millennium could be intimidated and ordered around as it was in the 1930s and 1950s. The reality was that a globalizing and dynamic Turkish Anatolian middle class was not willing to take orders from the authoritarian segments of society, whether they were Kemalist or religious. The arrogant and draconian policies and statements of the 1997 coup leaders led a large number of Turks of all ideological backgrounds to conclude that the military was against not only political Islam per se but also religion itself, and moreover against the very concept of civilian democratic rule in the country. This proved to be a fatal blow since the February 28 process only mobilized Turkish society and the dynamic new Anatolian middle class to finally demand representative government, the rule of law and elected civilian control over the military and bureaucracy.

After a series of ineffective and corrupt coalition governments between 1997 and 2002, early elections were scheduled in 2002 by Prime Minister Bülent Ecevit. In the 2002 elections, all three coalition parties failed to win the minimum 10 percent of the total vote in order to qualify for representation in the

Turkish parliament. The JDP, which was established by Recep Tayyip Erdoğan and Abdullah Gül, following the ban against the Welfare Party of Necmettin Erbakan by the constitutional court, emerged as the winner of the national elections. Once again, the Kemalist military and its civilian-secularist allies became alarmed about the threat of a renewed "fundamentalist takeover." In response, a group of generals again became involved in a series of clandestine activities to overthrow the elected civilian government. General Hilmi Özkök, who became the Chief of Staff in August 2002, resisted the efforts of the coup plotters and also used his power to rein in their clandestine activities, which he correctly realized would lead to uncontrollable backlash from a now sophisticated and mobilized Turkish middle class.

THE END OF KEMALIST MILITARY DOMINATION: THE ERGENEKON AFFAIRS

In response to the JDP's sweeping electoral victory in 2002, an organized set of clandestine coup plotting was once again set forth within military ranks known as the Ergenekon network.[22] Ergenekon is one of the alleged clandestine nationalist military-civilian networks with close ties to security forces, especially the military. According to the charges of the prosecutor, the members of the organization aimed to ferment unrest by killing politicians and leaders, and ultimately sought to overthrow the JDP government because of its roots in political Islam. Today over 800 people have been indicted by the court with some seemingly charged on a questionable basis for being outspoken in their criticism of the JDP. Nonetheless, the data revealed at the court proceedings have clearly indicated the desire and plans of a certain clique within the military to topple the JDP government. Because of a number of sinister plans such as Operation Sledgehammer, which even sought to ignite a war with Greece in order to justify military intervention as a prelude to destroying the JDP, as well as the Gülen movement, the movement finally responded to the threat of persecution by seeking an alliance with political parties, NGOs, and liberals groups to end the role of the military in Turkish politics once and for all. Indeed, the short-sighted policies and antidemocratic threats of the military turned a large sector of the Turkish population decisively against it. Today, both the conservative JDP government and the Gülen movement have finally come together, and are using all necessary means to push the military back into the barracks, and to exert final democratic civilian control over the governance of the country. A retired Turkish general complained that "the movement's newspapers, radios, and TV stations are acting with a sense of vengeance in order to silence all anti-Gülen groups or voices."[23] A number of articles sympathetic to Kemalist circles also echo similar feelings.[24] Indeed, presently, the Gülen movement-affiliated media and some public intellectuals have been more critical than any other group about the military's involvement in politics and the numerous cases of corruption and abuse brought against high-ranking generals. This criticism does not target the military as an institution, or even question the need for a powerful military, but rather aims to redefine the mission of the military as the protection of the territorial unity of the country rather than the protection of an ossified ideology, which had become an obstacle to progress and the modernization of the country. A colonel who is on active duty offered this assessment:

> The Gülen movement is doing an excellent job by exposing the shortcomings and irregularities within the military and especially the corrupt lifestyle of generals. Daily *Zaman* has covered how ordinary soldiers have been used for the personal needs of generals or their wives. Whenever I read their coverage which says "we send these soldiers to serve the country, not as busboys or waiters in your house" I am delighted. It is about time to expose this sickening level of corruption! I know those generals and the higher echelons of the military are trying to defend themselves by presenting daily *Zaman* as anti-Kemalist or anti-military, but I don't believe it. The Office of Chief of Staff has not been doing its job. We need these media exposures to correct and discipline the military. I like what *Zaman* newspaper is doing.[25]

Another young army officer based in Istanbul stated:

> The *cemaat* [Gülen movement] is our ombudsman. They are doing an excellent job by covering irregularities within the military. You need this media attention on the military to curtail the extravagant lifestyle of the generals. They are not only disconnected from ordinary people, but also from the officials within the military as well. This is the reason why there is not much reaction from the lower level of military officers when generals are jailed! Let me tell you this: the *cemaat*'s media coverage of the military is disturbing and sometimes it makes me angry. However, they play a positive role in forcing the army to become transparent and accountable to civilian authority.[26]

Indeed, there was virtually no reaction to the arrest of a large number of generals from the young officers (*genç subaylar*).

A newly retired colonel said:

> The military is too involved in politics at the expense of our mission. The military has to realize that we are the army of a Muslim nation. Islam is an integral part of our history and identity. We should not be afraid of Islam and things will get better as the military returns to the barracks and builds bridges with the people.[27]

The younger generation of officers has a more accommodating understanding of the role of Islam in Turkish history and identity, and they stress the centrality of civil society, democracy and human rights as vital for a modern Turkey. A prominent member of the Gülen movement told me:

> We love our army. I was even pro-MHP [the Nationalist Movement Party] when I was in college. I have always admired my army, but not these generals who are corrupt, ineffective, fat reds. They are alien to this society and they have destroyed the legitimacy of the army among the people. How could I possibly respect them if I'm hearing that as part of this Sledgehammer Plan they are talking about destroying a mosque? They must have gone crazy![28]

However, there are other groups within the military who still regard the Gülen community as a sinister threat. A Major on active duty said:

> The purpose of the Gülen movement is to destroy the military's discipline, infiltrate the army in order to undermine the most secular institution which is mandated to protect the Kemalist nature of the state. Their purpose is to turn Turkey into today's Pakistan where the security institutions are penetrated by the Islamic groups, and there is a war amongst the Pakistani army, police force and intelligence agencies due to the infiltration of religious identity. We cannot allow this to happen in Turkey.[29]

A number of active and retired military officers with whom I spoke raised questions about the Gülen movement's attempts to turn the military into a police force where no major appointment, according to them, could be made without approval of a Gülenist network within the police force and intelligence agencies. Indeed, a series of clandestine military plans were leaked to the media targeting the Gülen movement.[30] In these plans, the military openly targets the movement, along with the elected government, as an "internal enemy" to be defeated and driven from power. As these secret plans were leaked by some pro-democracy military officers themselves, the Gülen movement finally became more aggressive against the top-echelons of the military.

CIVILIAN GOVERNMENTS AND THE JDP

Despite the tensions with the secular military, Gülen has remained distant from Islamic parties in Turkey, and has tried to simultaneously maintain ties with the center-right parties, including the social democratic leader Bülent Ecevit. Moreover, Gülen had a cool relationship with the leading late Islamist politician,

Necmettin Erbakan, who headed (directly or indirectly) three successive generations of Islamist movements and parties going back to the 1970s: the National Salvation Party (*Milli Selamet Partisi*), the Welfare Party, and now the Virtue (*Fazilet*) Party. Gülen has always opposed the idea of an overtly Islamic political party, on several grounds. First, such overt entry into religious politics leads, by definition, to the compromising of faith. Gülen would prefer to exercise influence from a more indirect position, untainted by political log-rolling. Second, entry into politics would shift priorities away from moral principles and ideals toward the goal of winning power—which then drags personal politics, rivalries, and other extraneous factors into the equation. Third, because of the tense standoff between the Turkish military and the Islamic community, any Islamic party in power risks heightening military opposition to the overall Islamic agenda in Turkey.

When Turgut Özal first became the prime minister of Turkey in the 1980s, Gülen developed a close relationship with him. Özal, arguably the most important Turkish political figure since Atatürk, undertook a major series of reforms, which brought Turkey into the world economy via privatization and an opening of the economy that resulted in an extraordinary flowering of Turkish entrepreneurship that is still ongoing. After Özal's death, Gülen established good relations with Turkey's first female Prime Minister Tansu Çiller, whose True Path Party (*Doğru Yol*) also enjoyed much support from conservative and religious elements in the country, including Nurcu followers. But Gülen later became disillusioned with Çiller and her corruption and extremely opportunistic policies, which courted the military as often as it did religious circles.

Gülen also had closer ties with the coalition government of Bülent Ecevit and Devlet Bahceli of the MHP. In fact, the lower echelons of the MHP are more religiously oriented than the upper echelons, and see Turkish nationalism as inextricably entwined with the glories of Turkey's Ottoman Islamic past. Due to the military-imposed policies to cleanse Islam from the public sphere, many conservative Turks who voted for the MHP became disillusioned. Since the party leadership supported the military's crackdown against religion, and did not oppose the anti-headscarf campaign and the proposed laws to purge the bureaucracy of all those with religious affiliations, many among its Anatolian voter base abandoned the MHP and also felt alienated from the Gülen community. The followers of the Gülen movement tend to be pragmatic in their political choices, voting on issues, and local alliances. Religion is not the sole criterion for their support, but they will not support candidates who are openly hostile to religion and they prefer "clean" and politically untarnished candidates. Within that context, votes can go to nearly any party or candidate.

In order to understand the current changing nature of the political engagement of the Gülen community (i.e., its close alliance with the JDP), one needs to understand the changing sociopolitical context, as well as the pressure from the military to eliminate the movement. Since the late 1980s and 1990s, the civilian governments, especially the Motherland Party (ANAP) of Turgut Özal, Tansu Çiller of DYP, and Bülent Ecevit Social Democrats (DSP), have all defended the activities of the Gülen movement from Kemalist hard-liners, for it had strictly adopted a quietist strategy and preferred to focus on informal ties with politicians seeking to remain equidistant from all political parties. This strategy radically changed after the 2002 elections in reaction to the aggressive tactics of the military to overthrow the JDP government and also to criminalize the social and cultural activities of the Gülen movement. What factors explain this shift from appeasement and accommodation? There are several points that shed light on the current shift. One of them is the collapse of the center-right parties as a result of the 1997 military intervention that targeted their grassroots by eliminating conservative-religious networks. Moreover, a series of secret military plans were leaked to the public. These plans sought to destroy the Gülen movement by falsely linking it to terrorism and illegal activities.[31] This perception of common threat facing both the JDP and the Gülen community created an alliance against the aggressive Kemalist military and bureaucratic establishment. Third, the harmonization laws, which were required for European Union membership, helped to create a freer political environment for the Gülen movement and others to more openly engage in political activities and its support of the JDP due to its commitment to the EU process, continued democratization and the rule of law.

Although there are major differences in approach between the JDP and the Gülen movement when it comes to politics, they are in a symbiotic relationship from which both have often, but not always, benefited. This expedient relationship is a source of concern, if not a fear, for more secular sectors of Turkish society. Although the Gülen movement reluctantly supported the JDP in 2002 elections due to its skepticism about the JDP's overtly political Islamist roots and concerns over the international reaction to an electoral victory of a pro-Islamic party, it became the major supporter of the JDP by the next election cycle in the 2007 and 2011 elections. As the Kemalist establishment and its media outlets openly sought to launch another "soft coup," the Gülen movement this time abandoned appeasement, and used its means to support the JDP. In spite of this new alliance confronting a common enemy, there are several policy areas over which the Gülen movement and the JDP are in conflict. Some important JDP ministers are not happy with the involvement of the Gülenist activists in policy making. Prime Minister Erdoğan, who is not a follower of the Gülen movement, and does not want to share power with it, seeks to maintain some distance from it by supporting Cemil Çiçek and Beşir Atalay, two outspoken critics of Gülen. Since the Gülen movement's relations with other parties are in a lamentable state at present, and Erdoğan is wildly popular with its rank and file, he is assured that Gülen lacks an alternative party to the JDP.

The Gülen community has been a main supporter of the JDP government in terms of votes and support in its powerful media outlets. The movement has closely allied itself with the government to promote desired legal and administrative changes. Some JDP government ministers have publicly expressed their opposition against the movement's lobbying activities, and also the recruitment of pro-Gülenist bureaucrats within the state. According to US Embassy reports released by Wikileaks and some retired police chiefs, the Gülen movement is controlling the national police force, and they claim that the movement has also been targeting the judicial branch to gain influence.[32] It is a growing concern on the part of the old establishment that such control over the national police force in Turkey will increase the likelihood that journalists and scholars would face harassment, or even imprisonment, if they dared to write critically of the Gülen movement. On the basis of my interviews, I would argue that the movement is indeed more influential within the police force, but claims of its control of the police force are quite exaggerated.

In recent years, there have also been criticisms about the influence of the Gülen movement from within the JDP government as well. For instance, Cemil Çiçek, the current speaker of the Parliament, and Beşir Atalay, the former Minister of the Interior and current Deputy Prime Minister, also stated that the Gülen community is involving itself in the decision-making processes and also recruiting their own followers into the bureaucracy. Indeed, in both cases the Gülen community has been lobbying on a number of issues.[33] Neither Çiçek nor Atalay are used to such direct challenges and input from social movements, and they both represent the "old ways of governing the country," that is, governing without the input of civil society. In my interviews in Ankara, I was surprised to hear how some bureaucrats and ministers were quite critical of the movement. They all criticized the movement's "lobbying efforts" on a number of issues. These bureaucrats and politicians believe that the "bureaucracy" knows what is best for the society and no "lobbying group" should interfere in their decision. A high ranking advisor to the Minister of Interior said:

> The movement wants to tell us what is good for the public. When they make an argument in the name of the "public" they mean what is good for them. We the bureaucrats and the JDP are above all these small interest groups and can have much healthier judgements of what is good for the public. There is an increasing anger against the movement within the Erdoğan government because they interfere with almost every regulation or appointment. I think the perception that the Turkish police force is heavily recruited by the followers of the movement is very dangerous for the credibility of the police force in the country.[34]

When I told the advisor, who happens to be a bureaucrat as well, that it is perfectly normal for the Gülen movement to lobby on public policy as it understands the public interests, he said "yes, but there are no other groups out there in Ankara as powerful as the Gülen movement to balance their power." The relations between Gülen and the state bureaucracy is a process of ideological struggle, of debate, move and counter-move that have been taking place on a number of levels in the society and the state.

This represents a major paradox in the current JDP government. They appreciate the support of the Gülen movement, but they are very unhappy with the constant engagement of the movement in policy formulation. The old guard of the state treats all forms of grassroots movements and pressure as a threat to the autonomy of the state. There are major disagreements between the old guard, which stresses that the public good is best defended and defined by the bureaucracy and the new understanding of bottom-up politics; that the public is the people and they should organize and get the bureaucracy to do what is best for them. The main source of disagreement between the movement and the current JDP government is over the role of social groups in politics and the movement's insistence that electoral success does not bring an end to politics. The movement has been successful not only in pushing the military back into its barracks and demilitarizing the political landscape, but also in introducing a new form of politics by actively engaging with decision makers to shape the policies of the government. The movement believes that the bureaucrats are there to serve the needs of the public and are not in a position to define what is good for the public from on high.

The Gülen movement has distanced itself from the government on a number of foreign policy issues as well: controversially, they do not support the JDP government's very popular critical stance toward the aggressive regional policies of Israel's Likud bloc because of an attitude of appeasement and exaggerated fears of the power of the Israeli lobby to harm Turkey. The Gülen movement is also critical of the government's waning enthusiasm for becoming a member of the EU. Gülen has always defended Turkey's integration with European institutions, especially the EU.[35] His pro-EU vision is based on social, economic and political reasons. Gülen regards the EU as a major democratizing factor and pillar of support for human rights and civilian rule. I would like to summarize my conversation with Gülen in the following way: democracy is necessary to control radicalism and integrate marginal groups into the political and economic system. The EU is essential for the consolidation of democracy in Turkey. Thus, moderation requires Turkey's entry into the EU. Gülen has rejected the arguments of the anti-EU coalition; that EU membership would lead to cultural and religious assimilation of Turkey, and that there is no way to overcome inherent "Christian animosity" against Islam. Gülen has disagreed with these two common arguments heard from radical Islamic and nationalistic groups. Gülen genuinely sees interaction with diverse cultures, and positive encounters with the Abrahamic faiths, as a source of dynamism and a way of rejuvenating the universal aspects of Islam.

CONCLUSION

Fethullah Gülen has become the most dominant religio-political leader of Turkey because he come to understand a wider range of ideational and material factors relevant to national and international politics and the prevailing waves of social transformation. Gülen's actions have always had limited objectives, and he has never punched above his weight. His main policy has always been to coopt, rather than humiliate, his critics or adversaries. While Gülen has been vernacularizing modernity in Islamic terminology, his secularist critics are still wedded to the nineteenth-century concepts of politics as administration, secularism as the new lifestyle, scientism and positivist social engineering.

The Gülen movement's understanding of politics and the political process differentiate it from the military and bureaucratic elite. Its main political objective is to transform society by raising the moral consciousness of individuals. By raising moral consciousness, the movement hopes to cleanse the bureaucracy of widespread corruption, increase the efficiency and transparency of state institutions, reinvigorate public work ethic to serve the people in order to enhance the legitimacy of the state, and create opportunity spaces for marginalized sectors of the Anatolian population.

10

The Critics of the Movement

> They do not view the world through the lens that we do. They do not believe in the hereafter as we do. The values that are dear to us mean nothing to them. We seek the hereafter, paradise, divine beauty, and say that we do it to please God without any other motive. But they see nothing other than this world. We are not motivated by fame, glory, position, or money. But they make those the center of their lives. We say that one should not be deceived by this transient world, and that we should do whatever we do in this ephemeral world with the hereafter in mind and to please God. But they think and believe exactly the opposite. We know that the tastes of this world are like poisonous honey and that pleasures are always accompanied by woes. We believe that all pleasures, legitimate or illegitimate, try us in this world. But they do not understand such beliefs.
>
> GÜLEN[1]

Both within Turkey and outside it, there exists an intense debate over the ultimate aims of the Gülen movement. Critics of Gülen insist that the goal of the movement is to establish hegemony over Turkish civil society, some going as far as to assert the movement is laying the groundwork for seizing the state. However, so far this study has indicated that the movement is motivated neither by the desire to establish societal hegemony nor to seize control of the Turkish state. Rather, it seeks to shape society and politics by developing and strengthening a sense of morality and virtue among believers and between communities, the state, and humanity as a whole. By turning piety into an action, the

Gülen movement has without doubt been a major influence upon social, political and economic life in Turkey and beyond. It is this influence, which is in some unchecked manner, that has energized both its rivals and critics.

The main source of this tension is a diametrically opposed conception of the role and nature of civil society. The critics of the Gülen movement maintain a rigid understanding of civil society, arguing that it is, and should be, bound together by mutual interests and individualistic rights-based associations rather than by primordial ties such as religion or ethnicity. Moreover, civil society, for them, is a site that exists in order to enhance individual freedoms and thus a necessary instrument to sustain a secular lifestyle. This perspective also presupposes that the state, as a moral and enlightened institution, must play a role of protecting liberty and preventing primordial identities and associations from gaining strength in society. They argue that the Gülen movement's notion of civil society embodies uncivil exclusionary ideas and trends, such as religious and ethnic solidarity, and that these influences on the state inhibit the development of democracy. By referring to the appeals made to Kurdish and Islamic identity, they regard these movements as a threat to a liberal concept of civil society. Their main target has been a communitarian concept of civil society and democracy. Indeed, some, if not all, ethnic or religious-based movements are authoritarian and communalist; and some of these are even prone to violence. These movements repress pluralism and threaten to close spaces for the development of individualism.

The second vision of civil society is a mixture of civil and primordial ties that emphasizes the positive role of religion in the formation of social capital. Turkish socioreligious groups argue that they, along with Sufi networks, empower associational life, build bridges between diverse faiths and cultures, and sustain moral values that are necessary for civil society. The Gülen movement, in fact, presents a compelling case for the examination of the social effects of pietistic activism, and its role in motivating social action for the realization of the common good. The quest for a meaningful life is at the center of the current Islamic revival in many Muslim countries. The revival is not only about identity and morality, but stresses justice above all. Just like many religious leaders, Gülen identifies greed, egoism, fear and ignorance as the sources of human sufferings. The Gülen movement with its amorphous networks utilizes existing opportunity spaces in education, commerce, the media and politics to redefine social relations, and similarly, it utilizes the boundary between the state and society, to foster dialogue between cultures. Gülen's understanding of Islamic activism is based on compassion and mercy as the two critical values for enhancing civil society. These two competing visions of civil society are at the center of the current debate raging over the influence of the Gülen movement. It needs to be examined in detail why some leftists, Alevis, Kurds, and even rival

Islamists take a hostile stance against the movement. Does the Gülen community foster or impede the thickening of civil society? What does this debate over the role of the movement tell us about the nature of civil society in Turkey?

KEMALIST SECULAR CRITICS

This first group includes secularists, such as the Kemalists, and some leftist intellectuals, who demand the complete exclusion of religious groups and claims within civil society and politics, and who sternly resist any change to the status quo. They regard the movement as a threat to their "well-off" position and also to their lifestyle. For instance, most of the members and the followers of the Republican Peoples Party (CHP) regard the movement as a threat to secularism, democracy and civil society. The Doğan Media Corporation, a conglomerate with deep ties to the Kemalist military and state institutions (which often received preferential treatment in bidding for state contracts and was accused of involvement in large-scale tax evasion), undertook a public media campaign in support of the February 28, 1997, "soft coup", which claimed that all Islamic movements were a threat to liberal values and civil society.

The secular sector, which includes a large number of scholars and intellectuals, caricatured the movement as an Islamist political force with the goal of Islamizing society and the state. Scholars such as Binnaz Toprak, a leading political scientist, and legal scholar Ahmet İnsel, as well as some pro-establishment journalists, tend to explain the success of the movement in terms of the weakening of the social state and the search for identity in anomic urban centers. They claim that as a result of neoliberal economic policies, the Turkish state, like others in the developing world, had made severe cuts in social services. The Gülen movement became successful by stepping in to fill this gap by providing a number of vital social services. Toprak's field study about the Islamization of everyday life and practices in Anatolia, and the marginalization of Turkey's "other" identities (Alevi and Kurds) and ideological (secular/leftist) groups, led to a major debate.[2] In fact, the Islamically conservative government has not only been consolidating its own economic power through government bids, public land sales and access to state bank credits, it has also been creating its own separate cultural milieu. This critique further argues that the movement also plays an important role in raising political consciousness and encouraging people to vote for the JDP. Yet, there is almost no room for dissent within the movement itself, and all followers are asked to vote en masse for the JDP. This "guided" political education allegedly indicates that the Gülen movement has not fully internalized individual-centric liberal democracy and seeks to subordinate individual wills to the larger goals of the community.

Turkey's secular left intellectual elite have been incapable of adequately comprehending the Gülen movement because they have framed it within their own rigid ideological presumptions and perspectives. Such a shallow and dogmatic understanding, for example, is typified by Ahmet İnsel, who presents himself as the guru of leftist political academicians. Rather than trying to understand the sociological origins of the movement and the reasons for its appeal and success, he ironically mimics the same sort of the criticism of the Kemalist coup leaders in trying to criminalize the movement. He states:

> Gülen is the product of the struggle against the Communist foundations of the 1960s. Look.... The deep state sees everything acceptable as long as it is under their control. If something goes beyond its control, then that immediately becomes a threatening element. Gülen has a claim to be "educating a golden generation." This is Turco–Islamic elitism. Just as the Jesuit priests had.... "We will educate a golden generation in the schools. Later we will dominate the world with these elites, we will govern it." That is his idea.[3]

According to İnsel, it is actually the Kemalist "deep state" that created the Gülen movement, and Gülen seeks to "rule" the world by educating a new generation. İnsel, who is also a columnist in daily *Radikal*, believes that the Gülen movement is behind the government's policies on the Kurdish question, and accuses it of masterminding the arrest of pro-PKK (the Kurdistan Workers' Party) activists, scholars and journalists. When in October and November 2011, the Turkish police arrested several hundred people due to their alleged ties with the PKK, İnsel openly accused the Gülen movement of being the architects of these "anti-democratic" policies.[4] This baseless claim is not only absurd, but also paranoid and indicative of the intellectual poverty of many of Turkey's leftist intellectuals and their inability to understand the role of religious networks and social movements within their own country. They seldom carry out fieldwork or familiarize themselves with sociological theory and literature outside of a narrow Marxist purview and thus have the tendency to explain almost everything from either an ideological lens or from the angle of conspiracy theories.

As the writer Bill Park aptly argues:

> [T]he more one perceives the movement as a more-or-less hierarchical, disciplined, and "conspiratorial" organization that seeks to penetrate and undermine the Turkish state and society from within, the more one is inclined to adopt an essentially political interpretation of the movement's activities. This is precisely the model of the Gülen movement that many in Turkey's elite hold, and fear. On the other hand, although the movement's lack of transparency and the weakness of its internal democracy and

capacity for self-criticism are unsettling, this does not necessarily render it an extremist phenomenon.[5]

In fact, in an interview in Nişantaşı, Istanbul, a secularist academic, who teaches in a private university said:

> I am very unhappy about the future of our civil society. Wherever I turn in Istanbul, I see the activities of Islamic groups and their associations. Even in our university, I have just found out that the majority of our students, who have scholarships due to their high university scores, are staying in Gülen community run dormitories. This is shocking! The University provides them with a scholarship to foster critical thinking and expects the students to become open-minded and defend a secular lifestyle. I do not understand why they are staying in these dormitories. Their stipend is enough for them to rent an apartment.[6]

Indeed, many secularists and some liberals consider these communitarian networks as undermining the formation of a vibrant civil society. When I interviewed one of these students, who was actually staying in a Gülen-run dormitory, he said:

> I stay in this dormitory fully knowing that it is run by the Gülen community. Look! This is my decision to stay here not my family's or someone else's. So I have decided to stay here because in this dormitory I feel that I am attached to a community, and that I'm part of a group, and I have a sense of solidarity with other students here, and we are all involved in some communal activity of the movement. Here you learn to care for other people. I do not understand how my staying here in this dormitory undermines civil society. On the contrary, the solidarity and cooperative work skills I learn here would help civil society. The problem of our secularist intellectuals is that they really neither know Turkish society nor the social importance of religion. They live in their egocentric prison and think that society is only based on the reconciliation of conflicting interests of different groups.[7]

Some criticism of the insular nature of these Gülen communities is valid. Although such communal networks provide the necessary glue for civil society, they seldom reach out to other groups in order to build bridges. While the students who stay in these dormitories are all respectful and clean-cut, they also seem to have limited social contact with people of different worldviews and lifestyles.

I shall summarize the criticism of the Gülen movement under four categories on the basis of my interviews: (a) the movement does not encourage critical thinking and individualism; it is communitarian and prevents critical thinking by stressing Islamic-based values; and it seeks to create a conservative society; (b) the movement provides grassroots support for the perpetuation of social conservatism, it is politically partisan supporting the JDP, and it is part of the governing coalition; (c) the solidarity and powerful networks of the movement lead to the "othering" of other groups and exclude them from the processes of social mobility as the movement seeks to control key state positions such as the ministry of interior, national education, higher education and justice; (d) it promotes patriarchal values that are not limited to traditional gender relations while by stressing hierarchy based on one's position within the Gülen community.

The high level of group coordination, success, efficiency and influence make many people think the movement is a hierarchical organization with clear headquarters and directors; however, there is no central headquarters or board of directors. Then, one might fairly ask how to explain the group's coordination and efficiency. The answer is that this is achieved via a shared and internalized cognitive map of worldview, lifestyle and action. The followers of the movement share common sensibilities and attitudes, and dress and behave in similar ways. This inner uniformity, which critics contend stifles individualism, also explains the movement's success and patterns of conduct in diverse localities. They are motivated by shared ideas and patterns of action and a strong sense of solidarity, which increases as they gain economic success and political influence. In this sense, they are not very different from the Mormon Church in America, absent the clear hierarchy.

THE CONTROVERSIAL CASES OF AHMET ŞIK, NEDIM ŞENER, AND HANEFI AVCI

Critics of the movement, including scholars and journalists who treat it primarily as a political force, argue that it seeks to infiltrate state institutions such as the national police force, the ministry of education and the judiciary. They also insist that the movement intimidates its critics either by using the police force to prosecute them, or, if they are in the bureaucracy or private sector, by preventing their upward social mobility. They all point out journalist Ahmet Şık's statement during his detention by the police that "whoever touches [the Gülen movement] gets burned."[8] By referring also to the controversial cases of the journalist Nedim Şener and Hanefi Avcı,[9] who ran afoul of the movement and the police, the secularist critics argue that the movement is flexing its muscle to intimidate and silence its critics and alternative voices. Şık, Şener, and

Avcı all have written separate critical books on the Gülen movement, and all three have run afoul of state prosecutors and the police. Upon reading these three books, I found them to be unimpressive from an analytical perspective, relying mainly on hearsay and anecdotal evidence to support their claims of a Gülenist conspiracy. The books genuinely reflect an alarmist view about the power and role of the Gülen movement in Turkey by those who have been tied to the Kemalist ancien régime, and are now witnessing their own power fade away. The arrest of these three writers, however, seems to be not only related to the books they have written critical of the Gülen movement, but also due to their past close engagements with certain networks of the the pro-coup "deep-state." These networks use legal and illegal means to attack and criminalize all of those seen as challenging the authority of the Kemalist establishment. For instance, the popular website known as Odatv, with which Şener and Şık have been associated, became a major source of misinformation and scurrilous attacks on scholars, journalists and politicians critical of the Kemalist military-bureaucratic establishment.[10] It would thus be naïve to conclude that these two journalists, and a former police chief, were arrested solely because of their anti-Gülen writings given the fact that there are dozens of books published in Turkey that are not only critical of the movement, but also very derogatory toward Gülen himself.[11] In these cases, however, there has been no censorship or prosecution of the writers.

Following the arrest of these journalists and writers, both domestic and international media outlets became openly critical of the Gülen movement and its alleged efforts to censor critics. In response, however, Gülen has rejected the accusation that he was behind the arrest of the journalists, or that he had worked to block the publication of their books.[12] Turkey's opposition leaders, Kemal Kılıçdaroğlu of the Kemalist Republican Peoples Party (CHP), and Devlet Bahçeli of the far right National Movement Party (MHP) have openly criticized the Gülen movement, and Bahçeli has even demanded that Gülen stop his activities within the police force.[13] Following this barrage of criticism, Gülen issued the following statement to Hüseyin Gülerce, who sees himself as the spokesperson of the movement in Turkey, and who also writes a regular column in the daily *Zaman*, the flagship newspaper of the movement, saying:

> Why are others hostile to the movement? Why do they plan plots and attack the movement anytime they have the chance? We should take a look at ourselves. Are there any mistakes in our methodology and style? Is it because we have faults in our approach, because we are negligent or because we see certain people as the "opposite front," that there is a hostile view toward us? It is wrong to immediately blame people without first considering these possibilities and without first confronting and

questioning ourselves. I wish those people had good intentions for us and told us what our shortfalls are with the intention of helping us to improve ourselves. On the other hand, we should question our actions, confront ourselves and ask, "What are we missing, what do we need to do." I wish they would tell us what it is that we're missing, whether its reading, talking, comparative reading or making sacrifices, without insulting and offending us. We would consider it guidance. We would see it as a guide to improving ourselves, to improving the people within this movement. We would easily kiss the hands [an act of respect] of people who extend them with the purpose of showing us the way.[14]

In recent years, the movement has gradually become a controversial force in Turkey's already polarized society. Critics of the Gülen movement regard it as dangerous mainly because it presents a new and alternative form of modernity and civil society that is in harmony with religion and the Ottoman past. It also opens new opportunity spaces for the hitherto marginalized traditional Turkish Anatolian majority in high levels of the bureaucracy, security forces, judiciary, universities, and business, and finally it seems poised to cement the JDP's dominance of Turkish electoral politics far into the future, marking a decisive end to Kemalist hegemony over Turkish state and society. With the JDP's consolidation of power under the popular leadership of Prime Minister Erdoğan, the Gülen movement has finally agreed to a closer alliance with it, becoming in the process an indispensable source of political and economic support. Ironically, this will likely mean that some of the fears of the Kemalist ancien régime in Turkish state and society will come true. Just as they used the reigns of power to promote like-minded individuals to the commanding heights of politics, the military, and the economy, the Gülen communities' influence will only expand in state and society institutions as it moves officially closer to the dominant Turkish Muslim democratic political center now consolidated by the JDP. According to some anecdotal evidence, there are "representatives" of the movement in prominent levels of state institutions, and they are poised to promote like-minded followers as the Kemalists had done before them.

ALEVI CRITICS OF THE GÜLEN MOVEMENT

As the Kemalist secular establishment decisively alienated the Anatolian Turkish Sunni heartland, they increasingly came to fall back upon a long marginalized but sizable segment of the Turkish population represented by the heterodox Alevi community. The Alevis are the second-largest religious community in Turkey, following the Sunnis.[15] They are a multiethnic religious group that includes both Turks and Kurds and that constitutes between 15 to 20 percent of

Turkey's total population. The Alevis are a syncretic religious community in that their belief system combines elements of Shiism, Turkish shamanism, and even some Christian doctrines, while lacking a standardized textual tradition and ritual practice. The Alevi belief system varies from region to region, and until the 1960s, most Alevis lived in rural Anatolia. However, presently, they are found in large numbers in urban settings as well and have become increasingly mobilized and educated. During the leftist political activism in the 1960s, many educated Alevis became involved in Marxist political movements, which played a critical role in the politicization and articulation of the Alevi identity. Interestingly, many of the Alevi professionals and intellectuals who had been active in the revolutionary movements subsequently traded in their leftist convictions and converted into ethno-religious entrepreneurs. Therefore, it is important to note that modern Alevi political consciousness evolved within the leftist movement of the 1970s, and as a response to urbanization, industrialization, and education coupled with a keen appreciation of the discrimination their community had faced within a stridently Sunni Ottoman state. Until the 1960s, Alevi identity and traditions existed in separate, oral-based, often isolated communities, which protected the community from outside influence. However, with economic development, expanding political participation, and educational opportunities in urban centers, new forms of Alevi political consciousness evolved. Today, Turkish society is divided by ethnic (Kurdish vs. Turkish), sectarian (Alevi vs. Sunni), and ideological (Kemalist secular vs. Muslim democratic) cleavages.

Alevis differentiate themselves from Sunni Muslims by, among other things, not abiding by the Sunni-Hanafi conception of shari'a and associated religious practices. Alevis do not perform the five daily prayers, fast during Ramadan, nor do they make a pilgrimage to Mecca. They also reject the authority of the *ulema* or establishment of Islamic scholars. Because of their heterodox beliefs and practices, Alevis have historically been a target of discrimination and marginalization. The Turkish Sunni majority tended to portray Alevis as "outcasts" or "heretics" and even "unbelievers." Many Sunni Muslims, including the supporters of the Gülen movement, regard the Alevi sect as being theologically "wrong" and the official Sunni religious establishment still refuses to recognize them as an official and distinct religious minority.[16] Thus, when we analyze the relations between the Alevis and the Gülen community, we must keep in mind the larger history of misperceptions and prejudices between the two communities. Although, having said this, it should be noted that Gülen himself has advocated for more rights for the Alevi community, and has asked his followers to establish schools and university exam prep centers, such as Haydar and Düzgün, in Alevi-inhabited areas for their advancement. Indeed, the most prestigious high school in the heavily Kurdish-Alevi city of Tunceli is *Muzur Fen Lisesi* (high school), which was established by the movement. Despite initial hostile local reactions, the school has been able to garner the support of many Alevis due to its academic excellence. The Gülen communities' Abant platform organized its 13th meeting titled "Alevism: Historical, Cultural, Folkloric, and Contemporary Dimensions" on March 17-18, 2007. After defining Alevism, as an "interpretation" within Islam centered on the Prophet Muhammad, his cousin and son-in-law Ali, and certain Sufi masters of Anatolia, the meeting called upon the Turkish state to finally provide legal status to the *cemevis* (Alevi houses of worship). Nonetheless, the final communiqué of the meeting was sharply criticized by prominent Alevi organizations because it sought to define Alevi identity from a Sunni Islamic perspective.[17] Indeed, few Alevis themselves chose to participate in the meeting.

Since there is no universally recognized religious authority or center, most Alevis are organized in terms of associations and foundations. There are more than 300 such Alevi associations, and all attempts at establishing a unified federation have failed due to the internal and theological divisions within the group. A few of these associations have developed closer ties with the Gülen community such as the Cem Foundation of İzzettin Doğan, which represents the economic elite of Alevis, and has developed very positive ties with the movement. Doğan himself said:

> I know Fethullah Gülen. He is a person that I respect. I see him as a thinker and a philosopher who is interested in Islamic issues. We have met several times and he has visited me. He has made positive contributions to the construction of *cemevis* [Alevi places of worship]. As you might remember, years ago, he said, "*Cemevis* should be constructed next to mosques." This is a considerably important statement. Furthermore, he is open to discussion. In this regard, I have never had any doubts about Gülen's ideas.[18]

Indeed, in his book *Vuslat Muştusu* (Good News of Reunion), Gülen deconstructs popular Sunni misperceptions about the Alevi community. Yet, there is a gap between Gülen's understanding and acceptance of the Alevi community and that of his own Sunni grassroots, which still tends to look down on them.

İzzetin Doğan aside, however, most of the other Alevi associations are very skeptical of the Gülen movement, and they are hostile to its expanding power. Some of the Alevi elite is extremely critical of the Gülen movement in three areas: (1) the movement does not officially recognize Alevi Islam as legitimate; (2) the movement seeks to assimilate Alevi religious identity through a set of strategies to convert Alevi youth to Sunni Islam; and (3) the movement seeks to exclude and marginalize Alevis in key state positions and uses its media outlets to dehumanize them as atheists and heretics.

During my interviews in Istanbul, an Alevi bookstore owner, played for me a you-tube video of Gülen's speech on the Alevis.[19] In that speech, Gülen characterizes the Alevis of Tunceli as being intermixed with Armenians and other Christian doctrines and accuses them of atheism (*dinsizlik*). Moreover, he also showed me the latest issue of *Alevi Rapor*, which identifies ongoing human rights violation against Alevis by the Turkish state.[20] The first page had a section with a subheading entitled "the Alevi community is targeted by the Gülen movement." The analysis, by referring to an article published in the *Turkish Review* journal in January 2011, argues that the Gülen movement is seeking to dehumanize and marginalize the Alevi community.[21] In fact, this particular article in the journal was not only derogatory against Alevis but also reflected a deeper ideological chasm that emerged in recent Turkish politics. The article claimed that "the Kemalist regime had a carefully organized sectarian agenda. Educated members of the Alevi community were co-opted for significant posts in the army and the higher bureaucracy, including the judiciary." The article claims that Kemalist secularism "allowed an Alevi elite to lead the large Sunni masses." The *Alevi Rapor* analysis indicates that the bitter conflict between Kemalist secularists and Turkish Muslim democratic political movements has increasingly taken on a sectarian tone. If one examines the evolution of the Gülen movement's position on the Alevis, one sees a paradigmatic shift and moderation. The new discourse of Gülen on the Alevi rights and concerns, which is different from two decades ago, recognizes the authenticity and autonomy of the Alevi interpretation of Islam as legitimate, and he calls upon the government to address the genuine concerns of the Alevis in order to consolidate the social cohesion of the society.[22]

There are several critical articles, which have been issued from within the Alevi community about the Gülen movement-led "Islamization" process of the Turkish state. The Alevis have also accused the movement of marginalizing Alevis and excluding them from the political and economic processes. The representation of the Alevi minority continues to lag in state institutions and higher education and there is a growing radicalization of Alevi political consciousness. However, I would argue that the present Sunni–Alevi polarization is more a result of the policies of the JDP rather than the Gülen movement. It is further compounded by the fact that some Alevi community leaders have taken strident positions in support of Kemalism and the right of the military to overthrow civilian governments in its defense. The association of a number of prominent Alevi leaders and intellectuals with Kemalist authoritarianism has significantly set back progress in intercommunal relations. However, the close connection between the Gülen movement and the governing party (JDP) also makes the movement a target for the disenchanted Alevi community.

THE KURDISH OR MUSLIM QUESTION

Altan Tan, a current member of Parliament of the pro-Kurdish DTP, wrote the following in *Today's Zaman*:

> DTP circles maintain that the AK Party [JDP] and religious groups like the Fethullah Gülen community are seeking to gain control over the Kurdish people with charitable acts. According to this argument, the Kurdish people, who suffer from constant and prevailing poverty, remain ambivalent between adherence to their national identity and their reliance on economic aid. The Islamic groups exploit their despair to promote their agendas.
>
> This same argument points a finger at the Fethullah Gülen community in particular. It is said that the activities of this community in Diyarbakır and other cities in the region attract the attention of desperate and poor families who are concerned about the future of their children. Smart and talented Kurdish children are picked by this community and provided with financial support during their studies. At the same time, their Kurdish identity is deliberately undermined through propaganda.[23]

The third group critical of the Gülen movement and its activities are the Kurdish nationalists within Turkey.[24] They too have long-standing grievances against the Turkish Republic and this has continued with their struggles against the military and various governing parties. Although the JDP has taken historic and significant steps toward improving the political and cultural rights of Turkish Kurds, many activist and politicized Kurds believe that the JDP has not gone far enough to meet their demands for political equality and the sharing of sovereignty. Moreover, the growing closeness between the JDP, the Gülen community and religious Turkish Kurds greatly worries many secular Kurdish nationalists. Unlike the Kemalists, the Gülen community has never been intolerant toward Muslims of other ethnic backgrounds, viewing them as fellow believers who shared a common Ottoman Islamic bond. After all, Said Nursi himself was a Kurd, and many of those in the southeast of the country who later rebelled against the harsh homogenizing policies of the Kemalist state in the 1930s did so more in defense of their Muslim faith than out of ethnolinguistic consciousness or enmity toward ethnic Turks. A nationalist Kurdish intellectual who lives in the United States argues that "Fethullah, a shrewd leader, does not directly affiliate himself with politics but instead shapes policies behind the scenes and counsels his followers behind closed doors about ways to implement his directives.... Gülen tries to assimilate Kurds by emphasizing the Ottoman ideology in his school, causing many Kurds to see themselves as Osmanlı rather than as Selahattin Kurdi."[25]

Although the Kurdish sector of the population is divided on religious and political grounds, the secular nationalist Kurds, along with followers of Hizbullah, a radical Islamist group that justifies the use of violence, are quite critical of the movement.[26] Since 2004, there has been increasing hostility between the nationalist Kurdish organizations sympathetic to the PKK and the Gülen movement. Many secular or Marxist Kurdish nationalists in Diyarbakır, the largest Kurdish inhabited city, consider the movement as a potent threat and rival to Kurdish secessionist nationalism as it has often succeeded in bringing Turkish and Kurdish Muslims together in a warm embrace within the movement itself.[27] A Kurdish lawyer said:

> I know the movement is the rival organization to Kurdish nationalism. However, I support the education activities of the movement. It also tried to build bridges between the two people. I think stressing Islam as a shared identity is important. It is Islam that prevents the balkanization of Diyarbakır. But the movement should not let itself become the arm of some oppressive forces within the Turkish state. Since the 2011 elections, many of my friends have become more critical of the movement. They now treat it as the vehicle of the Turkish state to deny our separate Kurdish identity.[28]

A well organized and significant number of Kurds support the activities of the Gülen movement in the Kurdish inhabited cities of the southeast. A Kurd who considers himself a follower of the Gülen movement said:

> [T]he only hope we have in this region is the Gülen community. It not only provides the best schools for our kids but also provides some breathing room between the security forces and the PKK. We are all Muslims and have lived together for over 1,000 years. The roots of this senseless violence in this region are ignorance, poverty and intolerant bureaucrats.[29]

The movement has mobilized its networks and resources by establishing schools, reading rooms, hospitals, and humanitarian aid organizations in order to stress a common Ottoman Muslim heritage and identity while undermining and containing the influence of the PKK.[30] There is a tireless competition over the souls and loyalty of the Kurdish youth in southeast Turkey. The JDP government now also provides all the necessary means for the movement to counterbalance not only the PKK but the Kurdish Hizbullah as well. An active duty colonel in the Turkish Army, imbued with traditional Kemalist values, and who serves in Ağrı, a Kurdish populated city, said: "I changed my view of the Gülen movement after I came to Ağrı and saw what the Gülen people were doing there to rebuild the moral fabric of the society and offer a first-rate education for the region's children. We should have started doing this 30 years ago." The Turkish state officials in the region also greatly appreciate the activities of the Gülen movement, in coordination with moderate and religiously inclined Kurds who are also strongly opposed to violence, whether from the PKK or the Turkish military.

The Gülen movement operates several schools in Kurdish inhabited cities. In addition to these high schools, there are a growing number of "tutoring centers," such as those in Diyarbakir where 29 centers, also known as *okuma odaları*, can be found. Such schools and tutoring centers are now the main avenue of upward mobility, allowing Turkish Kurds to enter the ranks of economic and political leadership not only in the southeast, but also other parts of the country as well. A parent whose children were attending such a Gülen school related the following:

> These schools provide the best possible education. Not just education, but they also protect them from joining any illegal organizations. They teach them how to be respectful and become good Muslims. I am very happy that I can afford to send my two sons to these schools.[31]

Indeed, these schools are the only ones in the region that provide proper science and foreign language (English) education. In addition to education, they also seek to shape the moral character of these students and promote their sense of pride as both Kurdish Muslims and citizens of Turkey. No Turkish secular or even Kurdish groups operate such private schools in these cities. Wealthier Turkish Kurds, who maintain close ties with the state, also provide financial support to these Gülen schools.

Interestingly, the Gülen movement also has close ties with the Kurdish regional government in Iraq. There are 15 Gülen schools in Arbil, Sulaymaniya, Dohuk and Kirkuk, and there are over 2,500 students studying in the various Gülen schools.[32] The Gülen movement is the most active trans-border network between Turkey and the Kurdish regional government in Iraq. Moreover, the largest private university in Iraqi Kurdistan, known as Işık University, was established by the movement in Erbil.

The Gülen movement is seeking to reconstitute the historic ties among the various Muslim ethnic groups in Turkey by stressing a common historic, cultural and religious past. However, while secular Kurdish nationalists regard the Gülenist as still excessively Turkish, many Turkish nationalists accuse the Gülenist of being too cosmopolitan and not Turkish enough. This unresolved conflict goes back to the origins of the Kemalist Turkish Republic. In seeking to overthrow Turkey's Ottoman Muslim heritage and identity, the Kemalists also effectively undermined the bonds that had held traditional Anatolian Turkish and Kurdish Muslim society together. The Turkish Republic alternatively neglected the population of the southeast, or subjected it to harsh campaigns of assimilation, which targeted both their ethnolinguistic identity and culture, as well as their religious faith. Ironically, it was the ham-fisted policies and the ideological rigidity of the Kemalist military-bureaucratic establishment that would prove to be the best recruiting agent for the nascent PKK insurgency led by Abdullah Öcalan.

Initially, the PKK's militant Marxist-Leninist ideology, ruthless elimination of dissent and cult of personality surrounding the leader, held little natural appeal to traditional Turkish Kurds. However, because Kemalist ideology viewed both Kurdish and Muslim identity as a threat to be eliminated, the Turkish state could never carry out an effective hearts and minds strategy in the southeast, instead it helped to greatly fuel the insurgency by relying mainly on brute force. It is the unique ability of Muslim democratic movements like the Gülen community to bridge the ethnic divide, and restore the moral fabric of southeastern Anatolian society that makes it such a potent threat to hard-liners in both the PKK and the Turkish "deep-state." For this reason, the PKK, as well as Turkish Hizbullah media outlets, regularly perceive the movement and its activities as a threat. In turn, the Gülen movement's newspapers and TV stations always portray the PKK as a ruthless atheist organization, and a tool of hostile foreign powers and enemies of Islam.

In July 2008, the Gülen organizers of the annual Abant Platform had to cancel a planned conference entitled "The Kurdish Question" to be held on July 5–6, in Diyarbakır because of threats by the PKK.[33] The conference was then held in the city of Abant.[34] With this conference, the Gülen movement also presented its preferred solution to the Kurdish Question within Turkey in terms of individual rights, consolidation of democracy and the right to education in one's mother tongue. In this vein, the Gülen community is not only active with its schools and reading-room networks throughout Kurdish inhabited cities but also via a dense network of charitable organizations, such as the Association of *Kimse Yok Mu* (Is No One Out There?).[35]

In terms of restoring interethnic harmony in Turkey, the goal of the Gülen movement is to dilute and contain radical and exclusivist manifestations of both ethnic Kurdish and Turkish nationalism through shared ties to Islamic faith and culture. Related to this is the goal of consolidating Turkish democracy and economic development, and the Gülen community sees the cycle of terrorism and harsh state oppression as major impediments to the realization of their broader goals. A regional leader in Diyarbakır told the author:

> As long as we have terrorism and ethnic violence, there will be a legitimate reason to justify spending on military and police force. Moreover, the

chaos will prevent the liberalization of the constitution and the political environment. Thus, if you want to stop the deepening of democracy and the making of a new liberal constitution as the JDP government desires, you need to promote violence. Thus, the PKK violence is an obstacle to our democratization and economic development. So the Gülen community sees the PKK as the biggest threat to its goals.[36]

In terms of a political approach to the Kurdish question, the Gülen movement is in favor of individual and community-based cultural rights for all citizens and groups, but against strong federalism or regional autonomy in the southeast along ethnic lines.

Since 2010, the Gülen movement has launched an ideological counterattack against the PKK and Kurdish Hizbullah as representing forces of *"fitne"* within Muslim society. The Arabic term *fitne* means seditious behavior to undermine order and a destructive mode of thinking and feeling. In an interview in Nuremberg, Germany, a pro-Kurdish nationalist activist said:

[T]he state is using the Directorate of Religious Affairs and the Gülen movement to delegitimize Kurdish nationalism by portraying it as *fitne*. As far I am concerned, we see the movement as the fifth column, i.e., internal resistance, against the Kurdish nationalist movement. The movement is the ideological enemy of our independence. It mixes Turkish nationalism, Ottoman memory and Islam to deny our identity.[37]

However, not all politically mobilized Turkish Kurds think this way. Within the Gülen movement, there is a small but very vocal number of Turkish Kurdish grassroots supporters. Many conservative Kurds are very suspicious and critical of the PKK and its Marxist-Leninist background, and they believe that an Islamic identity and common heritage, respecting ethnic and linguistic diversity, is the only arena that would allow all the various Muslim ethnic groups in Turkey to truly coexist. A Kurdish citizen from the city of Van said:

I voted for Erdoğan. I voted for him because we need peace and we can only have peace with Islam. Neither Kurdish nor Turkish nationalism are a solution. We need the philosophy of Said Nursi and Fethullah Hocaefendi. All our problems stem from the lack of proper education. The followers of Hocaefendi are working day and night to educate the people of our region. Our hope is the Islam of Anatolia.[38]

Indeed, the JDP government of Prime Minister Erdoğan and the Gülen movement both share this same eclectic Islamic vision which, in sharp contrast to past Kemalist attempts at ideological, cultural and ethnic homogenization, believes that the solution to the Kurdish Question in Turkey should be a reactivated Muslim solidarity based on the common Ayyubid, Seljuk and Ottoman heritage. Both the JDP and the movement believe that Islamic identity and Islam-centric community building would lead Turkish Kurds away from separatism.[39] In short, the JDP government and the movement are against ethnic federalism and support a solution through de-secularization (i.e., re-Islamization), and de-ethnic-nationalization (re-Ottomanization), and stress a solution that is based on both allowing individual and communal rights within a broader shared religious and cultural tradition.[40] Indeed, Turkey's pro-Islamic forces are using the abject failure of the Turkish Republic to deal with the bitter Kurdish conflict to accuse Kemalism itself of having undermined and betrayed the cohesion of Turkish state and society with their ham-fisted policies. Ironically, the JDP governments' "Kurdish Opening" in this vein often finds itself assailed for threatening to blur ethnic identities and faultlines within the nation by both hard-liners in the PKK, as well as those in the Turkish military and nationalist parties such as the MHP.

ISLAMIST CRITICS OF THE GÜLEN MOVEMENT

As noted, the Gülen movement used to maintain a visible distance from Turkey's political Islamic groups. In fact, the major criticism against the movement in the past used to be that "it has wrongly directed itself to non-political areas. The future of Turkey will be decided through political struggle, and the Gülen movement, by not participating in this political struggle, is betraying the Islamic cause." Due to this non-activist political attitude, most of those Turkish Muslims who were critical of the potential divisive role of political Islam supported or sympathized with the movement as a counterforce to the overtly politicized Islamic movement of Necmettin Erbakan, known as the National Outlook Movement.

Erbakan, who died in 2011, as well as many Sufi groups, and some prominent Muslim intellectuals, were all very critical of the Gülenists on a number of issues.[41] Mehmet Şevket Eygi, a conservative leading Muslim columnist, regularly criticizes the activities, intentions and networks of the Gülen movement. He, along with other nationalistic Islamic groups such as Haydar Baş, a Sufi group with TV stations and several publications, sharply criticize the movement as being a tool of the JDP or the American government.[42] Some Islamic groups believe that the Gülen movement is "occupying state institutions" and "controlling" the economic centers of the country, and they criticize the exclusionary tactics of the movement. In Istanbul, a supporter of the JDP said, "It was a big mistake that the JDP closely allied itself with the movement. By doing this, it angered many pro-Islamic groups, since they do not like the movement, and also it led to the distancing of some Kurds from the party." When I asked him why Islamists criticize the Gülen movement, he said:

> "The movement is too powerful, too political and their followers are all over the state institutions and they also have major companies in the economic domain against financial institutions such as Asya Finans and many hospitals. Moreover, the Gülen movement is too pro-American and even supports Israel."

On May 31, 2010, the "Freedom Flotilla," which consisted of six ships, sought to break the controversial Israeli blockade of the Gaza Strip by carrying humanitarian relief to the long-suffering Palestinians there. Israeli forces attacked the unarmed Mavi Marmara in international waters killing nine Turks including a teenager who happened to be an American citizen. The unrestrained and violent nature of the Israeli attack against the unarmed crew sparked outrage around the world and was met with universal condemnation. Yet Gülen criticized the pro-Islamic humanitarian organization's attempt to lift the siege of Gaza and the subsequent bloody confrontation on the high seas with Israeli forces, for being provocative and unproductive, many Islamist as well as secular groups in Turkey accused Gülen of "appeasement."[43]

Whereas the majority of global opinion supported efforts to end the humanitarian disaster in Gaza and joined in the Turkish government's outrage over the killing of unarmed civilians, Gülen chose to controversially criticize the flotilla for trying to deliver humanitarian aid without the legal consent of Israel. This criticism led many religious and secular Turkish groups to sharply attack Gülen as being "the puppet of the CIA and Israel." Kadir Mısıroğlu, a popular Islamist historian, also sharply criticized Gülen and accused him of "being on the side of the unbelievers. He (Gülen) lost his Islamic identity and engaged in high politics."[44] Gülen's efforts to appear "moderate" and "conciliatory" in the face of the Israeli assault struck many Turkish and Islamists observers as being "appeasement" and refusal to "speak truth to power" in defense of moral principles and international norms, as was done by the Turkish government, for example.

Gülen's controversial and deferential behavior, however, was in keeping with his past behavior and actions when confronted by Kemalist hard-liners in the military. As both a tactic and strategy, he favors conciliation and mediation over conflict and challenge. He also prefers negotiated settlements to domestic and international conflicts, and is wary of the tactics of disruptive civil disobedience to bring about social change. Nonetheless, while Gülen garnered plaudits in this instance from the American neoconservatives in Washington, for many others it appeared unseemly and revealed his dislike of violence, even if it frustrates the larger Muslim public opinion.

For his part, Gülen wants to put the stability and prosperity of Turkey before any religious or ideological purity. Gülen is always leery of confrontational tactics and stances going back to his early negative experiences with the Kemalist state. Gülen prefers to build a "big tent" that would be supported by diverse groups such as liberals, Kurds, Alevis, and other religious traditions. Gülen wants to keep this coalition or "big tent" together on the basis of preserving public order and freedoms of each group against the threat of anarchy and conflict. He seeks to foster the same approach in dealing with international conflicts as well. His strategies for dealing with conflict are usually based on gradualism and a reflection of the prevailing political and intellectual climate rather than strictly adhering to rigid principles without regard to outcomes.

Critics of the Gülen movement often accuse it of simply seeking power and of having become a political rather than merely a religious and social welfare movement. When I raised this criticism before key followers of the movement, they argued:

> Yes, there is a gradual politicization of the movement and also closer identification with the governing Justice and Development Party because the pressure from the military and secular circles to eliminate the movement, along with other Islamic voices forced us to get involved more in politics.[45]

CONCLUSION

Stephen Kinzer, a prominent journalist for *The New York Times*, who has covered Turkish politics since the 1990s, also argued that many people in Turkey fear to scrutinize the sources of "the power of Fethullah Gülen, a shadowy but immensely influential Turkish religious leader."[46] Indeed, several books and many diplomatic cables all examine different aspects of the increasing power of the movement within the Turkish state and economy. Kinzer, like many writers, recognizes how difficult it is to fully understand the ultimate goals and policies of the movement, since it resists many forms of scrutiny or simple categorization.

When I was visiting Washington, a respected sociologist of religion asked me:

> Since you study the Gülen movement, I have a question. One thing about the followers always puzzles me. I know them here in Washington, DC. They are very nice, genteel, and clean people with little intellectual curiosity and almost no ability to engage intellectually about social or political issues. Yet it baffles me how these dull personalities could establish such a

powerful movement. I know they are hard-working and reverent—yet utterly boring. Tell me what is going on here. Who is behind them?

This is a correct description of many in the movement but it is utterly wrong to think that there is another hidden "force behind the movement." I tried to answer the question by referring to my home state, Utah, and its hardworking Mormon faithful, who are also idealistic, but not always sophisticated, and imbued with a mission. This has allowed them to emerge as a highly successful political and economic force in the United States like the American Jewish community. However, it also means that at times their very cohesion works against self-critical awareness or inclusion of others. Like the Mormon symbol of the beehive, they are builders and shapers with incredible work ethics and cohesion. Yet, they are often very shy about discussing their own beliefs and cautious with outsiders. The structural effect of the movement in terms of its collective identity goes beyond individual autonomy or questioning minds.

The Gülen movement started as a religious movement with fairly modest goals. Today, the movement has evolved and has become one of the most powerful forces not only in Turkey, but in several other Muslim countries as well with its schools, business networks, media outlets, NGOs and close connections with politicians. For instance, some of the American followers of the movement are regular contributors to several American political elections. Like American Evangelicals and Jews, they are using their rights to participate in the political system and shape civil society. Thus, it is a religiously rooted and morally guided movement with the purpose of influencing public policies where they are able. The movement never condones violence and always condemns it in any form. However, according to some opponents of the movement in Turkey, it has proven to be intolerant of its critics. Some argue that as the movement became more powerful, it has moved away from a soft and conciliatory tone to more confrontational and assertive one.

An increasing number of educated Turks argue that the Gülen movement, which relies on tight networks and resources, is seeking to control every state institution. Thus, the noticeably increasing power of the movement has become a source of fear for some secular groups. This fear, in turn, has mobilized its critics to organize and confront its expanding influence. Gülen has been a source of hope and fear for Turkey's bourgeoning civil society. Those who are concerned about secularism and a "modern" way of life see the Gülen movement as the main threat to the Kemalist reforms. However, legitimate concerns have often turned into paranoia by considering all forms of anti-Kemalist opposition to be the evil design of Gülen. Elisabeth Özdalga aptly summarizes this "paranoia" by arguing that Gülen's "opponents consider Gülen to be someone who is almighty, controlling everything, and has latent powers disregarding any political authority."[47]

Some of these criticisms are based on diverse personal interactions with the followers and networks of the movement. The Gülen movement consists of people with mixed intrinsic and extrinsic beliefs.[48] The former includes those who live according to their belief and see their faith as an ultimate value in itself. Religion, for them, is the intense feeling in the heart, and the reason why they need to set the best possible exemplary conduct. The latter includes those who treat religion as an instrument to realize worldly goals such as gaining comfort and security, feeling socially included, gaining prestige and having access to economic and political gains. These two forms of people coexist within the movement and the balance is moving toward the second group as the movement has gained access to more power and resources.

Since the Gülen movement functions within the framework of neoliberalism, and a bourgeoning civil society in which consumerism and ownership are defining features, its supporters and sympathizers have differing expectations. These structural conditions limit and shape the followers as much as, if not more than, the very teachings of Gülen himself. In other words, while Gülen seeks to mold selfless individuals who act with the purpose of serving God by negating their ego, the modern capitalist system in which consumerism, ownership, and self-importance are highlighted, are in direct conflict with the spiritual side of these ideals. Indeed, the followers of the movement are under siege by these socioeconomic temptations. The tension between the structure, agency and the expanding opportunity spaces in the economy and in politics have further encouraged some followers to stress worldly gains over spiritual ones. There are diverse people within a large movement who are either motivated by wealth and power or by spiritual hunger to define the meaning of the good life.

Due to these mixed motives, the movement is too *Islamist* and conservative for some social democrats and the secularist military, too *liberal* and pro-American for Islamists, too *Turkish* nationalist for the Kurdish nationalists, too *Sunni-Hanefi* for the Alevis, and too worldly for some Sufi-oriented Muslims. Gülen has been trying to restrain these contending forces by identifying the biggest threat to national unity and economic development as the lack of popular democracy, and the attempts of the authoritarian establishment to preserve the status quo.

As the movement has become a more powerful political force in Turkey due to changing political and security conditions, its flexibility, which was once provided by diverse groupings and sympathetic networks, has been in fact reduced.

A unified and forceful movement could be powerful enough to defeat its opponents, and this unchecked power has forced its opponents to form a "front" against the movement. Gülen before the Ergenekon case was successful in forming alliances with diverse groups in Turkey to prevent a common front from developing against the movement. Today, the name of the Gülen movement in Turkey (and outside it) is equated with a power struggle for control of state institutions. The movement is not a bridge but rather a source of fear for Turkey's deeply divided society. Due to increasing skepticism among the secular educated elite, the Gülen movement needs to undertake a mission of reassurance. They need to learn how to share power in state institutions, with more emphasis on merit and less on religious solidarity in job recruitments and promotion, the movement is still learning how to become more critical of the JDP and the Erdoğan government over corruption and the exclusion of marginalized Alevis and the lack of progress on the Kurdish issue as well.

Conclusion

Unbelief was an uncommon sentiment and esoteric term in Europe of the Middle Ages, whereas today it is a challenge to sustain religious belief in much of the industrialized world.[1] The sense that we are living in a secular age cannot be detached from past developments in European history and, yet, it must be included in theological discourses outside of Europe and Western Christianity. The apparent shift, which has taken place over the course of the last few centuries, is leading to today's postmodern age of secularism and skepticism; while liberating in some ways, it has also come with certain costs. What has been "lost" in this transition are certain organic certainties and solidarities that helped to weld traditional societies. Nature, humanity and the cosmos were once viewed as manifestations of God. The prevailing secular age is instead defined by certain macro-forces of modernity, faith in science and technology, nationalism and democracy, and globalized market economies. Individualism, instrumental rationality and scientific-technocratic solutions have become the organizing principles of our modern lives. However, despite Friedrich Nietzsche's famous dictum in the late nineteenth century, this modern age has not led to the death of God in the public sphere, but rather belief has been continuously recast and remolded as our faith in modern Prometheuses has also proved wanting. The defining features of modernity have changed the background conditions of belief and faith.[2] In a similar vein, the nascent Islamic Enlightenment in Turkey is also the unintended by-product of this secularizing and modernizing age. It is a reaction to official ideologies and impersonal forces that seek to exclude spiritual longings and insist on limiting our lives and imaginations to the here and now, with their rigid focus on the material aspects of being.

Secularization, the defining feature of modernity, has not evolved as sociologists have anticipated. Although modernity is fueling tangible material progress in this world, it is under constant challenge by both the forces of tradition and religion and also those stemming from the disquiet caused by relativism and nihilism.

It is important to keep in mind that there is no single universal path or model of modernity, but rather several alternative and competing ones. The paradox of the return of a certain form of Islam as Turkey becomes more modern, and politically and economically developed is not easily theoretically addressed. In the republican period of Turkish history, Islam became the most important indicator of backwardness, while a Kemalist/Jacobin style of secularism was regarded as the marker of modernity and progress. For a long time, being secular in Turkey was interpreted as being hostile or at least indifferent to religion. This study of the vitality of contemporary forms of Islam in Turkey indicates modernity and secularism deeply transform religious beliefs and practices but are also in turn transformed themselves as new societal needs and challenges are thrown up. What we are witnessing today in Turkey is the deep cross-fertilization and mutual transformative power of secularism, modernity and Islam. This evolution of a vernacularized Turkish Muslim modernity also has profound implications for much of the rest of the Muslim world as well.

The Gülen movement currently plays an important role in the evolution of new modernized interpretations and practices of Islam. Indeed, both the ruling class and the population of Turkey today are much more overtly Islamic in identity than several decades ago. However, this is an Islam deeply marked and transformed by the forces of secularism and modernization with which it had to painfully contend. The vast majority of Turkish Muslims today reject medieval forms of censure and punishment, as well as compulsion in religion. Rather, they stress the values of pluralism, democracy and the rule of law often over and against an authoritarian secularist establishment.[3] In this Islamically inflected milieu, the citizens of Turkey are becoming more enlightened and more religious at the same time. The post-Özal expanding opportunity spaces in the public sphere have encouraged Muslim intellectuals and leaders such as Fethullah Gülen to develop more accessible and reflexive forms of Islam that have to be able to hold their own with critical nonreligious actors and ideologies both within and outside of Turkey. This increasing accessibility, reflexivity and vernacularization of Islam have been crucial in accounting for the sweeping political and socioeconomic changes we are witnessing in Turkey today.

The lectures and writings of Fethullah Gülen, which cover social issues, religious concerns, art, education and science, share an underlying ambition to mold an Islamic understanding that can meet the challenges posed by modernity. Qur'anic concepts and principles must be mediated and justified through social and cultural public spheres inhabited by many varieties of believers and nonbelievers alike. There is also an attendant shift in emphasis among contemporary Turkish Muslim thinkers from traditional theological deliberations to modern social theories and also practical applications. Moreover, for Gülen, Islamic revival and Turkish secularism are inherently intertwined with each other; one could not have existed without the other.

This recast and recontextualized form of Islam has unmistakably reentered the public sphere, not with the intention to return to an imagined golden age of the past, but rather to fill the void left by certain failures of Kemalism, itself one variety of secularism, and in order to reincorporate a plethora of voices marginalized with the formation of the republic. In Turkish life, Islam is increasingly more important than politics. This recast modern Turkish Islam is imbued with vitality not as an instrument to challenge modernity but rather as a necessary means of integration to fill voids left by both the successes and failures of Kemalist secularism and modernity. Religious expressions and practices proved mutable and were recast to uphold core values of democracy, human rights and pluralism. Islam in this modern democratic environment has become a source for generating meaning, norms and solidarity. In other words, we are witnessing the integration of religion into a democratic and secular society as a moral force that functions to enhance civil society and uphold universalistic norms and values not unlike those produced in the Western secular Enlightenment. In different historical and socioeconomic contexts outside of Turkey, of course, the politics of Islamic revivalism have produced altogether different and dismal results.

For Gülen, religion is not an instrument for completely overthrowing the secular order, nor is it a space for retreat and private contemplation. Rather, Gülen envisions it as a value-giving normative system and as a set of beliefs and practices about how to shape a just society and restore social solidarities sundered by modernity and capitalist development. In other words, Islam for Gülen is about striving for just and harmonious societies and restoring faith in norms and values that transcend material and individualistic concerns and interests.

Gülen believes that the fundamental problem of postcolonial Muslim societies, including that of Turkey, are their authoritarian and self-serving "native alien" elites and the fragmentation of society along ethnic, religious, class and ideological faultlines that their corrupt rule fosters. Indeed, one of the most important problems of modern Turkey is elite factionalism and segmentation. The elite have difficulty in working and cooperating with each other. This is an outcome of Turkey's fragmented social structure. Unlike in much of the successful East Asian "tiger economies," where the developmental state, consensus politics and societal corporatism proved successful, in Turkey (and far more in much of the rest of the Muslim-majority world), deep-seeded societal conflicts and self-serving elites dependent on external Western military and political power proved the norm.[4] Normative conflicts in Turkish society have deep historical roots. Turkish society is highly segmented along ethnic and religious lines and along differing modes of lifestyles.

Gülen's prescriptions to resolve these societal conflicts have been threefold: to institute a new cultural and educational philosophy drawing on a modernized Ottoman Islamic ecumenism; to support economic development and the emergence of an Anatolian Turkish middle class (à la "the Protestant ethic") via success in mastering science, technology and the market to equip Muslims with the necessary modern tools to emerge as major actors on the global stage like their Western and East Asian counterparts; and to foster a new open Habermasian public sphere to allow competing and marginalized societal voices to engage in communication and understanding. In this vein, Gülen is also extremely optimistic about the impact of new information technology in terms of empowering people, thickening civil society through building practical and normative bridges between people, and allowing them to challenge authoritarian rule. In this regard, it should be noted, he was quite prescient in foreshadowing the crucial role played by social media and public spaces in allowing the youth of the Arab Spring to shake the ossified dictatorial order in the Middle East to its very core.

Gülen's educational system primarily emphasizes the training of the "heart" and the controlling of desire, while the "mind" or the intellect for most lay followers is only given secondary consideration. Gülen and his followers believe that those who have the "trained heart," filled with spiritual intuition (religious disposition), are ready to please God by striving to improve human welfare. The Gülen movement stresses the religious values of charity, pragmatism (middle way), frugality and economic productivity as the guiding principles to build a "dynamic Muslim society." Gülen's movement consists of pietistic Muslims whose ultimate references are actions that are pleasing to God and his creation. They recognize that other-worldly salvation does not come at the expense of earthly conditions and progress. They utilize religious values and dispositions in their daily life with the goal of bettering material and political conditions of society. Thus, for the Gülen movement, there is a close alliance between the forces of pietism and social activism. Gülen wants to awaken the youth through a sense of collective purpose to do what is good and empower society. He believes that all people are potentially captive to desires, appetite, selfishness and traumas from the past. In fact, these deep psychological neuroses rob many of their sense of humanity and idealism and block the enormous potential of the heart and mind. Thus, Gülen always calls on his followers not to see themselves as individuals, but rather as a part of a community and struggle to transform community through exemplary conduct. One becomes a part of the Gülen community by giving his/her time, energy and resources to those who are in need. One of the most critical concepts of Gülen's worldview is compassion (*merhamet*) to those in need, be they Muslims or not.

Gülen has always called for a modernized democratic Turkish state and society without having to imitate Westernization, a society that presents an exemplary sociopolitical system derived from its own deep cultural, religious, and historical wellsprings. The Gülen movement is not about the poor or the oppressed but rather about the empowerment of people, raising religious social consciousness by bringing spirituality back to the center of daily public life. Although on the surface, one might conclude that Gülen's endeavors amount to the Islamization of society, I would argue that this is inevitably as much an internal rationalization and secularization of Islam, whether Gülen or his followers intend it or not. The cross-fertilization between the sacred and the secular is inevitably leading to more rationalized and modern forms of religious belief and practice, at least in the Turkish case. In other words, the Gülen movement may be, like Protestant deism, a way station to a religiously informed modernity not that alien to forms of secular humanism. I would argue that it has the potential to be the beginning of religious Enlightenment in its Turkish and wider modern Islamic context where we are witnessing a new era of Muslim religious revival deeply embedded in modern processes of neoliberal market reforms and middle classes, open public spheres, democratic governance, modern education and technology-driven globalization.

By studying the movement, one can learn the patterns of interaction among religion, modernity, the public sphere, identity, civility (*adab*) and politics. The movement demonstrates that it is possible to simultaneously be a pious and modern Muslim. Emerging from the Kemalist state-secular tradition, along with the oppositional writings of Said Nursi, the Gülen community neither rejects Western modernity nor fully assimilates into it. It has instead created its own form of modernity that recasts Islam without discarding it. It is modernity with new forms of religion (Islam), and not without, as the Kemalists had sought. The Gülen movement can thus best be understood within the framework of the literature of the "multiple modernities" as defined by Shmuel Noah Eisenstadt: "[A]ttempts by various groups and movements to re-appropriate and redefine the discourse of modernity in their own new terms."[5] The movement is certainly not antimodern, and, furthermore, it seeks to create its own "Muslim" alternative modernity by framing science and the public sphere with its own idioms. Through its scientific discourse, the Gülen movement contests the atheistic notion of science, which may cast radical doubt on all traditional faiths but itself must become a faith-based belief system when it overreaches (as in the popular writings of Richard Dawkins or Stephen Hawking), in trying to prove the unprovable contention that there is indeed no providential order or force behind the creation of the Cosmos. In conclusion, the Gülen movement emerged as a vital agent in the transformation of modern Turkey by supporting dialogue between different cultures, ideologies and religions while giving

Turkey's conservative masses the confidence to engage with a much wider world. As a merchant in Konya said, "With *hizmet*, we can become what we were once again and become what we are: Turkish Muslims."

In terms of the future of the Gülen movement, the fate of other powerful Islamic movements in the past offers a useful precedent and a cautionary tale. Prior to Fethullah Gülen and his community, the most powerful Turkish Islamic group was led by the Nakşibendi Sufi leader, Mehmet Zahid Kotku. Following his death in 1980, however, the movement gradually dissolved into irrelevance. The new leader, Kotku's son-in-law, failed to maintain the movement as he lacked the institutions, as well as the necessary charisma and wisdom, to fill his father-in-law's shoes. Could a similar fate await the Gülen movement or has it established itself to a degree that it can function without its current charismatic leader? Given Gülen's charisma, learning and organizational skills, he will leave large shoes to fill. In addition, given his unelected leadership position and lack of a clear successor, there is currently no one in line to lead this transnational religious network of schools, finance and community services into the future. The Gülen movement, like previous Islamic movements in Turkey, is molded very much in the image and personality of its leader. When Gülen is gone, the faithful are likely to form a new "tent" around a new charismatic leader. However, given the lack of formal institutionalization, it is not clear whether the cohesion of the movement will be sustained in the future. Gülen's powerful legacy in shaping modern Turkish state and society, however, will likely endure for some time. His death will not mean the end of the project of Islamic Enlightenment he has sought to foster, but rather that the new Turkish religio-social movements that will arise will be heavily marked by the current one. This was true of Bediuzzaman Said Nursi himself, whose charisma and influence carried forth in important ways within the Gülen movement, even though the Kemalist state had sought to cast him into oblivion by burying him in an unmarked grave after long years of harsh solitary confinement. In a globalizing world, our identities, norms, values, and networks are constantly renegotiated as a result of encounters with other ways of seeing and being. In this sense, Islam and modernity will continue to be in a process of becoming.

Notes

INTRODUCTION
1. Farid Noor, ed., *New Voices of Islam* (Leiden: ISIM, 2002), 25.
2. Immanuel Kant, "What is Enlightenment." In *On History*, ed. and translated by Lewis Beck (New York: Macmillian, 1964), 1-10.
3. Karl Popper, *The Open Society and its Enemies, Vol. 2, The High Tide of Prophecy* (London: Routledge & Kegan Paul, 1945), 303.
4. Ernst Cassirer, *The Philosophy of the Enlightenment* (Princeton: Princeton University Press, 1968); Peter Gay, *The Enlightenment: An Interpretations, Vol. 1 The Rise of Paganism* (London: Weidenfeld & Nicolson, 1967); *Vol. 2, The Science of Freedom* (London: Weidenfeld & Nicolson, 1970); Jonathan Israel, *Radical Enlightenment: Philosophy and the Making of Modernity, 1650 1750* (Oxford University Press, Oxford, 2001); Lewis Hichman, *Hegel's Critique of the Enlightenment* (Gainesville, FL: 1984), chapter 5. H. R. Trevor-Roper, "The Religious Origin of the Enlightenment," in his *Religion, Reformation and Social Change*, 3rd edn (London: Martin Secker & Warburg Ltd,1984).
5. J. G. A. Pocock, *Barbarism and Religion: The Enlightenment of Edward Gibbon, 1737–1764* (New York: Cambridge University Press, 2001), 5.
6. David Sorkin, *The Religious Enlightenment: Protestant, Jews, and Catholics from London to Vienna* (Princeton: Princeton University Press, 2008).
7. Albert Hourani, *Arabic Thought in the Liberal Age, 1798-1939* (Cambridge: Cambridge University Press, 1983), 103-192.
8. Niyazi Berkes, *The Development of Secularism in Turkey.* (New York: Routledge, 1998).
9. Cited in Sorkin, *The Religious*, 12. Cited from [Antoine Adrien] Lamourette, Pensées sur la Philosophie de la foi, xviii-xix. CF. Pensées sur la Philosophie de l'incrédulité, 253, 263, and Les Délices De La Religion, Ou Le Pouvoir De L'évangile Pour Nous Rendre Heureux, ix.
10. Fethullah Gülen, *The Statue of Our Souls: Revival in Islamic Thought and Activism.* Somerset, NJ: Light, 2006), 31.

11. J.G.A. Pocock, *Virtue, Commerce, and History: Essays on Political Thought and History, Chiefly in the Eighteenth Century* (Cambridge: Cambridge University Press, 1985).
12. John Voll, "Renewal and Reform in Islamic History," in *Voices of Resurgent Islam*, ed. John Esposito (New York: Oxford University Press, 1983), 32–47.
13. For the meaning of *hizmet* in Islamic-Ottoman history, see Etienne Copeaux, "Hizmet: A Keyword in Turkish Historical Narrative," *New Perspectives on Turkey* 13 (1996): 91–114.
14. Brian Knowlton's interview with Gülen, *Turkish Review* 1:2 (2011): 52.
15. The Gülen movement had a troubling and cordial relationship with "*Türkmenbaşı*" Saparmurat Niyazov, the former leader of Turkmenistan, who was one of the most oppressive and bizarre leaders of Central Asia. His "sacred" book, the *Ruhname*, which was meant to rival the Bible and the Qur'an, was translated by *Muhammed* Cetin, who earned an award for cultural service to Turkmenistan. See more, http://www.sierraf.org/activity_details.php?id=30; Ilan Greenberg, "When a Kleptocratic, Megalomaniacal Dictator Goes Bad," *New York Times*, January 5, 2005.
16. The most prominent website is: http://www.fethullahGülen.org. This comprehensive website includes the writings and speeches of Fethullah Gülen, as well as his interviews and news from the national media about him. The website is available in nine languages, including Spanish, Arabic, German, and Danish. The other prominent websites are: http://www.herkul.org;http://www.sizinti.com.tr;http://www.rumiforum.org. Cyberspace provides a transnational opportunity space for the movement, which unites followers of the movement from different parts of the world and gives coherence and cohesion to the statements and positions of Gülen.
17. Bayram Balcı, *Orta Asya'da İslam Misyonerleri: Fethullah Gülen Okulları* (Istanbul: İletişim, 2005); Bayram Balcı, "Fethullah Gülen's Missionary Schools in Central Asia and their Role in the Spreading of Turkism and Islam," *Religion, State & Society* 31 (2003): 151–177; Bekim Agai, *Zwischen Netzwerk und Diskurs—Das Bildungsnetzwerk um Fethullah Gülen (geb. 1938): Die flexible Umsetzung modernen islamischen Gedankenguts* (Hamburg: EB-Verlag 2004); Bekim Agai, "Fethullah Gülen and his Movement's Islamic Ethic of Education," in *Turkish Islam and the Secular State*, ed. M. Hakan and John Esposito (Syracuse, NY: Syracuse University Press, 2004), 29–49; Bekim Agai, "Fethullah Gülen and his Movement's Islamic Ethic of Education," *Critique* 11:1 (2002): 27–47; Berna Turam, *Between Islam and the State: The Politics of Engagement* (Stanford, CA: Stanford University Press, 2006).
18. Joshua Hendrick, "Globalization and Marketized Islam in Turkey: The Case of Fethullah Gülen" (Ph.D. diss., University of California, Santa Cruz, 2009); Berna Arslan, "Pious Science: The Gülen Community and the Making of a Conservative Modernity in Turkey" (Ph.D. diss., University of California, Santa Cruz, 2009); Heon Chou Kim, "The Nature and Role of Sufism in Contemporary Islam: A Case Study of the Life, Thought and Teachings of Fethullah Gülen" (Ph.D. diss., Temple University, 2008).
19. "Gülen Inspires Muslims Worldwide," *Forbes' Oxford Analytical*, January 8, 2008; *New York Times*, May 4, 2008; *Le Monde*, November 5, 2006; *International Herald*

Tribune, January 8, 2008; *The Economist*, January 3, 2008 and March 6, 2008; *Foreign Policy* (2008) ; Suzy Hansen, "The Golbal Imam," *The New Republic*, November 10, 2010; Greg Toppo, "Objectives of Charter Schools with Turkish Ties Questioned," *US Today*, August 18, 2009.

20. Helen E. Ebaugh, *The Gülen Movement: A Sociological Analysis of a Civic Movement Rooted in Moderate Islam* (Springer, 2009). Etyen Mahcupyan, a columnist in *Zaman* daily, argues that:

>Ebaugh's book unfortunately lacks depth. As a matter of fact, her presentation in Istanbul, clearly showcasing the loopholes in her argument and style, suggested to the audience that such an intellectual depth should not be expected from her works. In her interview with *Zaman*, she explained that the Gülen movement emerged out of fears, also shared by the public, that widespread currents of Marxism and feminism were about to control the youth. Her explanation that what lies at the heart of the Gülen movement is Turkish hospitality should also be regarded as a farcical commentary. Her book also commands similar shallowness. The main sources for her book are a set of interviews but the author refrained from talking with Fethullah Gülen since she was afraid of losing her objectivity. This is another way of saying that the author is simply afraid of comprehending what the movement is.

Mahcupyan further criticizes the leaders of the Gülen movement for using considerable resources to promote the book. Muhammed Cetin, *The Gülen Movement: Civic Service without Border* (New York: Blue Dome, 2010); Mehmet Enes Ergene, *Tradition Witnessing the Modern Age: An Analysis of the Gülen Movement* (New Jersey: Tughra Books, 2008); John Esposito and İhsan Yılmaz, *Islam and Peacebuilding: Gülen Movement Initiatives* (New York: Blue Dome, 2010). Cetin, Ergene, and Yılmaz are three prominent intellectuals of the Gülen movement and their works while informative tend to lack a critical edge.

21. Some of the academic conferences sponsored by the Gülen movement included: Louisiana State University (2006), University of Texas at San Antonio (2007), University of Oklahoma (2006), Southern Methodist University (2006), Rice University (2005), University of Southern California (2009), Erasmus University (2007). All these conferences were entirely funded by the movement itself. The papers and programs of these conferences are also available on the Gülenists websites.

22. Stephen Schwartz, "The Real Fethullah Gülen," Prospect, July 26, 2008, accessed April 9, 2010, http://www.prospectmagazine.co.uk/2008/07/therealfethullahglen/; Guy Rodgers, "Fethullah Gülen: Infiltrating the U.S. through Our Charter Schools?" accessed April 9, 2010, http://www.actforamerica.org/index.php/learn/email-archives/1069-fethulla-Gülen-infiltrating-us-through-our-charter-schools/.

23. A report issued by the Center for American Progress details the contemporary networks and sources of anti-Islamism and bigotry in America, see *Fear, Inc: The Roots of the Islamophobia Networks in America* (Washington, DC, 2011).

24. Michael Rubin, "Turkey's Turning Point: Could There be an Islamic Revolution in Turkey?" National Review Online, April 14, 2008, accessed February 27, 2009, http://www.meforum.org/1882/turkeys-turning-point/.

25. For some idea of the conspiratorial neoconservative take on the Gülen movement, see Rachel Sharon-Kreskin, "Fethullah Gülen's Grand Ambition," *Middle East*

Quarterly 16: 1 (2009): 55–66; Soner Cagaptay, "What's Really Behind Turkey's Coup Arrests?" *Foreign Policy*, February 25, 2010.
26. More on the defining features of this new Turkey, see M. Hakan Yavuz, ed., *The Emergence of a New Turkey: Democracy and Ak Parti* (Salt Lake City: University of Utah, 2006).
27. M. Hakan Yavuz, *Secularism and Muslim Democracy in Turkey* (New York: Cambridge University Press, 2009).
28. By *ihlas*, Gülen means sincerity and "purity of intention" in one's action and devotion to God.
29. John Wall et al., *Paul Ricoeur and Contemporary Moral Thought* (London: Routledge, 2002).
30. For basic works on Said Nursi, see Şükran Vahide, *Islam in Modern Turkey: An Intellectual Biography of Bediüzzaman Said Nursi* (Albany: State University of New York Press, 2005); Ibrahim Abu-Rabi, ed., *Spiritual Dimensions of Bediüzzaman Said Nursi's Risale-i Nur* (Albany: State University of New York Press, 2008); Şerif Mardin, *Religion and Social Change in Modern Turkey: The Case of Bediuzzaman Said Nursi* (Albany: State University of New York Press, 1989); M. Hakan Yavuz, *Islamic Political Identity in Turkey* (New York: Oxford University Press, 2003), 151–178; Colin Turner and Hasan Horkuc, *Said Nursi* (London: I. B. Tauris, 2009).
31. More on the political aspects of the movement, see Eldar Mamedov, "Fethullah Gülen Movement—A View from Brussels," *Hürriyet Daily News*, May 27, 2010.
32. Interview in Istanbul, July 6, 2009.

CHAPTER 1

1. There are two fundamental sources for Gülen's life story. The first one was his interviews about himself and put together later as a book, see. Latif Erdoğan, *Fethullah Gülen Hocaefendi: Küçük Dünyam* (Istanbul: AD Yayıncılık, 1995) and the second source is Ali Ünal and Alphonse William, *Advocate of Dialogue: Fethullah Gülen* (Fairfax, VA: Fountain Publication, 2000), which includes a sizable section about his life. Both Erdoğan and Ünal are very close associates of Gülen.
2. Ünal and William, *Advocate of Dialogue*, 9.
3. Erdoğan, *Küçük Dünyam*, 13.
4. See further M. Hakan Yavuz, "Nasıl bir Türkiye," *Milliyet*, August 11, 1997; and Yavuz, "Nurluk Millileşiyor," *Milliyet*, September 18, 1996.
5. Halil İnalcık, "Erzurum," *Encyclopedia of Islam*, ed. P. Bearman et al. (Leiden: Brill, 1965), 2:712.
6. Charles Issawi, "The Tabriz-Trabzon Trade, 1830–1900: Rise and Decline of a Route," *International Journal of Middle East Studies* 1:1 (1970): 18–27.
7. Rubina Peroomian, "A Call Sounded from the Armenian Mountains," in *Armenia Karin/Erzerum*, ed. Richard G. Hovannisian (Costa Mesa, CA: Mazda, 2003), 189–222.
8. B. G. Williams, "Hijra and Forced Migration from Nineteenth-Century Russia to the Ottoman Empire," *Cahier du Monde russe* 41:1 (2000): 79–108; W. Brooks, "The Politics of the Conquest of the Caucasus, 1855–1864," *Nationalities Papers* 24:4 (1996): 649–660; W. Brooks, "Russia's Conquest and Pacification of the Caucasus: Relocation Becomes a Pogrom in the Post-Crimean War Period," *Nationalities*

Papers 23:4 (1995): 675–686; Justin McCarthy, *Death and Exile: The Ethnic Cleansing of Ottoman Muslims, 1821–1922* (Princeton: Darwin, 1995); A. W. Fisher, "Emigration of Muslims from the Russian Empire in the Years after the Crimean War," *Jahrbücher für Geschichte Osteuropas* 35 (1987): 356–371; Austin Jersild, *Orientalism and Empire: North Caucasus Mountain Peoples and the Georgian Frontier, 1845–1917* (Montreal: McGill-Queen's University Press, 2002); M. Pinson, "Demographic Warfare—An Aspect of Ottoman and Russian Foreign Policy, 1854–1866" (Ph.D. diss., Harvard University, 1970).

9. Simon Payaslian, "The Death of Armenia Karin/Erzerum," in *Armenia Karin/Erzerum*, ed. Richard G. Hovannisian (Costa Mesa, CA: Mazda, 2003), 339–364. This article is based on the assumption that the "Turks are genocidal people" and the entire book does not see any positive aspects of Ottoman history or the victimization of Ottoman Muslims. Another dynamic was that Armenians were by now much better educated thanks to the role of Christian missionaries and supported by Western countries; moreover, Georgian Armenians also had ideological and economic connections to prepare for pro-Russian Armenian nationalism; Russia became the source of all evil in the eyes of the Muslim population and this will help during the Cold War to prepare anticommunist and nationalist Turkish population and Gülen was raised in this milieu.
10. On July 23, 1919, the Congress in Erzurum decided to mobilize forces for the liberation of the homeland.
11. Mehmet Kırkıncı, *Bediüzzaman'ı Nasıl Tanıdım?* (İstanbul: Zafer, 1994), 21–22, 35–37.
12. Ünver Günay, *Erzurum ve Cevre Köylerinde Dini Hayat* (Istanbul: Dergah, 1999).
13. D. Heller, *The Children's God* (Chicago: University of Chicago, 1986), 32.
14. Erdoğan, *Küçük Dünyam*, 41.
15. Interview with Gülen, Üsküdar, Istanbul, April 25, 1996.
16. Muzafer Arslan was born in İspir, Eruzurm in 1928. He moved to Izmir in 1950 and was introduced to the writings of Said Nursi. He moved to Manisa in 1954 and joined a Nurcu reading circle. He soon gave up attachments to worldly things and never married, dedicating himself, like a Catholic priest, to the service (*hizmet*) of *Risale-i Nur* in terms of its publication and distribution across Anatolian cities and villages. Since these books were illegal in Turkey at the time, he also had to spend a lot of time in police stations and jails with his books.
17. Erdoğan, *Küçük Dünyam*, 47.
18. Alastair MacIntyre, "A Mistake about Causality in Social Sciences," in *Philosophy, Politics, and Society*, ed. P. Laslett and W. Runciman (Oxford: Oxford University Press, 1967), 52.
19. Eyup Can, *Fethullah Gülen Hocaefendi ile Ufuk Turu* (Istanbul: Doğan Kitap, 1996), 25.
20. Hikmet Çetinkaya, *Fethullah Gülen'in 40 Yıllık Serüveni* (Istanbul: Günizi Yayınları, 2004), 149.
21. For Gülen's intellectual evolution, M. Hakan Yavuz, *Islamic Political Identity in Turkey* (New York: Oxford University Press, 2003), 179–206.
22. Erdoğan, *Küçük Dünyam*, 49.
23. Ibid., 122.

24. For more on the "Turkish-Islamic synthesis" between the state and traditional Muslim society, see İbrahim Kafesoğlu, *Türk-Islam Sentezi* (Istanbul: Aydınlar Ocağı, 1985).
25. Ziya Öniş, "Turgut Özal and His Economic Legacy: Turkish Neo-Liberalism in Critical Perspective," *Middle Eastern Studies* 40:4 (July 2004): 113–134.
26. İbrahim Kafesoğlu, *Türk-İslam Sentezi*; Bozkurt Güvenç, *Dosya Türk-Islam Sentezi* (Istanbul: Sarmal Yayınları, 1991).
27. See the founding charter of the Intellectuals' Hearth Association, *Aydınlar Ocağı Derneği Tüzüğü* (İstanbul: Aydınlar Ocağı Yayınları, 1989), 7; see further Mustafa Erkal, "21 Yüzyıla Doğru Milli Kültürlerin Geleceği ve Bazi Çelişkiler," in *İslamiyet, Millet Gerçeği ve Laiklik* (İstanbul: Aydınlar Ocağı, 1994).
28. Ali Bulaç, *Din-Kent ve Cemaat Fethullah Gülen Örneği* (Istanbul: Ufufk Kitap, 2007), 139.
29. For more on his run-out, see http://tr.fGülen.com/content/view/7854/74/.
30. During the 1980 coup, the military issued an arrest warrant for Gülen for allegedly violating Article 163 of the Penal Code, which prosecuted alleged offenses against the official doctrine of state secularism. Gülen remained a fugitive and kept a low profile and this warrant was removed by Özal in 1983.
31. In Gülen's television interview, he sharply criticized Erbakan and political Islam; see "Hocaefendi'den güncel yorumlar," *Zaman*, April 16, 1997.
32. Gülay Göktürk, "Devletin inayetiyle," *Sabah*, June 25, 1999.
33. More on Ecevit's defense of Gülen, see *Zaman*, March 14, 1998; Nazlı Ilıcak, "Fethullah Gülen'in Gönül Penceresinden," *Akşam*, March 13, 1998.
34. Filiz Baskan, "The Political Economy of Islamic Finance in Turkey: The Role of Fethullah Gülen and Asya Finans," in *The Politics of Islamic Finance*, ed. Clement M. Henry and Rodney Wilson (Edinburgh: Edinburgh University Press, 2004), 236.
35. Ertuğrul Özkök, "Fethullahçılık ve Tarikat" and "Hoca Efendi anlatıyor," *Hürriyet*, January 23–30, 1995; Nuriye Akman, "Fethullah Hoca anlatıyor," *Sabah*, January 30, 1995.
36. Turkish channel ATV, June 18, 1999. http://www.meforum.org/2045/fethullah-Gülens-grand-ambition#_ftnref47.
37. The file of 2000/124 Second State Security Court in Ankara.
38. More on the media attack, see *Milliyet*, June 21–28, 1999; *Sabah*, June 21–29, 1999; *Turkish Daily News*, June 21, 1999.
39. More on the West Working Group, see Jeremy Salt, "Turkey's Military Democracy," *Current History* 98 (1999): 72–78.
40. *Zaman*, June 21–27, 1999.
41. Brian Knowlton's interview with Gülen, see *Turkish Review*, 1:2 (2011): 47.
42. Ibid., 46.
43. Martha Woodall and Claudio Gatti, "FBI Investigating Gülen Schools in the US," *Philadelphia Enquirer*, March 23, 2011.
44. Nuriye Akman, *Gurbette Fethullah Gülen* (Istanbul: Zaman, 2004).
45. Nevval Sevindi, *Fethullah Gülen ile New York Sohbeti* (İstanbul: Sabah Kitapçılık, 1997); Mehmet Gündem, *Fethullah Gülen'le 11 Gün* (Istanbul: Alfa Basım, 2005).
46. *Fethullah Gülen v. Michael Chertoff, Secretary, U.S. Dept. of Homeland Security, et al*, Case 2:07-cv-02148-SD, US District Court for the Eastern District of Pennsylvania.

47. Some articles in the West on the Gülen movement have been particularly shallow and superficial. A good example is Suzy Hansen, "The Global Imam," *The New Republic*, November 10, 2010.
48. "Fethullah Gülen: A Farm Boy on the World Stage," *The Economist*, May 6, 2008.

CHAPTER 2

1. Paul Tillich, *Systematic Theology*, 1951–63, 3 vols. (Chicago: University of Chicago Press, 1963); *The Courage to Be* (New Haven: Yale University Press, 1952).
2. Gülen, *Fountain*, 53 (January–March 2006), accessed April 5, 2011, http://www.fountainmagazine.com/article.php?ARTICLEID=751/.
3. Fethullah Gülen, "Mana kökleriyle irtibatlı kahramanlar yetiştirmeliyiz," *Zaman*, November 18, 2010.
4. Marshall Hodgson defines Islamicate as something that "would refer not directly to the religion, Islam, itself, but to the social and cultural complex historically associated with Islam and the Muslims, both among Muslims themselves and even when found among non-Muslims" *Venture of Islam* (Chicago: University of Chicago Press, 1977), 59.
5. M. Hakan Yavuz, "Is There a Turkish Islam? The Emergence of Convergence and Consensus," *Journal of Muslim Minority Affairs* 24 (2004): 1–22. This article examines seven diverse ethno-cultural zones of Islam. Each zone's understanding of Islam is primarily informed by national culture and diverse historical and economic factors.
6. For a more critical treatment of Gülen's community, see M. Hakan Yavuz, "Nasıl bir Türkiye," *Milliyet*, August 11, 1997.
7. For more on the debate on the Islam in Turkey, see Eyup Can, *Fethullah Gülen Hocaefendi ile Ufuk Turu* (Istanbul: Doğan, 1996), 33; Nur Vergin, "Türkiye Müslümanlığı ve Sözde Türk İslamı," *Yeni Yüzyıl*, September 6, 1998; Ismail Kara, "Ha Türk Müslümanlığı, ha Türk-Islam Sentezi," *Milliyet*, September 7, 1997.
8. Hans Urs von Balthasar and Edward T. Oakes, *The Theology of Karl Barth: Exposition and Interpretation* (Edinburg: Ignatius Press, 1992).
9. Interview in Istanbul, May 10, 2009.
10. Charles Taylor, *Sources of the Self: The Making of the Modern Identity* (Cambridge, MA: Harvard University Press, 1992); Michael Walzer, *The Spheres of Justice* (New York: Basic Books, 1984).
11. Ali Ünal and Williams Alphonse, *Advocate of Dialogue: Fethullah Gülen* (Fairfax, VA: The Fountain, 2000), 57–58.
12. My interview with Gülen in Philadelphia, October 12, 2000.
13. For more on Gülen's views on Iran, Arabs, and Turkish Islam, see the interview with Gülen in *Yeni Yüzyıl*, July 19–28, 1997.
14. Anthony Giddens, *Conversations with Anthony Giddens: Making Sense of Modernity* (Stanford, CA: Stanford University Press, 1998), 94.
15. Gülen's experience in the West has been much more positive than that of Sayyid Qutb. Qutb had a very negative experience in the West and come to the conclusion that it was not the model to be emulated.
16. Nuriye Akman's interview with Gülen, *Sabah*, January 26, 1995, accessed October 12, 2011, http://tr.fgulen.com/content/view/7851/74/.

17. Nuriye Akman's interview with Gülen, *Sabah*, January 26, 1995, accessed October 12, 2011, http://tr.fgulen.com/content/view/7851/74/.
18. For books on Soroush, see Mahmoud Sadri and Ahmad Sadri, *Reason, Freedom, and Democracy in Islam: Essential Writings of Soroush* (New York: Oxford University Press, 2002); Azzam S. Tamimi, *Rachid Ghannouchi: A Democrat within Islamism* (New York: Oxford University Press, 2001).
19. Yavuz Cobanoğlu, "Fethullah Gülen'de Sosyal Ahlak Tasavvuru" (Ph.D. diss., Ege Universitesi, Izmir, 2008), 96–108.
20. Zeki Sarıtoprak's interview with Gülen, *Muslim World* 95 (2005): 451.
21. Ibid., 452.
22. Bekim Agai, "Discursive and Organizational Strategies of the Gülen Movement," accessed April 5, 2011, http://www.fethullahgulen.org/conference-papers/294-the-fethullah-gulen-movement-i/2132-discursive-and-organizational-strategies-of-the-gulen-movement.html/.
23. Fethullah Gülen, *Hoşgörü ve Diyalog İklimi* (İstanbul: Merkur Yayıncılık, 1998).

CHAPTER 3

1. M. Hakan Yavuz, *Islamic Political Identity in Turkey* (New York: Oxford University Press, 2003), 133–150.
2. For an analysis of Fethullah Gülen's *Ufuk Turu*, see Nilüfer Göle, "Muhafazakarlığının Manalandırdığı Modernlik," in Eyup Can, *Fethullah Gülen Hocaefendi ile Ufuk Turu*, (Istanbul: Doğan Kitap, 1996), 207.
3. Gülen's interview in *Sabah*, January 29, 1995; Can, *Ufuk Turu*, 111.
4. Robert W. Hefner and Muhammad Q. Zaman, eds., *Schooling in Islam: The Culture and Religion of Modern Muslim Education* (Princeton: Princeton University Press, 2006).
5. Dale F. Eickelman and James Picatori, *Muslim Politics* (Princeton: Princeton University Press, 2004).
6. Fethullah Gülen's biography, accessed May 12, 2010, http://www.fgulen.com/.
7. Joe Lauria, "Reclusive Turkish Imam Criticizes Gaza Flotilla," *Wall Street Journal*, June 4, 2011.
8. Ahmet Yaşar Ocak, ed. *Sufism and Sufis in Ottoman Society* (Ankara: Türk Tarih Kurumu, 2001).
9. Interviews with Gülen, Istanbul, April 25, 1997; and Philadelphia, April 12, 2000.
10. Interview in Istanbul, May 8, 2010.
11. Interview in Istanbul, May 11, 2010. The Committee of Union and Progress (CUP) was established in 1889 by four college students (Ibrahim Temo, Abdullah Cevdet, Ishak Sükuti, and Hüzeyinzade Ali) with the purpose of saving the state through restructuring Ottoman society according to modern positivism and laws.
12. Interview in Istanbul, May 11, 2010.
13. Ibid.
14. Ibid.
15. Almost all Nurcu groups use "*iman hizmeti*" (service to faith) in order to describe the Nur movement. Said Nursi described his own efforts and writings as "*iman hizmeti*" (serving for faith). In the case of Gülen, he omits "faith" (iman) and just

uses *hizmet* due to his sensitivities about appealing to modern public culture in Turkey.
16. Etienne Copeaux, "*Hizmet*: A Keyword in the Turkish Historical Narrative," *New Perspectives on Turkey* 14 (1996): 97–114.
17. Interview in Istanbul, May 28, 2011. Those "longed ones" are mentioned in the statement of prophet Muhammad. I summarized this hadith in the first page of this chapter.
18. Fethullah Gülen, *Ölçü veya Yoldaki Işıklar* (Istanbul: Nil, 1985), 208; cited in Ali Ünal, *Bir Potre Denemesi: M. Fethullah Gülen* (Istanbul: Nil, 2002), 211.
19. Ünal, *Bir Potre Denemesi*, 267.
20. Yavuz, *Islamic Political Identity*, 187.
21. Fethullah Gülen, *Key Concepts in the Practice of Sufism: Emerald Hills of the Heart* 2 (Somerset, NJ: The Light, 2004), 235.
22. Elisabeth Özdalga, "Worldly Asceticism in Islamic Casting: Fethullah Gülen's Inspired Piety and Activism," *Critique* 17 (2000): 83–104.
23. Max Weber, "The Protestant Sect and the Spirit of Capitalism," in *From Max Weber: Essays in Sociology*, ed. H. H. Gerth and C. Wright Mills (New York: A Galaxy Book, 1958), 302–322.
24. Interview in Aydın, June 5, 2011.
25. Interview in Ankara, July 16, 2010.
26. Interview in Ankara, July 18, 2010.
27. Ibid.
28. Interview in Istanbul, July 22, 2010.
29. Robert Putnam, *Making Democracy Work: Civic Tradition in Modern Italy* (Princeton: Princeton University Press, 1993); Francis Fukuyama, "Social Capital and Global Economy," *Foreign Affairs* 74 (1995): 89–103.
30. Fethullah Gülen, "Düşünce ve Aksiyon İnsanı," *Zaman*, November 27, 1994.
31. Fethullah Gülen, "Beklenen Geçlik I, II," in *Çağ ve Nesil: Zamanın Altın Dilimi IV* (İzmir: TÖV, 1992), 125–132.
32. Fethullah Gülen, "Dünya Muvazenesinde Bir Millet," in *Çağ ve Nesil I* (İzmir: TÖV, 1992), 88–92.
33. Erol N. Gülay, "The Gülen Phenomenon: A Neo-Sufi Challenge to Turkey's Rival Elite," *Middle East Critique* 16:1 (2007): 37–61.
34. Max Weber, *The Sociology of Religion* (Boston: Beacon, 1963), 116–117.

Chapter 4
1. B. Russell, *Education of Character* (New York: Philosophical Library, 1961), 158.
2. M. Hakan Yavuz, "Towards an Islamic Liberalism?: The Nurcu Movement and Fethullah Gülen," *Middle East Journal* 53:4 (1999): 599; and M. Hakan Yavuz, "Orta Asya'daki Kimlik Oluşumu: Yeni Kolonizatör Dervişler-Nurcular"*Türkiye Günlüğü* 33 (1995): 160–164.
3. Ali Ünal and Williams Alphonse, *Advocate of Dialogue: Fethullah Gülen*, (Fairfax, VA: The Fountain, 1999), 305.
4. Bekim Agai, "Islam and Education in Secular Turkey: State Policies and the Emergence of the Fethullah Gülen Group," in *Schooling Islam: The Culture and Politics of*

Modern Muslim Education (Princeton: Princeton University Press, 2006), 149–171.
5. Much of the criticism of the Gülen movement has to do with the emergence of these new alternative elites who challenge the status and privilege of the Republican/Kemalist elite.
6. Ünal and Williams, *Advocate*, 148.
7. Bekim Agai, "Fethullah Gülen and his Movement's Ethic of Education," *Middle East Critique* 11:1 (2002): 27–47.
8. Gülen, *Fasıldan Fasıla 3* (Izmir: Nil Yayınları, 1996), 214; Eyup Can, *Fethullah Gülen ile Ufuk Turu* (Istanbul: Doğan Kitap, 1996), 43.
9. Gülen says that *hizmet* or *davet* (the call for Islam) are not fixed, but that they must be practiced in relation to time and place. This is what distinguished his position from a fundamentalist's approach. Fethullah Gülen, *Fasıldan Fasıla 2* (Izmir: Nil, 1995), 67.
10. Ünal and Williams, *Advocate*, 308–309.
11. Gülen was seeking to realize Mehmet Akif Ersoy's (1873–1936) dreams to cultivate a new generation (*Asım'ın Nesli*). Akif, Safahat (Gülen has been preaching about a project of "Golden Generation" (*Altın Nesil*), which is similar to the one mentioned by Akif.
12. Fethullah Gülen, *Ölçü veya Yoldaki Işıklar 4*, 8th edn. (Izmir: T.Ö.V., 1998), 87.
13. Ünal and Williams, *Advocate*, 103.
14. Ibid., 313.
15. Agai, "Fethullah Gülen," 33.
16. Yavuz, *Islamic Political Identity in Turkey* (New York: Oxford University Press, 2003), 193.
17. M. Hakan Yavuz, "The Gülen Movement: The Turkish Puritans," in *Turkish Islam and the Secular State*, eds. John Esposito and M. Hakan Yavuz (Syracuse: Syracuse University Press, 2003), 19–47.
18. Interview in Istanbul, August 5, 2010.
19. Richard L. Gawthrop, *Pietism and the Making of Eighteenth-Century Prussia* (New York: Cambridge University Press, 1993).
20. Interview in Istanbul, August 5, 2010.
21. Interview in Paderborn, July 1, 2010.
22. Interview in Cologne, July 2, 2010.
23. Ibid.
24. Interview in Istanbul, June 3, 2010.
25. Interview in Istanbul, June 4, 2010.
26. Paulo Freire, *Pedagogy of the Oppressed* (New York: Continuum, 1972), 77.
27. On şahs-ı manevi, see Mehmet Enes Ergene, *Tradition Witnessing the Modern Age* (Somerset, NJ: Tughra, 2008), 162–163.
28. Ibid., 162.
29. Ibid., 97.
30. Ergene does not fully understand the Ottoman history of this period. He presents a unified and romantic vision. His presentation of the Tanzimat period is very much derived from the radical Islamist perspective at odds with Gülen's own writings.
31. Ergene, *Tradition*, 105.

32. İsmail Ünal, *Fethullah Gülen'le Amerika'da Bir Ay*, (Istanbul: Işık Yayınları, 2001), 140.
33. Interview in Istanbul, June 4, 2010.
34. Özlem Kocabaş, "Scientific Careers and Ideological Profiles of Science Olympiad Participants from Fethullah Gülen and Other Secondary Schools in Turkey" (MA thesis, Middle East Technical University, 2006), 4, accessed October 18, 2011, http://etd.lib.metu.edu.tr/upload/12607217/index.pdf/.
35. Interview in Skopje, July 21, 2010.
36. Ibid.
37. Interview in Sarajevo, August 3, 2011.
38. Interview in Sarajevo, August 4, 2011.
39. The Gülen movement established Bosna Sema Educational Foundation in 1996 and opened five high schools and International Burch University in war-torn country. These schools have over 2,000 Bosnian students. The Foundation remodeled the old Serbian military garrison in Vraca neighborhood and turned it into a multinational high school. More on the schools, see http://www.bosnasema.com/index.php?p=7.
40. Fethullah Gülen, *Prizma I* (Izmir: Nil Yayınları, 1998), 63–67.
41. Interview in Istanbul, July 28, 2011.
42. Interview in Istanbul, August 10, 2011.
43. Ahmet İnsel, "Altın Nesil, Yeni Muhafazakarlık ve Fethullah Gülen," *Birikim* 99 (1997): 67–75; Ömer Laciner, "Postmodern Bir Dini Hareket: Fethullah Hoca cemaati," *Birikim* 76 (1995): 9–11.
44. Elizabeth Özdalga, "Secularizing Trends in Fethullah Gülen's Movement: Impasses or Opportunity for Further Renewal?" *Middle East Critique* 12 (2003): 72.
45. Kocabaş, "Scientific Careers," 41–42, 50.
46. "Bildung" not only implies the dimension of teaching but also that of learning ("*sich bilden*"), not only knowledge and skills but also values, ethos, personality, authenticity, and humanity.
47. Edward J. Lazzerini, "Ismail Bey Gasprinskii and Muslim Modernism in Russia, 1878–1914" (Ph.D. diss., University of Washington, 1973).
48. Adeeb Khalid, *The Politics of Muslim Cultural Reform* (Berkeley: University of California Press, 1998).
49. Fethullah Gülen, *Pearls of Wisdom*. (Somerset, NJ: The Light, 2005). http://talkislam.com/iquotes/quote.php?nNewsId=14370&nCatId=256.

CHAPTER 5

1. Fethullah Gülen, *Enginliğiyle Bizim Dünyamız: İktisadî Mülâhazalar* (Istanbul: Nil Yayınları, 2009). This book consists of Gülen's sermons that were delivered in the late 1970s and early 1980s. The collection of articles provides Gülen's views about social and economic life.
2. Bryan S. Turner, "Islam, Capitalism and the Weber Theses," *British Journal of Sociology* 61 (2010): 147–160.
3. Maxime Rodinson, *Islam and Capitalism* (New York: Pantheon, 1974).
4. In one of my meeting with Fethullah Gülen in America, I summarized for him Max Weber's view and asked him his opinion about Weber's argument. He said:

Weber mixes doctrine and history. He is right that sometimes "the warrior group" became dominant but that was the outcome of a historical context in some specific time and place. It cannot be reduced to the doctrine of Islam. Moreover, Islam is the religion of cities and commerce, not a "warrior religion." The origins of the underdevelopment and colonization of Muslim lands are rooted in the social, historical, and most importantly international context. Although I do not share Weber's conclusions, from what I have known about his writings, his method of understanding through interpretation is very important. Interview, on June 7, 2008.

5. Toby E. Huff and Wolfgang Schluchter, eds., *Max Weber and Islam* (New Brunswick, NJ: Transaction, 1999), 15.
6. Elizabeth Özdalga, "Worldly Asceticism in Islamic Casting: Fethullah Gülen's Inspired Piety and Activism," *Critique: Critical Middle Eastern Studies* 17 (2000): 87.
7. Selcuk Uyar, "'Islamic Puritanism' as a Source of Economic Development: The Case of Fethullah Gülen Movement," in *International Conference Proceedings: Muslim World in Transition: Contributions of the Gülen Movement* (Leeds: Leeds Metropolitan University, 2007), 176–186.
8. Max Weber, *The Protestant Ethic and the Spirit of Capitalism* (Los Angeles: Roxbury Publishing, 2002).
9. Fethullah Gülen, "Asceticism," *Key Concepts in the Practice of Sufism: Emerald Hills of the Heart* 1 (Somerset, NJ: The Light, 2006), 42–43.
10. A follower of Gülen, who stresses asceticism in his daily and family life, told me, "There is a close relationship between freedom and ascetic life. Asceticism frees one's soul from worldly desires and temptations, appetite and this 'worldliness' (*dünyevileşme*) brings slavery and devotion to the wealth and property. This, in turn, leads to the loss of freedom."
11. Elizabeth Özdalga, "Secularizing Trends in Fethullah Gülen's Movement: Impasse or Opportunity for Further Renewal," *Critique: Critical Middle Eastern Studies* 12:1 (2003): 62.
12. Berger defines "elective affinity" as the convergence between "certain ideas and certain social processes seek each other out." Peter Berger, "Charisma and Religious Innovation: The Social Location of Israelite Prophecy," *American Sociological Review* 28 (1963): 940–950.
13. Interview in Istanbul, July 16, 2010.
14. Interview in Istanbul, July 18, 2010.
15. Ibid.
16. Interview in Istanbul, July 19, 2010.
17. Filiz Baskan, "The Political Economy of Islamic Finance in Turkey: The Role of Fethullah Gülen and Asya Finans," in *The Politics of Islamic Finance*, ed. Clement M. Henry and Rodney Wilson (Edinburgh: Edinburgh University Press, 2004), 216–239.
18. http://ishad.org.tr/kurumsal/index.php?anahtar=hakkimizda.
19. http://www.hursiad.org.tr/Is/Index.aspx.
20. http://www.tuskon.org/?yenilisan=en.

Chapter 6

1. Giancarlo Bosetti and Klaus Eder, "Post-Secularism: A Return to the Public Sphere," *Eurozine*, August 17, 2006 [online journal], accessed March 7, 2010, http://www.eurozine.com/articles/2006-08-17-eder-en.html.
2. Jürgen Habermas, *The Structural Transformation of the Public Sphere: An Inquiry into a Category of Bourgeois Society* (Cambridge, MA: MIT Press, 1989), 27.
3. The public sphere in France means "the space where the State exerts its authority for the benefit of all and at the service of all." Blandine Chelini-Pont, "Religion in the Public Sphere: Challenges and Opportunities," *Brigham Young University Law Review* 3 (2005): 615.
4. Jürgen Habermas, *Between Naturalism and Religion: Philosophical Essays* (Cambridge: Polity Press, 2008).
5. John Rawls, "The Idea of Public Reason Revisited," in *Collected Papers* (Cambridge, MA: Harvard University Press, 1999), 575. Public reasoning is "argument addressed to others: it proceeds correctly from premises we accept and think others reasonably accept to conclusions we think they could also reasonably accept" (593–594).
6. The public sphere, as a contested zone over identity, authority, and resources, either seeks to discipline diverse opinions and practices or facilitates their emancipation from hegemonic discourses by empowering them with new ideas. By counter public, I mean a public with a different normativity and sense of justice and the good life. Moreover, the counter public under certain conditions absorbs the "official" public because the goal of the counter public is to change the normative foundations of the official hegemonic public. My understanding of the counter and "official" publics is very much informed by the Turkish experience.
7. Jürgen Habermas, "Religion in the Public Sphere," trans. Jeremy Gaines, *European Journal of Philosophy* 14:1 (2006): 9–10 [article online], accessed March 8, 2011, http://www.law.nyu.edu/clppt/program2006/readings/Habermas.Religion.pdf.
8. Ibid., 11.
9. Christa Case, "Germans Reconsider Religion," *Christian Science Monitor*, September 15, 2006 [newspaper online], accessed November 6, 2006, http://www.csmonitor.com/2006/0915/p01s01-woeu.html.
10. Virgil Nemoianu, "The Church and the Secular Establishment: A Philosophical Dialog between Joseph Ratzinger and Jürgen Habermas," *Logos: A Journal of Catholic Thought and Culture* 9 (2006): 20, 22.
11. Peter Rowe, "Spotlight on Public Role of Religion," *The San Diego Union-Tribune*, March 3, 2005 [newspaper online], accessed December 1, 2006, http://www.signonsandiego.com/uniontrib/20050303/news_lz1c3role.html.
12. On this point and the broader relationship between Islam, secularism, and democracy, see the valuable theoretical contribution made by Nader Hashemi, *Islam, Secularism and Liberal Democracy: Toward a Democratic Theory for Muslim Societies* (New York: Oxford University Press, 2009).
13. Safa Mürsel, *Bediüzzaman Said Nursi ve Devlet Felsefesi* (İstanbul: Yeni Asya, 1995); Yavuz Bahadıroğlu, *Bediüzzaman Said Nursi* (İstanbul: Yeni Asya, 1993); İbrahim

Canan, *İslam Aleminin Ana Meseleleri: Bediüzzaman'dan Çözümler* (İstanbul: Yeni Asya, 1993).
14. Habermas, *Structural Transformation*.
15. Bedri Gencer, "The Rise of Public Opinion in the Ottoman Empire (1839–1909)," *New Perspectives on Turkey* 30 (2004): 115–154.
16. Brian Knowlton's interview with Gülen, *Turkish Review* 1:2 (2011): 50.
17. The *Zaman* newspaper first was published on November 3, 1986.
18. *Zaman* is published in Germany in Turkish, Azerbaijan (8 pages and only one page is Turkish), Kazakhstan (8 pages; 6 Kazak and 2 Turkish), Kyrgyzstan (8 pages; 6 Kyrgyz; 2 Turkish), Turkmenistan (6 pages; 1 Turkish; 5 Turkmen), Tatarstan (4 pages; 1 Turkish; 3 Tatar), Boshgortastan (5 pages; 4 Baskurt; 1 Turkish), Bulgaria (16 pages; 12 Turkish; 4 Bulgarian), Romania (16 pages in Turkish) and Macedonia (8 pages; 6 Turkish; 2 Macedonian).
19. Blue Dome Press publishes books and journals to promote the Gülen movement. More see, http://www.bluedomepress.com/.
20. See, for example, his essay, "Tahrib edilen tabiat," *Zaman*, June 25, 1994.
21. For more on the debate over the Abant Declaration, see Kerem Çalıskan,"Fethullah Hoca ve Laiklik," *Yeni Yüzyıl*, July 21, 1998. Some scholars criticized the Declaration as a sign of the politicization of Islam, see Yakup Kepenek, "Abant Bildirgesi," *Cumhuriyet*, July 27, 1998; Ahmet Tasgetiren, a prominent Islamist writer, argues that "Gülen is seeking to facilitate the task of the secularists military establishment by distorting Islam" in "Abant'in Cözemediği Sorun," *Yeni Safak*, July 27, 1998.
22. For the full text of the Abant Declaration and debate, see Mehmet Gündem, *Abant Toplantıları I: Islam ve Laiklik* (Istanbul: Gazeteciler ve Yazarlar Vakfı, 1998), 269–272.
23. *Abant Platformu 4: Çoğulculuk ve Toplumsal Uzlaşma* (Istanbul: GYVY, 2001).
24. "The Declaration of the Abant Platform, July 2001," in *Abant Platformu 4*, 316.
25. Interview in Ankara, June 24, 2009.
26. Interview in Istanbul, June 2, 2009.
27. Interview in Ankara, June 4, 2009.
28. The Dialogue Eurasia Platform also publishes the DA Magazine both in Russian and Turkish. It includes a series of articles to stress the common heritage and concerns between the former Soviet republics and Turkey. The magazine also stresses the relations between the Orthodox Church and Islam.
29. Accessed March 10, 2010, http://www.abantplatform.org.
30. Interview in Ankara, June 4, 2004.
31. Interview in Istanbul, June 1, 2009.
32. Ibid.
33. Interview in Istanbul, June 6, 2009.
34. Interview in Istanbul, June 7, 2009.
35. Nadia Urbinati, "'Laicité in Reverse': Mono-Religious Democracies and the Issue of Religion in the Public Sphere," *Constellations* 17 (2010): 4–21.

Chapter 7

1. More on secularism, see *Secularism and Muslim Democracy in Turkey* (New York: Cambridge University Press, 2009), 144–170.

2. Niyazi Berkes, *The Development of Secularism in Turkey* (New York: Routledge, 1998).
3. Bekim Agai, "Fethullah Gülen and his Movement's Islamic Ethics of Education," *Critical Middle Eastern Studies* (Spring 2002): 31.
4. The Tanzimat reforms brought a series of changes to consolidate state power and prevent the decline of the Ottoman Empire. Namık Kemal (1840–1888) and Şinasi (1826–1871) were the two most important intellectuals who defended Islamic modernization, along with constitutionalism and the sovereignty of the people. Namık Kemal was the first Ottoman intellectual to develop a liberal Islamic project by stressing the concept of rights and seeking to vernacularize them in Islamic terms. Şinasi, who published *Tasvir-i Efkar*, in 1860, was much more positivist in orientation and stressed the role of science in rebuilding Ottoman society through educating the masses. Şinasi was deeply influenced by the positivist ideas of Ahmet Rıza. Namık Kemal, Şinasi, and Said Halim Paşa blamed the traditional *ulema* stating that they had betrayed the rich Islamic tradition of scientific inquiry. The conservative backward attitude of the *ulema* turned educated Muslim elites against them and they demanded far-reaching reforms in education and religious leadership. Said Halim was in favor of the modernization of the Ottoman state and society but vehemently against a slavishly imitative Westernization. In other words, Said Halim identified the lack of scientific research and thinking as the cause of the Muslim decline and backwardness and argued that this state of affairs brought about the occupation of Muslim countries. This European colonialism, in turn, had destructive implications, leading to Muslim anger and repulsion of anything to do with Europe. Said Halim Pasha, "The Reform of Muslim Society," *Islamic Culture* (Haydarabat) I, 1 (1927): 111–135; Said Halim Pasa, *Buhranlarımız ve Son Eserleri* (Istanbul: Iz, 2003); Hasan Kayalı, "Islam in the Thought and Politics of Two Late Ottoman Intellectuals: Mehmed Akif and Said Halim," *Archivum Ottomanicum* 19 (2001): 309; Ahmet Seyhun, *Said Halim Pasha: Ottoman Statesman and Islamist Thinker* (Istanbul: Isis, 2003), and Küdret Bülbül, *Bir Devlet Adam ve Siyasal Düsünür Olarak Said Halim Pasa* (Ankara: Kadim, 2006).
5. Auguste Comte (1798–1857) is regarded as the founder of positivist philosophy. Émile Durkheim (1858–1917) rejected this vulgar positivism using the scientific method of natural sciences to attempt to understand social events. He insisted that the study of social facts required a separate scientific methodology.
6. M. Şükrü Hanioğlu, "Blueprints for a Future Society: Late Ottoman Materialists on Science, Religion, and Art," in *Late Ottoman Society: The Intellectual Legacy*, ed. Elisabeth Özdalga (Abingdon: Routledge/Curzon, 2005), 28.
7. Mehmet Akgün, *Materyazilniin Türkiye'ye Girişi ve İlk Etkileri* (Ankara: Kültür ve Turizm Bakanlığı Yayını, 1988); Ekrem Işın, "Osmanlı Materyalizmi," *Tanzimat'tan Cumhuriyete Türkiye Ansiklopedisi*. c. 2 (Istanbul: İletişim Yayınlan, 1985), 363–370; Murtaza Korlaelci, *Pozitivizmin Türkiye'ye Girişi ve İlk Etkileri* (Istanbul: İnsan Yayınları, 1986); Şerif Mardin, *Jön Türklerin Siyasi Fikirleri 1895–1908* (Istanbul: İletişim Yayınları, 1989); *Meclis-i Mebusan ve Ayân Reisi Ahmed Rıza Bey'in Anıları* (Istanbul: Arba Yayınlan, 1988); C. Parkan Özturan, *İlk Türk Materyalisti Beşir Fuad'ın Mektupları* (Istanbul: Arba, 1987); Orhan Okay, *Besir Fuat: İlk Türk Pozitivisti ve Naturalisti* (Istanbul: Dergah, 2008).

8. Erol Nazim Gülay, "The Theological Thought of Fethullah Gülen: Reconciling Science with Islam" (MA thesis, Oxford University, St Anthony College, 2007), 15.
9. Şerif Mardin, *Religion and Social Change in Turkey: The Case of Bediüzzaman Said Nursi* (Albany: State University of New York Press, 1989), 214.
10. Nursi, *The Words*, 13th Word, trans. Ş. Vahide, 169, http://www.nursistudies.com.
11. George Becker, "Pietism's Confrontation with Enlightenment Rationalism: An Examination of the Relation between Ascetic Protestantism and Science," *Journal of the Scientific Study of Religion* 30:2 (1991): 141.
12. Ibid., 142.
13. Asharite occasionalism removes the possibility of human free will by arguing that every human act is willed by God. In other words, all our actions and fate is predetermined by God and thus we should not be responsible of our actions. Toby E. Huff, *The Rise of Early Modern Science: Islam, China, and the West*, 2nd edn. (Cambridge: Cambridge University Press, 2003).
14. Fethullah Gülen, *Understanding and Beliefs: The Essential of Islamic Faith* (Izmir: Kaynak, 1997), 309.
15. Ibid., 308.
16. Ibid., 307.
17. Ibid., 318–319.
18. Ibid., 334.
19. Ibid., 335.
20. Agai, "Fethullah Gülen," 31.
21. Gülen, *Understanding and Beliefs*, 288–300.
22. Ibid., 303–304.
23. Ibid., 333.
24. İrfan Yılmaz et al., *Yeni Bir Bakış Açısıyla İlim ve Din* (Izmir: Nil Yayınları, 1998), 10.
25. Fethullah Gülen, *Günler Baharı Soluklarken* (Istanbul: Nil Yayınları, 2002), 98–99.
26. Gülen, *Kendi Dünyamıza Doğru*, 142.
27. Thomas K. Carr, *Newman and Gadamer: Toward a Hermeneutic of Religious Knowledge* (Atlanta: Scholar Press, 1996).
28. Ibid., 70.
29. Clifford Geertz, "Religion as a Cultural System" in , *Anthropological Approaches to the Study of Religion* ed. M. Banton (London: Methuen, 1968), 28.
30. For one of the best studies of Gülen's views on science, see Gülay, "The Theological Thought of Fethullah Gülen."
31. Although Gülay is critical of my "internal secularization of Islam" thesis, I think he has misunderstood Nursi and Gülen's position on science. Both of them seek to marshal science to provide a secure ground for the claims of the Qur'an, 5–7.
32. Sükran Vahide, "Toward an Intellectual Biography of Said Nursi," in *Islam at the Crossroads*, ed. Ibrahim Abu-Rabi (Albany: State University of New York Press, 2003), 14.
33. Kelton Cobb, "Revelation, the Disciplines of Reason, and Truth in the Works of Said Nursi and Paul Tillich," in *Islam at the Crossroads*, 135.
34. Said Nursi, Risale-i Nur Collection, accessed June 10, 2011, http://www.nursistudies.com/risale.php?kid=1&sno=420.
35. Fethullah Gülen, "Question for Today," *The Fountain* 8 (1994).

36. Fethullah Gülen, "A Comparative Approach to Islam and Democracy," *SAIS Review* 21:2 (2001): 136.
37. Gülen, *Pearls of Wisdom*, accessed June, 12, 2011, http://talkislam.com/iquotes/quote.php?nNewsId=14364&nCatId=255.
38. Ibid.
39. Fethullah Gülen, "Humanity, Science, and Globalization," *The Foundation* 41:January–March (2003), accessed June 14, 2011, http://en.fgulen.com/a.page/books/a1218.html.
40. Fethullah Gülen, "The Concept of Science and Technology," 2004, accessed June 12, 2011, http://en.fgulen.com/a.page/books/essentials.of.the.islamic.faith/the.holy.quran/a691.html.
41. I am grateful to Mujeeb R. Khan for these insights.

CHAPTER 8

1. Lucien F. Cosijns, *Dialogue among the Faith Communities* (Lanham, MD: Hamilton Books, 2008), 4.
2. Norman Daniel, *Islam and the West: The Making of an Image* (Oxford: Oneworld, 1993).
3. Giulio Basetti-Sani, *Louis Massignon (1883–1962): Christian Ecumenist; Prophet of Interreligious Reconciliation*, trans. Allan Harris Cutler (Chicago: Franciscan Herald Press, 1974); Mary Louise Gude, *Louis Massignon: The Crucible of Compassion* (Notre Dame, IN and London: University of Notre Dame Press, 1996), 55. In fact, the close engagement with Islam helped Massignon to discover his own Christian value and caused his "conversion" to Christianity.
4. Paul Knitter, *No Other Name?: A Critical Survey of Christian Attitudes toward the World Religions* (Maryknoll, NY: Orbis, 1985).
5. Charles Taylor, "Liberal Politics and the Public Sphere," in *Philosophical Arguments* (Cambridge, MA: Harvard University Press, 1995).
6. James Coleman, "Social Capital in the Creation of Human Capital," *American Journal of Sociology* 94 (1988): 95–120.
7. Mark Granovetter, "The Strength of Weak Ties," *American Journal of Sociology* 78 (1978): 1360–1380.
8. Hans Küng and Karl-Joseph Kuschel, *A Global Ethics: The Declaration of the Parliament of the World's Religions* (New York: Continuum Press, 1995).
9. Alan Race, *Christians and Religious Pluralism: Patterns in the Christian Theology of Religions* (London: SCM Press, 1983); Jaques Dupuis, S.J., *Toward a Christian Theology of Religious Pluralism* (Maryknoll, NY: Orbis Books, 2002). He modifies these typologies from a Catholic perspective.
10. Eygi is also a leading anti-Semitic in Turkey, see Mehmet Şevket Eygi, *Iki Kimlikli, Esrarlı ve Çok Güçlü Bir Cemaat: Yahudi Türkler Yahut Sabetaycılar* (Istanbul: Zvi-Geyik Yayınları, 2000).
11. The best book on Nursi's theology of dialogue, see Ian Markham, *Engaging with Bediüzzaman Said Nursi: A Model of Interfaith Dialogue* (Farnham, England: Ashgate Publishing, 2009).
12. Karl Rahner, *Foundations of Christian Faith* (New York: Crossroad, 1978), 311–318. Rahner did not actually promote interfaith. Many scholars criticized Rahner's

concept of "anonymous." Nursi, unlike Rahner, closely studied other religions and proposed a framework for interfaith dialogue.
13. John Moffitt, "Interreligious Encounter and the Problem of Salvataion," *Christian Century*, November 17, 1976, 1001–1002.
14. Said Nursi in "A Call to the People of the Book," 23rd Word from the Risale-I Nur Collection, 2007 edition, 73–75.
15. As quoted in Osman Cilaci, "Comments on the Holy Bible in the Risale-i Nur," in *A Contemporary Approach to Understanding the Qur'an: The Example of the "Risale-i Nur"* (Istanbul: Sözler, 2000), 585.
16. Thomas Michel, "Muslim-Christian Dialogue and Co-operation in Bediüzzaman's Thought," In *A Contemporary Approach to Understanding the Qur'an: The Example of the Risale-I Nur* (Istanbul: Sözler Nesriyat, 2000), 557.
17. Wilfred Cantwell Smith, *Toward a World Theology: Faith and the Comparative History of Religion* (Philadelphia: Westminster Press, 1981); Diana Eck, "Prospect for Pluralism: Voice and Vision in the Study of Religion," *Journal of American Academy of Religion* 75:4 (2007): 743–766; Martin Marty, *When Faiths Collide* (Malden, MA: Blackwell Publishing, 2005).
18. John Hick, *An Interpretation of Religion: Human Response to the Transcendent* (New Haven: Yale University Press, 2005).
19. Martin Buber, *I and Thou*, trans. Ronald G. Smith (New York: Scribner, 2000).
20. MR Bawa Muhaiyaddeen, *Islam and World Peace* (Philadelphia: Fellowship Press, 1987). A Sri Lankan Sufi (d. 1986) and offered a most comprehensive vision of interfaith dialogue by stressing that we are all creatures of God and share the same humanity. He does not advocate the ecumenical blending of religions but rather calls upon people to accept the fact that all paths seek to reach God.
21. Reynold A. Nicholson, ed., *Selected Poems from the Divani Shamsi Tabriz* (London: Cambridge University Press, 1898), 15–17, 81–85.
22. Talat Halman, "Turkish Humanism and the Poetry of Yunus Emre," accessed June 12, 2011, http://dergiler.ankara.edu.tr/dergiler/18/838/10609.pdf.
23. The best book on the interfaith dialogue of the Gülen Movement is Ahmet Kurucan, *Nicin Diyalog?: Diyaloğun Temelleri* (Istanbul: Işık, 2006). Kurucan's perspective on dialogue is informed by the writings and conversations with Gülen.
24. I would like to thank Dr. Abdullah Antepli of Duke University for reading this paper several times and bringing the difference between theological and sociological diversity to my attention.
25. Ali Ünal and Alphonse Williams (compiled), *Fethullah Gülen: Advocate of Dialogue* (Fairfax, VA: Fountain, 2000), 244–245. This book is compiled from Gülen's interviews, speeches, and writings. This book provides the most complete vision of Gülen.
26. P. Valkenberg, "Fethullah Gülen's Contribution to Muslim–Christian Dialogue in the Context of Abrahamic Cooperation," accessed June 16, 2011, http://www.fethullahgulenconference.org/houston/proceedings/PValkenberg.pdf.
27. Fethullah Gülen, *Love and the Essence of Being Human*, 2nd edn. (Istanbul: Journalists and Writers Foundation Publications, 2004), 171.
28. Ibid., 157.

29. Hans-Georg Gadamar, *Truth and Method*, 2nd rev. edn. (1st English edn, 1975), trans. by J. Weinsheimer and D. G. Marshall (New York: Crossroad, 1989).
30. Zeki Saritoprak, "Said Nursi on Muslim–Christian Relations Leading to World Peace," *Islam and Christian–Muslim Relations* 19:1 (2008): 31. Zeki Saritoprak and Sidney Griffith, "Fethullah Gülen and the People of the Book: A Voice from Turkey for Interfaith Dialogue," *Muslim World* 95 (July 2005): 329–340.
31. Fethullah Gülen, *Toward a Global Civilization of Love and Tolerance* (Somerset, NJ: The Light, 2004), 10–11.
32. Ibid. 11.
33. Fethullah Gülen, *Örnekleri Kendinden Bir Hareket* (Istanbul: Nil, 2004), 187.
34. Ibid., 188.
35. Gülen, *Love*, 78.
36. Ibid., 50.
37. Fethullah Gülen, *Toward a Global Civilization of Love and Tolerance* (Istanbul: Light, 2004), 33.
38. Ibid., 37.
39. Ünal and Williams, *Advocate of Dialogue*, 203–204.
40. Ibid., 14–34.
41. Ibid., 242.
42. Gülen, *Love,* 207.
43. Interview in Berlin, Germany, July 13, 2009.
44. Interview in Chicago, June 12, 2009.
45. Interview in Salt Lake City, October 13, 2011.
46. "Fethullah Gülen Met with Pope John Paul II," *The Turkish Times*, March 1, 1998.
47. The Foundation organized an international "Abraham Symposium" in Urfa and Istanbul on April 13–16, 2000.
48. Accessed June 14, 2012, http://kadip.org.tr/Hakkimizda/Detay/65/Our%20 Vision%20&%20Work%20Principles.
49. DIP organized a series of conferences in different parts of the world. Global Capitalism in Crisis Globalization and Business for the Common Good: Theology and Economics working together, October 10, 2002, Oxford, England; ENAR Conference on Tolerance, Combating Racism, Discrimination and Xenophobia, September 11–12, 2004, Brussels, Belgium; An Interfaith Perspective on Globalization for the Common Good, April 21–24, 2005, Kericho, Kenya; For Mutual Understanding and Peace: Religions in Cooperation, May 11–14, 2005, Goteborg, Sweden; Dialogue of Cultures as a Chance of Europe: "Culture, Identity, and Religion," May 27–28, 2005, Berlin, Germany; Thoughts on Culture of Living Together, Cultures and Civilizations Dialogue, June 14–16, 2005, Rabat, Morocco; Meeting of Civilizations in Antioch, September 25–29, 2005, Antioch, Turkey; Dialogue of Civilizations and World Peace Meeting, October 5–9, 2005, Rhodes, Greece; Fast Breaking Ramadan Dinner at European Parliament, October 10–11, 2005, Brussels, Belgium.
50. Ünal and Williams, *Advocate of Dialogue*, 193.
51. Ibid., 205.
52. Interview in Washington, DC, October 13, 2011.

53. For a prescient analysis of this development, see Sener Aktürk and Mujeeb R. Khan, "How Western Anti-Muslim Bigotry Became Respectable," *Today's Zaman*, January 3, 2010.
54. Interview in Washington, DC, October 12, 2011.
55. Ibid.

CHAPTER 9

1. Steven A. Glazer, "Historical Setting," in *A Country Study: Turkey*, ed. Helen Chapin Metz (Washington, DC: Library of Congress, 1996), 36.
2. Delphine Strauss, "Turkey: Inspiring or Insidious," *Financial Times*, April 28, 2011.
3. Ergene argues that "Gülen is against the use of religion as a political ideology.... Throughout his life, Gülen has stayed away from involving himself in politics and has never sought political ends." Enes Ergene, *Tradition Witnessing the Modern Age* (Somerset, NJ: Tughra, 2008), 16–17.
4. Ali Ünal and Alphonse Williams, *Fethullah Gülen: Advocate of Dialogue* (Fairfax, VA: The Fountain, 2000), 149.
5. Erol N. Gülay, "The Gülen Phenomenon: A Neo-Sufi Challenge to Turkey's Rival Elite?" *Critique: Critical Middle Eastern Studies* 16 (2007): 37–61.
6. Alasdair MacIntyre, *After Virtue: A Study in Moral Theory* (Notre Dame, IN: University of Notre Dame Press, 1984), 244–245.
7. John Neuhaus, *The Naked Public Square: Religion and Democracy in America* (Grand Rapids, MI: Eerdmans, 1984), 22, 59, 61, 64.
8. I arrived at this idea of "conversation" from the writings of Michael Oakeshott. Gülen, like Oakeshott, is skeptical of strictly political solutions and especially revolutionary politics. Both Oakeshott and Gülen expect participants to share a tradition in order to form an intelligible exchange. Politics, for Oakeshott, should not be reduced to administration, social engineering, or scientific understanding. M. Oakeshott, *Rationalism in Politics and Other Essays* (Indianapolis: Liberty Press, 1991).
9. For more on the Turkish military, see William Hale, *Turkish Politics and the Military* (London: Routledge, 1993); Mehmet Ali Birand, *Shirts of Steel: An Anatomy of the Turkish Armed Forces* (London: I. B. Taurus, 1991); M. Sükrü Hanioğlu, "Civil-Military Relations in the Second Constitutional Period, 1908–1918," *Turkish Review* 12 (2011): 177–189.
10. Ersel Aydınlı, Nihat Ali Özcan, and Doğan Akyaz, "The Turkish Military's March toward Europe," *Foreign Affairs* 85 (2006): 77–90; Ersel Aydınlı, "A Paradigmatic Shift for the Turkish Generals and an End to the Coup Era in Turkey," *Middle East Journal* 63 (2009): 581–596.
11. For the impact of the defeat of the Balkan wars, see Fikret Adanır, "Non-Muslims in the Ottoman Army and the Ottoman Defeat in the Balkan war of 1912–1913," in *A Question of Genocide*, ed. Ronald Grigor Sunny, Fatma Müge Göçek, and Norman M. Naimark (New York: Oxford University Press, 2011), 113–125.
12. Sinem Gürbey, "Islam, Nation-State, and the Military: A Discussion of Secularism in Turkey," *Comparative Studies of South Asia, Africa and the Middle East* 29 (2009): 171–180.

13. Robert Olson, *The Emergence of Kurdish Nationalism and the Sheikh Said Rebellion, 1880–1925* (Austin: University of Texas Press, 1989); Kemal Üstün, *Menemen Olayı ve Kubilay*, 4th edn. (Istanbul: Çağdaş Yayınları, 1990). In this incident, a group of militant Muslims rebelled under the leadership of the Naksibendi Sheikh Dervis Mehmet in the city of Menemen and killed a military officer Mustafa Fehmi (Kubilay). These two religiously inspired incidents aroused Ankara to the fact that its radical reforms had not really taken root in society. Atatürk subsequently took a three-month visit to the countryside and came to the conclusion that his radical reforms had not really penetrated the periphery. Ahmed Hamdi Basar, *Atatürk'le Üç Ay ve 1930'dan Sonra Türkiye* (Istanbul: Tan Matbaası, 1945).
14. Ahmet Hamdi Akseki, *Askere Din Kitabı* (Istanbul: Ebuzziya Matbaası, 1945).
15. Fethullah Gülen, "Asker," *Sızıntı* (1979), accessed October 10, 2011, http://www.cagvenesil.com/fethullah-gulen-cag-ve-nesil/287-fethullah-gulen-cag-ve-nesil-asker.html/.
16. Andrew Mango, *The Turks Today* (London: John Murray Publisher, 2004), 97.
17. Carsten Bagge Laustsen and Ole Waever, "In Defence of Religion: Sacred Referent Objects for Securitization," *Millennium: Journal of International Studies* 29 (2000): 705–739; Ole Waever, "Securitization and Desecuritization," in *On Security*, ed. Ronnie D. Lipschutz (New York: Columbia University Press, 1995), 46–86.
18. Aydınlı, "A Paradigmatic," 586.
19. Hasan Cemal, "Asker herseye maydanoz olunca," *Milliyet*, September 17, 2011. Atilla Kıyat, a retired general, sharply criticized this process and how the military lost its legitimacy by isolating itself from its own society.
20. Jeremy Salt, "Turkey's Military Democracy," *Current History* (February 1999): 72–78.
21. Gülen gave a two-hour interview to Yalçın Doğan and defended the coup and asked the Welfare Party-led coalition government to resign, see "Fethullah Gülen'in Kanal D'deki Konuşması," in *28 Şubat Belgeler*, ed. Abdullah Yıldız (Istanbul: Pınar, 2000), 395–426; Gülen believes that the "soft coup" of 1997 accelerated the democratization of Turkey, see İsmail Ünal, *Fethullah Gülen'le Amerika'da Bir Ay* (Istanbul: Işık, 2001), 64.
22. Gareth Jedkins, *Between Facts and Fantasy: Turkey's Ergenekon Investigation* (Washington, DC: Silk Road Paper, 2009). Although the court case on the Ergenekon case is ongoing with a series of irregularities on the part of prosecutors; the case also reflects a long tradition in a sense, with contemporary undertones of the Young Turk struggle in Macedonia that was organized as a secret network to protect the "state" and the "country" against internal and external enemies. The coup-plotting current network was a Kemalist and nationalist reaction to three developments: the European Union's reluctance to accept Turkey as a full member and forcing Turkey to compromise its sovereignty without a clear road map of membership; the establishment of a semi-autonomous Kurdish state in Iraq and the radicalization of the Kurdish population in Turkey; and the electoral victories of the pan-Islamic JDP and its policies to water down Kemalism and ethnic Turkish nationalism.
23. Interview in Ankara, July 10, 2011.

24. See, for example, Soner Cagaptay, "What's Really behind Turkey's Coup Arrests?" *Foreign Policy*, February 25, 2010, accessed May 8, 2010, http://www.foreignpolicy.com/articles/2010/02/25/whats_really_behind_turkeys_coup_arrests.
25. Interview in Ankara, July 9, 2011.
26. Interview in Ankara July 10, 2011.
27. Interview in Istanbul July 8, 2011.
28. Ibid.
29. Interview in Ankara July 10, 2011.
30. For more on the military hard-liners plans to eliminate the JDP and the GM, see "Turkey and its Army," *The Economist*, June 18, 2009; *Today's Zaman*, June 12, 2009, October 28, 2009; *Turkish Daily News*, November 10, 2009.
31. Mehmet Baransu, "AKP ve Güleni Bitirme Planı," *Taraf*, June 12, 2009; and "Turkey and its Army," *The Economist*, June 18, 2009.
32. Wikileaks Report from the US Consulate from Istanbul says:

Deep and widespread doubts remain, however, about this movement's ultimate intentions. We have anecdotal evidence of the pressure that the various circles of his movement put on people they have drawn in, for instance severe pressure on businessmen to continue to give money to support Gülenist schools or other activities. We have multiple reliable reports that the Gülenists use their school network (including dozens of schools in the United States) to cherry-pick students they think are susceptible to being molded as proselytizers and we have steadily heard reports about how the schools indoctrinate boarding students. These facts, when coupled with the Gülenists' penetration of state institutions, including the TNP [Turkish National Police] (as reflected in Istanbul Legat's meeting—Ankara septel [Separate Telegram] will address the impact this development has had on police anti-terrorism efforts), hint that a much harder line, a sense of worldwide Islamist proselytizing mission, lies just under the surface. In short, the Gülenists' efforts to mold future generations through their international school network (which exists throughout Turkey, Asia (e.g., Afghanistan and Pakistan), and Africa, in addition to the U.S.) and their documented effort to infiltrate not just Turkish business circles but governmental institutions as well have raised questions about whether their moderation would continue if they gained a preponderant voice in Turkish Islam.

Accessed August 24, 2011, http://www.hurriyetdailynews.com/n.php?n = turkish-daily-starts-wikileaks-coverage-with-gulen-community-2011-03-17.
33. When Cemil Çiçek was the Minister of Justice, he prepared the new "Law for the Struggle with Terrorism." The movement was critical over the loose definition of terrorism, crime of terrorism, and financial sources of terrorism. It lobbied very hard to change the law. Eventually Prime Minister Erdoğan, under the pressure from the movement, asked Abdullah Gül, then the Minister of Foreign Affairs, to prepare the law. For more on the lobbying activities of the movement, see daily *Zaman*, September 8–11, 2005. Indeed, according to a high-ranking leader of the movement, Çiçek told the followers of the movement that "you are a religious community. You should be involved in religious affairs, and also your educational programs. Why are you getting involved in the law-making process? This is the

task of the state and all religious groups should remain outside the process." In the end, the movement prevailed and the law was amended according to their desires. Even this event shows the blurred boundary between a religious movement and political action group. The Gülen movement is a religiously rooted, politically active, religio-political movement. Atalay also had several confrontations with the movement over the appointments of some bureaucrats and the movement's attempt to discredit him as "pro-Iranist" and "pro-Islamists (Milli Görüşcü)."

34. Interview in Ankara, June 26, 2010.
35. M. Hakan Yavuz, "Islam and Europeanization in Turkish-Muslim Socio-Political Movements," in *Religion in an Expanding Europe*, ed. Peter J. Katzenstein and Timothy A. Byrnes (Cambridge: Cambridge University Press, 2006), 225–255; Hasan Kösebalaban, "The Making the Enemy and Friend: Fethullah Gülen's National Security Identity," in *Turkish Islam and the Secular State: The Gülen Movement*, ed. M. Hakan Yavuz and John Esposito (Syracuse, NY: Syracuse University Press, 2003), 170–183.

Chapter 10

1. Cited in Ahmet Kurucan, "İnanmayacaklar," *Zaman*, April 17, 2010.
2. Binnaz Toprak et al., *Türkiye'de Farklı Olmak* (Istanbul: Metis, 2009), 195–211. This book includes an in-depth study (Being Different in Turkey—Alienation on the Axis of Religion and Conservatism) of the "neighborhood pressure" in Turkey on Alevis, secular groups, and some Kurds. Many scholars and journalists criticized the methodology of the study. The main argument of the study is that Turkish society today is much more polarized around competing normative orders and some groups are increasingly marginalized and excluded from mainstream politics and social life. The report examines the processes of "othering" in diverse Anatolian cities, and it claims that both the JDP and the Gülen movement are behind the marginalization of the groups who are labeled "different." Because of these findings, Toprak and her report became a target of criticism from conservative and Islamic media outlets. The report is indeed lacking in two important ways. First, it only focuses on the exclusion of the leftists, Alevis, and Kurds, and ignores the systematic exclusion of conservative Sunni Muslims by the Kemalist establishment with considerable support from segments of the left and the Alevi community. In other words, the report casts traditional Sunni Muslims as oppressive and ignores the fact that historically in modern Turkey, the main source of oppression and exclusion were the "secular fundamentalists" of the Kemalist establishment itself. Second, the study is ahistorical and it only focuses on the current situation without proper historical contextualization. It concludes that the "exclusionary" tactics are more common under the JDP government, without comparing JDP rule with that of various more establishment parties. The study would have made a major contribution if it had examined the current situation in historical context and compared the current situation to the February 28 process and earlier post-coup regimes in which larger sectors of conservative Muslim majority were systematically excluded from social, economic, and administrative positions. A most telling example of such intolerance and exclusion was, of course, the flagrant denial of access to higher education and government jobs to conservative Sunni women who chose to wear

the headscarf. For more on the report and Toprak's attempt at rebuttal, see the "Epilogue," accessed August 12, 2011, http://www.aciktoplumvakfi.org.tr/pdf/tr_farkli_olmak.pdf/.
3. Ahmet İnsel interviewed by Neşe Düzel, "Fethullahcıları Derin Devlet Yarattı," *Taraf*, January 14, 2008.
4. Ahmet İnsel, "Heyulanın dönüşü," *Radikal*, November 1, 2011.
5. Bill Park, "The Fethullah Gülen Movement," *MERIA Journal* 12 (2008), accessed June 9, 2011, http://www.worldsecuritynetwork.com/documents/Movement.pdf/.
6. Interview in Istanbul June 21, 2011.
7. Interview in Istanbul June 23, 2011.
8. In 2011, the Turkish court arrested the two investigative journalists, Nedim Şener and Ahmet Şık, on the grounds that they provided media support for an attempt to organize a coup d'état against the JDP government. However, some sectors of the public believe that these two journalists were arrested because of their critical views of the Gülen movement. Şener wrote a book, showing the degree to which the Gülen movement had infiltrated the state bureaucracy, and Şık was in the process of writing a critical book on the Gülen movement. They were arrested and jailed on the basis of campaigning for a military coup as part of the Ergenekon plot. The Istanbul police force was accused of being more concerned in seeking to "arrest the manuscript of Ahmet Şık," titled, *İmamın Ordusu* (The Imam's Army, i.e., Gülen's Army) rather than in preventing a coup. The manuscript is yet to be published, but the prosecutor in the Ergenekon case, who has become increasingly suspect in light of these and other questionable arrests, ordered the Turkish police to search the homes of scholars, journalists, and even coffee shops, to find the critical manuscript. The fact that both Şener and Şık had been independent and critical media voices in the past against the excesses of the Kemalist "deep state" added to suspicion that their current prosecution had little to do with the Ergenekon conspiracy.
9. In 2010, one of Turkey's most prominent police figures, Chief Hanefi Avcı wrote a book critical of the Gülen movement: Hanefi Avcı, *Haliç'te Yaşayan Simonlar: Dün Devlet Bugün Cemaat* (Ankara: Angora, 2010). He alleged that the Gülen movement increasingly controlled the police force, and he provided a long list of such anecdotal evidence. After his book became a best-seller in Turkey, Avcı was removed from his job and even jailed on the basis of his alleged ties with an illegal leftist organization. Avcı wrote this book when he was on active duty as the Eskisehir Police Chief. It sold 400,000 copies in the first six months after it was published, and it purported to demonstrate how the followers of Gülen have influence in critical state institutions such as the police, the judiciary, and the universities where hitherto only loyal Kemalists were allowed in. Demonstrating anxiety over these changes from the ancien régime and the ongoing "Ergenekon Trials" of those accused of plotting to overthrow the JDP government, the book argues that the Gülen movement and its underground police force are destroying the careers and reputations of anyone who stands in their way with the help of illegal wiretappings, corruption, and intimidation. Critics of Gülen and the JDP believe that Avcı's arrest demonstrates the sinister power of the Gülen community and its control over the national police force. However, other journalistic and public investigations showed

that Avcı himself was not a disinterested observer of the Gülen community but had himself worked very closely with establishment media circles that had controversial ties with the Kemalist "deep state." According to the prosecutor of the Ergenekon case, certain sections of Avci's book were written not by him, but rather by journalist friends such as Nedim Şener and Ahmet Şık.
10. For more on the anti-Semitism of Odatv and its chief editor Soner Yalçın, see Rıfat Bali's "What is the Efendi Telling Us?" accessed October 15, 2011, http://www.rifatbali.com/images/stories/dokumanlar/what_is_efendi_telling_us.pdf/.
11. For instance, Hikmet Cetinkaya, a leading journalist of the Kemalist daily *Cumhuriyet*, who has constantly portrayed the movement under a very negative light, has written several books on the Gülen movement. His writings are shallow and sensationalistic in the style of tabloid journalism seeking to sow fear about the power of the movement. However, it is noteworthy that he has never faced censorship or prosecution for expressing his views. Cetinkaya's *Fethullah Gülen'in Kırk Yıllık Serüveni* (Fethullah Gülen's 40 Year Journey) lacks any contextualization or deep background study of the origins and goals of the movement. His second book, *Fethullah Gülen, ABD ve AKP* (Fethullah Gülen, the USA, and the JDP), seeks to portray Gülen as an agent of the US government and the CIA. Another controversial book, which is as alarmist as Cetinkaya's, seeks to also perpetuate such fear and was written by Merdan Yanardağ. Yanardağ's book, titled *"Türkiye Nasıl Kuşatıldı?"* (How Turkey is Besieged), also claims that the Gülen movement is under the control of the CIA. One of the better critical books with some official documentation is by Saygı Öztürk, *Okyanus Ötesindeki Vaiz* (Istanbul: Doğan Kitabevi, 2010). Emin Çölaşan, a hard-line critic of Gülen, wrote the introduction to this book and he succinctly summarizes the gist of accusations against the movement. Although this book includes several reports by the Turkish police force and the National Intelligence Agency (MIT), the book shows how diverse factions within the bureaucracy often use the Gülen community to either hinder or facilitate the promotion of some officials. To date, however, there is no single scholarly study in Turkey about the movement overall. Most of the books either seek to advocate on behalf of the Gülen movement and present it as a network of selfless volunteers and idealists or seek to present the movement as a clandestine radical Islamist movement that seeks to infiltrate the state in order to create an Iranian-style Islamic Republic.
12. For the statement by Gülen, see *Zaman*, March 28, 2011.
13. Bahçeli's statement, see *Zaman*, April 1, 2011. Aytekin Gezici, *Okyanus Ötesi Gerçeği* (Istanbul: Anatolia, 2011), 80–100. Both Kurdish nationalists, as well as Turkish nationalists, are critical of the Gülen community, viewing it as drawing away potential supporters with its eclectic Ottomanism, which seeks to overcome ethnic divides in the country. The Turkish nationalist party criticizes the community for being too pro-American, and for serving American interests in the Central Asia and other places, while also being sympathetic to Kurdish cultural demands and supporting the JDP.
14. Hüseyin Gülerce, "Eksiğimizi söyleyenin, elini öperiz," *Zaman*, March 30, 2011.
15. For the most comprehensive studies on the Alevis, see İsmail Engin and Franz Erhard *Aleviler/Alewiten*, Vols. 1–3 (Hamburg: Deutsches Orient Institut, 2001);

Paul White and Joost Jongerden, eds., *Turkey's Alevi Enigma: A Comprehensive Overview* (Leiden: Brill, 2003); David Shankland, *The Alevis in Turkey: The Emergence of a Secular Islamic Tradition* (London: Routledge, 2003); John Shindeldecker, *Turkish Alevis Today* (Istanbul: Sahkulu Sultan Külliyesi, 1996); and Ali Yaman and Aykan Erdemir, *Alevism-Bektashism: A Brief Introduction* (London: Alevi Cultural Centre & Cem Evi, 2006).

16. Göksel Bozkurt, "EU Monitors Alevi Reform," *Turkish Daily News*, December 19, 2007, accessed May 2, 2008, http://www.turkishdailynews.com.tr/article.php?enewsid=89912/.
17. During the last day of the meeting, Reha Camuroğlu and Ali Yaman criticized the meeting on the basis of seeking to define Alevi faith for Alevis from the perspective of the dominant Sunni understanding. More criticism came from those Alevi organizations that refused to participate in the meeting, see Turan Eser, the secretary-general of the Alevi and Bektasi Federation, accessed August 9, 2011, http://www.alevibektasifederasyonu.org.tr/.
18. Hüseyin Gülerce, "Alevis Respect Gülen," *Today's Zaman*, June 19, 2008.
19. Mustafa Pekoz, "Fethullah Gülen'in Kürt ve Alevi Düşmanlığı," *Birgün*, August 23, 2010, accessed July 12, 2011, http://www.dailymotion.com/video/xei7oz_fethullah-gulen-yn-kurt-ve-alevy-du_shortfilms/. However, to be fair, this speech by Gülen differentiates the Alevi community into several groups. After defining Alevis as a Muslim group with a different interpretation of Islam, Gülen criticizes the most radical elements in the Alevi community for rejecting faith in God and the Qur'an. This would, of course, be true for those Alevis who remained committed to Marxism from the period of the 1960s and 1970s.
20. Alevi Rapor, July 2011. This report identifies human rights violations against Alevis in the media, popular culture, and politics and was published by the largest and most influential Federation of Alevi and Bektasis.
21. Gökhan Bacık, "The Fragmentation of Turkey's Secularists," *Turkish Review*, January 2011.
22. Gülen's responses to questions on the Alevi interpretation of Islam, see accessed October 7, 2011, http://www.alevihaberajansi.com/index.php?option=com_content&task=view&id=2057&Itemid=50.
23. Altan Tan, "Is Secularism the Last Trump Card of Ethnic Politics," *Today's Zaman*, December 13, 2007.
24. Nevzat Cicek, "PKK, Gülen hareketinden ne istiyor," *Milat*, November 4, 2011.
25. Aland Mizell, "Erdoğan's AKP, Fethullah Gülen's opium, and the Kurdish Question," *KurdishMedia.com*, March 15, 2005.
26. For more on the Hizbullah's anti-Gülen campaign, see Hizbullah's official website (http://hurseda.net); for more on Hizbullah, see M. Hakan Yavuz and Nihat Ali Özcan, "The Kurdish Question and the JDP," *Middle East Journal* 13:1 (2006): 102–119.
27. Emine Ayna, co-president of the pro-Kurdish Democratic Society Party, regularly criticizes the Gülen movement and its cooperation with the JDP. She argues that the "campaign against the Kurdish nationalists is carried out by the JDP-Gülen coalition," *Radikal*, April 22, 2009; she also argues that "The JDP relies on the Gülen community to exploit religious feeling of the Kurds," *Radikal*, December 3, 2008.
28. Interview in Istanbul, June 20, 2011.
29. Interview in Ağrı, June 23, 2010.

30. Nicolas Birch, "Turkey: The Country's Biggest Religious Movement Educates Kurds, and not Everyone Is Happy," http://www.eurasianet.org/departments/insightb/articles/eav030309a.shtml.
31. Interview in Diyarbakır, June 26, 2010.
32. *Zaman*, October 22, 2008.
33. Nasuhi Güngör, "The Gülen Cemmati, Kürt Sorunu ve 'Tek Türkiye,'" *Star Gazetesi*, September 26, 2008.
34. There are several articles and a summary of the discussion of the Abant Meeting on the Kurdish issue, see Daily *Zaman*'s coverage between July 4–7, 2008.
35. The charitable association *Kimse Yok Mu* was established in 2004, and it has been active in Turkey and in Palestine, Bangladesh, Pakistan, Sudan-Darfur, Myanmar, and in Haiti.
36. Interview in Diyarbakir, June 26, 2010.
37. Interview in Diyarbakir, July 12, 2009.
38. Interview in Van, June 23, 2010.
39. For a useful theoretical comparative analysis of ethnicity in Turkey, see Sener Aktürk, "Regimes of Ethnicity: Comparative Analysis of Germany, The Soviet Union/Post-Soviet Russia, and Turkey," *World Politics* 63:1 (2011): 115–164.
40. The movement's daily *Zaman* newspaper organized a series of panels to find a solution to the problem. See Salih Boztaş, ed., *Kürt Sorunu* (Istanbul: Zaman Gazetesi, 2007). The participants were Mumtazer Türköne, Ali Bulaç, Sedat Laçiner, Ümit Fırat, and Nihat Ali Özcan. Except the last two names they all have organic ties with the movement. Fırat was the only Kurd who participated in the debate.
41. See a series of essays on the difference between the National Outlook Movement of Erbakan and the Gülen movement, Cüneyt Ülsever, *Hurriyet Daily Newspaper*, June 14–16, 2010. Ülsever lays out the political involvement of the movement and argues that this represents a major break from the traditions of the movement.
42. Haydar Baş is a leader of a small but effective nationalist-Islamic group. The group has its own TV station, newspaper, and magazine. It is the most vicious anti-Gülen group in Turkey. They accuse Gülen of being an agent of American imperialism and alternatively an agent of the Vatican. For more on the nationalistic aspects of this movement, see Ahmet T. Kuru, "Globalization and Diversification of Islamic Movements: Three Turkish Cases," *Political Science Quarterly* 120:2 (2005): 253–274.
43. See Joe Lauria, "Reclusive Turkish Imam Criticizes Gaza Flotilla," *Wall Street Journal*, June 4, 2010 [online], accessed June 12, 2011.http://online.wsj.com/article/SB10001424052748704025304575284721280274694.html
44. Mısırlıoğlu's interview in http://www.medyaradar.com/haber/gundem-44654/tarihci-kadir-misiroglu-fethullah-guleni-hedef-aldi-video.html.
45. Interview in Istanbul, August 24, 2011.
46. Stephen Kinzer, "Triumphant Turkey?" *New York Review of Books*, July 19, 2011.
47. Elisabeth Özdalga, *Islamcılığın Türkiye Seyri: Sosyolojik Bir Perspektif* (Istanbul: Iletisim, 2006), 255.
48. This distinction is made by G. M. Allport, "The Religious Context of Prejudice," *Journal of the Scientific Study of Religion* 5 (1966): 447–457.

Conclusion

1. Charles Taylor, "Modernity and Closed World Structures Talk on the Occasion of Receiving the Josef Pieper Prize," accessed October 24, 2011, http://josef-pieper-arbeitsstelle.de/fileadmin/documents/online-artikel/Taylor%20-%20J.%20Pieper%20Prize.pdf/.
2. Muhammed Khalid Masud, Armando Salvatore, and Martin van Bruinessen, eds., *Islam and Modernity: Key Issues and Debates* (Edinburg: Edinburg University, 2009).
3. M. Hakan Yavuz, "Islam without Shari'a," in *Shari'a Politics: Islamic Law and Society in the Modern World*, ed. Rober Hefner (Bloomington: Indiana University Press, 2011), 46–178.
4. In some cases, like Syria, the external power propping up despotic rule in the Muslim world was the Soviet Union or Russia. In other cases, like that of the despotic monarchies of the Persian Gulf or Mubarak's Egypt and the Algerian junta, these brutal regimes relied on vital backing from the United States, Britain, and France.
5. Shmuel N. Eisenstadt, "Multiple Modernities," *Daedalus* 129:1 (2000): 24.

Selected Bibliography

Abu-Rabi, Ibrahim. *Islam at the Crossroads: On the Life and Thought of Bediuzzaman Said Nursi.* Albany: State University of New York Press, 2003.
——. *Spiritual Dimensions of Bediüzzaman Said Nursi's Risale-i Nur.* Albany: State University of New York Press, 2008.
Adanır, Fikret. "Non-Muslims in the Ottoman Army and the Ottoman Defeat in the Balkan War of 1912–1913." In *A Question of Genocide*, ed. Ronald Grigor Sunny, Fatma Müge Göçek, and Norman M. Naimark, New York: Oxford University Press, 2011.
Agai, Bekim. "Fethullah Gülen and his Movement's Islamic Ethic of Education." *Critique: Critical Middle Eastern Studies* 11 (2002): 27–47.
——. "The Gülen Movement's Islamic Ethic of Education." In *Turkish Islam and the Secular State: The Gülen Movement*, ed. M. Hakan Yavuz and John Esposito. Syracuse, NY: Syracuse University Press, 2003.
——. "Islam and Education in Secular Turkey: State Policies and the Emergence of the Fethullah Gülen Group." In *Schooling Islam: The Culture and Politics of Modern Muslim Education*, ed. Robert W. Hefner and Muhammad Qasim Zaman. Princeton: Princeton University Press, 2007.
——. *Zwischen Netzwerk und Diskurs—Das Bildungsnetzwerk um Fethullah Gulen"(geb. 1938): Die Flexible Umsetzung Modernen Islamischen Gedankenguts.* Hamburg: EB-Verlag, 2004.
Akgün, Mehmet. *Materyazilmin Türkiye'ye Girişi ve ilk Etkileri.* Ankara: Kültür ve Turizm Bakanlığı Yayını, 1988.
Akman, Nuriye. *Gurbette Fethullah Gülen.* Istanbul: Zaman, 2004.
Akseki, Ahmet Hamdi. *Askere Din Kitabı.* Istanbul: Ebuzziya Matbaası, 1945.
Aktürk, Şener. "Regimes of Ethnicity: Comparative Analysis of Germany, the Soviet Union/Post-Soviet Russia, and Turkey." *World Politics* 63: 1 (2011): 115–164.
Allport, G. M. "The Religious Context of Prejudice." *Journal of the Scientific Study of Religion* 5 (1966): 447–457.
Arslan, Berna. "Pious Science: The Gülen Community and the Making of a Conservative Modernity in Turkey." Ph.D. diss. Santa Cruz: University of California, 2009.

Avcı, Hanefi. *Haliç'te Yaşayan Simonlar: Dün Devlet Bugün Cemaat*. Ankara: Angora, 2010.

Aydınlı, Ersel. "A Paradigmatic Shift for the Turkish Generals and an End to the Coup Era in Turkey." *Middle East Journal* 63 (2009): 581–596.

Aydınlı, Ersel, Nihat Ali Özcan, and Doğan Akyaz. "The Turkish Military's March toward Europe." *Foreign Affairs* 85 (2006): 77–90.

Bacık, Gökhan. "The Fragmentation of Turkey's Secularists." *Turkish Review* 1 (2011): 12–17.

Bahadıroğlu, Yavuz. *Bediüzzaman Said Nursi*. Istanbul: Yeni Asya, 1993.

Bakar, Osman. "Gülen on Religion and Science: A Theological Perspective." *Muslim World* 95 (2005): 359–372.

Balcı, Bayram. "Fethullah Gülen's Missionary Schools in Central Asia and their Role in the Spreading of Turkism and Islam." *Religion, State & Society* 31 (2003): 151–177.

——. *Orta Asya'da İslam Misyonerleri: Fethullah Gülen Okulları*. Istanbul: İletişim, 2005.

Balthasar, Hans Urs Von, and Edward T. Oakes. *The Theology of Karl Barth: Exposition and Interpretation*. Edinburg: Ignatius Press, 1992.

Baransu, Mehmet. "AKP ve Güleni Bitirme Planı." *Taraf*, June 12, 2009.

Barton, Greg. "Turkey's Gulen Hizmet and Indonesia's Neo-modernist NGOs: Remarkable Examples of Progressive Islamic Thought and Civil Society Activism in the Muslim World." In *Political Islam and Human Security*, ed. Fethi Mansouri and Shahram Akbarzadeh. Newcastle: Cambridge Scholars Press, 2006.

Başar, Ahmed Hamdi. *Atatürk'le Üç Ay ve 1930'dan Sonra Türkiye*. Istanbul: Tan Matbaası, 1945.

Basetti-Sani, Giulio. *Louis Massignon (1883–1962): Christian Ecumenist; Prophet of Interreligious Reconciliation*. Chicago: Franciscan Herald Press, 1974.

Baskan, Filiz. "The Fethullah Gülen Community: Contribution or Barrier to the Consolidation of Democracy in Turkey?" *Middle Eastern Studies* 41 (2005): 849–861.

——. "The Political Economy of Islamic Finance in Turkey: The Role of Fethullah Gülen and Asya Finans." In *The Politics of Islamic Finance*, ed. Clement M. Henry and Rodney Wilson. Edinburgh: Edinburgh University Press, 2004.

Becker, George. "Pietism's Confrontation with Enlightenment Rationalism: An Examination of the Relation between Ascetic Protestantism and Science." *Journal of the Scientific Study of Religion* 30:2 (1991): 139–158.

Berger, Peter. "Charisma and Religious Innovation: The Social Location of Israelite Prophecy." *American Sociological Review* 28 (1963) 940–950.

Berkes, Niyazi. *The Development of Secularism in Turkey*. New York: Routledge, 1998.

Birand, Mehmet Ali. *Shirts of Steel: An Anatomy of the Turkish Armed Forces*. London: I. B. Taurus, 1991.

Birch, Nicolas. "Turkey: The Country's Biggest Religious Movement Educates Kurds, and not Everyone Is Happy." Accessed June 8, 2010. http://www.eurasianet.org/departments/insightb/articles/eav030309a.shtml.

Bosetti, Giancarlo, and Klaus Eder. "Post-Secularism: A Return to the Public Sphere." *Eurozine*, August 17, 2006 [online journal]. Accessed March 7, 2010. http://www.eurozine.com/articles/2006-08-17-eder-en.html.

Bozkurt, Göksel. "EU Monitors Alevi Reform." *Turkish Daily News*, December 19, 2007. Accessed May 2, 2008. http://www.turkishdailynews.com.tr/article.php?enewsid=89912.

Boztaş, Salih. *Kürt Sorunu*. Istanbul: Zaman Gazetesi, 2007.

Brooks, W. "The Politics of the Conquest of the Caucasus, 1855–1864." *Nationalities Papers* 24:4 (1996): 649–660.

——. "Russia's Conquest and Pacification of the Caucasus: Relocation Becomes a Pogrom in the Post-Crimean War Period." *Nationalities Papers* 23:4 (1995): 675–686.

Buber, Martin. *I and Thou*. New York: Scribner, 2000.

Bulaç, Ali. *Din-Kent ve Cemaat Fethullah Gülen Örneği*. Istanbul: Ufuk, 2007.

Bülbül, Kudret. *Bir Devlet Adamı ve Siyasal Düşünür Olarak Said Halim Paşa*. Ankara: Kadim, 2006.

Cağaptay, Soner. "What's Really behind Turkey's Coup Arrests?" *Foreign Policy*, February 25, 2010.

Can, Eyüp. *Fethullah Gülen Hocaefendi ile Ufuk Turu*. Istanbul: AD Yayıncılık, 1997.

Canan, İbrahim. *İslam Aleminin Ana Meseleleri: Bediüzzaman'dan Çözümler*. Istanbul: Yeni Asya, 1993.

Carr, Thomas K. *Newman and Gadamer: Toward a Hermeneutic of Religious Knowledge*. Atlanta: Scholar Press, 1996.

Casanova, Jose. *Public Religions in the Modern World*. Chicago: University of Chicago Press, 1994.

Case, Christa. "Germans Reconsider Religion." *Christian Science Monitor*, September 15, 2006.

Çalıskan, Kerem. "Fethullah Hoca ve Laiklik." *Yeni Yüzyıl*, July 21, 1998.

Cassirer, Ernst. *The Philosophy of the Enlightenment*. Princeton: Princeton University Press, 1968.

Cetin, Muhammed. *The Gülen Movement: Civic Service without Border*. New York: Blue Dome, 2010.

Çetinkaya, Hikmet. *Fethullah Gülen'in 40 Yıllık Serüveni*. Istanbul: Günizi Yayınları, 2004.

Chelini-Pont, Blandine. "Religion in the Public Sphere: Challenges and Opportunities." *Brigham Young University Law Review* 3 (2005): 611–627.

Çicek, Nevzat. "PKK, Gülen hareketinden Ne Istiyor." *Milat*, November 4, 2011.

Cilacı, Osman. "Comments on the Holy Bible in the Risale-i Nur." *Contemporary Approach to Understanding the Qur'an: The Example of the "Risale-i Nur."* Istanbul: Sözler, 2000.

Cobanoğlu, Yavuz. "Fethullah Gülen'de Sosyal Ahlak Tasavvuru." Ph.D. diss., Ege Universitesi, 2008.

Cobb, Kelton. "Revelation, the Disciplines of Reason, and Truth in the Works of Said Nursi and Paul Tillich." In *Islam at the Crossroads: On the Life and Thought of Bediuzzaman Said Nursi*, ed. Ibrahim Abu-Rabi. Albany: State University of New York Press, 2003.

Coleman, James. "Social Capital in the Creation of Human Capital." *American Journal of Sociology* 94 (1988): 95–120.

Copeaux, Etienne. "Hizmet: A Keyword in Turkish Historical Narrative." *New Perspectives on Turkey* 13 (1996): 91–114.

Cosijns, Lucien F. *Dialogue among the Faith Communities.* Lanham, MD: Hamilton Books, 2008.

Daniel, Norman. *Islam and the West: The Making of an Image.* Oxford: Oneworld, 1993.

Dupuis, Jaques S.J. *Toward a Christian Theology of Religious Pluralism.* Maryknoll, NY: Orbis Books, 2002.

Ebaugh, Helen R. *The Gülen Movement: A Sociological Analysis of a Civic Movement Rooted in Moderate Islam.* Dordrecht: Springer, 2009.

Eck, Diana. "Prospect for Pluralism: Voice and Vision in the Study of Religion." *Journal of American Academy of Religion* 75:4 (2007): 743–766.

Eickelman, Dale F., and James Picatori. *Muslim Politics.* Princeton: Princeton University Press, 2004.

Engin, İsmail, and Franz Erhard. *Aleviler/Alewiten.* Vols. 1–3. Hamburg: Deutsches Orient Institut, 2001.

Erdoğan, Latif. *Fethullah Gülen Hocaefendi: Küçük Dünyam.* Istanbul: AD Yayıncılık, 1995.

Ergene, Mehmet Enes. *Tradition Witnessing the Modern Age: An Analysis of the Gülen Movement.* Somerset, NJ: Tughra Books, 2008.

Erkal, Mustafa. "21 Yüzyıla Doğru Milli Kültürlerin Geleceği ve Bazı Çelişkiler." In *İslamiyet, Millet Gerçeği ve Laiklik.* Istanbul: Aydınlar Ocağı, 1994.

Esposito, John, and İhsan Yılmaz. *Islam and Peacebuilding: Gülen Movement Initiatives.* New York: Blue Dome, 2010.

Eygi, Mehmet Şevket. *İki Kimlikli, Esrarlı ve Çok Güçlü Bir Cemaat: Yahudi Türkler Yahut Sabetaycılar.* Istanbul: Zvi-Geyik Yayınları, 2000.

Fisher, A. W. "Emigration of Muslims from the Russian Empire in the Years after the Crimean War." *Jahrbücher für Geschichte Osteuropas* 35 (1987): 356–371.

Fukuyama, Francis. "Social Capital and Global Economy." *Foreign Affairs* 74 (1995): 89–103.

Gadamar, Hans-Georg. *Truth and Method.* 2nd rev. edn. (1st English edn., 1975). Trans. by J. Weinsheimer and D. G. Marshall. New York: Crossroad, 1989.

Gail, Minault. "Urdu Political Poetry during the Khilafat Movement." *Modern Asian Studies* 8 (1974): 459–471.

Gay, Peter. *The Enlightenment: An Interpretations.* Vol. 1, *The Rise of Paganism.* London: Weidenfeld & Nicolson, 1967.

——. *The Enlightenment: An Interpretations.* Vol. 2, *The Science of Freedom.* London: Weidenfeld & Nicolson, 1970.

Geertz, Clifford. "Religion as a Cultural System." In *Anthropological Approaches to the Study of Religion,* ed. Michael Banton. London: Methuen, 1968.

Gencer, Bedri. "The Rise of Public Opinion in the Ottoman Empire (1839–1909)." *New Perspectives on Turkey* 30 (2004): 115–154.

Gerth, H. H., and C. Wright Mills, eds. *From Max Weber: Essays in Sociology.* New York: Oxford University Press, 1958.

Gezici, Aytekin. *Okyanus Ötesi Gerçeği.* Istanbul: Anatolia, 2011.

Giddens, Anthony. *Conversations with Anthony Giddens: Making Sense of Modernity.* Stanford, CA: Stanford University Press, 1998.

Glazer, Steven A. "Historical Setting." In *A Country Study: Turkey,* ed. Helen Chapin Metz. Washington, DC: Library of Congress, 1996.

Göktürk, Gülay. "Devletin İnayetiyle." *Sabah*, June 25, 1999.
Göle, Nilüfer. "Türk Muhafazakarlığının Manalandırdığı Modernlik." In *Fethullah Gülen Hocaefendi ile Ufuk Turu*, ed. Eyüp Can. Istanbul: AD Yayıncılık, 1997.
Granovetter, Mark. "The Strength of Weak Ties." *American Journal of Sociology* 78 (1978): 1360–1380.
Greenberg, Ilan. "When a Kleptocratic, Megalomaniacal Dictator Goes Bad." *New York Times*, January 5, 2005.
Gude, Mary Louise. *Louis Massignon: The Crucible of Compassion*. Notre Dame and London: University of Notre Dame Press, 1996.
Gülay, Erol N. "The Gülen Phenomenon: A Neo-Sufi Challenge to Turkey's Rival Elite." *Middle East Critique*, 16:1 (2007): 37–61.
——. "The Theological Thought of Fethullah Gülen: Reconciling Science with Islam." MA thesis, Oxford University, St Anthony College, 2007.
Gülen, Fethullah. *Advocate of Dialogue*. Fairfax: The Fountain, 2000.
——. "Asker." *Sızıntı* (1979) Accessed October 10, 2011. http://www.cagvenesil.com/fethullah-gulen-cag-ve-nesil/287-fethullah-gulen-cag-ve-nesil-asker.html/.
——. "Beklenen Geçlik I-II." *Çağ ve Nesil: Zamanın Altın Dilimi IV*. İzmir: TÖV, 1992.
——. "The Concept of Science and Technology." 2004. http://en.fgulen.com/a.page/books/essentials.of.the.islamic.faith/the.holy.quran/a691.html.
——. "Dünya Muvazenesinde Bir Millet." *Çağ ve Nesil I*. İzmir: TÖV, 1992.
——. "Düşünce ve Aksiyon İnsanı." *Zaman*, November 27, 1994.
——. *Enginliğiyle Bizim Dünyamız: İktisadî Mülâhazalar*. Istanbul: Nil Publications, 2009.
——. *Günler Baharı Soluklarken*. Istanbul: Nil Yayınları, 2002.
——. *Hoşgörü ve Diyalog İklimi*. Istanbul: Merkur Yayıncılık, 1998.
——. "Humanity, Science, and Globalization." *The Foundation* 41 (2003): 6–8.
——. *Key Concepts in the Practice of Sufism: Emerald Hills of the Heart*, Vol. 1. Somerset, NJ: The Light, 2006.
——. *Key Concepts in the Practice of Sufism: Emerald Hills of the Heart*, Vol. 2. Somerset, NJ: The Light, 2006.
——. *Love and the Essence of Being Human*. 2nd edn. Istanbul: Journalists and Writers Foundation Publications, 2004.
——. "Mana Kökleriyle İrtibatlı Kahramanlar Yetiştirmeliyiz." *Zaman*, November 18, 2010.
——. *Ölçü veya Yoldaki Işıklar*. Istanbul: Nil, 1985.
——. *Örnekleri Kendinden Bir Hareket*. Istanbul: Nil, 2004.
——. *Pearls of Wisdom*. Somerset, NJ: The Light, 2005.
——. "Question for Today." *The Fountain*, 8 (1994): 3–6.
——. *The Statue of Our Souls: Thought and Activism*. Somerset, NJ: Light, 2005.
——. *Toward a Global Civilization of Love and Tolerance*. Istanbul: Light, 2004.
——. *Understanding and Beliefs: The Essential of Islamic Faith*. Izmir: Kaynak, 1997.
——. *The Statue of Our Souls: Revival in Islamic Thought and Activism*. Somerset, NJ: Light, 2006.
Gülerce, Hüseyin. "Alevis Respect Gülen." *Today's Zaman*, June 19, 2008.
——. "Eksiğimizi Söyleyenin, Elini Öperiz." *Zaman*, March 30, 2011.
Günay, Ünver. *Erzurum ve Cevre Köylerinde Dini Hayat*. Istanbul: Dergah, 1999.

Gündem, Mehmet. *Abant Toplantıları I: Islam ve Laiklik.* Istanbul: Gazeteciler ve Yazarlar Vakfı, 1998.

——. *Fethullah Gülen'le 11 Gün.* Istanbul: Alfa Basım, 2005.

Güngör, Nasuhi. "The Gülen Cemmati, Kürt Sorunu and 'Tek Türkiye.'" *Star Gazetesi,* September 26, 2008.

Gürbey, Sinem. "Islam, Nation-State, and the Military: A Discussion of Secularism in Turkey." *Comparative Studies of South Asia, Africa and the Middle East* 29 (2009): 171–180.

Güvenç, Bozkurt. *Dosya Türk-Islam Sentezi.* Istanbul: Sarmal Yayınları, 1991.

Habermas, Jürgen. *Between Naturalism and Religion: Philosophical Essays.* Cambridge: Polity Press, 2008.

——. "Religion in the Public Sphere." *European Journal of Philosophy* 14 (2006): 1–25.

——. *The Structural Transformation of the Public Sphere: An Inquiry into a Category of Bourgeois Society.* Cambridge, MA: MIT Press, 1989.

Hale, William. *Turkish Politics and the Military.* London: Routledge, 1993.

Halman, Talat. "Turkish Humanism and the Poetry of Yunus Emre." Accessed June 12, 2011. http://dergiler.ankara.edu.tr/dergiler/18/838/10609.pdf.

Hanioğlu, M. Şükrü. "Blueprints for a Future Society: Late Ottoman Materialists on Science, Religion, and Art." In *Late Ottoman Society: The Intellectual Legacy,* ed. Elisabeth Özdalga. Abingdon: Routledge/Curzon, 2005.

——. "Civil–Military Relations in the Second Constitutional Period, 1908–1918." *Turkish Review* 12 (2011): 177–189.

Hansen, Suzy. "The Golbal Imam." *The New Republic.* November 10, 2010.

Hashemi, Nader. *Islam, Secularism and Liberal Democracy.* New York: Oxford University Press, 2009.

Hefner, Robert W., and Muhammad Q. Zaman, eds. *Schooling in Islam: The Culture and Religion of Modern Muslim Education.* Princeton: Princeton University Press, 2006.

Heller, D. *The Children's God.* Chicago: University of Chicago, 1986.

Hendrick, Joshua. "Globalization, Islamic Activism, and Passive Revolution in Turkey: The Case of Fethullah Gülen." *Journal of Political Power* 2 (2009): 343–368.

——. "Globalization and Marketized Islam in Turkey: The Case of Fethullah Gülen." Ph.D. diss. Santa Cruz: University of California, 2009.

——. "Media Wars and the Gülen Factor in the New Turkey." *Middle East Report* 260 (2011): 40–46.

Hick, John. *An Interpretation of Religion: Human Response to the Transcendent.* New Haven: Yale University Press, 2005.

Hourani, Albert. *Arabic Thought in the Liberal Age, 1798-1939.* Cambridge: Cambridge University Press, 1983.

Huff, Toby E. *The Rise of Early Modern Science: Islam, China, and the West.* 2nd edn. Cambridge: Cambridge University Press, 2003.

Huff, Toby E., and Wolfgang Schluchter, eds. *Max Weber and Islam.* New Brunswick, NJ: Transaction, 1999.

Huntington, Samuel P. (1993). "The Clash of Civilizations?" *Foreign Affairs,* 72 (1993): 22–49.

———. *The Clash of Civilizations and the Remaking of World Order*. London: Touchstone, 1998.
İnalcık, Halil. "Erzurum." *Encyclopedia of Islam*, Vol. 2, ed. P. Bearman et al. Leiden: Brill, 1965.
İnsel, Ahmet. "Fethullahcıları Derin Devlet Yarattı." *Taraf*, January 14, 2008.
———. "Heyulanın Dönüşü." *Radikal*, November 1, 2011.
Israel, Jonathan. *Radical Enlightenment: Philosophy and the Making of Modernity, 1650–1750*. New York: Oxford University Press, 2001.
Işın, Ekrem. "Osmanlı Materyalizmi." *Tanzimat'tan Cumhuriyete Türkiye Ansiklopedisi*. c. 2, Istanbul: İletişim Yayınları, 1985.
Issawi, Charles. "The Tabriz-Trabzon Trade, 1830–1900: Rise and Decline of a Route." *International Journal of Middle East Studies* 1:1 (1970): 18–27.
Jedkins, Gareth. *Between Facts and Fantasy: Turkey's Ergenekon Investigation*. Washington, DC: Silk Road Paper, 2009.
Jersild, Austin. *Orientalism and Empire: North Caucasus Mountain Peoples and the Georgian Frontier, 1845–1917*. Montreal: McGill-Queen's University Press, 2002.
Kafesoğlu, İbrahim. *Türk-Islam Sentezi*. Istanbul: Aydınlar Ocağı, 1985.
———. *Türk-İslam Sentezi*. Istanbul: Ötüken, 1999.
Kara, İsmail. "Ha Türk Müslümanlığı, Ha Türk-Islam Sentezi." *Milliyet*, September 7, 1997.
Kayalı, Hasan. "Islam in the Thought and Politics of Two Late Ottoman Intellectuals: Mehmed Akif and Said Halim." *Archivum Ottomanicum* 19 (2001): 307–331.
Kepenek, Yakup. "Abant Bildirgesi." *Cumhuriyet*, July 27, 1998.
Kim, Heon Chou. "The Nature and Role of Sufism in Contemporary Islam: A Case Study of the Life, Thought and Teachings of Fethullah Gülen." Ph.D. diss., Temple University, 2008.
Kinzer, Stephen. "Triumphant Turkey?" *New York Review of Books*, July 19, 2011.
Kırkıncı, Mehmet. *Bediüzzaman'ı Nasıl Tanıdım?* Istanbul: Zafer, 1994.
Knitter, Paul. *No Other Name?: A Critical Survey of Christian Attitudes toward the World Religions*. Maryknoll, NY: Orbis, 1985.
Knowlton, Brian. "Interview with Gülen." *Turkish Review* 1 (2011): 50–54.
Korlaelci, Murtaza. *Pozitivizmin Türkiye'ye Girişi ve İlk Etkileri*. Istanbul: İnsan Yayınları, 1986.
Kösebalaban, Hasan. "The Making of Enemy and Friend: Fethullah Gülen's National Security Identity." In *Turkish Islam and the Secular State: The Gülen Movement*, eds. M. Hakan Yavuz and John Esposito. Syracuse, NY: Syracuse University Press, 2003.
Küng, Hans, and Karl-Joseph Kuschel. *A Global Ethics: The Declaration of the Parliament of the World's Religions*. New York: Continuum Press, 1995.
Kuru, Ahmet T. "Globalization and Diversification of Islamist Movements: Three Turkish Cases." *Political Science Quarterly* 120 (2005): 252–274.
Kurucan, Ahmet. "İnanmayacaklar." *Zaman*, April 17, 2010.
———. *Nicin Diyalog?: Diyaloğun Temelleri*. Istanbul: Işık, 2006.
Lauria, Joe. "Reclusive Turkish Imam Criticizes Gaza Flotilla." *Wall Street Journal*, June 4, 2011.
Laustsen, Carsten Bagge, and Ole Waever. "In Defence of Religion: Sacred Referent Objects for Securitization." *Millennium: Journal of International Studies* 29 (2000): 705–739.

Lewis, Bernard. *Cultures in Conflict: Christians, Muslims, and Jews in the Age of Discovery.* New York: Oxford University Press, 1995.
——. *The Emergence of Modern Turkey.* 2nd edn. London: Oxford University Press, 1968.
MacIntyre, Alastair. *After Virtue: A Study in Moral Theory.* Notre Dame: University of Notre Dame Press, 1984.
——. "A Mistake about Causality in Social Sciences." In *Philosophy, Politics, and Society*, ed. P. Laslett and W. Runciman. Oxford: Oxford University Press, 1967.
Mamedov, Eldar. "Fethullah Gülen Movement—a View from Brussels." *Hürriyet Daily News*, May 27, 2010.
Mango, Andrew. *The Turks Today.* London: John Murray Publisher, 2004.
Mardin, Şerif. *Jön Türklerin Siyasi Fikirleri 1895–1908.* Istanbul: İletişim Yayınları, 1989.
——. *Religion and Social Change in Modern Turkey: The Case of Bediuzzaman Said Nursi.* Albany: State University of New York Press, 1989.
Markham, Ian. *Engaging with Bediuzzaman Said Nursi: A Model of Interfaith Dialogue.* Farnham: Ashgate Publishing, 2009.
Marty, Martin. *When Faith Collide.* Malden, MA: Blackwell Publishing, 2005.
McCarthy, Justin. *Death and Exile: The Ethnic Cleansing of Ottoman Muslims, 1821–1922.* Princeton: Darwin, 1995.
Michel, Thomas. "Muslim-Christian Dialogue and Co-operation in Bediüzzaman's Thought." In *A Contemporary Approach to Understanding the Qur'an: The Example of the Risale-I Nur.* Istanbul: Sözler Nesriyat, 2000.
——. "Sufism and Modernity in the thought of Fethullah Gülen." *Muslim World* 95 (2005): 342–358.
——. "Turkish Islam in Dialogue with Modern Society: The Neo-Sufi Spirituality of the Gülen Movement." *Concilium* 5 (2005): 71–80.
Mizell, Aland. "Erdoğan's AKP, Fethullah Gülen's Opium, and the Kurdish Question." KurdishMedia.com—March 15, 2005.
Muhaiyaddeen, Bawa. *Islam and World Peace.* Philadelphia: Fellowship Press, 1987.
Mürsel, Safa. *Bediüzzaman Said Nursi ve Devlet Felsefesi.* Istanbul: Yeni Asya, 1995.
Nemoianu, Virgil. "The Church and the Secular Establishment: A Philosophical Dialog between Joseph Ratzinger and Jürgen Habermas." *Logos: A Journal of Catholic Thought and Culture* 9 (2006): 20–22.
Neuhaus, John. *The Naked Public Square: Religion and Democracy in America.* Grand Rapids, MI: Eerdmans, 1984.
Nicholson, Reynold A., ed. *Selected Poems from the Divani Shamsi Tabriz.* London: Cambridge University Press, 1898.
Noor, Farid, ed. *New Voices of Islam.* Leiden: ISIM, 2002.
Nursi, Said. *Risale-i Nur Kulliyatı.* Istanbul: Sözler, 2001.
Oakeshott, Michael. *Rationalism in Politics and Other Essays.* Indianapolis: Liberty Press, 1991.
Ocak, Ahmet Yaşar. *Sufism and Sufis in Ottoman Society.* Ankara: Türk Tarih Kurumu, 2001.
Okay, Orhan. *Beşir Fuat: İlk Türk Positivisti ve Naturalisti.* Istanbul: Dergah, 2008.
Olson, Robert. *The Emergence of Kurdish Nationalism and the Sheikh Said Rebellion, 1880–1925.* Austin: University of Texas Press, 1989.

Öniş, Ziya. "Turgut Özal and His Economic Legacy: Turkish Neo-Liberalism in Critical Perspective." *Middle Eastern Studies* 40:4 (July 2004): 113–134.

Özdalga, Elisabeth. "Following in the Footsteps of Fethullah Gülen." In *Turkish Islam and the Secular State: The Gülen Movement*, ed. M. H. Yavuz and J. L. Esposito. Syracuse, NY: Syracuse University Press, 2003.

———. "The Hidden Arab: A Critical Reading of the Notion of 'Turkish Islam.'" *Middle East Studies* 42 (2006): 551–570.

———. *İslamcılığın Türkiye Seyri: Sosyolojik Bir Perspektif*. Istanbul: İletisim, 2006.

———. "Redeemer or Outsider? The Gülen Community in the Civilizing Process." *Muslim World* 95 (2005): 429–446.

———. "Secularizing Trends in Fethullah Gülen's Movement: Impasse or Opportunity for Further Renewal." *Critique Middle East Studies* 12 (2003): 61–73.

———. "Worldly Asceticism in Islamic Casting: Fethullah Gülen's Inspired Piety and Activism." *Critique Middle East Studies* 17 (2000): 83–104.

Özturan, A. Parkan. *İlk Türk Materyalisti Beşir Fuad'ın Mektupları*. Istanbul: Arba, 1987.

Öztürk, Saygı. *Okyanus Ötesindeki Vaiz*. Istanbul: Doğan Kitabevi, 2010.

Park, Bill. "The Fethullah Gülen Movement." *MERIA Journal* 12 (2008). Accessed June 9, 2011. http://www.worldsecuritynetwork.com/documents/Movement.pdf/.

Payaslian, Simon. "The Death of Armenia Karin/Erzerum." In *Armenia Karin/Erzerum*, ed. Richard G. Hovannisian. Costa Mesa, CA: Mazda, 2003.

Pekoz, Mustafa. "Fethullah Gülen'in Kürt ve Alevi Düşmanlığı." *Birgün*, August 23, 2010. Accessed July 12, 2011, http://www.dailymotion.com/video/xei7oz_fethullah-gulen-yn-kurt-ve-alevy-du_shortfilms.

Peroomian, Rubina. "A Call Sounded from the Armenian Mountains." In *Armenia Karin/Erzerum*, ed. Richard G. Hovannisian. Costa Mesa, CA: Mazda, 2003.

Pinson, M. "Demographic Warfare—An Aspect of Ottoman and Russian Foreign Policy, 1854–1866." Ph.D. diss., Harvard University, 1970.

Pocock, J. G. A. *Barbarism and Religion: The Enlightenment of Edward Gibbon, 1737–1764*. Cambridge: Cambridge University Press, 1999.

———. *Virtue, Commerce, and History: Essays on Political Thought and History, Chiefly in the Eighteenth Century*. Cambridge: Cambridge University Press. 1985.

Popper, Karl. *The Open Society and its Enemies*. Vol. 2, *The High Tide of Prophecy*. London: Routledge & Kegan Paul, 1945.

Putnam, Robert. *Making Democracy Work: Civic Tradition in Modern Italy*. Princeton: Princeton University Press, 1993.

Race, Alan. *Christians and Religious Pluralism: Patterns in the Christian Theology of Religions*. London: SCM Press, 1983.

Rahner, Karl. *Foundations of Christian Faith*. New York: Crossroad, 1978.

Ramadan, Tariq. *To be a European Muslim*. Leicester: The Islamic Foundation, 1999.

———. *Western Muslims and the Future of Islam*. Oxford: Oxford University Press, 2004.

Rawls, John. *Collected Papers*. Cambridge, MA: Harvard University Press, 1999.

Rodgers, Guy. "Fethullah Gülen: Infiltrating the U.S. Through Our Charter Schools?" Accessed April 9, 2010. http://www.actforamerica.org/index.php/learn/email-archives/1069-fethulla-Gülen-infiltrating-us-through-our-charter-schools.

Rodinson, Maxime. *Islam and Capitalism*. New York: Pantheon, 1974.

Sadri, Mahmoud, and Ahmad Sadri. *Reason, Freedom, and Democracy in Islam: Essential Writings of Soroush.* New York: Oxford University Press, 2002.
Said Halim Pasa. *Buhranlarımız ve Son Eserleri.* Istanbul: İz Yayınları, 2003.
——. "The Reform of Muslim Society." *Islamic Culture* (Haydarabat) 1 (1927): 111–135.
Salt, Jeremy. "Turkey's Military Democracy." *Current History* 98 (1999): 72–78.
——. *The Unmaking of the Middle East: A History of Western Disorder in Arab Lands.* Berkeley: University of California Press, 2008.
Saritoprak, Zeki. "Said Nursi on Muslim–Christian Relations Leading to World Peace." *Islam and Christian-Muslim Relations* 19:1 (2008): 25–37.
Saritoprak, Zeki, and Griffith, Sidney. "Fethullah Gülen and the People of the Book: A Voice from Turkey for Interfaith Dialogue." *Muslim World* 95 (2005): 329–340.
Saritoprak, Z., and Ünal, A. "Interview with Fethullah Gülen." *Muslim World* 95 (2005): 447–467.
Schwartz, Stephen. "The Real Fethullah Gülen." Prospect, July 26, 2008. Accessed April 9, 2010. http://www.prospectmagazine.co.uk/2008/07/therealfethullahglen.
Sevindi, Nevval. *Contemporary Islamic Conversations: M. Fethullah Gülen on Turkey, Islam, and the West.* Albany: State University of New York, 2008.
Seyhun, Ahmet. *Said Halim Pasha: Ottoman Statesman and Islamist Thinker.* Istanbul: Isis, 2003.
Shankland, David. *The Alevis in Turkey: The Emergence of a Secular Islamic Tradition.* London: Routledge, 2003.
Sharon-Kreskin, Rachel. "Fethullah Gülen's Grand Ambition." *Middle East Quarterly* 16:1 (2009): 55–66.
Shindeldecker, John. *Turkish Alevis Today.* Istanbul: Sahkulu Sultan Külliyesi, 1996.
Smith, Wilfred Cantwell. *Toward A World Theology: Faith and the Comparative History of Religion.* Philadelphia: Westminster Press, 1981.
Sorkin, David. *The Religious Enlightenment: Protestant, Jews, and Catholics from London to Vienna.* Princeton: Princeton University Press, 2008.
Strauss, Delphine. "Turkey: Inspiring or Insidious." *Financial Times*, April 28, 2011.
Tamimi, Azzam S. *Rachid Ghannouchi: A Democrat within Islamism.* New York: Oxford University Press, 2001.
Tan, Altan. "Is Secularism the Last Trump Card of Ethnic Politics?" *Today's Zaman*, December 13, 2007.
Taşgetiren, Ahmet. "Abant'in Cözemediği Sorun." *Yeni Safak*, July 27, 1998.
Taylor, Charles. "Liberal Politics and the Public Sphere." In *Philosophical Arguments.* Cambridge, MA: Harvard University Press, 1995.
——. *Sources of the Self: The Making of the Modern Identity.* Cambridge, MA: Harvard University Press, 1992.
Tillich, Paul. *The Courage to Be.* New Haven: Yale University Press, 1952.
——. *Systematic Theology.* 1951–63. 3 vols. Chicago: University of Chicago Press, 1963.
Tokat, Harun. *Önden Giden Atlılar.* Istanbul: Ufuk Books, 2007.
Toppo, Greg. "Objectives of Charter Schools with Turkish Ties Questioned." *US Today*, August 18, 2009.
Toprak, Binnaz. *Türkiye'de Farklı Olmak.* Istanbul: Metiş, 2009.

Trevor-Roper, H. R. *Religion, Reformation and Social Change.* 3rd edn. London: Martin Secker & Warburg Ltd, 1984.
Turam, Berna. *Between Islam and the State: The Politics of Engagement.* Stanford, CA: Stanford University Press, 2006.
Turner, Bryan S. "Islam, Capitalism and the Weber Theses." *British Journal of Sociology* 61 (2010): 147–160.
Turner, Colin, and Hasan Horkuc. *Said Nursi.* London: I. B. Tauris, 2009.
Ülsever, Cüneyt. *Hürriyet Daily Newspaper,* June 14–16, 2010.
Ünal, Ali. *Bir Potre Denemesi: M. Fethullah Gülen.* Istanbul: Nil, 2002.
Ünal, Ali, and Alphonse Williams. *Fethullah Gülen: Advocate of Dialogue.* Fairfax: Fountain, 2000.
Urbinati, Nadia. "'Laicité in Reverse': Mono-Religious Democracies and the Issue of Religion in the Public Sphere." *Constellations* 17 (2010): 4–21.
Üstün, Kemal. *Menemen Olayı ve Kubilay.* Istanbul: Cağdaş Yayınları, 1990.
Uyar, Selcuk. "'Islamic Puritanism' as a Source of Economic Development: The Case of Fethullah Gülen Movement." In *International Conference Proceedings: Muslim World in Transition: Contributions of the Gülen Movement.* Leeds: Leeds Metropolitan University, 2007.
Vahide, Şükran. *Islam in Modern Turkey: An Intellectual Biography of Bediüzzaman Said Nursi.* Albany: State University of New York Press, 2005.
———. "Toward an Intellectual Biography of Said Nursi." In *Islam at the Crossroads,* ed. Ibrahim Abu-Rabi, Albany: State University of New York Press, 2003.
Valkenberg, P. "Fethullah Gülen's Contribution to Muslim–Christian Dialogue in the Context of Abrahamic Cooperation." Accessed June 16, 2011. http://www.fethullahgulenconference.org/houston/proceedings/PValkenberg.pdf.
Vergin, Nur. "Türkiye Müslümanlığı ve Sözde Türk Islami." *Yeni Yüzyıl,* September 6, 1998.
Voll, John O. "Renewal and Reform in Islamic History: Tajdid and Islah." In *Voices of Resurgent Islam,* ed. John Esposito. New York: Oxford University Press, 1983.
Waever, Ole. "Securitization and Desecuritization." In *On Security,* ed. Ronnie D. Lipschutz. New York: Columbia University Press, 1995.
Wall, John. *Paul Ricoeur and Contemporary Moral Thought.* London: Routledge, 2002.
Walzer, Michael. *The Spheres of Justice.* New York: Basic Books, 1984.
Weber, Max. *The Protestant Ethic and the Spirit of Capitalism.* Los Angeles: Roxbury Publishing, 2002.
———. *The Sociology of Religion.* Boston: Beacon, 1963.
White, Paul, and Joost Jongerden. *Turkey's Alevi Enigma: A Comprehensive Overview.* Leiden: Brill, 2003.
Williams, B. G. "Hijra and Forced Migration from Nineteenth-Century Russia to the Ottoman Empire." *Cahier du Monde Russe* 41:1 (2000): 79–108.
Woodall, Martha, and Claudio Gatti. "FBI Investigating Gülen Schools in the US." *Philadelphia Enquirer,* March 23, 2011.
Yaman, Ali, and Aykan Erdemir. *Alevism-Bektashism: A Brief Introduction.* London: England Alevi Cultural Centre & Cem Evi, 2006.
Yanardağ, Merdan. *Turkiye Nasıl Kuşatıldı?* Istanbul: Siyah ve Beyaz Yayınları, 2009.
Yavuz, M. Hakan. "Nurluk Millileşiyor." *Milliyet,* September 18, 1996.

———. "Nasıl bir Türkiye." *Milliyet*, August 11, 1997.

———. "Search for a New Contract: Fethullah Gülen, Virtue Party, and the Kurds." *SAIS Review* 19 (1999): 114–143.

———. "Towards an Islamic Liberalism? The Nurcu Movement and Fethullah Gülen in Turkey." *Middle East Journal* 53 (1999): 584–605.

———. "Being Modern in the Nurcu Way." *ISIM Newsletter* 6 (2000): 7, 14.

———. "The Gülen Movement: The Turkish Puritans." In *Turkish Islam and the Secular State: The Gülen Movement*, ed. M. H. Yavuz and J. L. Esposito. Syracuse, NY: Syracuse University Press, 2003.

———. *Islamic Political Identity in Turkey*. New York: Oxford University Press, 2003.

———. "Is There a Turkish Islam? The Emergence of Convergence and Consensus." *Journal of Muslim Minority Affairs* 24 (2004): 1–22.

———. "The Gülen Movement." Religioscope. July 21, 2004. http://religion.info/english/interviews/article_74.Html.

———. *The Emergence of a New Turkey: Democracy and Ak Parti*. Salt Lake City: University of Utah, 2006.

———. "Islam and Europeanization in Turkish-Muslim Socio-Political Movements." In *Religion in an Expanding Europe*, ed. Peter J. Katzenstein and Timothy A. Byrnes. Cambridge: Cambridge University Press, 2006.

———. *Secularism and Muslim Democracy in Turkey*. New York: Cambridge University Press, 2009.

Yılmaz, İrfan. *Yeni Bir Bakış Açısıyla İlim ve Din*. İzmir: Nil Yayınları, 1998.

Zürcher, E. J. *Turkey: A Modern History*. London and New York: I. B. Tauris, 2007.

———. "Young Turks, Ottoman Muslims and Turkish nationalists Identity politics 1908–1938." *Ottoman Past and Today's Turkey*, ed. Kemal Karpat. Leiden: Brill, 2000.

Index

Abant Platform Conferences, 17–18, 136, 143–149, 230, 235
Abduh, Muhammad, 3–4, 6
afterlife (*ahiret*), 32, 46, 53, 77, 83, 101, 102, 125, 164
Ağa, Şamil, 29
Agai, Bekim, 11, 64, 155
Akif, Mehmet, 258n11
AKP. *See* Justice and Development Party (JDP)
Al-Afghani, Sayyid Jammaludin, 3–4
Al-Bannah, Hassan, 3
Al-Farabi, 171
al-Nahda Party (Tunisia), 62
Albanians, 110
Alevis, 18–19, 127, 222–223, 228–231, 239, 241, 242
Alparslan, 187
Arab Spring, 5, 150, 246
Aristotle, 93, 201
Armenians, 26–28, 231
Arslan, Muzaffer, 30
Article 163 (Turkish penal code), 36, 39
Arvasi, Abdulhakim, 72
Aseo, David, 192
Asrın Getirdiği Tereddütler (Gülen), 102
Association for Solidarity in Business Life (İŞHAD), 126
Association of *Kimse Yokmu* (Is Anybody There?), 235
Asya Finance Corporation, 90, 126, 238
Atalay, Beşir, 17–18, 218

Atatürk, Mustafa Kemal, 9, 25, 28, 95, 155. *See also* Kemalism
Avcı, Hanefi, 226–227
Aydınlı, Ersel, 210
Aymaz, Abdullah, 86
Ayna, Emine, 274n27
Azerbaijan, 13, 107

Ba'athism, 4
Baba, Rasim, 29–30
Bahçeli, Devlet, 227
Balcı, Bayram, 11
Balkans: Gülen movement in, 11, 57–58, 81, 83, 92, 96, 106–107, 110–111, 126, 129
  Ottoman Empire and, 27–28, 81–82, 205–206
  Treaty of Sèvres and, 38. *See also* Bosnia-Herzegovina
Barth, Karl, 54
Bartholomeos (Orthodox Patriarch of Istanbul), 192
Baş, Haydar, 237, 275n42
Bayram, Ali, 11, 86
Beck, Glenn, 12
Bektaş, Osman, 30
Bitlis province (eastern Anatolia), 26
Bosetti, Giancarlo, 133
Bosna Sema Educational Foundation, 259n39
Bosnia-Herzegovina, 5–6, 81–82, 107, 111
Buber, Martin, 179

Businessmen's Association for Freedom (HÜRSİAD), 126
Butler, Joseph, 165–166
Büyükcelebi, İsmail, 86
Buzan, Barry, 209

Calvinism, 121
Camurcu, Kenan, 20
Canada, 193
capitalism: asceticism (*zuhd*) and, 117–123
  education and, 125
  enterprise Islam and, 125
  Gülen movement and, 17, 52, 56, 76, 117–119, 121, 124, 126–129, 241, 245
  Islamic bourgeoisie and, 119–121
  modernity and, 59
  motivational factors and, 118–119
  Nursi and, 125–126
  social welfare and, 122–125, 128
  Weber and, 17, 80, 101, 117–118
Carr, Thomas K., 166
Cassirer, Ernst, 5
Caucasus, 28, 38, 57, 126, 145, 193
Cem Foundation, 230
cemiyet (human world), 33
Central Asia, Gülen movement in, 11, 57–58, 81, 83, 92, 96, 106, 126, 129, 145, 193
Cetinkaya, Hikmet, 273n11
Cevdet, Abdullah, 157
Çiçek, Cemil, 217–218, 270n33
Çiller, Tansu, 216–217
civil society: European Enlightenment and, 8
  Gülen movement and, 8, 41, 52, 54, 61–62, 73, 79–80, 90, 127–128, 135, 144, 174, 222, 225, 228, 240
  individualism and, 222
  Kemalism and, 223, 225
  religion and, 135, 174, 222, 225. *See also* public sphere
"Clash of Civilizations" (Huntington), 173
Clinton, Hillary, 45

Cobb, Kelton, 167
Coleman, James, 175
Committee of Union and Progress, 77
Crimean War, 27

Dadaş Islam, 26, 28
Darwinism, 34, 171
Dawkins, Richard, 157, 247
Demirel, Süleyman, 41
democracy: Gülen movement and, 41, 44–45, 47, 50, 55, 61–63, 65, 120, 127, 135, 145–146, 219, 235, 244
  Islam and, 62–63, 138, 153, 245
  Islamic bourgeoisie and, 62, 120
  minority rights and, 62
  modernity and, 59–60
  secularism and, 152–153
  Turkey and, 16, 18, 219, 222–223, 235–236
Democrat Party (DP), 207
Democratic Left Party (DSP), 217
dershanes (Nursi), 100–101, 109, 143
Dialogue Eurasia Platform, 145, 193
Divine Book of Creation, 161
Diyarbakir (Turkey), 84, 233–235
Doğan Media Corporation, 137
Doğan, Izzettin, 230
DTP (pro-Kurdish political party), 232
Dumanlı, Ekrem, 86

Ebaugh, Helen E., 259n20
Ecevit, Bülent, 41, 43, 199, 212, 215–217
Edirne (Turkey), 27, 34–35, 57
education in the Gülen movement: *abi* (elders) and, 101–103, 112
  as vehicle for reform and, 8, 92, 94–95, 98–101, 114
  critical thinking and, 104–105, 107–108, 113–114
  criticisms of, 113–115
  discussion and, 101–103
  dormitories (*yurt*), 97, 106, 113, 225
  gender and, 105, 114
  "golden generation" and, 40, 93–99, 104, 116, 168, 202, 224

international scope of, 96, 102–104, 106–107, 110–111, 235
Kurdish communities and, 84, 233–234
lighthouses (*Işıkevler*), 35–36, 42, 93, 96–97, 100–106, 113, 136
merchant class (*esnaf*) and, 94–95
moral guidance and, 76–77, 98–99, 101–105, 109–114, 234
networks in, 95–97
non-Muslim students and, 110–111
Nursi's writings and, 105, 111
reading and, 101–102
rehber (leaders) and, 103
religious aspects of, 6–7, 73–74, 93–94, 98, 102–103, 115, 165
science and, 6–7, 76, 92, 95–98, 113–114, 234
socioeconomic development and, 93–94
summer camps and, 35, 99–100
teachers and, 98–99, 105–107, 109–111
temsil (setting good examples) and, 109–110
Efendi, Lutfi, 29
Efendi, Ramiz, 29
Efendi, Sıddık, 30
Efendi, Solakzade Sadık, 30
Eickelman, Dale F., 74
Einstein, Albert, 152
Eisenstadt, Shmuel Noah, 247
Elder, Klause, 86, 101–102, 104
Emre, Yunus, 179–180, 185
Enlightenment. *See* European Enlightenment; Islamic Enlightenment
enterprise Islam, 125
Erbakan, Necmettin: Gülen movement and, 37, 97, 199, 204, 210, 212, 215–216
Islamic political movement of, 37, 97, 142, 199, 204, 207, 216, 237
prime ministry of, 209, 212
Welfare Party and, 204, 210, 213, 216
Erdoğan, Latif, 86

Erdoğan, Recep Tayyip: Gülen movement and, 217–218, 236, 242
Justice and Development Party (JDP) and, 13, 213, 228
prime ministry of, 16, 217, 228, 236, 242
Ergene, Mehmet, 108–109
Ergenekon network, 142, 213, 242
Erzurum (Turkey), 25–28
eser (lasting good deeds), 79, 87, 121, 124
esnaf (small merchants), 87, 94–95, 120
Esposito, John, 11, 13
European Enlightenment: education and, 115
Islamic Enlightenment and, 6–7, 50, 72–73, 95, 245
religion and, 5–6
values of, 5, 8–9
Young Turks and, 156
European Union, 50, 217, 219
Evren, Kenan, 38, 208
Eygi, Mehmet Sevket, 176, 237

Fadlullah, Sayyid, 178
Fatih University, 212
Fazilet (Virtue) Party, 41, 216
fazilet (virtue), 41
February 28 "soft coup" (1997), 41, 149, 209, 211–212, 223
Fidas, George, 45
fitne (seditious behavior), 236
Freire, Paulo, 105–106
Fuat, Beşir, 157
Fuller, Graham, 45

Gadamer, Hans-Georg, 165, 183
Gasperinski, Ismail, 114
Gay, Peter, 5
Germany, 37, 79, 102–104
Geylani, Abdulkadir, 26
Ghannoushi, Rachid, 4, 62
Ghazali, 20
Giddens, Anthony, 59
globalization, Gülen movement's approach to, 18–20, 45–46, 134, 146, 189, 247

Gökalp, Ziya, 3
"golden generation," 40, 93–99, 104, 116, 168, 202, 224
Golden Generation Worship and Retreat Center, 43
"the good life": Gülen movement and, 14, 17, 19–20, 52–56, 61, 65, 88, 93, 96, 105, 113–114, 116, 122, 142, 150, 157, 188, 201–203, 241
Nursi on, 93, 113, 116
Granovetter, Mark, 175
Gül, Abdullah, 59, 213
Gülen movement (GM): *adab* (good morals) and, 15, 247
achievement and, 54–55, 72–73, 80
Alevis and, 127, 229–231
Arabs and, 58
Balkans and, 11, 57–58, 81, 83, 92, 96, 106–107, 110–111, 126, 129
bildung (character formation) and, 15–16, 35, 76
businesspeople and, 54–55, 60, 73, 80, 87–89, 94–95, 120–122, 124–126
capitalism and, 17, 52, 56, 76, 117–119, 121, 124, 126–129, 241, 245
cemaat (community) and, 31, 88
Central Asia and, 11, 57–58, 81, 83, 92, 96, 106, 126, 129, 145, 193
civil society and, 8, 41, 52, 54, 61–62, 73, 79–80, 90, 127–128, 135, 144, 174, 222, 225, 228, 240
communalism and, 14–15, 48, 51, 54–55, 58–59, 63–64, 80
communications technology and, 7–8, 39–40, 74, 76–77, 85–86, 89
comparison to *sahabah* (companions of Prophet Muhammad), 71
dava (good example) and, 20, 89
democracy and, 41, 44–45, 47, 50, 55, 61–63, 65, 120, 127, 135, 145–146, 219, 235, 244
emotional aspects of, 29, 39, 57, 89, 172
Erbakan and, 37, 97, 199, 204, 210, 212, 215–216
Erdoğan and, 217–218, 236, 242

eser (lasting good deeds) and, 79, 87, 121, 124
European Union and, 219
Germany and, 79–80
globalization and, 18–20, 45–46, 134, 146, 189, 247
"good life" and, 14, 17, 19–20, 52–56, 61, 65, 88, 93, 96, 105, 113–114, 116, 122, 142, 150, 157, 188, 201–203, 241
Gülen's leadership role in, 71, 73–75, 89, 248
himmet (charity) and, 8, 56, 60, 75, 77, 80–82, 85, 87, 100
hizmet (service) and, 8, 10, 36, 49, 75–80, 98–99, 122, 168, 202–203
ihlas (religious worldview) and, 15, 76–77, 80
individualism and, 14–15, 55, 142
insan-ı kamil (perfected human being) and, 15, 35, 48, 51, 113
interfaith dialogue and, 11, 19, 73, 173–174, 179–196
Islamiyet (Muslim civilization) and, 51–52, 59
Justice and Development Party (JDP) and, 13, 45, 59, 65, 75, 115, 127, 142, 147, 198, 204–205, 213, 216–219, 223, 226, 228, 231–232, 236–239, 242
Kurds and, 58, 84, 127, 145, 224, 232–238, 241–242
lobbying and, 218–219
media presence of, 84–86, 90, 97, 129, 141–142
modernity and, 10–11, 14, 31–34, 46–47, 50, 52, 54–55, 57, 59–61, 63–67, 95, 97, 104–105, 134–135, 153, 171–172, 203, 244–245, 247
Nursi's influence and, 12, 15, 30–35, 66, 93, 97, 105, 158, 162, 166, 198, 249
Occidentalism in, 108
Ottoman legacy and, 18, 25, 46, 51–52, 56–58, 73, 75, 86, 93, 104–105, 108, 113, 127, 187, 194, 203, 232–233, 237, 246

öze dönüş (sacred center) and, 51
piety and, 8, 9–10, 13–14, 31, 58, 76, 80, 89, 93, 100–102, 120, 123, 221–222, 246
police force and, 215, 218
political engagement and, 199–204, 209–210
private property and, 53
public sphere and, 134–139, 141, 143–151, 200, 202, 244, 246
Qur'an and, 14, 51–52, 56, 63, 66, 72, 78, 102, 105, 142, 160–165, 167–168, 170, 180, 186–187, 190, 244
science and, 6–9, 35, 56, 76, 92, 95–98, 152–153, 158, 160–165, 167, 169–172, 202, 246–247
secularism and, 11–13, 57, 65, 72, 95, 223–227, 240–241
social networks in, 83–86, 88–89, 91, 129
structure of, 17, 74–76, 86–90
Sufism and, 10, 172, 237
tecdid (dynamic renewalism) approach and, 9
temsil (setting good examples) and, 80
theology of action (*aksyion*) and, 32–34, 44, 46–50, 53, 73, 76–77, 99, 103–104, 121, 168, 182, 221–222
tolerance and, 9, 11, 17–18, 20, 44, 65–66, 80, 85, 124, 153, 182, 186–188, 190, 193, 202
Turkish military and, 208–215, 219, 227–228, 238–239, 241
Turkish nationalism and, 57–59, 64, 73
United States and, 11, 83, 96–97, 129, 141, 145, 148, 193–194, 240
view of history and, 56–59
view of the state and, 38, 42, 56, 61–62
Western thought and, 72–73, 142, 168. *See also* education in the Gülen movement
Gülen movement, critics of

Gülen movement, critics of: Alevis and, 230–231, 241
alleged plots and, 227–228
education issues and, 113–115, 224
Gülen's response to, 221, 227–228
individualist perspective and, 65, 226
interfaith dialogue issues and, 194–195
Islamists and, 40–41, 237–239
Kurds and, 232–235, 241
neoconservatives and, 11, 12
secularists and, 11–13, 40–43, 57, 65, 95, 223–227, 240–241
Westernization issues and, 108
Gülen, Fethullah: Ankara State Security Court case against, 39, 42–43
as *alim* (religious scholar), 72–74
as *Hocafendi*, 9, 72, 75
as norm entrepreneur, 62
as storyteller, 112–113
as teacher, 35
communism and, 38, 39
education of, 29–30
February 28, 1997 "soft coup" and, 41–43, 59, 61, 96–97, 149
formative period (1941–1948) of, 25–30
Germany and, 37
imam duties of, 34–37, 57
political views of, 37, 40, 200–201, 215–216
prison sentence of, 36, 39
Qur'an and, 14, 56, 63, 66, 72, 142, 160–164, 167–168, 170, 180, 186–187, 190
Sufism and, 26, 29–30, 44, 52
Turkish military and, 35, 39
United States and, 9, 43–46, 59, 61, 84, 97, 109, 180. *See also* Gülen movement (GM)
Gülen, Necdet, 45
Gülerce, Hüseyin, 86, 227

Habermas, Jürgen, 17–18, 135–139, 143, 149–150

hadith, 14, 51, 187
Hagee, John, 195
Hanbal, Muhammad Ibn, 4
Hanioğlu, Sükrü, 156–157
Hanım, Munise, 29
Hanım, Rafiya, 29
hasbi (expectations), 49
Heidegger, Martin, 92
Hick, John, 179
himmet (charity): businesspeople and, 60, 81–83, 125
   Gülen movement and, 8, 56, 60, 75, 77, 80–82, 85, 87, 100
   meetings and, 80–82
   motivation for, 82–83
   sources of, 82–83
Hizbullah, 233, 235–236
hizmet (service): afterlife and, 77, 83
   businesspeople and, 125
   Gülen movement and, 8, 10, 36, 49, 75–80, 98–99, 122, 168, 202–203
   social capital and, 78
   Turkish society and, 77
Hoca, Fethullah, 171, 248
Hocaefendi (religious scholar), Gülen as, 9, 75
Hudaybiyya, Treaty of, 190
Huff, Toby E., 118
Huntington, Samuel, 108, 153
Hürriyet, 42

Ibn Rushd, 20
Ibn Taymiyyah, 4
Ibn-i Erkam, 100
ihlas (religious moral worldview), 15, 31–32, 77, 80
Indonesia, 5
insan-ı kamil (perfected human being), 15, 48, 51, 113
İnsel, Ahmet, 114, 223–224
Intellectuals' Hearth Association (Aydınlar Ocağı), 38–39
Intercultural Dialogue Platform (IDP), 145, 192
Interfaith Dialogue for World Peace, Inc. (IID), 193

interfaith dialogue: criticisms of, 194–195
   definition of, 174
   exclusivism and, 176–177, 180
   good example (*temsil*) and, 173–174, 189, 195
   Gülen movement and, 11, 19, 73, 173–174, 179–196
   inclusivism and, 177–178, 180
   intrafaith dialogue, compared to, 194
   love and, 184–186
   male domination of, 194
   models of, 176–181
   Nursi and, 177–178
   pluralist approach to, 178–181
   public sphere and, 174–176
   Race's typology of, 176
   recognition and, 174, 188–189
   shared language of common concerns and, 189–191
   silence and, 195
   social cohesion and, 173–175, 186
   tolerance and, 173–174, 182, 186–188
   United States and, 193
   Vatican II and, 176–177
International Institute of Islamic Thought (IIIT), 171
interpretivists. *See* modernists
Iqbal, Muhammad, 3–4, 6
Iran, 12, 27, 64, 82, 194
Iraq, 234
Işıkevler. *See* lighthouses
Islam: capitalism and, 3, 125
   democracy and, 62–63, 138, 153, 245
   modernity and, 10, 13, 32, 16, 60, 134–135, 244
   occasionalism and, 160
   "Protestantization" of, 10, 61, 118, 123, 247
   secularism and, 3–4, 18, 153, 155
   vernacularization of, 10, 15, 26, 61, 86, 118, 138, 150, 168, 244
   Weber on, 117–118. *See also* Gülen movement; Nurcu movement; Qu'ran; Sufism

Islamic Enlightenment: European
    Enlightenment and, 6–7, 50,
    72–73, 95, 245
  Gülen and, 7–9, 153, 248
  Islamic bourgeoisie and, 119–121
  Nursi and, 5–8, 66, 153
  socioeconomic conditions and, 6
  Sufism and, 5
  Tanzimat period and, 6
  Turkey and, 7–9, 119–121, 243
  values of, 5–7. See also European
    Enlightenment; Gülen movement;
    and Nurcu movement
Islamism, 10, 15–16, 40–41, 66, 97, 153,
    155, 205, 207–208. *See also*
    political Islam
Islamiyet (Muslim civilization),
    51–52, 59
Israel, 75, 219, 238
Izetbegovic, Alija, 4

Jackson, Sherman, 178
Jadidist movement, 114–115
jihad, 20, 117
John Paul II, 159, 192
Journalists and Writers Foundation
    (JWF), 90, 143, 145
Justice and Development Party (JDP):
  Alevis and, 231
  businesspeople and, 204
  coup attempt against, 213, 217
  Erdoğan's leadership of, 13, 213,
    218, 228
  Gülen movement and, 13, 45, 59, 65,
    75, 115, 127, 142, 147, 198, 204–205,
    213, 216–219, 223, 226, 228,
    231–232, 236–239, 242
  Israel and, 75, 219
  Kurds and, 232–233, 236–237
  liberal reforms and, 16, 87, 142,
    217, 236

Kant, Emmanuel, 5, 20, 60, 73
Karakoç Sezai, 34
Kaya, Alaaddin, 86
Kemal, Namık, 3, 4, 6, 263n4

Kemalism, 4, 41, 72, 94, 205, 207–208,
    231, 237, 245. *See also* Ataturk,
    Mustafa Kemal; secularism
Khan, Sayyid Ahmad, 3–4, 21
Khulifat, 4
Kinzer, Stephen, 239
Kılıçdaroğlu, Kemal, 235
Kırık Mızraplar (Gülen), 59
Kırkıncı, Mehmet, 28, 38
Kısakürek, Necip Fazıl, 34
Kocabaş, Özlem, 110, 114
Kotku, Mehmet Zahid, 72, 248
Krauthammer, Charles, 12
Küng, Hans, 173, 176
Kurban Bayramı (Muslim festival of
    sacrifice), 126
Kurds: Gülen movement and, 58, 84,
    127, 145, 224, 232–238, 241–242
  Justice and Development Party
    (JDP) and, 232–233, 236–237
  PKK (Kurdistan Workers' Party),
    233–236
  Turkish military and, 208, 209,
    232, 235

laikcilik (laicism), 154
Lamourette, Adrian, 6
Lewis, Bernard, 108
lighthouses (*Işıkevler*), 35–36, 42, 93,
    96–97, 100–106, 113, 136
Likud Party (Israel), 219
literalists, 4, 20
Lutfi, Muhammad, 29

Macedonia, 13, 107, 110
MacIntyre, Alasdair, 32, 201
madrasas/medrese (Islamic seminaries),
    35, 42, 74, 80
Malaysia, 5–6
Mango, Andrew, 209
Mardin, Şerif, 159
Mattson, Ingrid, 178
Mavi Marmara flotilla incident
    (2010), 238
Mawdudi, Maulana, 3
Mendelssohn, Moses, 115

Menderes, Adnan, 207
Menemen Rebellion (1930), 206
Meral, Riza Nur, 86
Mevlevi, 26
Milli Gazete, 176
Mısırlıoğlu, Kadir, 238
modernists, 4, 16, 107–108. *See also*
    Gülen movement; Nurcu (Nur)
    movement
modernity: capitalism and, 59
  definition of, 59–60
  democracy and, 59–60
  Gülen movement and, 10–11, 14,
    31–34, 46–47, 50, 52, 54–55, 57,
    59–61, 63–67, 95, 97, 104–105,
    134–135, 153, 171–172, 203,
    244–245, 247
  Islam and, 10, 13, 32, 16, 60,
    134–135, 244
  Nurcu movement and, 64, 66, 155
  positivism and, 60, 64
  secularism and, 10, 60, 243–244
  state-led modernization projects
    and, 64
  Turkey and, 9–10, 16, 244
  vernacularization and, 47, 63–64,
    118, 134, 220, 244
Mormons, 226, 240
Motherland Party (ANAP), 217
Muhaiyaddeen, 179
Muhammad: Alevism and, 230
  as example of perfect human being,
    15, 29, 46, 113, 118
  history and, 56
  immediate followers of, 4, 71
  logos and, 49
  revelation and, 180
MÜSIAD, 126
Muzaffer, Chandra, 124

Nasr, Syed Hussein, 179
National Outlook Movement, 237
National Salvation Party (Milli Selamet
    Partisi), 216
Nationalist Movement Party (MHP),
    199, 215–216, 227, 237

neoconservatives, 11, 12, 108, 195, 238
Neuhaus, John, 201
Newman, John, 165–166
Nurcu (Nur) movement: antico
    mmunism and, 34
  Gülen's differences from, 31–32
  Gülen's exposure to, 30–31, 36
  modernity and, 66, 155
  public sphere and, 40, 138
  social networks and, 85
  Turkish government and, 34, 36, 217
  view of the state and, 37–38
Nursi, Bediüzzaman Said: after
    life and, 32
  capitalism and, 125–126
  cemaat (community) and, 31, 88
  education and, 94, 96–97, 99–101,
    104, 109, 114, 143
  "good life" and, 93, 113, 116
  ihlas (sincerity) and, 31–32
  iman (faith) and, 31–32
  incarceration of, 198
  influence on Gülen movement and,
    12, 15, 30–35, 66, 93, 97, 105, 158,
    162, 166, 198, 249
  interfaith dialogue and, 177–178
  Islamic Enlightenment and, 5–8,
    61, 153
  Kurdish ethnicity of, 30, 232
  leadership role of, 75, 88, 220
  mana-yı harfi (indicative meaning),
    159
  mana-yı ismi (material existence),
    159
  modernity and, 64
  politics and, 31–32
  Qur'an and, 31–32, 159, 166–168,
    177–178
  science and, 155–156, 158–159,
    162–163, 167–169, 171–172
  vicdan (conscience) and, 33
  World War I and, 28. *See also* Nurcu
    (Nur) movement

Oakeshott, Michael, 268n8
Öcalan, Abdullah, 235

Odatv, 227
"the other," 12, 19, 65, 179, 186–188
Ottoman Empire: Alevis and, 229
　Arab populations and, 58
　Armenians in, 27–28
　Balkans and, 27–28, 81–82, 110, 205–206
　Christians in 27
　decline of, 6, 27–28, 32, 37, 154–156
　Gülen movement's views of, 18, 25, 46, 51–52, 56–58, 73, 75, 86, 93, 104–105, 108, 113, 127, 187, 194, 203, 232–233, 237, 246
　Intellectuals' Hearth Association and, 39
　Islam and, 19, 156
　Jadidist movement and, 114–115
　Kemalism and, 36, 72, 95, 139–140, 154, 234–235
　positivism and, 19, 157–158
　Russian Empire and, 26–28
　science and, 19, 154–158, 205
　Tanzimat period and, 6, 9, 27, 94, 154–155, 205
　Young Ottomans, 156
　Young Turks, 103, 156. *See also* Turkey
Özal, Turgut: Gülen and, 40, 216
　liberal reforms of, 9, 16, 38–40, 119, 128, 133, 140, 204, 208–209, 216
　Motherland Party and, 217
　religion and, 39–40, 208–209
Özdalga, Elizabeth, 114, 120, 123, 241
Özkök, Hilmi, 213

Pahlavi, Reza Shah, 4, 25
Park, Bill, 224–225
Paşa, Said Halim, 158, 263n4
Pascal, Blaise, 152
Persian Empire, 26–27, 194
piety: activist form of, 8, 9–10, 14, 31, 76, 80, 93, 123, 221–222
　Gülen movement and, 8, 9–10, 13–14, 31, 58, 76, 80, 89, 93, 100–102, 120, 123, 221–222, 246
　Nursi and, 93

Pipes, Daniel, 12
PKK (Kurdistan Workers' Party), 233–236
Pocock, J. G. A., 5
political Islam, 41, 89, 142, 205, 208–209, 212–213, 237. *See also* Islamism
Popper, Karl, 5
positivism: Islamic reactions to, 158–161, 163, 169, 178, 202
　Kemalist secularization and, 25, 33, 39, 46, 93, 171, 205, 220
　modernity and, 60, 64
　Ottoman era and, 19, 157–158
　scientific positivism, 152, 154, 156–157
public sphere: Abant Platform Conferences and, 136, 143–149
　definition of, 136
　economic reforms' impact on, 133–134, 140
　Gülen movement and, 134–139, 141, 143–151, 200, 202, 244, 246
　Habermas and, 17–18, 135–137, 139, 143, 149–150
　interfaith dialogue and, 174–176
　media and, 133–134, 136, 140–142, 147–148, 151
　Nurcu movement and, 40, 138
　Ottoman Empire and, 139
　religion and, 18, 133–141, 143–151, 155, 206, 211, 216, 244–246
　secularism and, 137–140, 147, 151
　Turkey and, 133–134, 137–149, 155, 200, 202, 211, 216, 244, 246. *See also* civil society

Qur'an: Gülen movement and, 14, 51–52, 56, 63, 66, 72, 78, 102, 105, 142, 160–165, 167–168, 170, 180, 186–187, 190, 244
　literalist interpretations of, 4, 20
　modernist interpretations of, 4, 16, 107–108
　Nursi and, 31–32, 159, 166–168, 177–178

Rabbani, 20
Race, Alan, 176
Rahman, Fazlur, 4
Rahner, Karl, 177
Ramadan, Tariq, 178
Randal, Jonathon, 5
Refah (Welfare) Party, 41, 119, 142, 204, 209–210, 213, 216
Republican People's Party (RPP/CHP), 37, 206–207
Rida, Rashid, 3
Risale-i Nur Kulliyatı (Collected Epistles of Light) (Nursi), 15, 30
Rıza, Ahmet, 86, 157
Robertson, Pat, 195
Rodinson, Maxime, 118
Rubin, Michael, 12
Rumi Forum, 193
Rumi, Celaleddin, 179–180, 193
Russell, Bertrand, 92
Russian Empire, 26–28, 114

Safavid Dynasty, 194
Sahabah (companions of Prophet Muhammad), 30, 71
şahs-ı manevi (collective personality), 107–108
Saladin, 187
Salafism, 4, 16, 108, 194
Saudi Arabia, 4, 82
Schluchter, Wolfgang, 118
science: education and, 76, 92, 95–98, 113–114
  Gülen movement and, 6–9, 35, 56, 76, 92, 95–98, 152–153, 158, 160–165, 167, 169–172, 202, 246–247
  hakikat (search for truth) and, 160–161
  Nursi and, 155–156, 158–159, 162–163, 167–169, 171–172
  Ottoman Empire and, 19, 154–158, 205
  religion and, 18, 152–154, 157–165, 169–172
  secularism and, 18, 155
  Turkey and, 157, 206
secularism: compatibility with Islam and, 3–4, 18, 153, 155
  democracy and, 152–15
  Gülen movement and, 11–13, 57, 65, 72, 95, 223–227, 240–241
  Islamist challenge to, 155
  modernity and, 10, 60, 243–244
  Ottoman Empire and, 154–158
  positivism and, 25, 33, 39, 46, 93, 152, 154, 156–158, 163, 171, 205, 220
  public sphere and, 137–140, 147, 151
  science and, 18, 155
  Turkey and, 4, 7, 36, 66, 152 154–155. *See also* Kemalism
Şener, Nedim, 226–227
September 11, 2001 terrorist attacks, impact of,152, 173, 195–196
Sèvres Peace Treaty (1920), 38
Sharia law, 12, 40, 48
Shariati, Ali, 4
Shaykh Said Rebellion (1925), 206
Shias, 194
Şinasi, 263n4
Sirhindi, Ahmad, 3
Şık, Ahmet, 226–227
Sızıntı magazine, 38, 97
Sorkin, David, 5–6
Soroush, Abdolkarim, 3–4, 62
Sözler (Nursi), 159
Sufism: civil society and, 222
  Gülen and, 26, 29–30, 44, 52, 180
  Gülen movement and, 10, 172, 237
  Islamic Enlightenment and, 5
  lodges of, 29, 35, 75
  Nakşibendi order of, 120, 138, 208, 248
  renouncing of worldly concerns and, 32, 46, 117, 122, 241
  social justice and, 123
Sunna, 56, 63, 66, 72
şura (consultation), 62
şuur (moral consciousness), 77
talim (teaching modern sciences), 76

Tan, Altan, 232
Tanzimat (Ottoman reform period), 6, 9, 27, 94, 154–155, 205

Tataristan, 6
Taylor, Charles, 175, 189
Tekalan, Şerif Ali, 86
Tevfik, Baha, 157
Tevfik, Rıza, 157
tevhidi (unified) account of science and religion, 19, 154, 160
Tillich, Paul, 47–48
Tokat, Harun, 86
tolerance: Gülen movement and, 9, 11, 17–18, 20, 44, 65–66, 80, 85, 124, 153, 182, 186–188, 190, 193, 202
  Habermas on, 137, 139
  interfaith dialogue and, 173–174, 182, 186–188
Topçu, Nurettin, 34
Toprak, Binnaz, 223
True Path Party (Doğru Yol, DYP), 216–217
Tunahan, Süleyman Hilmi, 72
Tuncay, Mete, 145
Tunisia, 64
Turam, Berna, 11
Turkey: anti-terror law in, 43, 212
  anticommunism and, 34, 37–38
  capitalism in, 9, 117–118, 120, 122–123, 128
  coups in, 37–38, 41, 149, 198, 205, 207–209, 211–212, 223
  democracy in, 16, 18, 219, 222–223, 235–236
  European Union and, 50, 217, 219
  Islam and, 33, 38–39, 72
  Islamic Enlightenment and, 7–9, 119–121, 243
  merchant class in, 9, 54–55, 60, 73, 80, 87–89, 120–123, 124–127, 140, 204
  modernity and, 9–10, 16, 64, 72, 244
  nationalism and, 38–39, 57
  public sphere in, 133–134, 137–149, 155, 200, 202, 211, 216, 244, 246
  secularism and, 4, 7, 9, 18, 36, 41, 66, 72, 94, 152 154–155, 205, 207–208, 231, 237, 245. *See also* Gülen movement; Ottoman Empire; Turkish military

Turkish Associations for the Struggle against Communism, 34
Turkish military: anticommunism and, 207–208
  coups by, 37–38, 198, 205, 207–208
  Ergenekon network coup attempt against JDP and, 213
  February 28, 1997 "soft coup" and, 41–43, 209, 211–212
  Gülen movement and, 208–215, 219, 227–228, 238–239, 241
  Islam and, 38–39, 205–211, 214–215, 217
  Kemalist ideology of 198, 205–207, 211
  Kurdish separatism and, 208, 209, 232, 235
  Western Working Group and, 211
Türkiye'de Farklı Olmak, 271n2
Turkmenbaşı (Saparmurat Niyazov), 250n11
TÜSIAD, 126
TUSKON (Turkish Confederation of Businessmen and Industrialists), 89, 122, 124, 126

ulema (Muslim religious scholars), 66, 72–73, 150, 156, 208, 229
umma (community of believers), 20, 50, 59
United States: Gülen and, 9, 43–46, 59, 61, 84, 109, 180
  Gülen movement in, 11, 83, 96–97, 129, 141, 145, 148, 193–194, 240
  neoconservatives in, 11, 12, 108, 195, 238

Vahide, Şükran, 167
Vatican II, 176–177
vernacularization: Enlightenment and, 6
  Islam and, 10, 15, 26, 61, 86, 118, 138, 150, 168, 244
  modernity and, 47, 63–64, 118, 134, 220, 244
Vuslat Mustuşu (Good News of Reunion) (Gülen), 230

Waever, Ole, 209
Wahab, Muhammad Abdul, 4
Wahabism, 58
Wahid, Abdur Rahman, 4
Weber, Max: Calvinism and, 121
  capitalism and, 17, 80, 101, 117–118
  communalized society and, 88, 117
  elective affinities and, 17, 90–91, 123
  Islam and, 117–118
  rationalization and, 55–56

Welfare Party. *See* Refah (Welfare) Party
World Parliament of Religions, 176

Yahya, Harun (Adnan Hoca), 171
Yeşil, Mustafa, 86
Young Ottomans, 156
Young Turks, 103, 156
Yusuf, Hamza, 178

zakat (alms tax), 83
Zaman (Turkish newspaper), 84, 90, 141, 148, 232